9/23

Space in the Tropics

MW00806047

Space in the Tropics

From Convicts to Rockets in French Guiana

Peter Redfield

UNIVERSITY OF CALIFORNIA PRESS
Berkeley · Los Angeles · London

University of California Press
Berkeley and Los Angeles, California

University of California Press, Ltd.
London, England

Library of Congress Cataloging-in-Publication Data

Peter, Redfield, 1965–.
Space in the tropics : from convicts to rockets in
French Guiana / Peter Redfield.
    p.   cm.
Includes bibliographical references and index.
ISBN 0-520-21984-8 (cloth : acid-free paper) —
ISBN 0-520-21985-6 (pbk. : acid-free paper)
1. Human geography—French Guiana—
History.   2. Centre spatial guyanais.   3. Penal
colonies—French Guiana—Devil's Island.
4. Human ecology.   5. Economic development—
Environmental aspects.   I. Title.
GF532.F74 R43   2000
304.2′8′09882—dc21   Catalog Number
99-056834   CIP

Manufactured in the United States of America

09   08   07   06   05   04   03   02   01   00
10   9   8   7   6   5   4   3   2   1

Contents

Illustrations

FIGURES

MAPS

(following page xvi)

Acknowledgments

By now this meditation on place has crossed many settings and climes. I have carried French Guiana with me from Cayenne to Berkeley, California, through the Mediterranean coast of France, an *arrondissement* or two of Paris, a village or two in the former Czechoslovakia, and the blue coastline of Martinique. Then it was on to other Californias—the woods of Santa Cruz, the high desert of Deep Springs, and a beachfront in Santa Monica—before winter wind in Cambridge, Massachusetts, weathered hills in Jerusalem, summer heat in Austin, faded brick in Baltimore, and now a stand of quiet pines near a town named for Ralegh. Given the theme of the work, I must admit that extensive dislocation has filtered my view of the tropics described—and yet, though it may have muted certain sights and sounds, contrast with these other places has sharpened the focus and lent acuity to the description of movement. Along the way, from place to place and sentence to sentence, the assistance and inspiration of numerous people have proved invaluable. Authorship is rarely a singular condition, and in a project focused on context a gesture toward biography seems only fair for the reader. The Russian name of the first satellite, *Sputnik,* can be translated as "Fellow Traveler"; in this sense I claim a constellation of companions, without whose influence my trajectory would have been quite different.

First, I acknowledge my family, who have given me constant encouragement, as well as confirmation that life can be lived in idiosyncratic ways. To my maternal grandparents, Jean and William Wolfe, I owe an undergraduate education, to my parents, Margaret and Charles Redfield, a belief in the possibility of virtue, and to my brothers, Marc and Tim, a sense of expanding, disparate, horizons.

On an institutional level, Harvard and Berkeley served as centers of gravity in my educational career. I began this work as a dissertation for the University of California at Berkeley's Department of Anthropology. Given the unusual nature of this project, I am particularly grateful to those entities that granted me material support, including the University of California at Berkeley, its anthropology department, the Camargo Foundation, and the National Science Foundation (Award #9400155). Additional assistance in publication came from the University Research Council of the University of North Carolina at Chapel Hill. Individuals within institutions make them habitable, and thus I thank all those who took the time to try to teach me, and particularly those who encouraged exploration beyond the ready lines of thought. Nancy Scheper-Hughes, Aiwha Ong, Bill Simmons, and Meg Conkey helped guide me through the maze of an advanced degree, while Randy Starn added a particularly inspiring touch of humanity and history; Paul Rabinow combined encouragement and a critical eye as advisor, insisting that anthropology can be both rigorous and free.

I first considered French Guiana through forgotten books in the Berkeley and Stanford libraries. The timely visits of Brackette Williams and Richard and Sally Price to California provided a more revealing introduction to the literature of the Caribbean. Brackette inspired me to think critically about the geography of theory (as well as everything else), while Rich and Sally came to play multiple roles as hosts, ethnographic guides, and mentors. Their attentiveness to detail yet openness to scholarly experimentation was of immeasurable value in this unorthodox foray through Atlantic history.

At Berkeley it was my privilege to have remarkable student contemporaries whose humor and care proved priceless. In particular, John Leedom, John Nelson, Misha Klein, and Søren Germer provided me with occasional materials, and Jennifer Cole and Mark Pedelty read early portions of this manuscript. Lucien Taylor and Ilisa Barbash shared an interest in the Caribbean as well as images, and Alice Bullard tirelessly discussed the gloomy record of colonies and prisons. Other friendships also echo between the lines, some too striking to ignore. I would never have begun to understand the world, let alone anything French, without having known Pamela Cheek, or learned how to persevere without Jono Mermin, physician, philosopher, and constant counsel. Throughout, Eric San Juan reminded me of sardonic shadows behind scholarship; Daniel Labovitz and C. L. Anderson, of the enthusiastic potential of written words; and Rachel King, of climes warmer than our old apartment. Amid a lively Camargo troop (thank you Anne-Marie, Elinor, Michael, Rebecca, and Vaheed), I especially acknowledge Anna Kirkpatrick, who showed me why Provence is worth painting, and Molly Westling, who encouraged me to contemplate nature with a careful eye.

Research in France was greatly assisted by Sylvie Claire at the Centre des Archives d'Outre-Mer (CAOM), M. Habfast, and (particularly) Mme. Lemoine at the European Space Agency. For their help in French Guiana I must thank Ken Bilby, Arthur Othily, Ron Pederson, M. Rocheteau, Diane Vernon, and the late Kris Wood, as well as D. Lammers and the late M. Hauzer at the Centre Spatial Guyanais. Others will remain nameless here but ever in my memory. I am further grateful to the space agencies for having provided me with a generous torrent of brochures, and to the unsung authors of minor tracts and pamphlets whose labor fills the notes and bibliography. When in transit I benefited from the warm hospitality of Rich Williams, Holly Kogut, the Tomášková family, Suzie England and the entire Berkshire clan, Jerry and Sarah Petersen, Guy Wheeler, Marc Petrusa, and particularly Catherine Benoît, who has doubled as genial host and insightful colleague. Above all, Alex Miles and Anne-Marie Bruleaux offered me both a professional and a social welcome, providing shelter as well as advice and ideas. I could never have accomplished this project without them, the Reuters bureau and Departmental Archives of Guyane, or Alex's fondness for *le benching*.

While working and reworking this text I have benefited from additional institutional homes. Deep Springs College—that inspiring, infuriating experiment—could not escape mention, or the remarkable students, staff, and faculty I encountered there, including Andreas Kriefall's crusade for Hegel, and the lingering ghost of Julian Steward. The Center for Cultural Studies of Science Technology and Medicine in the University of California at Los Angeles's Department of History hosted me for a year, and I likewise thank its faculty and students, especially Sharon Traweek, who shows the rare courage of being quietly different. The Department of History of Science, Medicine, and Technology at Johns Hopkins University also lent me an intellectual hearth, and I thank that community, especially Sharon Kingsland, Bill Leslie, and Harry Marks, who will always want a better book. Cletus Knowles,

David Munns, Jesse Bump, and Greg Downey lent critical assistance at one of several final hours. Finally, the University of North Carolina at Chapel Hill's Department of Anthropology has provided an environment where critical thought and civility are regarded as virtues. I am grateful to my new colleagues, faculty and student alike, for that privilege. At different points portions of this work were delivered at Harvard University's History of Science Department, the University of Chicago's Department of Anthropology, the University of Texas at Austin's Department of Anthropology, and the Massachusetts Institute of Technology's Program in Science, Technology, and Society, as well as meetings of the American Anthropology Association, the American Ethnological Society, and an interdisciplinary conference on Materializing Culture at Stanford University. I am most grateful to those audiences for their comments and interventions.

Elements of chapter 5 and chapter 6 appeared in different form in *Science, Technology and Human Values,* and I thank Sage Publications for permission to reproduce them. Between the lines of illustration credits, Des McTernan at the British Library and Susan Snyder at Berkeley's Bancroft Library were exceptionally helpful in locating images at their respective institutions. At the University of California Press I am especially grateful to Stan Holwitz, who saw what this book might be. An author could not ask for more thoughtful responses than the ones provided by my two readers, or more careful copyediting than that exacted by Carolyn Hill's sharp eye and light touch. Additional help in steering the manuscript into print came from Scott Norton, Lynn Meinhardt, and Janet Reed.

Other people who provided a timely word, reading, or reference or encouragement over the years—some flashing by like comets, others in steadier orbits like moons—include Warwick Anderson, Mario Biagioli, Jean-Jacques Chalifoux, Lawrence Cohen, Jonathan Culler, James Faubion, Jim Ferguson, Mike Fischer, Joan Fujimura, Reynal Guillen, Deborah Heath, Gabrielle Hecht, David Hess, Louis and Rolande Honorien, Bruno Latour, Gerard Prost, Vernon Rosario III, Kamala Visweswaran, Sam Wilson, Nigel Wright, and Stacia Zabusky.

Around again to an inner plane, I thank Silvia Tomášková, the sort of friend who thinks of seven unexpected things before breakfast, and who has taught me more about motion than I imagined possible. Near or far, we have traveled this cycle together, long after helping that hedgehog across the road. And now between us, laughing, our Zoë Sofia—smallest, dearest wonder of my world.

The Edge of the World

A book I read as a child showed a ship at the edge of the world, sails full and crew aghast. The image fascinated me, combining as it did the knowable and the familiar—waves and a small wooden vessel—with the unknowable and, indeed, inconceivable—that which lay beyond the fall. Only when grown would I realize that part of this fascination stemmed from growing up in a world that thought itself to have no edge, or at least none so terrifyingly near in experience. A globe floating through vast, abstract darkness, movements approximated by formulae, suggests no clear or catastrophic boundary, no abrupt and extraordinary limit to the everyday.

Years later, when discussing French Guiana, a number of people half-jokingly described it to me as lying *au about du monde,* at the "ends of the earth." One time when I heard this remark, on the terrace of a central and influential bar in Cayenne, eyes partly closed against bright tropical light and aided by a small glass of rum, I took the metaphor literally and tried to imagine what the ends of the earth might look like. Where, after all, is one left when a map runs out? A walled frontier, a cliff, a blank expanse? Would the edge seal in a seam, or, as in a medieval engraving of earth meeting sky, would another, hidden universe stretch beyond? Against certain knowledge of the world's spherical form, the exercise of thinking this way seemed far more foreign than the flat, slow air around me, and my attention returned to the conversation at hand.

Yet the memory of these images, the edge and the ends, resurfaces when struggling to frame the material before me. How is it that a small wedge of the South American continent, long claimed by a major European power and still administered by it, could present a profile of wilderness at the end of the twentieth century? How might this same location on the globe have proved useful for such an unlikely combination of purposes as the resettlement of convicted criminals and the launching of rockets? French Guiana remains a remarkably insignificant artifact of the political landscape—rarely noticed by most of France, let alone anyone else—as well as one of the least settled regions of the world. It has also hosted two exceptional experiments of the French state: the historical penal colony known in English as "Devil's Island," which operated between 1852 and 1946, and the contemporary space center that launches the European consortium rocket Ariane, responsible for transporting a good half of the commercial satellites orbiting our globe. In both of these projects we glimpse edges of the world, as it were, different ends of the earth. On the one hand lies the colonial fall of thousands of men into the heat of tropical purgatory, and on the other the triumphant rise of a rocket into a cold and calculating heaven. The moral decay of social death fills one horizon, and the technical might of pure machinery fills the other. Yet the hands layer and the vision blurs, for these disparate events occur in the same geographic setting, separated only by the passing of years. At the margins of significance, far from the central circuitry of human affairs, things come together and the ground falls away. At different ends of a critical century paths lead up into orbit and down to the grave.

Does it matter where things happen? Or more precisely, what might it reveal that different things happen in the same place? In the following pages I take these questions seriously, both at face value and in detail, examining French Guiana and its shifting roles as penal colony and launch site. Asking such questions by way of a case study of French Guiana leads to an exploration of nature and technology in a corner of the world where they lie richly entangled on the surface. En route one moves back and forth across many frontiers of what might be "modern," from a number of seemingly disconnected directions, all the while passing repeatedly over the same horizon. The northeast corner of South America, where a vast array of trees meets a slow and placid quadrant of the Atlantic, provides a field of high contrast for envisioning future and past while building the present. Over the last four centuries a procession of people, most arriving from Europe and usually

convinced of their unique status as civilized moderns, have claimed political authority over this region, defining its boundaries and certifying
its labels. I will follow this population through their encounters with
place, concentrating on their activities in the mid–nineteenth century
and onward, when the symbolic and material tools they bring to their
tasks become most acute. In particular I wish to focus on ways these
self-proclaimed modernizers perceive the possibilities of this point on
the planet: how they attempt to live in it and make use of it, what they
accept about its previous definitions, and what they seek to redefine, in
and around the lives of people already there. Amid surrounding issues
of administration and representation lies the context crucial to understanding how the present came to be, how a rocket arrived in the rain
forest, and how an unlikely pair of projects quite literally found common ground between an era of empire and an age of global connection.
Thus we can pass from the vivid terror of adventurous, avaricious European sailors to search for other images, ones that we might take as
less imaginary but no less disturbing: the edges of our own lives, and
those of the lives around us.

In pursuing this project I have made an effort to write in a fairly
common tongue, with a minimum of specialized vocabulary or allusions. While I believe that the material addresses a number of concerns
that resonate with what anthropologists call "theory," I prefer to leave
that language largely below the surface, lest it disturb a primary narrative claim: this is a true story about real, if unexpected, things. The theoretical interest of this story lies in its incongruity, its combination of
familiar fragments into an unusual pattern. At such times analysis is
best served by description, with a minimum of overt intervention, for
when facts are unexpected they disrupt interpretive assumptions and in
doing so can "speak for themselves"—not in the preemptive tones of
positivist certainty, but in the uneasy echoes of limiting doubt. I call this
approach to material "thinking through the world," suggesting that
carefully positioned, theoretically informed description brings into
view objects that are otherwise too often lost between the fault lines of
knowledge, and that in their very existence these objects reattach material culture to discourse and technology to the fabric of life. Although
this failure to neatly fit expected patterns creates problems of reading
and expectation, some of which I address in chapter 1, I would make
clear from the outset that the incongruity is intentional and multiple;
I have chosen to present an uncomfortable knot where different patterns cross, and the result is unlikely to satisfy any of those following

particular threads. With this in mind I provide a governing voice to guide the main text and I assign the words of others to a constellation of positioned quotations, footnotes, and epigraphs. The resulting work is one of unstable gravity, written with fluid vocabulary, dense metaphors, and shifting frames. In a tidier world it would be two or three books rather than one. But French Guiana's passage between "empire" and "globe" has been neither tidy nor pure, particularly along its edges. To defer connections risks deferring the essence of historical and contemporary experience, as well as forgetting its limits. Thus what the following pages may lack in order I hope they make up in interest; writing about tools I would recall that language is a very special one, a device of conjuring as well as calibration, a fragile reminder of the edge of understanding. For in the end we are still falling on this round planet of ours, forward and forward, day by day.

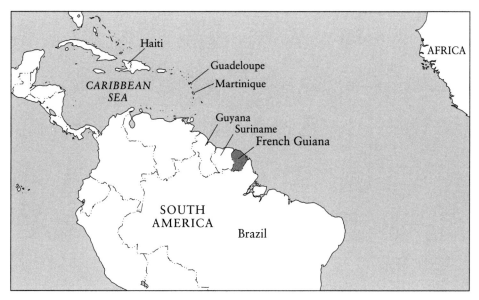

Map 1.   French Guiana in geographic context

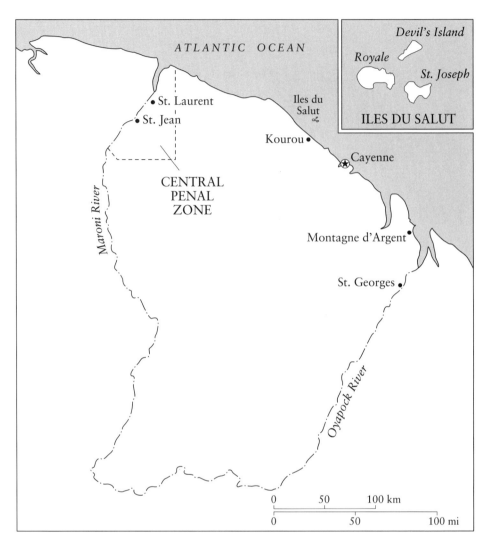

Map 2.   The penal colony in French Guiana

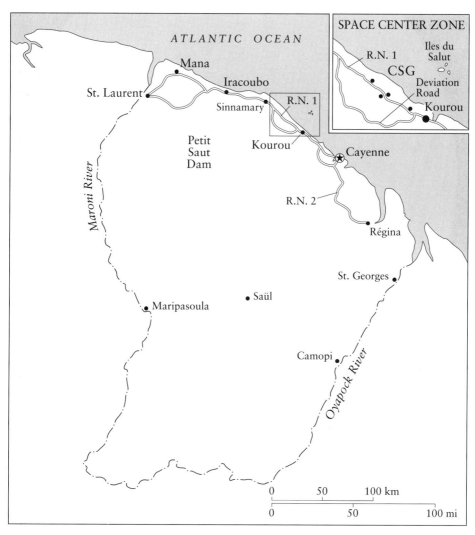

Map 3. The space center in French Guiana

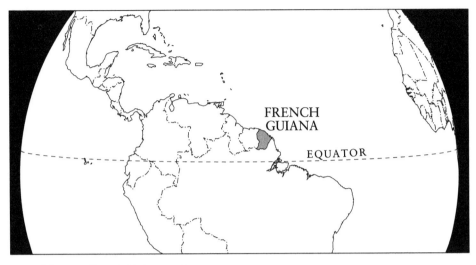

Map 4.   French Guiana and space

Figure 1.   Devil's Island from guard post, 1990

PART I

Islands and Disciplines

All of us, without exception, live on islands. But some of
these islands on our planet are so much larger than others.
Hendrik Willen Van Loon,
Van Loon's Geography, *1940*

First another story, familiar if not quite true: A man, shipwrecked, finds himself alone on an unknown island. Relying on memory and ingenious improvisation, he struggles to survive, reinventing things necessary to his way of life from materials at hand. Over the years he solves problems of ever-increasing complexity, gradually becoming familiar enough with his new surroundings to call them his own. By the time others arrive to live with him, the island lies somewhere between craft and nature, and his claim to mastery rests on substance. Even when he sails off, those who remain will follow his pioneering routines, enlarging the new tradition he left behind and remarking on the wonder of his deeds.

The story is that of Robinson Crusoe, the protagonist of an early-eighteenth-century travel tale who slipped out of the emerging form of the English novel back into cultural myth. I introduce Crusoe here for several reasons, including that he is familiar and fictional and thus provides us with all the clarity and attendant misunderstanding inherent in any model. Crusoe is an old friend to social theory, called upon to represent a pure form of individual existence outside society, as well as a key experiment in literature, marking a transition between fantastic and realistic representation. More crucially for the ensuing discussion, the story combines key general elements—nature, technology, and colonialism—in a setting where political economy and morality weave together, where men are men without women, and where space and individual identity are most clearly aligned. Crusoe's island exile embodies improvisation beyond the limits of design, a central theme of this work. Crusoe returns us to a time before industrial manufacture and global development policies, and his island returns us to the tropics, a zone of uncertainty circling the middle of the globe. Here, categories of "material" and "symbolic" action blur as one man struggles to rebuild his world. Mundane details and final purpose fill his head as this earnest amateur finds salvation by solving problems at the edge of his experience.

Still another reason to recall our man on the island can be found at a further metaphorical remove. Echoes of Crusoe's travails reverberate in stories told about knowledge and practice, including technologies and academic disciplines. Many historical figures have occupied islands since his, moving from castaway to pioneer as they rebuild a small piece of the world in their own image. The island constitutes a space of world imagining and world building, a limited domain within which some semblance of certainty and control can be maintained. Whether literal landmass or metaphorical field of expertise, an island has clear borders and a horizon on all sides. Along these borders we find techniques and their limits most clearly exposed, as the certainty of systematic order confronts the possibility of other conditions and alternative solutions. In taking Crusoe as our guide we return to a state of natural artifice where the manufacture of knowledge becomes an obvious craft.

Positioning this initial image of the lonely castaway in colonial history provides us with a frame against which to interpret French Guiana and the apparitions of a penal colony and space center within it. It also permits us to reflect on disciplinary boundaries, readerly expectations, and the dilemmas of anthropology in the face of modern technology and an intensifying set of worldly connections.

Robinson Crusoe, Anthropology, and the Horizon of Technology

Thence emerged the story of Robinson, in the way a dream
might occur. When this dream was published, however, all
Europe realized that it had been dreaming it.

Octave Mannoni, Prospero and Caliban, *1950*

They would make their islands in their own image.

Greg Dening, Islands and Beaches, *1980*

ROBINSON CRUSOE
AND THE IMPROVEMENT OF ISLANDS

Since its introduction to the reading public in 1719, Daniel Defoe's *The
Life and Strange Surprizing Adventures of Robinson Crusoe, of York,
Mariner* has worked its way through numerous additions, translations,
and recastings, inspiring not only architects of grand theory but also
small children, especially boys. From early best-seller and example of
the English novel, it has become a cultural referent and childhood classic. Indeed, it is as deserving as any work of the label "modern myth,"
a fact pointed out by a number of the book's readers, including Virginia
Woolf. And what readers it has had! This is, after all, the only volume
Rousseau would give his ideal pupil, Emile, and the work that Marx invokes in crucial and biting fashion at the beginning of *Capital*. While
few now know that the book had sequels (let alone read them), and not
many recall much about its narrative beyond the protagonist's ma-
rooning on an island, that central image has reverberated far and wide:[1]
Crusoe, washed up on an unfamiliar shore, facing the world alone.

Several facts are worth underlining before turning to the work itself.
First, while *Robinson Crusoe* can be called fiction, it was written at a
moment of transition in genre and presents itself as an authentic story,
striving to evoke the believable over the fantastic. A number of historical accounts of marooned sailors surround Defoe's text (the most famous being that of Alexander Selkirk); the narration is focused on

ROBINSON CRUSOE.

Figure 2.   Frontispiece to French *Robinson Crusoe*, 1720

everyday problems of Crusoe's condition, convincing in outline, if not in every detail; and the preface proclaims it a "just History of Fact" without "any Appearance of Fiction." Second, Crusoe has numerous adventures before arriving on the island, and has more after leaving; he is taken slave before he takes his own, and founds a plantation in Brazil before his fateful voyage. As a general portrait of an era his fictional biography represents something beyond the idiosyncratic; this is the morning of the great age of sugar production, of the painful triangle between Europe, Africa, and the Americas, and Defoe himself was quite interested in the colonialism of his day. Third, the work was immensely popular at the time of its appearance and was quickly translated into other languages (the first French edition appeared in 1720), even as its themes would be reworked and rewritten across the ensuing centuries.[2] Thus while *Robinson Crusoe* may be an English novel, one influential in reflecting and defining national character as well as the novel form, it also echoed throughout Europe. Eventually, in a twist particularly germane to this story, it inspired Jules Verne, the French father of science fiction, who in turn served as a hero to rocketeers.[3]

Taken as a literary work, *Robinson Crusoe* has been read in a number of ways. Two of the most influential traditions are those that treat his exile on the island as a spiritual or psychological trial and those that focus on his behavior as economic man, the classic bourgeois stripped of society.[4] Here I will move between these traditions to concentrate on an essential condition of the character salient to this study: Robinson Crusoe, at the center of his story, is a man out of place, learning to improvise. Marooned on a small tropical island, his horizons limited and surrounded by exotic flora and fauna, this nontechnical man (he has always traveled as a merchant) must rebuild his life. Alone for most of his years of exile, he lives with constant thoughts of elsewhere, repenting his past, dreaming of liberation, and dreading cannibals. And yet by the time he acquires his man Friday (not to mention his later retinue of Spanish and English sailors) he has become sovereign and—in an odd way—native, dictating not only the political terms of the island's administration but also the technical terms of its settlement. He builds himself a world, one between England and the tropics, one that bears the mark of his hand.

Here then is our key figure. To allow him something of the fullness of history I will continue reading the fiction where he found form, noting elements that bear on our theme. Crusoe marooned is a man painfully displaced. Yet he has, in some senses, always been so, a point worth underscoring. As he tells us on the opening page of his tale his father was a "Foreigner of Bremen," and the very name "Crusoe" is a corruption of "Kreutznaer." Throughout his life he craves adventure, physical as well as economic. Robinson goes against his father's designs to place him in the "upper Station of *Low Life*," that condition between labor and luxury "most suited to human Happiness."[5] Time and time again, when settled in one locale or another, he uproots himself and sails off. Yet his sojourn on the uncharted isle, his furthest displacement beyond the bounds of society, in the end brings him closest to home. Once wedded to his island, he can never leave it, returning at the end of the book to inspect it again and bearing everywhere its mark on him. For, when all is said and done, it is the central experience of his life, the one that defines him as a character.

Crusoe, despite his taste for adventure, does not remain an explorer; he becomes, however unwillingly, a colonist. This condition separates his account from many earlier travel tales of adventurers and merchants, Odysseus to Sinbad.[6] Our Englishman not only encounters the exotic but must learn to live with it on a daily basis, in a state of uneasy mastery. The explorer has come to rest, and in proving himself cosmopolitan, he reworks his body and soul: the island inspires Crusoe to his closest encounter with both spiritual anguish and the material conditions of life. It is here that he (who has never been a religious paragon) begins again to pray, here that he (who has never been a skilled worker) learns, slowly and awkwardly, to husband the land and to make all he needs. Following his shipwreck he is initially beset with the terror of his predicament, and his condition of isolation leads him to refer to his setting as the "Island of Despair."[7] Sick, he loses track of time, even as he relentlessly calculates it, and his attempt to flee the place only leads him to embrace it more fully. Yet he takes heart in his work, in his improvements. Defoe devotes pages to consider (if occasionally in haste) the technical aspects of Crusoe's struggle to reconstitute a familiar life. When the fatal footprint shatters Crusoe's sense of solitude, he finds new fears in the shape of cannibals and eventually gains a servant companion, rescued from their midst. Throughout he oscillates between faith and doubt, fear and hope, salvation and doom. His island is both kingdom and prison, and his presence on it reign or captivity, depending on his mood.[8]

Yet, for all that his shipwreck strands him in unfamiliar surroundings, bereft of human company, it simultaneously provides him with initial provisions and the means to reestablish technical mastery, including seeds as well as the essential Carpenter's Chest and Ammunition and Arms. Crusoe lands with a chest of tools as well as a rudimentary knowledge of their use. And for all that the island is exotic, an initially mysterious and threatening environment, it provides him with empty ground to claim for his own; its tropical climate supports game animals and allows the practice of agriculture.[9] Thus his efforts to civilize the island rest on imported elements both technical and natural. These are things he recognizes and holds onto, tools and ways of being that he will pass on to others, first his servant Friday and then the Spaniards and English mutineers who take his place. To live on his island is to live *as* Crusoe, to adopt his ways and habits, as well as to walk the same ground. However relentlessly focused on individuality, *Robinson Crusoe* revolves around a discovery of social order through its lack and the necessary conditions of its reimposition.

And what is this social order? Before us we have a single male, a European traveler aware of his national origin, language, and religion, categorizing others and himself, alternately certain and uncertain where sovereignty lies. He judges; he defers judgment; he calculates; he weeps. Born between high and low, he is placed by fate where he can act as both lord and bondsman. Separated from England, detached from his plantation in Brazil, he can imagine and experience himself beyond the edge of one identity or at the center of a new one. He learns to work, even while he learns to rule. He learns old techniques, even while he confronts a new and wild land. When he does acquire a servant he names him, while renaming himself as master. Social mobility and hierarchy emerge in tandem: one commoner becomes king, and another acquires the debt of life that will make him a slave. Furthermore, Crusoe is a man in a world of men; women hover only at the edges of his story.[10] His tools do not depend on women, and he has moved beyond them to construct his kingdom. The island creates a gender of absence; the terrifying prospect of his independence obscures sex and sensuality, and no other flesh impedes his path to God. For all his fear and doubt, Robinson is an eminently rational man. Thus when he returns to visit his island and his successors, he not only brings them additional tools, but, noting the "Improvement" they have made on the island and new children born of women captured from the mainland, apportions parts of the island to them. After binding others to his realm, Crusoe sails away again. The order he reasserts is that of the local sovereign, redistributing property and encouraging its material enlargement, preaching self-reliance, while dividing his subjects by rank and religion.[11]

Defoe's memoir for a marooned adventurer overflows with irre-pressible and singular detail. Yet it also provides us with key elements of the settler myth:

- The land is empty and waiting.
- Wilderness must be tamed into familiarity.
- Individuals are isolated and self-sufficient.
- Industry displays morality.
- Servants arrive afterward and are secondary.
- Attachment to homeland becomes defined through distance.
- Frontier masculinity is expressed in separation.
- Technical solutions conquer natural problems.
- Engagement with everyday problems underwrites independence.
- The goal of settlement is improvement, leaving more of value than one finds.

Amid these overlapping, interrelated points we find an emerging figure for modernization: the mobile man, a displaced agent carrying techni-cal knowledge to transform his surroundings. The most significant ac-tions of this agent occur in imagined isolation; they represent con-frontations between technology and nature *before* any confrontations between people. The existence of others obscured by a storm and an empty horizon, Crusoe's first fears are of "ravenous Beasts," not canni-bals, and before he has a servant he labors for himself.[12] Defoe's figure is a fiction, but an important one when considering castaways, colonists, and the worlds and histories they have made. Robinson Cru-soe, richly, imperfectly—mythically—is a "relentlessly 'modern' man."[13] And descendants of this "modern man," together with the universal space generated in his name, occupy many islands across the globe.

A RETURN TO OUR TOPIC

Before us now we have hints of the central themes of this work: tech-nology, nature, and development, amid the human experience of space and place. Defoe's Crusoe, attempting to reestablish order in alien sur-roundings and caught between spiritual anguish and material desire, finds himself through adventure, experiencing the fortunes of misfor-tune and rewriting mistakes. He does this apart from others, at a distance from the center of the place he sees as his origin, against the wilderness, and with the help of imported tools and improvised techniques. Refashioning his island, he builds a home and finds himself by tracing the margins of his world and becoming stranded at its very edge. It is there that he finds value in his life, even as he has acquired capital far from his birthplace, and it is there that he locates the site of his reconstruction. A northern man in the tropics, he lands in an exotic zone of possibility, a geographic space that strips away his everyday norms, exposing them through their absence. The island, then, is the land of displacement, its development the assertion of mobile cultural space over fixed location.

As the image of Crusoe on his lonely island suggests, nature and culture meet at their poles. Against unfamiliar wilderness the normal requires active definition; poised on the edge of the abyss, the castaway takes form by means of practical universality and a story of transcendence. From his experience we can distill twin languages of modernity, one economic and one moral. The first is more familiar under names such as *industry*, the second as *civilization*. In the late twentieth century these languages overlap and blur in the key term *development*, as well as twist into a variety of discourses surrounding it and opposing it.

Nevertheless, it would be a mistake to forget that within this general, floating, symbolic geography, Crusoe's shipwreck occurs at a most precise, earthly point. As Peter Hulme reminds us, *Robinson Crusoe* not only narrates colonial encounters, it does so within the context of the Caribbean, the raw entryway of the New World.[14] In Defoe's telling, Crusoe's island lies off the northeast coast of South America, just beyond the mouth of the Orinoco River, near Trinidad. Stretching to the south and east we find the long, flat expanse of the Guianas, the land passed by Crusoe on his voyage to shipwreck, the land to which we will shortly turn.

First, however, I will mimic our marooned protagonist and survey the pieces of the ship that brought me here. A chest of tools, definitions, and traditions will prove indispensable on our own analytic island. At any point language may falter, collapsing beneath the weight of other expectations. If we look closely we may also find footprints on our pristine beach and take fear and comfort, wondering who else may walk this shore. Before moving from the myth and theory of Crusoe to more historic Robinsons, let us sketch a chart before us on the sand, remembering other voyages and taking stock of received possessions.

OF METHODS AND DISCIPLINES

A particular problem arises when, instead of being a
discourse on other discourses, as is usually the case,
theory has to advance over an area where there are no
longer any discourses. There is a sudden unevenness of
the terrain: the ground on which the verbal language
rests begins to fail. The theorizing operation finds itself
at the limits of the terrain where it normally functions,
like an automobile at the edge of a cliff. Beyond and
below lies the ocean.

Michel de Certeau,
The Practice of Everyday Life, *1979*

Since this work takes shape along the rough edge of academic traditions, rather than smoothly within a single one, some genealogical ori-
entation is in order. I am by training an anthropologist and by inclination sympathetic to neighboring domains of history, geography, and
philosophy. Relations between nature and culture constitute a long-
standing concern for American anthropology, and in this sense I claim
ancestry within that lineage. However, the problem chosen and the approach taken vary from certain disciplinary conventions in both content and form: this is a study of displaced elements of modern life, and
one that is historical as well as ethnographic. All these points merit
elaboration.

ANTHROPOLOGY AND THE PROBLEM
OF MODERNITY

The philosophic traveller, sailing to the ends of the
earth, is in fact travelling in time; he is exploring the
past; every step he makes is the passage of an age.

Joseph Marie de Gérando,
The Observation of Savage Peoples, *1800*

American anthropology has long been an undisciplined discipline, un-
sure of its parameters as well as its parts and careening between the sciences and humanities in pursuit of the human.[15] Indeed, in an effort to
see the world whole, anthropology has done its best to sail over every
possible edge in space and time, pursuing overlapping questions of

human origins, human nature, and human difference. Yet amid this pursuit of the farthest facts, certain areas of the resulting map remain sketchy at best. Despite the legacy of many of its early and prominent practitioners, until relatively recently anthropological discussions tended to avoid direct confrontations with modern life, discreetly editing its effects.[16] When they have addressed what was once called "civilization," they treated it either as a larger and newer variant on traditional patterns or as a kind of terrifying, undiagnosed cancer eating them away. The point is not new, but its implications remain cogent. Even as the era of neglecting "uncivilized" cultures has partly passed in the university amid a remarkable expansion of historical and literary canons over the last two decades, and even as categorizations of "traditional" and "modern" have been called into question, studies of modern phenomena—particularly modern material culture—have until recently focused on a generalized and highly abstract "West." By examining the boundary of this West, this study seeks to follow those within and without anthropology who have attempted to trace modern life through place and time and a world framed by legacies of empire.[17] In contrast to anthropological tradition, here the relevant intersections between nature and culture stem less from human adaptation to particular environments and more from human perception of particular environments together with active efforts to reconstruct them.

Since the adoption of Bronislaw Malinowski and Franz Boas as totemic figures, the practice of social and cultural anthropology has centered on fieldwork and the production of ethnographies—monographs written on the basis of direct experience with a particular group of people—a focus that recent debates over the status of ethnography as written genre have in many ways only served to underline.[18] Essentially, anthropology sought to solve methodological issues through sharply defined communities, by anchoring knowledge of a people in the knowledge of a place, by choosing a site and "being there." To know a community, went the logic, is to know its language and customs. In practice this principle translated into knowledge of a community in geographic terms, to locate it and map its boundaries within a larger area. Particularly with the vast expansion and increasing degree of specialization within anthropology following World War II and the rise of area studies, one was expected to master one's village and report back from it into a greater surrounding literature, becoming an Africanist, or a Latin Americanist, amid a community of scholars.

Despite historical and political questions one might well raise about the structure of such a system as a whole and about the effects of knowledge in relations of power, the move was a strong one from a technical and methodological standpoint.[19] Detail makes the everyday convincing, and localized knowledge comes from the ground. As its increasing diffusion into other domains suggests, the practice of ethnography retains a vital allure, the promise that if well done, it will offer rich rewards: moments of experience, an echo of different voices, and the crucial reminder that things could be otherwise.

Thus for the anthropological tradition, exotic islands (literal or otherwise) represent a natural habitat. In the metaphor of Defoe's adventurer, ethnographers sought an audience with Friday, pursuing his earlier "cannibal" experience. Their labor was the opposite of Crusoe's, concentrated on comprehension rather than conversion, on abandoning home rather than rebuilding it, and on learning language rather than teaching it. If they became governors, it was of textual atolls, their pages cleared of irregularities and defended by theoretical fortifications.

And yet a hallmark of modern experience is that it appears in mobile, shifting form, difficult to pin down.[20] The speed of migrations and the exactness of their recording limit the process of historical amnesia upon which "timeless" cultures are built, while the centrality of machines and standardization shifts focus away from human groups and their particular horizons. Documentation disenchants traditions, even as it registers individuals. Cities and suburbs have a different topography than villages or islands, and they group together disparate humans and tangle the webs of their relations. "Community" becomes a slippery object, sometimes a neighborhood, or a region, or an ethnic group. Even worse (from the perspective of a categorical purist), boundaries grow even more permeable as the number of people living between stable entities increases. To know a modern individual in any sort of convincing social detail, one must consider that person's position relative to a wide range of categories (race, ethnic affiliation, class, profession, education, gender, sexuality, and citizenship, to name a few) and an individual biography that may cross several divides. Furthermore, many of these categories are consciously invoked in everyday language by the actors themselves and are well documented, through writing, photography, and ever increasingly efficient technologies of preservation. The problem for anthropology at the end of the twentieth century is less frequently a lack of information than a determination of what information within an overwhelming deluge might be significant relative to the questions at hand.

Not a few attempts have been made to bring ethnographic methods to bear on modern experience, both within and outside the boundaries of academic anthropology. Yet even explicitly urban studies frequently work most successfully around metaphors of the village, rarely transcending them; after all, participant observation requires direct encounters and limited numbers. Having no direct recourse to the exotic, studies in urban settings labor under the double burden of having to represent both a personal transformative experience and an identifiable, locatable group in an "ordinary" setting, without an obvious literal or symbolic journey. In order to lay full claim on the Anglo-American ethnographic legacy, one must displace oneself, personally and culturally.[21] Thus direct attempts to find "the field" in the city often appear secondary activities, and both prestige and insight in ethnography tend to lie away from the center. Exceptions to this generalization certainly exist, but often in the form of works focused on internal margins, studies of the poor, of minority populations, of tightly woven neighborhoods, or of rural communities in industrial societies. Without the challenge posed by bridging physical and conceptual distance, the intellectual significance of the ethnographic act per se wears thin. To suggest at the beginning of the twentieth century that distant savages are as fundamentally human as the denizens of a London drawing room was a startling act. To remind someone at the end of the century that people in a New York subway or Paris metro have something in common with savages is much less surprising or, in itself, compelling. Life outside the academy has only become a more open tangle of partly crossed cultures since the critical months Malinowski spent stranded on the Trobriands. Bringing anthropology to bear on the West, like studying "up" the scale of social influence, involves more than merely reversing the direction of inquiry; it requires a more conscious selection of site and subject matter, questions and methods. For "ethnography," like "archaeology," properly names an approach to understanding, an activity, what practitioners do.[22] While the intellectual effort involved may not be simply reducible to technique, it depends on a significant set of techniques, and by very definition takes place on the ground and not in a vacuum. One crucial aspect of any empirical technique is finding a significant where and when in which to apply it.

COLONIAL HISTORY, GLOBALIZATION, AND SCIENCE STUDIES

Three current trends in anthropology have engaged modernity in distinct but significant ways, together framing this study. The first, which I will describe with the term *colonial history,* stems from the latest rapprochement between anthropology and history. Here the ethnographic project is reframed in the past, concentrating on colonial interactions in nineteenth-century European empires. Documents take precedence over oral testimony, but the analysis remains consciously cultural, and the scope both locally framed and implicitly comparative. Such an approach reveals the "modern" world as the product of overlapping imperial systems, with a vocabulary of concepts and practices emerging between metropoles and colonies. History no longer flows in one direction, because key categories of contemporary life—from nationalism to urban planning—evolve as much "overseas" as in Europe.[23]

The second trend recognizes the interconnectedness of human affairs captured in the term *globalization.* Growing out of earlier studies of world systems, this work adds a focus on electronic media, concentrating on cultural dimensions of international networks. Placing connections in the foreground weakens the force of immobile cultural geographies, allowing into view entities between nation-states: borders, migrants, and hybrid experience. Acknowledging the speed and range of cultural influences allows even remote areas an active present. In a new world order that prefers voyages to islands, and video to maps, ethnographies can witness the plurality of present. Far from representing a uniform norm, "modern" life incorporates ceaseless variation. Indeed, for all that shared systems of exchange may exist, one might better conceive of multiple modernities, intertwining paths rather than a smooth highway to the future.[24]

The third trend involves a direct engagement with the heart of modern practice: science and technology. Focused studies on laboratory life have located highly charged sites within much vaster networks of knowledge. Within the walls of the Salk Institute or the Stanford Linear Accelerator walk identifiable, frail humans. The very power of such inquiries reveals a critical point: they succeed by grounding the abstractions of science in localized action, reversing assumptions about the transcendent qualities of the white coat. By transforming the laboratory into a community subject to ethnographic study, they reveal a space that can only be understood with reference to other spaces, a local node along a global network. Such a space does not merely de-

mand context; it is, in a sense, made up of context, of mixtures and hy-
brids, people, machines, texts, and places, blends of technology and humanity. Thus a concentration on elements of science, technology, and
medicine quickly leads beyond laboratory walls.[25]

Collectively, these three strands of influence—colonial history, globalization, and science studies—carry one common message for anthropology: links have become unavoidable. The turmoil of the last few
decades over ethnography and the boundaries of anthropology's domain can be understood as a struggle over which links will be permitted, and which denied, as well as the means through which an object of
study should be delimited. Disciplinary tension emerges between rival
impulses to maintain competing analytic traditions (and their accompanying bodies of literature) and to account for the observable features
of contemporary reality.

COMPARISONS AND SHADOW HISTORIES

Debates over the direction of anthropology circle issues of comparison.
At stake is the degree to which the diversity of human experience can
be resolved into overarching principles. Simplified characterizations
usually identify two camps: on one side stand proponents of greater
universalism, often championing the extension of biological understanding, and on the other stand proponents of greater particularism,
often championing the demonstrable variation of cultural forms. While
the sympathies of this work lie more on the side of diversity than principles, it acknowledges the importance of comparison to any effort to
situate present experience. The real promise of work involving colonial
history and global forms is that its scope becomes more than particular
but less than universal in scale, allowing for partial and shifting comparisons. The additional promise of interpretive studies involving science and technology is that human bodies and tools no longer become
visible only in general laws; interpretation can confront the physicality
of life in all its concrete, disruptive plurality, recognizing the active
landscape that surrounds speaking subjects and the shifting winds of
discourse.

Such a perspective recalls anthropology's variegated heritage even
while confronting the disorientation of the present. Anthropology flows
not through clean laboratories but through unkempt fields, following no
certain texts or archives, only bits and pieces left by others and a faint,
vast shadow of humanism. It is, in essence, a tropical discipline, ever

disrupted by local conditions and threatened with unexpected break-downs. It constitutes the only corner of the academic court where personal experience has long been admissible as evidence and where the contingency of life is partially incorporated in the formulation of knowledge. Rather than constitute an impediment, this fluidity can itself represent a critical resource.[26]

Beyond ethnography, a key task for any anthropology concerned with modern life involves the writing of what I call "shadow histories," accounts of the very real alternatives to the primary ways things have been done or understood. A shadow is an offset imprint of varying shape and intensity. The realm of shadows contains partial differences, similarities, and overlaps, and it is in this world that we find reflections between interconnected varieties of human experience. The greatest illusion of history proper lies in the implication that past actions have singular roots or consequences, clearly visible under the proper light. The rigid architecture of defined expertise within the academic discipline of history rarely permits its practitioners to follow the edges of actions or to trace influences spanning centuries and continents, let alone to linger on insignificant islands. Anthropology's inheritance includes the freedom to define parameters of relevance, to ask impossible questions, and to provide partial answers. As well as documenting an ever-shifting geography of human activity in the present, its practitioners can confront modernity in reverse, sketching shadows of industry and reason filtering between places and times. In doing so they contribute a sense of motion to the study of humanity, destabilizing the balance of evolutionary models with disconcerting accumulations of historical fact.

THE HORIZON OF TECHNOLOGY

A boundary is not that at which something stops but, as
the Greeks recognized, the boundary is that from which
something *begins its essential unfolding.* That is why the
concept is that of *horismos,* that is, the horizon.

> *Martin Heidegger,* Basic Writings, *1954*

Yet the most telling justification for anthropological attention to comparative history is also the most nominal: disciplines are composed not only by what practitioners "do" but also by the stories they recount and those recounted around them. Generalist projects of the sort com-

mon to the postwar era may no longer dominate the academic agenda
of anthropology at elite institutions, but a sense of greater human history and motion pervades statements of ultimate ends in other disciplines and outside academic walls. Professional anthropologists have
no monopoly on anthropological tales. They are told all the time at the
beginning and end of stories, from student essays and scholarly studies
through corporate promotions and government documents, including,
as we shall see, in the context of prisons and rockets.

Here technology again proves particularly significant. Naive anthro-
pologies—general stories about a human condition—flow especially
around technologies, key symbolic markers in defining modern
chronology. In positioning past and present, the definition of an "Age"
plays a crucial role. Prehistory marches from Stone to Bronze to Iron;
the nineteenth century rides on Steam, Railroads, and Electricity; and
the twentieth century accelerates through Atoms, Space, and Computers.[27] When facing such a series of Ages—whole units that exclude by
virtue of their inclusivity—critics tend to focus either on flaws in their
parts or on excesses in their narration. While these strategies work well
within defined frameworks, they underestimate the ghostly power of
whole stories and the figures that operate within them, as well as the
material shadow of technical systems. The romantic holism of anthropology's legacy here comprises a critical resource, if transformed from
end goal into opening strategy. Rather than ignore naive vision, one can
take its questions seriously so as to transform and redirect them. A particularly naive empiricism, faithfully recording both forests and trees,
can produce the analytic restlessness requisite to unsettling the certainty of the present, and with it the Age.

THE LOCATION OF THIS WORK

What follows lies somewhere between colonial history and a study of a
distinctly globalizing technology, amid a shadowy field at the margins
of significance. It does not seek to be an ethnography per se, in the sense
of maintaining a constant anchor in a singular and present life-world of
a particular bounded human community. Instead, it adopts an ethnographic sensibility, and works along a particular seam of more general
histories of the present. An older order within anthropology placed its
villages minutely and pedantically, considered culture in terms of custom, symbol, and artifact, and acknowledged folk categories such as
"civilized" and "primitive." In recalling this tradition I do not advocate

nostalgic return to either imperial collecting or evolutionary thought. Rather, I would remember that people can be known through their things and the places they inhabit as well as through their words, and I suggest that crucial aspects of modernity involve space and tools as much as language and action.[28]

Following a particular variant of a universalizing culture through time, I seek to retain elements of the empirical force of the ethnographic tradition, while allowing for an account that addresses a wider range of mixed subjects and objects, living and dead: people, plants, machines, rain, myths, and bureaucratic files. If a problem of the modern is constantly one of framing, then a key, if sometimes forgotten, element in the narrative tradition of an older generation of ethnography—the crossed axes of history and geography against which the present moment is laid—becomes simultaneously complicated and crucial. As the local has become more obviously mobile and quickly reinvented, the limits of the community stretch around numerous sites and weave together a greater number of stories. Within a context such as contemporary French Guiana, to study even a "traditional" population in a careful way involves an expanded definition of the field, and a mobile ethnographer.[29] For this project I have chosen to concentrate on those crucial framing axes in order to both describe one frontier of the modern and explore the ramifications of modernity and its spatial technologies for the tradition of ethnography. The general strategy is a focus on a particular locale in order to describe the shifting cultural topographies of people passing through it.[30] The work thus constitutes an ethnographic prologue, extended and expanded to emphasize its significance, engaging history, ecology, and material culture. The subject of the work remains ever partly offstage, while the spotlight trains on the scenery. What most distinguishes Crusoe's heirs is not their peculiar customs but rather the mobile island they inhabit.

My methodology can be summed up by Lévi-Strauss's well-worn invocation of the humbler end of French technical expertise, the *bricoleur,* an amateur handyman found building structures from the "remains and debris of events," following problems between the joints and crevices to improvised solutions, and focusing on the available more than the appropriate.[31] I offer an account between empiricism and theory, based partly on fieldwork, partly on archival research, and partly on the work and thought of others: an assemblage constructed from notes taken on trips to French Guiana between 1990 and 1994, from notes taken in archives in both France and French Guiana, and from research conducted in a number of public and private libraries.[32] These are all familiar academic tools; what is less conventional is the manner of their combination and application in relation to the subject matter, and the elements they patch together. The result represents a mix of planning and improvisation undertaken within the concrete and changing circumstances of my life rather than a scripted adherence to a clear and universal technical standard. In addition to suggesting that such an approach is increasingly unavoidable in the contemporary world (both despite and because of relentless pressures toward standardization and specialization), I also contend that anthropology's most hopeful legacy lies in its resistance to a singularity of method and in a continuing, questioning search through every toolbox for the bits and fragments saved because "they may always come in handy." As these pages hope to suggest, bricolage is an essential element of life in the tropics (and in all environments other than those where things are designed)—one that even engineers have to learn. Indeed, in French Guiana, where small edges of life often go awry, *bricolage* is a relatively common term in everyday speech. After all, at the end of supply networks, a *bricoleur* can repair more than a technician.

TOOLS FOR THE READER

> To be sure, it would still remain to be asked if the
> anthropologist considers himself "engineer" or
> "bricoleur."
>
> > Jacques Derrida,
> > Of Grammatology, 1967

To take the metaphor of the *bricoleur* seriously—and further extend that of Crusoe—I must arrange the contents of our chest before us. Beyond disciplinary heritage and methodological practice, the improvising tinker requires a bag of resources, full of odds and ends of thought. It is this motley collection, not the clear plans of an engineer, that define the particular problem. Washed up with us from the sea of history are bits of language and earlier thought. The selection is not random—any more than the contents of any worker's bag—but it derives as much from context as from principle. This fact creates a problem of coherence and tautology: the general statements involved depend on particular history and experience, but narrating that history and experience requires the use and reworking of general terms to be comprehensible. In the face of this problem, I lay out a number of pieces and partial explanations and then draw a quick map before proceeding to describe the situation at hand. When on his island, Crusoe learned to mingle engineering and bricolage, to both plan and improvise; over the course of our narrative voyage we will do the same. Thus I offer a glossary of key concepts, adapted for a forgiving climate.

SPACE

Two senses of the term concern us: one involving the realm of rockets and satellites and the other involving the geometry of human experience. This unavoidable double meaning draws together "outer" space and the preoccupations of geographers and architects, suggesting that they may be connected. When speaking of space on the ground, I oppose it to *place,* the former suggesting neutral abstraction, and the latter localized specificity. This opposition, like others in this work, is far from stable.[33]

COLONIALISM

The sense of *colony* crucial here is that of a social extension in space, as suggested by the etymological roots of the term in settlement.[34] Most critical work on colonialism in recent decades focuses on the age of European empire in the late nineteenth and early twentieth century and on relationships of domination between colonizing and colonized populations. Following the vocabulary of biology and Crusoe, I concentrate on the ways that habitats are constructed and the work that goes into maintaining them. This shift in emphasis seeks not to erase histories of oppression but to recall two contextual facts about colonial practice: first, that colonies involve craft and nature as well as culture (that is to say, animals, plants, and machines as well as people), and second, that colonial projects, whatever their intentions, can fail.

NATURE

Nature here describes nonhuman flora and fauna, as conceived by humans. Because the setting involved is on the wild side, *civilization* constitutes an opposed term in addition to *culture* (with its ties to agricultural landscapes). Nature, like culture, is taken to be simultaneously real, historical, and interpreted. Humans are all natural, even modern ones, but they also live within technological environments and view and interact with nature differently depending on their location. Although French Guiana contains a number of biogeographical zones, this work will frequently blur them into one: the symbolically potent "rain forest."

TROPICS

As in common speech, *the tropics* here refers generally to the middle regions of the globe, especially their humid, forested sections. On a metaphorical level this phrase partially substitutes for *the third world*—that is to say, "developing" regions, largely composed of former colonies. While not always geographically accurate (any more than the terms *the Non-West* or *the South*), it serves as a reminder that people live and machines operate in different natural and cultural environments, even as it recalls a telling complex of metaphors inherited from empire.

TECHNOLOGY

Here I maintain some distinctions between *technology* and *technique*, with the former term restricted to complex systems associated with industrial manufacture, planning, and coordinated expertise, and the latter operating more loosely to describe all instrumental intervention in the world.[35] Material tools represent only the most visible part of any technical operation, the remainder being composed of knowledge, social relations, and sensibilities. While much of modern technology is increasingly aligned with various fields of science, the focus here rests less on invention or production of knowledge than on the other end of the future—the way grand things become normal and once-extraordinary notions shrink into everyday expectations. In this context the symbolic dimensions of material action, as well as its limits, inconsistencies, and breakdowns, are of particular concern.

MODERNITY

Much of what comes under the term *modernity* might also be described by the terms *capitalism* and *the state*—market exchange, industrial production, bureaucratic regulation, secular reason, social welfare, and compound machinery. However, *modernity* has advantages in this context, where profit is not always clear, where fields of political control overlap, and where the opposition involved is frequently as much to nature as to other forms of human organization understood as tradition. Modernity also suggests technology as the key marker of distinction and the defining agent of reality, underscoring the general artifice of neutrality. While this work compares contrasting modern systems, it also emphasizes their common characteristic of displacement.

PLACE AND PEOPLE

Most ethnographic accounts make explicit reference to a particular group of people, usually bounded by those hallmarks of culture, language and custom, or by descent. In the language of empire such groups are "native"—that is to say, composed of people in place. In French Guiana, a product of several colonial layers, the issue of who can claim such status grows complex.[36] For rhetorical ease in describing a setting that fits awkwardly into international norms, I move between the terms *French Guiana* and *Guyane* to describe the geographic region in question, and I follow local practice in using the male French adjective form *Guyanais*. The local terms *Métro* and *Créole* (without their diacritical marks) respectively name descendants of Europeans and mixed descendants of Africans, and the more scholarly terms *Maroons* and *Amerindians* respectively name the descendants of rebel slaves and the descendants of Native South Americans. *Metropolitan* designates the center of a political system, in this case usually meaning European France. Here I use the term *Guyanais* loosely, describing all those who might claim a home there, primarily Creoles, Amerindians, and Maroons.

Local vocabulary divides the "non-Guyanais" population into two general groups: people of European extraction and other immigrants (defined by their nation-state of origin, primarily Brazil, Haiti, and Suriname). This work concentrates on the former group, using the latter as a cautionary shadow against overly simple classification in a region of overlapping colonizations, displaced classes, and multiple (if unequal) Metropoles. Of interest here are people accepted as "moderns" in social interactions, and who expressly *lack* unquestioned attachment to their surroundings, living as outsiders with constant reference to elsewhere.[37] Figures cast in the role of agents of change play a particularly significant role in tracing bureaucratic and technical tendencies. While the majority of the Europeans involved are French, and the general peculiarities of colonial heritage involved derive distinctively from that national experience, I focus part of the time on mutual Anglo-French influences and part of the time on French-Euro tensions. Just as the category "native" here remains open, so too does the category "foreign."

SURVEYING THE TERRAIN

To clarify the material contained in the following pages, I provide the reader with two final tools: a thesis and a conceptual map.

THESIS

At its core this work addresses the greater ecology of modern expertise. The thesis is that modern categories of nature and technology can only be understood in relation to each other, and, further, that neither can be adequately understood without recourse to spatial terms. By focusing on a marginal case of colonial history and tracing the operation of two grand plans within it, key elements of different historical moments of a world system (here glossed as "Empire" and "Globe") come into view. Between them we witness a practical redefinition of human limits, one that shifts symbolic understandings and experiences of the world amid continuities of historical power. The labor of colonization involves dislocation and attempts to reorder nature as bodies are repositioned and landscapes altered. In partial contrast, the work of high technology involves continued mobility, as well as a profound spatial reconfiguration around dislocated expertise and standardized material culture. Both colonization and technological systems need to be understood through metaphors of ecology and architecture as well as through metaphors of society and culture. The human subject of technology inhabits an inherently cosmopolitan and active environment, amid inherited inequities and incomplete transformations wrought by prior systems. Thus whether or not people may be "modern," certain spaces clearly are, and amid their imperfect limits and small details the historical geography of the present comes into view.

A CHART OF THE WORK

The text is divided into four parts. The first includes introduction and background material, the second offers a case study of the penal colony, and the third presents a case study of the space center. The fourth part compares the penal colony and the space center, concentrating on intersections between nature, technology, and the work of development. Within these four sections are nine chapters, organized as follows.

Chapter 1 presents our key figure, Robinson Crusoe, and lays the terminological and disciplinary groundwork for the study.

Chapter 2 offers a historical sketch of development in French Guiana, beginning with El Dorado and continuing on through competing European settlements, early plantations, the disastrous attempt at a settler colony in 1763, deportation during the French Revolution, a return of a slave society, final emancipation, efforts to find alternate labor, the founding of the penal colony, a gold rush, two world wars, the end of transportation, the end of official colonial status, the founding of the space center, and other development projects. Around these particulars I sketch a frame within the context of the Caribbean and the New World, providing the essential setting of the case.

Chapter 3 returns to the early nineteenth century to examine the background to the founding of the penal colony in 1852, surveying prison debates, the model of Australia, the shifting background of emancipation and labor questions in French Guiana's plantation system against dilemmas of criminality in urbanizing France, and the reintroduction of deportation following the 1848 revolution. The latter part of the chapter covers the establishment of the penal colony and the techniques of its early administration, including the search for a successful site within French Guiana and the establishment of a rival institution in New Caledonia.

Chapter 4 addresses the later penal colony and issues of representation related to it, covering the Dreyfus Affair and sensational accounts of the early twentieth century, focusing on their international context. Nature here becomes destiny, and the tropics a site of degeneration rather than improvement, with the governmental norms deferred and racial, sexual, and environmental norms inverted relative to civilized Europe. The penal colony becomes a colonial site of terror, dislocated from its coordinates, even as it enters a long, uneasy equilibrium with the rest of French Guiana.

Chapter 5 shifts the focus to the establishment of the space center, covering the realization of outer space, the move from World War II to the Space Race, and France's search for a substitute launch site after the

Algerian War. Key to the story is the repositioning of the equator within a frame of reference of satellite technology. The chapter continues to sketch Kourou's first development in the 1960s and the basic structure of the contemporary space center.

Chapter 6 addresses the later space center and related issues of representation. It focuses on the successful Ariane program and the symbolism associated with rocketry and the Space Age, as well as local development and the ritual of launches. Technology here becomes destiny, and the tropics turn into a site of aesthetic pleasure. The space center, having served as a catalyst in the transformation of French Guiana, with unintended consequences, seeks to rewrite the area's past and reposition itself at various points as both a development project and an environmentally concerned agency. At the same time, it becomes a lightning rod for protest on the part of elements of the local population.

As a first step in bringing the penal colony and space center together, chapter 7 examines what "place" means in each context, tracing nineteenth-century climatic theories and obsessions with race, disease, death rates, and reproduction in the penal colony against the twentieth-century rise of ecological discourse and immigration concerns in French Guiana. It also addresses the aestheticization of nature surrounding the contemporary space center, focusing on ways of marking time in the tropics, from prison sentences to jungle tours, and comparing a search for authenticity to one for survival.

Chapter 8 moves from questions of nature back to related ones of technology and development, comparing ecologies of work in the penal colony and the space center and the place of improvisation within each design, as well as their status as separate states within states relative to the rest of French Guiana. Construction of a large dam at Petit Saut and debates over two roads in the summer of 1994 brought oppositions within Guyanais society to the surface, even while revealing the greater transformatory environment of the space enterprise. The shift from the rural settlements envisioned in the penal colony to the urban professional norms of the space center reflects wider trends of material culture and a new scale of mobility and connection affecting thought and practice.

Finally, chapter 9 returns to issues of colonial technology, the figure of Robinson Crusoe, and the importance of margins. Modernity, I suggest, is a spatial condition as well as a temporal one, its magic of speed and scale experienced from several directions. Reading Crusoe against

Hegel's master and slave, we see the significance of a working, mobile master; comparing moments of empire and global experimentation, we can identify both a proliferating impurity of categories and a continuing heritage of technological imbalance. The technical spaces and natural places at the edge of things provide testing grounds, room for mistakes, leftovers, and visions of the past and future; they thus give us reflective sites from which to glimpse the imperfect present. One such site lies at a juncture of the Caribbean and the Amazon, along a natural horizon of technology. There space and the tropics meet, between the foot of a launch tower and the ruins of a cell, alternate legacies of Crusoe's bold adventure.

CHAPTER 2

History on the Wild Coast

The Antilles and Guyane belong to a universe whose magical reflections invite endless vagabondage. Discovered and explored at the close of the fifteenth century, at the dawn of the Renaissance, they opened the gates of a New World to the daring European, landscapes of paradise. They regaled the adventurer with a legendary history, unfolding fabulous images before his eyes. To such beings, escaped from a rough and meager world, they revealed the sun of perpetual summer, abundant and novel foods, spaces to discover and enslave. But for this luxury the pioneers soon paid their tribute, in incurable sickness, in work rendered exhausting by the torrid climate, in solitude broken too rarely by a feminine presence.

> *Pierre Pluchon,*
> Histoire des Antilles et de la Guyane, *1982*

Myths are essential; French Guiana relies on them. Facts about the country do exist, but they are usually neglected; according to still another myth the facts are hard to obtain. When the French information officer in New York, N.Y. showed me her file on French Guiana, she apologized for its being so meager. "We have very few statistics from Cayenne," she explained, "because it is too hot to make statistics there."

> *David Lowenthal,*
> *"French Guiana: Myths and Realities," 1960*

COLUMBUS DAY 1992

October 12, 1992, on the Gregorian calendar marked the five hundredth anniversary of Columbus's arrival on that largest of islands, the New World. In Cayenne the occasion was commemorated with a general strike. Businesses closed and a protest march wound through the streets to the plaza before the prefecture and the old governor's palace. Although later the mood would turn uglier, with roadblocks and

C E P T / **ESPACE ET GUYANE** / **EUROPA** / **2,50** / **LA POSTE 1991** / **REPUBLIQUE FRANÇAISE** / **ANDREOTTO**

Figure 3.   French stamp, 1991

smashed windows, this first day of demonstration had almost a festive
air; despite the presence of police barricades and a helicopter overhead,
the initial widespread support for the affair—it had been endorsed by the
employers' association as well as the workers' unions—dampened any
immediate sense of confrontation. The crowd chanted slogans in
French about "the right to work for all" and waved signs about the
need for "real development" to replace colonization. One small boy
resting in the shade wore a T-shirt that read in English "Enjoy Shop-
ping," and a woman laughingly called out to an acquaintance in the
window above to come down and "join the people."

Only recently installed nearby, I observed the protest with bewildered amusement. Later in the week I would become acutely aware that I was white, that the vast majority of protesters were not, and that their anger was primarily directed against Metropolitan French bureaucrats and secondarily at Creole elected officials and Chinese merchants. On this first day, however, I was struck most by the smallness of the affair (like everything else in French Guiana relative to metropolitan norms) and the generality of its claims (the local economy is in poor shape, and the French state must fix it). After five centuries of European presence in the New World and the long painful history of colonial empire, this plea for French-directed development impressed me as an unlikely outcome.[1]

The strike lasted through the week, before negotiations produced the promise of a new aid package from Paris. In the protest's aftermath an air of bitterness lingered most strongly in neighboring Kourou, the space center town, where the barricades were last to come down and a prominent local official's car was burned. In Cayenne, people complained about the cancellation of the town's annual festival. But throughout Guyane, police lines and protest barricades vanished, and racial tensions that had openly flared subsided, as life resumed a more regular, languid pace. Despite the new initiatives, the local economy continued to stagnate and unemployment remained high. I returned to the archives to read about the past, yet the impression of this brief, tense present remained with me. How, I wondered, could a long colonial history, including periods of plantation slavery and penal colonization, lead to a demand of "the right to work for all"? As time passed and my research continued, I began to realize that an obsession with "development"—or rather its persistent absence—ran deeply through the soil of French Guiana, inseparable from the history of the colony beneath the department. Here I will sketch the background of that history, to better position the two projects that most concern us.

A PROMISE OF GOLD

The Empyre of *Guiana* is directly east from *Peru* towards the sea, and lieth under the Equinoctial line,
and it hath more abundance of Golde than any part
of *Peru,* and as many or more great Cities then euer
Peru had when it florished most. . . . I have been assured by such of the *Spanyardes* as haue seen *Manoa*
the emperiall Citie of *Guiana,* which the *Spanyardes*

call *el Dorado,* that for the greatnes, for the riches, for
the excellent seate, it farre exceedeth any of the world.

> *Sir Walter Ralegh,* The Discoverie
> of the Large, Rich, and Bewtiful Empire
> of Guiana, *1596*

We will begin our story not with Columbus but with another noted
sailor and another small wooden ship bobbing off to sea. Though Spanish eyes may first have discerned the shape of Europe's new western
edge, an English pen first set forth a central motif of its conquest. Composed over a century after Columbus's arrival in the Caribbean, Sir
Walter Ralegh's *The Discoverie of the Large, Rich, and Bewtiful Empire of Guiana* grandly proclaimed the great riches to be found in the
northeast section of South America.[2] The area he described ran south
from the mouth of the Orinoco River—not far from where Defoe
would later place Robinson Crusoe's fictive island—down what was
called the "Wild Coast" toward Brazil. Ralegh was sure that somewhere in the tangled forest away from the sea lay the great city of
Manoa, a fountainhead of wealth that would put Peru to shame. Although he returned to England with a cargo composed largely of enthusiasm, and although a second voyage in 1617 ended in disaster, his
account of the city of gold set the legend of El Dorado firmly in the history of the New World. Here was the driving dream: a hidden source of
wealth—wealth found, not created—just over the horizon.[3]

Most popular renderings of French Guiana history begin with El Dorado, and the reference runs through the accounts of several centuries.
For all that the French zone of the Guianas lay slightly to the side of
Ralegh's adventuring and the legendary location of Manoa, the sense of
richness in the land struck powerful chords. Gold, the metal of conquest,
has repeatedly lured those seeking a future in Guyane and still beckons
poor Brazilians and large international companies. However, we should
remember that Ralegh was not only interested in discovery. He was also
a pioneering figure (however unsuccessful) of North American settlement, standing at the beginning of the great phase of British and French
expansion. While Manoa would remain hidden, new sources of wealth
sprouted west of the Atlantic. As one of Ralegh's later editors wrote
when introducing the adventurer to his reading public in 1928, Ralegh is
"the link between the Elizabethan pioneer and the sober hewers of wood
and drawers of water of the seventeenth century, who built where the
others had led."[4] Thus we come across a crucial hinge in colonial practice: that between exploratory conquest and practical settlement.

As plunder and mining came to the Wild Coast, so did agriculture and the productive reformation of nature—the other end of Ralegh's dreams. During the seventeenth century, a number of European powers vied for footholds on the Guiana coast, with the Dutch, English, and French taking advantage of Spanish and Portuguese neglect. The first French expedition to what would become "their" Guiana took place in 1604, but they did not establish effective control until many decades later. After trials at other locations, early efforts centered on the island of Cayenne (a section of land separated from the rest of the mainland by estuaries and rivers). In 1664 an expedition by a French company captured Cayenne from the Dutch, only to lose it again three years later to an English raid. The French regained control in 1676 and gradually settled into full possession of the surrounding section of coast.

Even when they had fended off rival claimants, the French were not alone. At the time of European settlement, Guyane may have been inhabited by slightly under ten thousand Amerindians, principally Kaliña (Galibi) and Palikur. Indeed, the name *Guiana* most likely stems from Amerindian roots.[5] In addition, slaves were soon imported from Africa; the Compagnie de la France Equinoxiale already had possession of some 420 in 1665. The primary model of settlement adopted was the plantation, which required massed manual labor. Despite a number of experiments, the slave system remained dominant into the nineteenth century, and slaves of African descent soon outnumbered all other segments of the population.[6] Prior to their expulsion from the colony in 1762 (part of a general banishment from the realm of France), members of the Jesuit order worked prominently to establish plantation settlements.

Yet in recounting the plantation history of French Guiana, one must stress that the region continually languished at the edge of France's first colonial empire. In relative terms few slaves were imported, little capital was invested, and little was generated. Unlike the Caribbean islands, French Guiana missed the sugar boom; in the words of Marie-José Jolivet, for the area around Cayenne the period between 1677 and 1763 constitutes "a century of stagnation."[7] The contrast with other entities in the area becomes all the more striking given that the neighboring Dutch settlement grew to become one of the most important—and rich—plantation colonies of the eighteenth century.[8]

Two factors contributed to French Guiana's stagnation as a plantation colony. The first was a lack of labor; between 1715 and 1775 only 11 French slavers left Nantes for Cayenne, whereas 299 headed for

Martinique. Compared to the Caribbean the influx was a trickle rather than a flood, measured in hundreds, not thousands. Slave merchants were reluctant to transport their cargo to Cayenne, partly because it was a less than ideal harbor, difficult to navigate in a sailing ship, partly because it was well removed from other, larger French Caribbean colonies, and partly because the prevailing winds and currents discouraged journeys by way of those ports. The second factor contributing to the lack of success was a failure to adequately drain and cultivate the low ground—a swampy home to malarial mosquitoes—instead of concentrating efforts on the less fertile high ground. Only at the end of the eighteenth century would wide-scale drainage begin, even as the greater plantation system surrounding the enterprise started to crumble. Yet the central impulse discouraging growth in French Guiana came less from either of these factors than from the cyclical inertia of the situation: French Guiana remained small because it lacked labor, and it lacked labor because it remained small. This early inertia of insignificance foreshadowed ensuing developments while preserving the land as an open horizon for future dreams.[9]

SETBACKS AND SLOW DEVELOPMENTS

At the conclusion of the Seven Years' War in 1763, France lost much of its overseas empire, including Canada. As the largest landmass left under French rule, French Guiana became the subject of renewed colonial interest.[10] In a bid to revive imperial growth, the French made a disastrous attempt to settle large numbers of European peasants in the region around Kourou. Some twelve thousand immigrants arrived between 1763 and 1765, hoping to build a tropical Quebec up the coast from the slave plantations.[11] Poorly prepared and terribly administered—the expedition was even at odds with its established neighbor Cayenne—the venture collapsed amid widespread epidemics. By most counts at least half the colonists died.

Here visions of El Dorado mixed with a fantasy of Canadian industry. Those involved in the scheme sought to create a settler colony in the tropics, while those who participated found themselves in a confused version of the New World dream. One apocryphal account has a cook informing her master that she has just married in order to emigrate. "Oh, Sir," she gushes to him, "it's a new discovery, gold and silver mines have been found, diamonds, coffee, sugar, and cotton; one can make a fortune there in two years." Because some members of the elite, sporting plumes and flowing clothing, accompanied the stolid peasantry, the resulting spectacle even invited florid comparison between the "deserts" of Kourou and the gardens of Palais Royal in Paris.[12]

The effect of the Kourou expedition was to bolster suspicions that Europeans were incapable of colonizing Guyane and that the land and climate were deadly to them. Later documents related to decisions involving the settlement of Europeans in French Guiana refer to the Kourou disaster frequently, and the experience served as one of the basic elements in a new emerging myth to fit alongside that of El Dorado: the myth of French Guiana as a European tomb.[13] The expedition also left a local legacy, renaming a trio of islands off the coast of Kourou—a refuge during the epidemics—the Iles du Salut, or Islands of Salvation. In material terms, however, the experiment left little behind; a handful of settlers remained, but the focus of colonial efforts returned to the plantation model.

The upheaval of the revolutionary period in Metropolitan France also brought turmoil to the colonies. Most momentously, the slaves were freed in 1794, only to be reenslaved in 1802. Though Cayenne experienced minor insurrection, nothing on the scale of the uprisings in Guadeloupe or the future Haiti occurred. Instead, Guyane served as a site of deportation for several hundred enemies of the shifting regimes. As with the Kourou expedition, death rates among these exiles were high, further cementing the area's negative reputation as a land for European settlement, particularly when several accounts of their suffering became sufficiently disseminated. In 1809 the Portuguese, with English assistance, seized French Guiana. Five years later the territory was returned to France under the terms of the Treaty of Paris.[14]

THE MOMENT OF THE NINETEENTH CENTURY

As the revolutionary tides in France subsided, French Guiana experienced a moment of relative prosperity. Like the restoration of the Bourbons, it was to prove short-lived, but for a period around 1830 the slave population expanded to nineteen thousand, and production included spices, largely for local consumption, as well as export crops of cotton, sugar, and dye. However, in the face of growing cotton production in the southern United States and European sugar beet crops, French Guiana's moment of expansion came too little too late. Both plantation production and the slave population dwindled as the mid-century neared.[15]

In 1848 another surge of revolution finally swept slavery aside throughout the remaining French Empire. The effects in Guyane of this development were marked, as the former slaves left the plantations to practice subsistence agriculture (farming plots known as *abattis*). Unlike most other parts of the Caribbean, French or otherwise, here the population was so small and available land so vast that the plantation system disintegrated, leaving little economic structure in its wake. Thus no well-defined reinvented "peasantry" emerged. Inspired by the example of neighboring British Guiana, the remaining planter class and colonial officials sought to encourage immigration of contract laborers, recruiting Africans, Chinese, Indians, and even a few souls from the Madeira Islands. None of these experiments met with much success. Unlike Britain, France lacked an obvious source of colonial labor.[16] Instead of a renewed plantation system, two new forces came to define the local economy for much of the ensuing century—a penal colony and a gold rush. Established in 1852, the penal colony failed to live up to its initial billing as a substitute source of agricultural labor; however, in fits and starts, its lingering presence deeply influenced the flow of goods and services as well as the reputation of the colony. For its part, the gold rush gathered steam in the decades after finds in the 1850s and 1860s and brought thousands of free immigrants to Guyane, largely from the neighboring areas, especially the French and British West Indies.[17] It also became the focus of much of the export activity on the part of the civil population, who were lured by the promise of quick wealth, and it remains a significant part of the cultural mythology of Guyanais society. The image of the small-time *maraudeur* or *bricoleur*, pan in hand, finding his fortune in the face of mining companies, took an honored place in the Creole pantheon.[18] Although arbitration severed the French territory from grandiose claims south and east to the Amazon (Switzerland awarding the area to Brazil), as the twentieth century dawned this particular colony remained on its erratic course. Between a nonproductive criminal analog of the plantation and a revitalized quest for El Dorado, French Guiana's economy continued a peculiar, hollow evolution.

THE LONG CRISIS: COLONIALISM TO DEPARTMENTALIZATION

During the decades preceding World War II, the colony remained a remote appendage to the French body politic. A number of other ventures had been founded between gold and convicts, including the production of rum, rosewood, and balata gum. These economic activities met with some initial success, assisting in the creation of minor fortunes such as that of Jean Galmot, a populist local politician who came into conflict with the colonial administration, and whose death under mysterious circumstances in 1928 led to riots in Cayenne. In 1930 the colony was divided in two, the interior region, known as the Inini territory, passing directly under the control of the governor and a separate council. The goal of this operation was to encourage and facilitate the exploitation of the interior, an outcome that failed to materialize. However, the administrative separation of the Inini insulated its population (primarily composed of Amerindians, Maroons, and gold miners) from the events and policies of the coast.[19]

The world depression of the 1930s did little to aid French Guiana's economy. Gold production declined and the fragility of the colonial economy was left bare for all to see. Despite the tons of gold extracted since the nineteenth century, little significant industry or agriculture existed, and the gap between imports and exports failed to close. For all its lack of production and endemic corruption, the penal colony served as a source of revenue as well as cheap labor, a fact that led some locals to oppose its closure, even as others called for its suppression. In 1938 the French Assembly finally made the decision to phase out the operation, setting the stage for a new political and economic era. However, World War II intervened. Along with the rest of France's Atlantic colonies, Guyane was left stranded by the fall of France in 1940.[20] Under an administration sympathetic to the Vichy regime it faltered economically, cut off from supply routes and incapable of producing adequate supplies of food. The suffering in the penal colony during this period was particularly intense. In 1943, under continuing pressure from the United States and shifts in public opinion, the Vichy regime finally collapsed, and pro–Free French forces and sentiment took over. While this political shift failed to rekindle economic production, American subventions, partly in the form of the construction of two airfields, eased the crisis.[21]

The aftermath of the war brought French Guiana to an administrative watershed: the transition of its status from that of a colony to that of an "overseas department" (*département d'outre-mer,* or DOM) politically integrated into the French state. In March 1946 the special relationship of the significant remnants of France's first empire—Guyane, Guadeloupe, Martinique, and Réunion—with the Metropole was written into law. This shift, long sought by the political representatives of the "old colonies," ensured the legal status of their citizens as well as continuing economic links to France.[22] A prefect would replace the governor, and—in a triumph of cultural heritage and political will over geography—Guyane would at last truly become France. After the upheaval of the war, the future now promised a new beginning.

A BUREAUCRATIC LULL

"Bricolage must give way to technique.*"*
                                                    French colonial report, 1945[23]

A shift of some sort was clearly needed to integrate the region into greater France. In the 1946 census, French Guiana could only muster a population of 29,506, recording one of the lowest population densities on the planet. Cayenne was the only settlement of any significance, boasting 10,961 inhabitants. The rest of the population lived largely in small pockets along the coast, while the interior officially held only 6,509 persons. The population figures were down almost a quarter from prewar levels, and birth- and death rates were discouraging. The closure of the penal colony eliminated one source of new arrivals, and the gold fields no longer attracted the flood of fortune seekers of the glory days. Calls were made for a new wave of immigrants, echoing an earlier plea for Jewish refugees. However, no large-scale immigration ensued, and the pattern of population decline did not reverse until 1954.[24]

The economy faced other challenges besides the lack of adequate labor supply: infrastructure was scanty and disease endemic. Communication and transportation links between Cayenne and the other communities left much to be desired, and public health measures were minimal. The new administration identified these problems and sought to ameliorate both, attempting to improve the conditions of life while creating a model French society on the South American continent. In general, the public health campaign met with great success. The establishment of a network of clinics and radio telephones allowed widespread medical coverage, and a crusade to improve mother and infant care helped decrease infant mortality (although a moral campaign to reduce illegitimate births among the Creole population failed to achieve equivalent results). The local branch of the Institut Pasteur—established during the war in 1940—actively led a campaign against malaria, and DDT spraying began in 1949. This program soon claimed spectacular success, reducing the mortality rate by three-fourths over six months of the ensuing year. Other efforts targeted yellow fever and leprosy, and local health statistics continued to show significant improvement. At long last the specter of disease haunting Guyane began to fade.[25]

The search for an elusive "economic takeoff," in contrast, largely failed. The most significant growth in the local economy occurred in the public sector, which accounted for almost two-thirds of salaries in 1959. This dramatic increase stemmed directly from departmentalization, as administrative models derived from Metropolitan norms were applied overseas and bureaucratic positions, in the absence of alternatives, acquired a mark of social distinction. Because there were difficulties in luring trained personnel to remote locations, in 1957 the Metropolitan salary scale was augmented by a 40 percent bonus for those serving in overseas departments. This both exacerbated the gap between those on and off the public payroll and increased the attraction of administrative posts. At the same time this influx of surplus income encouraged the growth of consumer spending, and new commodities and services (including automobiles and electrical power) made their appearance. Although departmentalization improved the standard of living and general quality of life of the citizens of French Guiana, it only furthered dependence on France.[26] The economic hollow stretching between gold exploitation and the *bagne* in the prewar colony gaped only wider beneath the frame of the postwar welfare state.

POLITICAL HISTORY AND DEVELOPMENT PLANS

It never occurred to anyone that any large-scale enterprise could be put through successfully without the intervention of the State.

> *Alexis de Tocqueville,* The Old Régime
> and the French Revolution, *1856*

At the end of the 1950s local enthusiasm for the departmental experiment in French Guiana began to wane. As the Algerian War precipitated a constitutional crisis in France, a number of leftist political parties favoring greater autonomy emerged onto the local scene. The decade of the 1960s also witnessed several significant transformations of the social and economic landscapes, including the growing significance of migration issues and the establishment of the Guiana Space Center

(CSG) at Kourou in 1964. Migration cut both ways: large numbers of young Guyanais began leaving for the Metropole, just as foreign labor—encouraged by the new large-scale construction projects associated with the space center—began to arrive at last. Thus while the Guyanais Creole population established its own colony in urban France, the non-Creole population in Guyane grew. The space center contributed significantly to the development of the department's infrastructure, as bridges were completed and port and airport facilities improved in anticipation of its needs. It also brought with it a new kind of elite migrant: the well-educated and well-paid French technical worker, ready to rival the bureaucrat in levels of consumption. Moreover, as a major project of direct strategic importance to France, the space center created another pole of state activity to rival that of the departmental government. The abolition of the Inini territory in 1969 completed the drive toward integration and heralded the political emergence of populations who lived in the interior, primarily Maroons and Amerindians.[27]

The early 1970s ushered in a small burst of independence movements and political unrest, the peaks coming in 1971 and 1974. After the arrest of a number of militants the protests eventually fizzled, though underlying tensions remained. Despite efforts to revitalize the economy and modernize agricultural practice, production continued to sag. France's entry into the European Economic Community and treaties signed with Caribbean, African, and Pacific nations complicated the economic position of Guyanais agriculture, while shifting consumption patterns favored European staples of bread and potatoes over local manioc. In a lull of space activity in the middle of the decade, the government unveiled a new development initiative, the Plan Vert (Green Plan), which envisioned a new wave of industrious French colonists to serve, in the words of Prime Minister Jacques Chirac, as the "principal motor of development."[28] The document outlining the initiative includes a sequence about a young Metropolitan named "Henri" who arrives in French Guiana to seek his fortune. Learning to shoot a bow and arrow, cutting a tree, and inspecting a gold mine, Henri becomes aware of the range of possibilities awaiting in this yet-unconquered New World. Two centuries after the disastrous Kourou expedition, a ghost of the settler dream reemerges in these pages; on the cover of the document we see Henri paddling a canoe into the future, while a nameless, dark-skinned man toils dourly behind him.[29]

The Green Plan encountered strenuous local opposition and failed to achieve its envisioned goals. Independence groups denounced it as a form of potential "genocide," and at the same time the value of paper products (a planned focus of investment) fell sharply on the world market.[30] Out of over fifteen thousand application dossiers processed, fewer than a thousand found their way through the appropriate French ministries, and little new agriculture took root in Guyane.[31] Immigration, however, continued apace throughout the latter part of the decade and into the 1980s. Haitians arrived in large numbers, and, in the wake of the long conflict in the former Indochina, a group of Hmong were resettled in these distant tropics and encouraged to play the role of model horticultural minority.

Meanwhile, the space program rebounded with the newly designed Ariane rocket, which proved to be both a technical and a commercial success. As confidence grew and satellite contracts rolled in, the space complex and the neighboring community of Kourou expanded quickly, displacing the former penal colony hub of St. Laurent as French Guiana's second-largest town. Administratively, the Socialist Party victory in 1982 and the subsequent policy of "decentralization" led to increased local political authority and a new layer of bureaucratic offices. Economic production, however, continued to limp unhurriedly along. Wood, shrimp, and gold each showed signs of promise as an export product, but none posed much of a challenge to the public sector. Direct air links to Paris helped to generate modest European tourism, but nothing on the scale of Caribbean islands. In 1986 the outbreak of civil war in neighboring Suriname brought a new flood of refugees, largely Maroons, while the number of Brazilians crossing the other border began to soar. By the time of the 1990 census, the official population was over one hundred thousand. Coupled with endemic unemployment and an economy split between those enjoying a professional income and spending freely, those living at a more modest level of French welfare allowances, and those working unofficially and scraping along at a subsistence level, this demographic explosion threatened to drastically alter the shape of Guyanais society.

Thus by 1992 the stage was set: a standard of living and patterns of consumption geared to French norms went hand in hand with a dearth of agricultural or industrial production. Only bureaucratic agencies, the space center, and a black market centered on the labor of illegal aliens showed clear signs of vitality. After three centuries of European presence, gold, the plantation, the prison, the bureau, and the rocket had each left their different marks, composing a society of fragmentary frontiers, ordinary elements in unusual alignment. Before continuing to consider French Guiana in relation to its context, let us pause and consider its profile more carefully, five centuries after Columbus.

NATURAL FACTS

Since this work concerns itself with "nature," a brief litany of relevant facts is in order. The geographic region known on current maps as French Guiana (or *la Guyane française* lies between 51°30' and 54°30' West in longitude, and 2° and 6° North in latitude, encompassing somewhat under ninety thousand square kilometers (roughly thirty-five thousand square miles) of surface area. In human political terms it is located on the northeast coast of South America, above Brazil and beside Suriname, and is about the size of the state of Maine, or about a sixth the size of Metropolitan France.[32] The average annual temperature varies little, usually resting between 22° and 30° C (71.6° and 86° F), with a mean just under 27° C (80.6° F). Humidity remains persistently high (usually between 80 and 90 percent). Rainfall is heavy, totaling some 200 to 400 centimeters (79 to 157 inches) per year depending on locale, and falling most frequently during the periods between December and February and between May and July. The "dry season," which denotes the longest break in precipitation and the highest set of temperatures, usually occurs between August and December. The sun is bright and shines for an average of six hours a day. Because of Guyane's position relative to the shifting zone of intertropical convergence, it does not experience the cycle of hurricanes that afflict the Caribbean, and the ground is seismically stable. Indeed, the area constitutes an epitome of natural regularity: the measurable climate is methodically tropical, and the experience of it calm, warm, and sticky.[33]

While the coastal region includes savannas, mangroves, and marshlands, rich rain forest mantles the interior, composing some 90 percent of the surface area. Stretches around the coast settlements include thick secondary growth, but most of the forest is primary, dark, and strikingly open beneath high trees. Although hills rise amid the trees, from the air the topography appears relatively flat. An impressive number of rivers and streams wind through the forest to meet the calm and often muddy sea. The two largest of these, the River Maroni to the northwest and the River Oyapock to the southeast, mark the present-day boundaries with Suriname and Brazil respectively; both sport stretches of

Figure 4.   Governor's palace, Cayenne, 1990

rapids and widen impressively at the mouth.[34] The flora and fauna are rich, including hundreds of varieties of trees, numerous orchids, many birds, tarantulas, and beetles and other insects, not to mention such Amazonian staples as frogs, snakes, and caimans, or monkeys, sloths, and tapirs. Many species remain uncatalogued.[35] In the last decade of the twentieth century, French Guiana stands out as one of the least populated and obviously "natural" areas of the world, a large portion of its territory little affected by overt signs of human presence, a small vestige of Columbus's New World.

POLITICAL ECONOMY

As an economic entity, French Guiana is truly an outpost of France, officially importing and exporting most goods to and from that source. Imports easily outstrip exports, by a factor of about seven in 1992.[36] The productive sector of the economy includes exploitation of wood, fishing, agriculture, and mining, but no enterprise is significantly large. Unlike in the neighboring French islands of Martinique and Guadeloupe, tourism remains a minor factor, and the space center accounts for up to half of all economic activity. Almost a quarter of the workforce is unemployed, yet French Guiana contains about sixty thousand

Figure 5.   Creole house, Mana, 1993

automobiles, running over a mere five hundred or so kilometers of paved road.[37] None of these figures, of course, adequately account for the activity of illegal immigrants, private exchanges, or illicit trade over the borders with Suriname and Brazil.

As a political entity, French Guiana remains first and foremost a *département*, a unit established at the end of the eighteenth century in revolutionary France and perfected under Napoleon. Although the overseas departments retain certain distinct features, for most intents and purposes they live up to the legal claim of constituting an extension of France. As in Metropolitan departments, the French state is represented by a *préfet* (prefect). Not coincidentally, this official occupies the former colonial governor's palace on ceremonial occasions, serving for many practical purposes much the same role in the postcolonial department. The local political apparatus is complex and multiheaded, with numerous and occasionally overlapping spheres of authority.[38] One significant divide, however, frames Guyanais political disputes, that separating the local elected officials (*les élus*) from the professional administrators representing the French state in the prefect's office. Not only is this distinction frequently invoked in political rhetoric, but the career trajectory of the individuals involved differs widely; unlike the local politicians, but like the earlier colonial governor, a prefect can come from anywhere within the French system and, after staying a few years, departs again. Hence, for all that these officials represent the apex of political authority, their actual impact usually remains quite limited. Another potentially significant political fault line stems from Guyane's membership in the European Community. Although European elections proved less than popular in 1994, local politicians, particularly those with inclinations toward independence, have begun to realize that the European bureaucracy presents an alternative source of financial and political influence, one which can sometimes be set against that of France.

HUMAN PATTERNS

Three demographic facts distinguish the human geography of French Guiana. First, the population is very small, barely enough to fill a modest city in many parts of the world. Second, the population is nevertheless quite diverse, a result of centuries of colonial migration. And third, recent demographic growth, much of it coming from immigration, has significantly altered the ethnic landscape. Here I will enumerate only the major groups, and echo Ken Bilby's proviso that if one were to count all the finer distinctions made, the list could easily pass a hundred.[39] The Amerindian population found within the territory includes six groups: the Arawak, Emerillon, Kaliña (Galibi), Palikur, Wayana, and Wayampi. The ancestors of the Arawak and Kaliña, who today live on the coast and are the most integrated of the Amerindian communities, and possibly those of the Emerillon and Palikur, were present in Guyane when the French arrived. The forebears of the Wayana and Wayampi most likely entered French Guiana from Brazil at some point in the eighteenth or nineteenth century. The total population for all groups is something in the range of four thousand to five thousand persons, over half of whom are Kaliña. The Wayana, Wayampi, and Emerillon, all of whom live in the interior, remain the most distinct in terms of dress and cultural behavior.[40] The Europeans who arrived in the seventeenth through nineteenth century left few descendants, and the "Metropolitans" who currently live in French Guiana are more recent immigrants, mostly centered around Cayenne, the administrative center, and Kourou, the space town. That segment of the population known as "Creoles," the descendants of former African slaves, immigrants from elsewhere in the West Indies, and Europeans, comprises the largest single block. In addition to Creoles identified as "Guyanais," there are also Creoles from the French and British Antilles and a large and particularly distinct group of recent immigrants from Haiti. The descendants of African slaves (largely from the plantations of Dutch Guiana) who escaped to establish separate societies in the interior between the seventeenth and nineteenth centuries are known as "Maroons." Within French Guiana several groups of Maroons play significant roles, including the Aluku (who enjoy French citizenship) and the Saramaka, Ndjuka, and Paramaka, many of whom crossed the river into French Guiana following unrest in Suriname.[41] Brazilians, who have arrived in ever-increasing numbers throughout the 1990s, make up the fastest growing immigrant group, while the Chinese, despite their relatively small numbers, occupy a position of social prominence as a result of their near-monopoly on small food stores and related commerce.

An imperfect ethnic breakdown in 1985, prior to the major influx of Brazilians and Maroon refugees, ran as follows: Guyanais Creoles 43 percent, Haitians 22 percent, Metropolitans 8 percent, Maroons 6 percent, Brazilians 6 percent, French Antillian Creoles 5 percent, Amerindians 4 percent, Anglophone Caribbeans 3 percent, Chinese 1 percent, Hmong 1 percent, and Suriname Creoles 1 percent. Since that time the population has grown considerably, with a 1992 estimate of 131,000 and a 1994 figure of 150,000.[42] Taken as a whole the population is very young; more than half the inhabitants are under twenty-five years of age. The birthrate is almost seven times higher than the death rate, and if growth matches predictions, the total population will near 200,000 in the year 2000 census.[43]

Because my main focus is on actors arriving in the tropics from Europe, internal tensions surrounding identity in French Guiana remain muted in this work. However, it is important to note that a crucial social divide runs between the coast (where the vast majority of the population lives) and the interior (rarely visited by those who live on the coast). The status of "native" identity remains in question across this very divide: it is most often claimed by Guyanais Creoles in opposition to Metropolitan norms, but it is always hedged by the existence of "more natural" Amerindians and Maroons in the interior. In the face of continued immigration, the position of Guyanais Creoles—the dominant non-European segment of the population—has only grown more symbolically embattled.[44]

FRENCH GUIANA IN CONTEXT

The despair of classifiers, area studies programs, krem-
linologists in ill-fitting sombreros, North American
race relations experts, ambulant East European com-
missars and the CIA, the Caribbean region goes its
own way, richly researched but poorly understood.

Sidney Mintz, "The Caribbean Region," 1974

No Industrial Revolution, no revolution of any kind,
no Age of Anything, no world wars, no decades of tur-
bulence balanced by decades of calm.

Jamaica Kincaid, A Small Place, *1988*

Now let us return to a broader geographic and conceptual frame. For
all that French Guiana represents an anomaly (as most writers who
seek to describe it suggest), it is at the same time a microcosm of
larger trends and forces. In Guyane—so long a colony, so little developed—the loose ends of the New World dangle free. The most immediate geographic context into which to place French Guiana is that of
two neighboring political entities to the northwest, Suriname (former
Dutch Guiana) and Guyana (former British Guiana). While the physical region that they represent may extend further into Brazil and
Venezuela, in human terms the Guiana trio represents an exception to
most generalizations about the continent of South America, and as
such can be treated as a separate block. All three share a legacy of
non-Iberian European colonization and remained colonies long after
the rest of the continent became politically independent. All three remain relatively marginal in both political and academic terms. In traditions of area studies in social science they are usually classified—
inasmuch as they are classified at all—as part of an expanded
Caribbean, a tradition that I follow here. However, for all the similarity among the three, each of the Guianas has a particular history
and contemporary profile. A full comparison between them lies outside the scope of this project, but two points should be made. First,
the Guiana colonies built under the rule of the Dutch and English
greatly outweighed the French in wealth and standing throughout
most of their history; and second, this imbalance has reversed since
the departmentalization of French Guiana in 1946 and the later independence of Guyana (1966) and Suriname (1975). Whereas in the
past the French outpost was a poor cousin to the other two—the

margin of the margin—at present it is the rich relation and a window back into Western Europe.[45]

Another step back leads us to a more general frame of reference for French Guiana: the long, tense seam between Old and New worlds that runs through the Caribbean Sea. The Caribbean has had an uneasy career as a culture area in social science. The questions of anthropology in particular fall too close to home, lacking the comfortable veil of timeless purity. Even if the descendants of the pre-Columbian era have largely vanished, the effects of colonization are impossible to ignore.[46] Effects of history, in naked, painful form, lie around every corner. The traditions of the present can—with unnerving certainty, if not precision—be dated. Born amid conquest and slavery, at the intersection between Europe, Africa, and America, the defining features of the Caribbean are unquestionably modern. This modernity disabuses simple orders of space as well as time: even in its prenational origin the Caribbean is obviously transnational, the result of several migrations and intercontinental ties.

As Michel-Rolph Trouillot points out, the Caribbean has long served as an academic crossroads, lacking "gates on the frontier."[47] Disciplinary fences are loose, and large sections of the fence running between anthropology and history lie fallen. Questions cross back and forth, linking subjects even on their surface. From this perspective it is no accident that figures within the anthropology of the expanded Caribbean region have produced work beyond immediate ethnography, work that navigates between domains of present and past and falls outside simple geographic classifications.[48] Certainly it would be no overstatement to say that interest in political economy and the study of the Caribbean have led to each other, and the marriage of the two has produced much of the important work in the region. One of the central concepts in the analysis of the systems that brought the New World into being—the plantation—encourages a broader redefinition of the Caribbean area back into the New World, moving beyond the islands at its center to include the surrounding shore, Brazil, and the southern United States. Efforts to better define postplantation Caribbean "peasantries" in turn feed back into reconsiderations of European peasantries. In this modern tropics, between bright light and heavy rain, circular movements of theory, region, and discipline grow bold and thick.

Given the conditions of this regional map, it is only appropriate to include French Guiana within the Caribbean. Although Guyane is not a literal island, it exhibits many of the historical characteristics of one, and although it never felt Columbus's boot, the shadow of exploration still rests on its shore. A thinly inhabited forest, a backwater plantation, a failed settler colony, a dumping ground for undesirables, and a minor rush for gold—together these layers of colonial legacy give us a New World tableau in miniature. This miniature remains unfinished, for in French Guiana growth and decay do not separate neatly. As local rhetoric would have it, after more than three centuries of colonization, the real "conquest" of Guyane has yet to begin. The long frontier still lies open. In essence, French Guiana represents the margin of the Caribbean, a border outpost, a place where certainties unravel. It is also a space where the dreams of Columbus and Crusoe flicker on, amid the possibility of discovery, of planting one's foot, and of the wealth and dominion in claiming a New World.

Thus in beginning our analysis of a historical penal colony, an extant satellite center, and the common ground they share, we have before us fragments of familiar stories, shadows of elsewhere, and an open horizon of dreams. The longevity of this space—the social potential of an empty tropics—constitutes the crux of French Guiana's importance as a case, because "nature," the pure realm of open possibility, here comes directly into view across from "culture," the contending human and material technologies seeking to effect its transformation. The edge of modern development rises to the surface from under sediments of language and historical experience. Despite three centuries of active French presence, Guyane retains the aura of an unconquered realm, a land open to possibility. For those who discuss its future—particularly those susceptible to metaphors of virginity—the words of Ralegh ring ever fresh and true:

> To conclude, *Guiana* is a Countrey that hath yet her Maydenhead, neuer sackt, turned, nor wrought, the face of the earth hath not been torne, nor the vertue and salt of the soyle been spent by manurance, the graues haue not beene opened for gold, the mines not broken with sledges, nor their Images puld down out of their temples.[49]

Figure 6.   French Foreign Legion, Cayenne, 1994

PART 2

Colonial Ground

"I wonder if I shall fall right *through* the earth! How funny
it'll seem to come out among the people that walk with their
heads downwards! The Antipathies, I think—"
  Lewis Carroll, Alice's Adventures in Wonderland, *1865*

In the child's logic of digging through the Earth and out the other side,
the world reached can only be reversed. For all that astronomy might
predict a round globe, and the experience of voyagers affirm it, the implications are hard to fit with an everyday experience of singular flat-
ness. But in the antipodes the sprawl of European expansion came together, joining horizons and confusing common sense. The down and
under known as "Australia" also marks another end to empire quite
relevant for us: the classic penal colony, a great experiment tying the
labor of transported convicts to the development of wilderness. In settling their farthest shore, the British government sought to alleviate
dangerous pressures from within. It was an ingenious solution: the distance between colony and nation would turn the desperate criminal on
his or her head, creating a useful subject at the frontier of civilization.
The British experiment inspired the French to transport part of their
penal system overseas, in an effort to build Australia in the tropics. But
the French project failed as a settler colony, misreading its maps, and
instead found another end, a hole that led below without resurfacing.
As the century turned, the penal colony (the *bagne,* Devil's Island) lent
French Guiana its greatest specificity, but in geographic abstraction: a
vague, highly charged inversion of wider colonial ground, a land of
tropical punishment where European criminals fell and suffered along
with colonials, or even underneath them. In this space of punishment
we find a number of edges: boundaries of economics, moral behavior,
and race. Between them we also find a world reversed, a land of heads
bowed low, if not suspended downward.

CHAPTER 3

Botany Bay to Devil's Island

The explorer bent so close to the paper that the officer feared
he might touch it and drew it farther away; the explorer
made no remark, yet it was clear that he still could not deci-
pher it. "'BE JUST!' is what is written there," said the officer
once more. "Maybe," said the explorer, "I am prepared to
believe you."

Franz Kafka, "In the Penal Colony," 1919

PRISON DEBATES AND COLONIAL PUNISHMENT

In the summer of 1914, as European civility crumbled into war, Franz
Kafka began writing what was to become *The Trial,* his great indict-
ment of the mindless machinery of bureaucratic justice. By November
he had also penned "In the Penal Colony," a short, savage description
of a place and procedure of punishment.[1] At the center of that tale lies
an extraordinary apparatus, at once delicate and blunt, that slowly ex-
ecutes a prisoner by repeatedly writing his sentence on his body.
Kafka's narrative follows a gentlemanly traveler as he encounters this
perfectly literate form of execution in a decaying colony. The explorer
reluctantly witnesses the final, mad demise of the system and its exaggerated principles, amid a dismal environment of chronic lassitude.
Kafka's work thus provides a double frame for anyone contemplating
the follies of modern justice: in addition to the vast, demented calculus
of *The Trial,* he offers a smaller, more pointed nightmare of reason
gone astray in some distant tropics. This second narrative gives us two
key images: a metaphorical machine of literal punishment and an island
as shadowy as Crusoe's is exacting. Both prove apt figures for the next
part of our story.

Between the eighteenth and twentieth centuries, general European
attitudes toward punishment shifted at an official level. This shift—
both dramatic and incomplete—centers around the emergence of more
exact and self-consciously humane ways of identifying and treating

Figure 7.   Penal colony interior, St. Laurent, 1990

offenders. Public trials and prisons take the place of public torture and execution. Focus moves to the issue of whether malefactors might be reformed, their souls reclaimed in this life. The transformation is far from universal but clear enough to be recognizable; although torture and executions may continue, and suffering persist, the formal exercise of justice has acquired a new and technically dispassionate architecture. What one makes of this transformation is another matter.

The most provocative narration of modern penal history can be found in Michel Foucault's *Discipline and Punish*.[2] In the two decades since its publication this work has both exerted wide and varied influence and encountered furious opposition. A number of scholars across a range of academic disciplines have drawn inspiration from Foucault's genealogical account of modern power, even as more conventional studies of prison history have proliferated. The image of the Panopticon, Bentham's architectural ode to surveillance, has emerged from the dusty closet of history to travel across numerous pages of contemporary academic reference. At the same time some have expressed distaste for the work's fundamental interrogation of humanism, and others have questioned the historical fabric of its specific chronology, arguing for either more gradual or incomplete versions of penal transformation. Yet few would disagree that *Discipline and Punish* represents an inescapable reference point in any contemporary discussion of punishment.[3]

Here I accept the broad frame of Foucault's historical panorama, yet wish to reposition it against the backdrop of empire. The very specificity of one of its prominent details opens another horizon: beyond Bentham's Panopticon lies Australia, and beyond the modern prison lies the shadow of the penal colony. Although the Panopticon was never built, we should not forget that its inventor championed his project in opposition to a very real British experiment, the practice of penal transportation to the Pacific. And the penal colony was to remain a viable alternative to the penitentiary, not only in nineteenth-century Britain, but also in twentieth-century France (not to mention—in a somewhat different form—the Soviet Union). Even as techniques of confinement, isolation, and regulation grew refined in Metropolitan prison architecture, cruder structures of punishment took shape on the periphery. Foucault's analysis offers no direct space in which to locate them. *Discipline and Punish* makes only brief references to deportation as an alternative to the prison, calling the French case a "rigorous and distant form of imprisonment" and noting that it did little for the colonial enterprise and was of no real economic importance in either New Caledonia or Guiana.[4] But what might it mean to have a rigorous and distant form of imprisonment, located in a colony and continuing until the mid–twentieth century? To answer this we must turn from the bright light of the Panopticon and search in its shadows, for another, less perfect machine.

BENTHAM'S PANOPTICON
AND BRITISH TRANSPORTATION

Morals reformed—health preserved—industry invigor-
ated—instruction diffused—public burthens light-
ened—Economy seated, as it were, upon a rock—the
gordian knot of the Poor-Laws not cut, but untied—all
by a simple idea of Architecture!

> *Jeremy Bentham,*
> Panopticon, or The Inspection House, *1791*

An unexplored continent would become a jail. The
space around it, the very sea and air, the whole transparent labyrinth of the South Pacific, would become a
wall 14,000 miles thick.

> *Robert Hughes,* The Fatal Shore, *1986*

The practice of transportation did not emerge out of thin air. The penal colony has antecedents on the one hand in practices of slavery and forced labor in galleys, mines, and public works, and on the other in traditions of exile for political figures, nobles, and other members of fallen elites. Before being applied to penal colonies, the French term *bagne* was applied successively to those sentenced to rowing Mediterranean galleys and to performing hard labor in Metropolitan ports.[5] But the marriage of both labor and exile in the systematized deportation of large numbers of common criminals to New World settlements marks an extreme twist in the eighteenth and nineteenth century. In a world shaped by economic reordering, imperial expansion, and increasing bureaucratization, the transportation of common criminals away from Europe became a viable penal strategy, an alternative to execution and local prisons that would be formulated and practiced by more than one nation.

Indeed the stories of both the penitentiary and the penal colony are inextricably woven between national histories and empires. At the very least, any serious discussion must encompass Britain, France, and the United States, as varying currents of reform and counterreform ran across both the Channel and the Atlantic. Both Britain and France sought to rid themselves of malefactors by banishing them to the New World, whereas the fields of religious experimentation in the newly independent United States allowed for practical implementation of reform projects. These model prisons in turn—particularly those of Philadelphia and Auburn—enjoyed considerable influence in both British and French debates.[6] But it was in Britain that the organizational outlines of penal transportation took shape and came into conflict with the emerging penitentiary. The British context, therefore, merits closer examination.

The use of prison sentences as a sanction for legal transgression was rarely applied to offenders in England before the late eighteenth century. Instead, punishment more commonly took the form of hanging, whipping, or other physical abuse or transportation overseas. Faced with a growing and unpoliced population of petty criminals and political rebels, the British government found a solution to domestic problems by transferring criminals to the colonies in North America and the Caribbean. The scale of the operation was modest, something on the order of seven hundred felons a year in the mid–eighteenth century. Faced with the independence of the former American colonies, which eliminated their future utility as a penal repository, the British sought an alternative site for transportation. The commission formed in 1785 considered locations in West Africa and Southwest Africa before settling on Australia. Lacking the time to wait for a scouting mission to confirm reports from Cook's 1770 voyage, the first fleet of transports set sail in 1787 and landed at Botany Bay in the spring of 1788.

In all some 160,000 convicts were to make the Australian voyage into exile before the last ship pulled ashore in 1868. However, they did not come all at once, or under the same conditions. The bulk arrived between 1810 and 1840, after which transportation to the territory of New South Wales ceased. Following that point, convicts were redirected to marginal zones of the Australian colonial map, Van Dieman's Land (Tasmania), and finally Western Australia. These facts are important to recall when considering the rise and fall of voices urging reform of the system, for they remind us that the possibility of the penitentiary did not simply eliminate the penal colony and that the penal colony did not represent a singular or uniform effort of colonization. Rather, penal colony and penitentiary coexisted in uneasy competition, as did convict and free projects of colonization, and the demise of the latter was gradual and spatially defined.[7]

The system of transportation had numerous critics, many associated with the reforms that gave rise to the penitentiary. Although earlier precedents exist, the decade of the 1770s marks the first watershed of the English reform movement, including the publication of John Howard's influential survey, *The State of the Prisons,* in 1777 and the passage of Blackstone and Eden's Penitentiary Act in 1779.[8] During the ensuing decades, issues related to the proper forms of punishment occupied a significant place in British public debates, and one of the most prominent figures amid these discussions was Jeremy Bentham. A year after Howard's work, Bentham published a response to a draft version of Blackstone and Eden's bill. Bentham sought to eliminate elements of irrationality from systems of punishment, suggesting, among other things, a whipping machine that would eliminate variability in the force of the blows. Following a trip to visit his brother in Russia, he came up with the outlines of his most influential proposition of all, the system of total surveillance entitled the Panopticon, at about the same time as he learned of the decision to reestablish transportation to Botany Bay. Returning to England in 1788—even as the First Fleet anchored off the barren Australian coast—Bentham set out on a long endeavor to convince a government to build his proposed penitentiary, approaching the Irish and French as well as the English administrations. Setting forth his ideas in pamphlet form in 1791, he proclaimed an "Idea of a New Principle of Construction applicable to Any Sort of Establishment in Which Persons of Any Description are to be Kept Under Inspection," notably including workhouses, manufactories, madhouses, hospitals, and schools under its purview, in addition to prisons and penitentiaries.[9]

Bentham's struggle to convince the British government to build the Panopticon continued for two decades, almost achieving success before he admitted defeat in 1813 and finally received compensation for losses incurred. Throughout the effort he argued strenuously against transportation and the choice of Botany Bay, on the basis of both principle and economy. An opponent of colonies in general, he thought that New South Wales represented a too costly, too distant, and unexemplary form of punishment, far inferior to the penitentiary on every account, views he set forth in an appeal to the home secretary, Lord Pelham, circulated in 1802.[10] But Bentham's protest would not yet win the day; support for transportation ran strong. As he expressed in disgust: "Ask if the Colony presents any prospect of paying its own expenses—oh, but it is an engine of punishment, to be substituted for the Hulks—Ask whether as an engine of punishment it is not an expensive one—oh, but it is a colony to boot, and a fifth quarter of the globe added to the British empire."[11] This double logic supporting a combination of transportation, empire, and punishment continued to underwrite the Australian venture through the mid–nineteenth century. Although the penal colony encountered criticism for being too lenient as well as too harsh, it was the latter charge, coupled with the overflow of arguments against slavery and combined with the shifting economic structure of the penal apparatus, that finally led to its eventual decline.[12] Yet before it faded away the Australian system made a lasting impression and echoed across the English channel, where French officials sought solutions for their own dilemmas of crime.

THE MODEL OF AUSTRALIA: ANGLO INFLUENCE AND FRENCH PROPOSALS

Australia is the penal colony that we can cite as a
model, by reason of its choice of locale, the efforts
which prepared its colonization and the success that
crowns it each day.

French colonial official, 1845[13]

Although the French matched the British in early uses of deporting political undesirables and banishing criminals overseas, they developed penal colonies relatively late. In part this can be attributed to the differing fortunes of each empire as well as the differing composition of each national system of punishment. On the one hand the French government could not match Britain's imperial sweep following 1763, while on the other they had a functioning police force and the penal tradition of the *bagne* to help absorb malefactors. Furthermore, the upheaval associated with the French Revolution complicated questions of punishment directly at the center of national government, unlike the effects of the American Revolution on Britain. Yet it would be a mistake to think that interest in the penal colony ran low. Glowing references to Australia and proposals to establish an overseas prison appeared frequently during the first half of the nineteenth century.[14]

The first serious proposals to establish a "French Botany Bay," as one later author would put it, surfaced during the revolutionary period. The French Revolution brought a new penal code and opened the door to innovation in punishment, including the adoption of the guillotine in 1792, that infamous scientific advance in the art of decapitation. Debates began over the possibility of establishing a colony based on penal transportation or political deportation, and pamphlets appeared urging the adoption of the scheme, including one supporting the suitability of French Guiana for such a project because the "eternal springtime" of its climate would permit the realization of Plato's republic.[15] While other sites merited consideration—Corsica was also advanced for being underpopulated and underdeveloped—French Guiana emerged as an early favorite for the placement of a French penal colony.

In 1791 a doctor and naturalist named Leblond, who had been searching Guyane for quinine at the behest of Louis XVI, found himself deported from Cayenne back to France. There he did his best to counter the negative image of the colony left by the disastrous Kourou expedition, and he gave a speech proposing to solve urban misery by shipping indigents to work the rich tropical soil. Leblond's efforts were matched by those of Daniel Lescallier, who had likewise served in French Guiana, and who in the same year authored a work entitled "Exposé des moyens de mettre en valeur la Guyane française" (Exposition of the means by which to develop French Guiana). In it he points to the example the British have set in exporting offenders to the colonies, while inveighing against the legacy of the *bagnes* (in their ancestral galley form).[16] Here we have the outlines of a pattern that would be repeated in the decades that followed, a replication of the logic Bentham so despised, explicitly borrowed from the British example. Two problems could be solved at once by transporting criminals to the colonies: fallen citizens would moralize themselves through the toil of developing new lands.

The schemes put forward by Leblond and Lescallier came to rest in the same administrative limbo as the Panopticon, but the French Assembly was intrigued enough in 1792 to designate French Guiana as the site of deportation for priests who refused to accept state supremacy. The following year the Convention wistfully considered Madagascar as a site for the removal of beggars and vagrants, but because the British blocked the way the plan came to naught. Under the Directory, political exiles finally set sail for French Guiana in 1795. In addition to geopolitical realism, the naturalist urges of one of the directors and an effort to import the bread tree to the region may have contributed to the final choice of destination. Deportations continued through the rule of the Directory and into that of Napoleon. The total number of deportees was small—under seven hundred—but the experience left a bad taste; over half of the exiles died, and those who survived gave damning accounts of their suffering. In addition, the experiment was of little use in developing the colony, which was already disrupted by the temporary suspension of slavery. When the Portuguese government in exile in Brazil occupied French Guiana with English assistance in 1809, this first phase of deportation came to an end.[17]

The idea of a French penal colony, however, did not die. Indeed, the period between the restoration of the monarchy and the return of revolution in 1848 overflows with proposals on prisons and punishments. As recidivism came to be recognized as a social problem, religious reformist influence came again to the fore, and the prison became the standard of punishment.[18] Amid these writings, proposals related to transportation were well represented. In 1816 we find a lengthy report by a prominent bureaucrat, M. Forestier, entitled "Memoire sur le choix d'un lieu de déportation" (Memorandum on the choice of a site for deportation).[19] The report takes the basic logic of the transportation but frees it from a predetermined locale, seeking instead to establish the proper rational criteria with which to choose a penal depot. Therefore we will look at it more closely. Opening with a citation of the

English jurist Blackstone, the text places the project of transportation squarely within the realm of modern justice:

> Justice, which in centuries of ignorance always displayed itself armed with glory, has yielded before the voice of policy and humanity; a more just proportion has been established between trespasses and punishments, and society has become aware of how to make use of criminals expelled from its bosom. Thus it is that in almost all States, capital punishment is today reserved for serious offenders. England has given this system further development. Almost all crimes that entail the death penalty are punished by deportation. An immense continent offers the convicts a new homeland, a new existence, hopes of fortune and the prospect of forgiveness. And at the same time that this power spares and increases a population too small for its needs and its projects, it imparts movement to capital, as equally advantageous to private industry as to public fortune. . . . It is thus evident that it is necessary to follow the example of England and to found a colony based on deportation. Justice, ethics, and policy clamor for its establishment, and when so many interests tend toward the same goal, one must hasten to satisfy them.

Having adopted this principle, the question becomes one of how best to choose a site for this "colony based on deportation." In addition to "a healthy climate and a fertile ground," an algorithm of distance is crucial: the successful colony must be not too close, but also not too far, and represent a distinct settlement of its own. It requires:

> A proximity great enough so that the expense of transportation of convicts and things useful to their establishment is not excessive, and yet a removal considerable enough to create an obstacle, not only to their return, but also to communications with them, of which facility and frequency would not be without danger. A place circumscribed, isolated, distanced from [civil] colonial establishments, be they national or foreign, where the deported might find ways of escape or the opportunity to create turmoil, the seed of which already exists in the New World.

Next the report surveys possibilities within the diminished French Empire: French Guiana, Senegal, and the island of Madagascar, all of which had been long designated "in public opinion" as proper places for penal colonies. The respective advantages and disadvantages of each potential site are weighed. French Guiana offers fertile soil and a rich forest, but the climate is deadly to Europeans, and they are incapable of either hard labor or reproduction under "the fires of the equator." Furthermore, its open continental boundaries offer the possibility of escape, and the effect of white convicts on the racial hierarchy of the already established slave colony would prove disastrous:

> This spectacle can only weaken the conception of the superiority of the European race that is so important to maintain among slaves. . . . The colony of Guyane includes but a very small number of whites compared to blacks and mulattos. This multitude is contained only by the prestige of color; but if agitated by unruly men, for whom disorder is a necessity, what will become of this moral force? . . . Guyane will become the theater of the misfortunes and crimes that entailed the loss of Saint-Domingue [Haiti].

Senegal receives an equally negative rating, promising to turn into "a vast tomb" for Europeans, and while the author deems Madagascar the best option at this point, French control of the island remains uncertain. The British Empire represents an impressive and threatening competitor ("When one casts an eye on the map of the globe, one is frightened at the aspect of the multiplicity and extension of lands submissive to Great Britain"), but it serves also as a model for the organization of the future colony, which must not treat its constituents too harshly and threaten their survival ("In all cases, the government has to appear generous relative to the colonists, rather than to abandon them too abruptly to their own resources").

The central themes of this 1816 memorandum find repetition in many subsequent documents. A decade later the allusion to the British model became most clear in a project entitled "Le Botany-Bay Français." Expressing concern that the "century of civilization" would succumb to such errors as "modern philosophy, dogmas of the revolution, materialism, and indifference to religious matters," the author suggests consulting the legislation that produced British Australia and Russian Siberia to better understand the virtues of exile.[20] Running through the list of available French colonies, he regrets that France—"expropriated" by Britain—retains so few. Dismissing Martinique and Guadeloupe, on the grounds that their soil has been exhausted by cultivation, and "ungrateful" Senegal, with its sandy soil and fearsome sun, he turns to French Guiana as the proper location for France's Australia:

> Here, without contradiction, is virgin soil that calls for the arms of man, the propitious place where France must send its guilty and perverse children to make them industrious and upright men. . . . Guyane will be for France what New South Wales is for England; our colony will become like Sydney: citizen colonists and planters will derive great advantage from these slaves of the law.

He notes that similar proposals had met with local opposition ("quite justly"—who would want to live next to convicts?), but this could be solved by carefully separating the penal establishment from the plantation colony. Even the essential racism of plantation slavery, while constituting a formidable obstacle, can be overcome for the good of the nation:

> The white caste clings most singularly to the nobility of the epidermis; it cannot consent to place before eyes of a Negro a tableau of the degradation of a white. . . . If ever a Negro slave and rebel reproached his master, . . . [t]he colonist could not support this humiliation; the whip would fall from his hands. How much he himself would change color, if a man of color, free and crafty, pleased to show him at every turn his fellow [white] men chained and degraded! . . . A bad joke would suggest that we dye our convicts black before embarking them, seeing no middle course between an opinion so inherent to the country, and the necessity of colonizing it with our criminals. But no, the enlightened portion of the French residing in Cayenne will understand that the projected measure is of major interest; that it concerns nothing less than the repose of families and the morality of a nation of brothers, and that the small interests of self-esteem cannot stand in the way of such a great object. In addition, thanks to the abolition of the slave trade [1815 in France], these demarcations of vanity will diminish with time.

Such optimism proved premature; the penal colony remained in gestation, and the prejudice of race remained, as yet, unchallenged by the sight of white "slaves."

However, the debates continued, with questions related to the appropriateness of sending Europeans to work in French Guiana never far from their center. In 1826 a frigate received secret orders to scout the area between the Oyapock and Amazon rivers (then still claimed by France), seeking an equatorial Sydney. In contrast, an 1827 report on the English experiment rules out the slave-holding Antilles, favoring a project in the South Pacific.[21] At the same time, difficulties in obtaining an adequate labor supply after the suppression of the slave trade began to undermine objections to sending Europeans to a plantation colony. Noting the lack of legal means to increase slave numbers, a letter from the governor of French Guiana in September 1828 wondered "if the employment of a certain number of white convicts would be suitable to the cultivation of our land, without clashing too obviously with our colonial system."[22]

Under the new regime of Louis-Philippe in the 1830s, the discussion of issues related to prison reform expanded, and in the ensuing decade they came to a head. A lengthy debate pitted reformers who favored adopting cellular prisons (led by Alexis de Tocqueville and Gustave de Beaumont, deeply influenced by their American sojourn) against those who wished to revive transportation and others who defended the status quo. At the center of these discussions lay the question of what to do with the *bagnes*, the increasingly obsolete naval port prisons descended from the galleys. In Toulon, Brest, and Rochefort, some seven thousand convicts under sentence of hard labor shuffled monotonously between work in open air and imprisonment in common rooms. While the public ritual of leading new *bagnards* away in chains (*la chaîne*) had ended in 1836, the *bagnes* themselves remained at the lower end of the prison system, where incorrigibles languished at the edge of France. The reformers wished to suppress them, the transporters to remove them overseas, and the hard-line conservatives to keep them and increase the level of suffering. A lengthy legislative struggle dragged on, but before the modified reform proposal could be put to a final vote, the revolution again intervened.[23]

The political turmoil of 1848 would prove decisive in the history of the French penal colony. The upheaval in June produced some twelve thousand political prisoners for the regime to process, and the decision was eventually taken to provide for deportation to a "fortified enclosure" outside continental France. Although initially banned from the Mediterranean, the majority of these prisoners ended up there, while the government debated the merits of other sites, including the familiar options of Madagascar and Senegal as well as the arctic Kerguelen Islands. The list of proposals covering the Atlantic was truly remarkable, ranging beyond the standby, French Guiana, to the Dominican Republic, Haiti, Cuba, St. Pierre and Miquelon, and even Texas. The Pacific won the dubious distinction of welcoming this round of exiles when a handful of deportees headed for the newly annexed Marquesas Islands in 1850.[24]

Louis-Napoleon, still serving in the capacity of president of the republic, threw his weight behind the reform of the *bagnes* and the exile of criminals as well as political dissidents. "It seems possible to me," he declared near the end of 1850, "to render the punishment of hard labor more efficient, more moralizing, less expensive and more human, by using it to advance French colonization."[25] The movement in favor of transportation grew steadily, and a legislative commission proposed Africa as a suitable dumping ground. Then Louis-Napoleon's coup d'état reworked the political ground yet again and created another twenty-seven thousand or so political detainees. About ten thousand of them were deported to Algeria. Freed from the necessity of negotiating between factions, the emperor-to-be added French Guiana as a site of deportation by decree and prepared to ship the most dangerous agitators there. Furthermore, he set a commission of naval officers headed by Admiral Mackau to consider the question of the *bagnes* and the possibilities of transportation. The commission concurred with Louis-Napoleon's earlier recommendation to close the port prisons and move the convicts overseas and, after considerable research and some debate, designated French Guiana as the preferred location for the experiment. A considerable minority urged the annexation of the Pacific island of New Caledonia as an alternate site.[26]

The emperor wasted no time waiting for legislative approval of the choice. He announced an experiment by decree: convicts from the *bagnes* could volunteer to transfer to French Guiana, where, it was suggested, they would be able to work free of the chain gang and even marry. The response was gratifying: some three thousand *bagnards* expressed interest. The majority of them arrived in French Guiana before the end of the year. Meanwhile, a second commission headed by Rudel du Miral seconded Louis-Napoleon's proposal to close the *bagnes* and send their inmates to Guyane. The legislative debate focused more on the need to set a terrible example for evildoers than the need to reform or moralize them, and the motion passed overwhelmingly. The law establishing the conditions of penal transportation was ratified on May 30, 1854. One by one the Metropolitan *bagnes* closed—Rochefort in 1852, Brest in 1858, and Toulon in 1873. Their name, along with their constituents, moved across the ocean; as steam replaced sail in Metropolitan ports, further reducing the need for the raw, unskilled labor that had once powered galleys, a new *bagne* formed in the colonies. The era of the French penal colony was now open; the new French Empire had begun its Botany Bay, even as the British original wound to a close.[27]

COLONIAL LOGIC AND PENAL TRANSPORTATION

When then will France cure itself of the mania of
wanting to copy England? We have nothing to learn
from that country in matters of moralization. Instead
of copying its so-called reforms, let us propose models
for its imitation, as we did when we inaugurated the
regime of overseas transportation, for all that it had
been abandoned by England. Our neighbors will not
delay to follow our example.

Catholic newspaper, 1857[28]

Here I will pause for a minute and review the evidence before us. The idea of the penal colony flickers through prison debates in France from the revolution onward but only bursts into full flame in the mid– nineteenth century. Planning and discussion consciously takes Australia for its central model and frequently refers to the need to transport common criminals, but action is spurred primarily by a wave of political arrests, both in the experiment with deportation during the revolution and the founding of the new overseas system under the Second Republic and empire. Unlike the British case, the French penal colony grows less from criminal pressure and more from sudden political upheaval. The *bagnes*—marginal spaces on the edge of the nation, holding its "desperate" refuse—linger on, resisting reform until they finally yield to colonial transportation.

The double logic of the British system also drives the French imagination; proposals alternatively concentrate on a desire to punish criminals and rid the Metropole of their presence, on the one hand, and a hope of furthering the work of colonial expansion and economic progress, on the other. Within this logic the focus shifts between the need to colonize, the need to punish, and the need to reform, depending on context and the position of the author. Unlike the penitentiary, the penal colony is not a clear instrument of reason in punishment, neatly aligned with movements for reform. Yet it would be a mistake to discount the degree of possible reform envisioned for this colonial experiment.[29] Rather than a conservative punishment, the penal colony constitutes a hybrid, awkward development, part machine and part beast. It represents a kind of reform, a kind of modern punishment, but one that also reflects repression and the legacy of spectacle at a colonial distance. In the case of France, it shimmers with colonial fantasy, allowing future Australias to emerge on tropical horizons.

Here we come to an important point: unlike the penitentiary, the penal colony requires location. The specificity of the site matters; it is the very place that is to enact punishment and reform while itself undergoing transformation. The penal colony is in essence a geographic technique, deploying instruments of distance and density. By definition it should be at a remove, and relatively open, a separate clearing into which the crime of the center can flow. In discussing the choice of location for such an experiment, the various documents make clear these basic parameters. They describe additional criteria less uniformly: the need to prevent escapes (a logic that favors islands), the need to restrict communication (a logic that favors distance), the need to control costs (a logic that favors proximity), the need not to disrupt other colonial activities (a logic that favors empty land), the need not to disrupt slavery (a logic that conflicts with one dominant model of colonial labor and favors settler colonies over plantations), the need to transform a corrupt mass into moral individuals (a logic that also favors settler colonies over plantations), and—significantly if intermittently—the need to find a climate deemed racially appropriate (a logic that favors temperate zones over tropical ones for European prisoners). In application these abstract principles collide with the limitations of a restricted French sphere of influence and with the uncomfortable fact that the favored model, Australia, remains under British control. Rather, many of the most practical sites for a French experiment are located in the tropics.

Amid these discussions French Guiana plays a key, if ambiguous, role. Frequently it is the favored choice, yet always with qualifications and controversy. Past experience (primarily the ill-fated Kourou expedition and deportations during the revolutionary period) dictates caution, but openness invites speculation. The land is particularly alluring because of its perceived natural wealth, yet particularly threatening because of its perceived inappropriateness for Europeans. Its status prior to 1848 as a plantation slave colony brings questions of race tightly into focus. Thus the choice of French Guiana is never clean; for every approval there is a disavowal. In 1841 we find another suggestion that French Guiana really would be appropriate, while eight years later *Journal de la Marine* preferred Tahiti, where Europeans, it was said, could work even in full sunlight.[30] Even when the Mackau commission settles on Guyane, a number of commission members dissent in favor of the South Pacific.

Beyond potential conflicts of interest for some authors opposed to French Guiana's selection, we should also note their persistent reliance on a climatic theory of race. A letter from a former attorney general and governor of French Guiana to the Mackau commission typifies this viewpoint. Urging them not to place the penal colony there, he appends the text of a speech he had delivered six years earlier on the subject of penal colonization. Fully convinced of the appropriateness of Australia as a model, he stands by his racial reasoning, the intervening abolition of slavery notwithstanding. He believes that, amid the geographic criteria governing the selection of a penal colony, climate reigns supreme: "To transport convicts from a cold country to the torrid zone and there set them to hard labor would be to send them to a certain death."[31]

This principle of racial geography was about to be put to the test. The sudden end of slavery in 1848 removed the central objection to the placement of a penal colony in French Guiana: that it would corrupt the essential nineteenth-century racial code of master-slave relations by demonstrating that men with white skin could be subordinate and perform manual labor. Thus while the abolition of slavery may have hastened the end of Australian transportation, it contributed to the emergence of the French penal colony. Even as the emancipation of plantation slaves threw French Guiana into turmoil, a new bureaucratic entity and a new class of indentured Europeans appeared on its shores.

RUNNING A PENAL COLONY

"It's a remarkable piece of apparatus," said the officer
to the explorer.
> *Franz Kafka, "In the Penal Colony," 1919*

When the first shipment of convicts pulled into Cayenne in 1852, they received a warm welcome. The governor gave a speech promising a bright future, holding forth the lure of rural civil redemption:

> My friends, there is no more beautiful or richer country under the sun than this one. It is yours. The Prince Louis-Napoleon sends me to share it out among you. You will disembark, work, prepare the ground, construct cabins. During that time, I will cover the colony. I will choose plots in the most charming sites, the most fertile cantons; then these lands cultivated in common will be shared among the most deserving.[32]

In the interim it was decided to select the Iles du Salut—the same "Islands of Salvation" where the remnants of the Kourou expedition had fled in fear of disease—for the first penal installations. The convicts set to work clearing the ground and building housing.

By all accounts they worked with some efficiency, and a modicum of eagerness. As one official effusively wrote the minister of the navy in June:

> The convicts, filled with the warmest sense of debt to the government, have asked me how they could demonstrate their sentiment at this time. They are going to raise a column on the plateau of Ile Royale on which one can read the following inscription: "To repent, that is Salvation. To Louis-Napoleon, President of the French Republic, to Théodore Ducos, Minister of the Navy."[33]

For all the excess of such official enthusiasm, for all that the legislature may have argued for repression, for all that the political detainees may not have shared in any adulation of Louis Bonaparte (who was, however, remarkably popular in the national plebiscites of the era), we should not miss this moment of optimism amid the irony of later events. Imagine the first impression. Freed from the gloomy *bagnes* of France, released from the holds of ships after an Atlantic crossing, the convicts emerge, blinking, into bright tropical light. They are told that land will be theirs, that redemption is possible, and they are given immediate, concretely meaningful tasks. Around them the world is still in turmoil: a new Napoleon rules in Paris, slavery has ended, and the earlier plantation system lies in shambles. Few of them have traveled before this trip, few of them know much about Guyane beyond rumor. Armed with the unstoppable ardor of amnesia, the actors of the new drama, convicts and officials alike, can succumb to initial enthusiasm. For these first arrivals are, in their small, desperate way, volunteers.

Back in France the experiment continued to incite interest from more than one direction. Rumors flowed across the Atlantic, varying widely in perspective and detail. The apparent enthusiasm of the convicts upset those who wished transportation to be a fearsome penalty: "If things happen as is said, if convicts go to French Guiana as if they were going to the promised land . . . justice is sacrificed to philanthropy."[34] At the same time philanthropists and relatives of the convicts worried about potential terrors of the jungle. A publication in the French West Indies hastened to defend the region from popular misconceptions, claiming the climate of Cayenne to be "one of the mildest of the world," noting that fevers could be cured with the timely application of quinine, that snakes were actually rare, and that "at the slightest noise even tigers themselves flee before man."[35] Thus the removal of the *bagnards* to French Guiana, the article went on to stress, did not represent some plot of premeditated execution on the part of the government. Subsequent events, however, were to belie this optimistic realism, and the opponents of penal paradise would soon have little reason for complaint.

Because the Iles du Salut were of quite limited size and the flow of convicts from France continued unabated, the first installations could only serve as a temporary depot. In any case, to complete the reformatory vision of criminals transformed into an agricultural labor force, suitable locations had to be found on the mainland. The first of these was located to the southeast of Cayenne near the mouth of the Oyapock

River. Named "Montagne d'Argent" (Silver Mountain) after the silver-colored leaves of some local trees, the site had previously hosted an eighteenth-century Jesuit house and a sugar plantation, which the state acquired in October 1852. The setting appeared well suited with regard to confinement, being a peninsula joined to land by a large and almost impenetrable marsh, and hence functionally an island. Yet the actual occupation of the area was to prove disastrous: few preparations were made, the hygienic conditions quickly deteriorated, disease set in, and the death rate grew. Another camp established down the Oyapock River at St. Georges met with a similar fate.[36]

The death rates were not only startling but also carefully recorded. While some have suggested that official estimates are actually low, they were more than high enough to cause alarm and sat uncomfortably on the pages of official reports. Indeed, the documents of the day are full of statistics, mournful scorecards of survival. The budget of 1855, for example, notes that by the end of November 1853 a full 549 out of the 3,038 so far transported were dead, calculating a rate of 18 percent over nineteen months of activity, or 11 percent a year.[37] These figures did not pass unnoticed; they constituted a central topic of discussion between officials of the nascent penal colony and its parent ministry in Paris. For all that the legislation shifting the *bagnes* overseas may have intended the experience to be severe, reformatory conscience and the colonizing impulse objected to wholesale liquidation of prisoners. As the minister of the navy and the colonies wrote to French Guiana's governor in December 1854: "The figure of twenty-six dead for the month of November is quite rightly pointed out by you as a significant improvement relative to the situation last year, but not yet constituting a satisfactory proportion. The number of sick lends still further support to this observation."[38] He went on to express hope that shifting of the installation at Montagne d'Argent to "healthier" ground would improve conditions there. Unfortunately it did not. All told some eight thousand convicts crossed the Atlantic in the first five years of French transportation. As 1857 dawned the prison population was still only at thirty-six hundred; of the eight thousand transported bodies, half lay in tropical graves.[39]

The authorities experimented repeatedly, opening installations in new locations and shifting prisoners between them. They tried acclimating new arrivals through an intermediary stay on the islands, where death rates were generally lower. Echoing objections raised in the debates leading to the selection of French Guiana, a number of officials became convinced that European convicts were incapable of performing hard labor in the tropics, and they devoted much ink to expounding on their views. The heavy work of clearing and draining land was deemed appropriate for black prisoners, who were shifted to the camps in "unhealthy" areas under the theory (partly supported by limited observation) that they tended to survive better. As the chief physician of Cayenne wrote in his official report of 1854: "It is recognized that the white race can only take root in hot countries when preceded by the African, who prepares and sanitizes places by means of cultivation."[40] The racial theory ran deep—after all this is the immediate aftermath of plantation slavery, and the associations surrounding that era had not disappeared into thin air. Convicts of African descent received a different ration (substituting, among other things, manioc meal, fish, and rum for bread, meat, and wine). And on the list of those human forms meant to inhabit dangerous margins they ranked with categories of medical outcasts; in 1857 we find the governor contemplating whether to put black convicts or lepers at Montagne d'Argent.[41]

Yet the vast majority of convicts were of European rather than of colonial origin, and the central experiment of penal colonization revolved around the question of what to do with them. A shifting array of administrators reshuffled plans and operations. Installations were opened and—eventually, after long delays—closed. The most significant, St. Laurent, was located on the border with Dutch Guiana near the mouth of the Maroni River. Interest in the Maroni region stemmed in part from French observation of the Dutch settlement of Albina on the opposite bank. Inspired by this European success, an experiment involving a dozen white and a dozen black prisoners began in 1857. The convicts built a settlement on land previously occupied by an Amerindian village, preparing the way for the opening of a major settlement two years later. In 1860 a decree separated the surrounding territory from the rest of the colony, reserving it exclusively for penal use.[42]

It was at St. Laurent that the next step in plans to further colonization unfolded: women prisoners were imported, in hopes of fostering the emergence of convict families and consequently the growth of Guyane's population. In 1859 a first shipment of thirty-six women arrived. The beginning of the experiment was inauspicious; nearly a third died in the first six months. In all some nine hundred other women would eventually follow them there over the next half century. Although many of these *bagnardes* did marry, they failed to produce the anticipated offspring, and the dream of convict families multiplying into a full settler colony along the lines of Australia never came to pass.[43]

Similarly, the agricultural settlements failed to produce much of anything, let alone a landscape of reformed small farmers. Some of this failure can be attributed to the excessive levels of death and disease, and some to inefficient and inconsistent administration, for while efforts at colonization grimly carried on, the direction of the operation passed from hand to hand. All told, French Guiana was to have seventy-eight governors in seventy-seven years.[44] Work remained a central concern of the penal colony, touted for both its moralizing influence and its crucial role in the project of colonization. But the work carried out in French Guiana produced little of lasting value. Rather, the experiment proved a most efficient mechanism by which to quietly eliminate criminals far from home. By 1866 the penal colony had registered a total of 17,017 convicts, including 594 of colonial origin, 329 political prisoners, and 212 women. Out of this total 6,809 (40 percent) were dead, mostly from disease, 809 (4.8 percent) had escaped or disappeared, 1,770 (10.4 percent) had been allowed to return to France, and just 166 (1 percent) remained "voluntarily" in French Guiana, in addition to the active penal population of 7,466.[45] The real industry of the equatorial penal colony, it began to be clear, was imperfect death.

Local reaction to the displacement of the *bagne* in Guyane remained mixed. While some still held out hopes that it might prove the key to the expansion of the colony, others opposed the arrival of criminals in their immediate vicinity. A number of pleas and recommendations arrived at the Parisian ministry, including an 1862 article in a French economics publication (written by a resident of Cayenne under a pseudonym) that charged the penal administration with mismanagement.[46] The feelings of the less literate surface more rarely, but we can bear witness to a partial example: in 1856 residents of the town of Kourou sent a petition to Louis-Napoleon, protesting the selection of their district for a penal installation. Assuring their ruler that they were not against the "principle of transportation," they worried about what would become of their community of small farmers, threatened by the arrival of convicts: "We only protest today, Sire, against the arbitrary processes by which we are obliged to either take our risks and live in peril amid the prison population, or to abandon our lands without any remuneration, which would be the equivalent of complete ruin, or expatriation, for those few whose means still allow them the possibility!"[47] What they hoped for was "just and large" compensation, particularly if Kourou was destined to become the principal seat of transportation. On this occasion the eye of Paris focused elsewhere; Kourou remained a secondary installation of the *bagne,* significant enough to disrupt, minor enough to contribute little. Yet the signatures of the petitioners remain—some carefully scrawled, others blotted or apologetically written on the behalf of relatives—a faint, cautious protest on the border of great, misguided plans.

A COLONIAL RIVAL:
THE OPTION OF NEW CALEDONIA

In New Caledonia we have committed an anachronism
150 years in advance on our period; in Guyane the
anachronism is no less appreciable, but in the inverse
direction.

> *Military officer analyzing the*
> *French penal colonies, 1868*[48]

By 1857, even the emperor himself began to admit that the Guiana project was in trouble and that perhaps another site would prove more auspicious. Just after the original decision to open the overseas *bagne*, France had annexed the Pacific island of New Caledonia, the close second choice of the Mackau commission. Now that island beckoned again. The government dispatched a trial shipment of three hundred convicts and, when they seemed to do well, followed them with another in 1864. Meanwhile, conditions in French Guiana continued to be unsatisfactory with regard to either moralization or colonization. In 1867 the government announced that henceforth New Caledonia would serve as the repository for *bagnards* of European origin, while those from the colonies would continue to arrive in French Guiana. The racial logic was now sanctioned; white men required less severe conditions, such as in the "milder" tropics of New Caledonia. Those already in French Guiana would remain, but in the future only colonials would arrive to replace them.[49]

Here we have a clear turning point in the history of the penal colony: an official admission that the original rehabilitory project of colonial labor required modification and that the geographic calculus involved must be altered to account for race. A technical shift in administration might allow the apparatus of transportation to continue to promise something beyond sheer repression. Distinctions between kinds of humans would allow for a more humane—if severe—punishment. The dream of a French Australia would be transferred to an island lying off the coast of that very continent, while French Guiana would be reserved for those of more tropical origin. The move to suspend transportation of European prisoners to French Guiana marks the end of the generalized reformatory experiment, for all that convicts were still destined to arrive.

Yet the reform potential of the penal colony lingered in the minds of visionaries. One lengthy report sent to the minister by a military officer in 1864 still argued that the problem with the French Guiana project lay not in concept but in application—the "flourishing" and "opulent" success of British efforts proved as much. Rather than continue to treat the *bagnards* as exiled lepers, a new concentration on the moral and colonial dimensions of the project was in order through productive labor; as a concrete beginning, the report urged that the penal colony be placed under the direction of an agricultural engineer.[50] In 1868 an infantry officer serving in Saigon submitted an elaborate proposal to the emperor's office, which subsequently forwarded the document to the ministry of the navy. Entitled "Un Pénitencier doit être une véritable maison de santé morale" (A penitentiary must be a veritable house of moral health), the tract reviews the record of the French Guiana experiment and details recommended reforms based on the author's thirteen years of experience with a disciplinary battalion in Algeria and Senegal. Ascribing the failure in French Guiana to climatic limits of race and poor administration, the author suggests that a tropical penal colony is simultaneously a geographic and anthropological enterprise: "not only a question of modifying the ground, but indeed even the nature of man, and that is the work of generations."[51] In his view New Caledonia holds more promise as a site of transportation. However, he objects to what he sees as overly lax administration in the Pacific *bagne*. Expiation must come before rehabilitation, this colonial officer believes, to ensure "moral health." The key to success—yet again—is to be found in work and the proper organization of the convicts. Most intriguingly, the author includes a careful rendering of a layout of his ideal penal establishment: a cross composed of four barracks, with a guardhouse in the middle, gunsights trained along the axes. In the distant heat of Southeast Asia, amid discussions shifting over several seas, appears a tiny, colonial reflection of the Panopticon.

THE AUSTRALIAN MODEL: LOOKING BACKWARD

The opening of a French penal colony in the Pacific marked a period of limbo for the French Guiana *bagne* but did not put an end to either it or comparisons with Australia. An authorless draft of a report written sometime in the 1880s provides us with an extended critical comparison between the French and British systems.[52] Given its historical position and its elusive, removed rhetoric, the document is worth quoting in detail. It begins by noting that the system of transportation had proved up to ten times as expensive as the Metropolitan *bagnes,* and it castigates Louis-Napoleon's regime in particular for its decision to found a colony in Guyane. Nothing, the report suggests, could have been more foolish or naive:

> The idea of colonizing a country situated at the equator with the European workers would perhaps have been excusable two hundred years ago; it cannot be in our century. This senseless project, undertaken blindly, without reflection, and as if by surprise, in the aftermath of the coup d'etat of December second, has continued for thirty years, with a completely French ignorance of all things colonial. Theory and experience have condemned it highly. French Guiana was not a new, unknown country; for more than two centuries, the white race had tried at different times to till the soil of this country with its own hands, and every attempt of colonization with white laborers ended with the same disastrous result.

Yet the problems of judgment ran much deeper than geographic ignorance. The flaw of the French project was systemic in nature and hence the failure of the *bagne* preordained. The French sin lay in misunderstanding an essential English principle—private enterprise—as well as the entire model of penal transportation. Without that understanding, the report maintains, there could be no development:

> It has been said, and is still often repeated, that by transporting its convicts France has imitated the example of England. Nothing is more false than this assertion. Between the penal colonization system of the English and our own lies an immense difference. England told its convicts: "You have broken the social pact on which rests all civilized society; you have all gravely infringed the penal code; my duty is to shelter myself from your attacks. I do not want you consuming in a prison without producing. I condemn you to work. . . . Here is a new country, situated outside the tropics. Scientific consideration provides certainty that the European can live and work there. It is there that I am going to send you; through work you will be able to create for yourself there a place in the sun that you lack on the soil of old England. Do not forget, however, that you will have to count far more on yourself than on me. There already exists a New England of America; it is for you to work, to struggle, and to create here an Australian New England." A century has not yet passed since the day when Philip disembarked his convicts at Port Jackson, and the New England of the south exists today. It possesses cities that can be compared with more than one capital of Europe, and that have already their universal exhibitions. . . . To imitate England, France told its transportees: "It no longer suits me to maintain the national workshops in

the Metropole that, under name of *bagnes,* I have kept up until now. That which you do in military ports, free labor will do. I want to use you to aid the progress of French colonization. I will guide you and allow you to lack nothing. I am the State. For you, I will dip a free hand in the budget—that is to say, in the product of the work of honest France. I will spend on you far more than I spend on my most deserving servants. It is I who will undertake to help you die, marry, and feed and raise your children. You will have advantages and privileges that I have never granted and could not grant to other citizens, neither in the Metropole nor in the colonies; I will make every sacrifice for you; only . . . I place you in a country situated at the equator, where, for more than two centuries, theory and experience have more than amply demonstrated that men of your race can neither work, nor live, nor reproduce." We know what St. Laurent du Maroni is today. In a century, the virgin forest will have overwhelmed it without leaving a trace, and nobody will know that it existed.

Here, encapsulated in the language of personified states, we find a contrast between generational independence imagined in the British Empire and paternalistic dependence fostered by the French: where England made its erring children into men, the metaphor goes, France kept them permanently infantile. The model of Australia has become less a vision of the future than a template against which to judge the past; where England matched the proper system to the proper place and found prosperity, France misunderstood that system and misapplied it in an inappropriate setting. Of course the result was doomed, and only decay could ensue, never development. Nature, unchallenged by industrious culture, would take back its own.

THE PENAL COLONY AS PUNISHMENT

All my books . . . are little toolboxes, if you will. If
people are willing to open them and make use of such
and such a sentence or idea, of one analysis or another,
as they would a screwdriver or a monkey wrench, in
order to short circuit or disqualify systems of power,
including even possibly the ones my books came out
of, well, all the better.

Michel Foucault, 1975[53]

Let us return now to the Metropolitan clarity of the Panopticon and Foucault's suggestive, offhand dismissal of the penal colony as a "rigorous and distant form of imprisonment." Distant, yes, crucially over the horizon, but what might "rigorous" signify? To what degree are we to read the goal of the penal colony as repression, and to what degree reform? Bentham first proposed his inspection house as an alternative to the nascent Australian penal colony. He opposed transportation, viewing it as an uncertain as well as a morally and economically inefficient form of punishment, and continued to lobby against the practice after its adoption. Following Bentham, then, the Panopticon and penal colony become polar extremes, for where the Panopticon would perfect the architecture of internalization, the penal colony would represent an extreme of externalization. One effects change within the individual, where the other radically transforms the environment.

Carrying this thesis a step further we might ask if the penal colony represents an anachronism, a backward eddy in the flow of modern punishment.[54] Transportation certainly had close ancestors in chain gangs, convict labor on public works, and the isolation of lepers—all practices that Foucault places in his earlier, floating category of punishment. The prisoners endured physical abuse, and their fate was to some degree public, at least in Guiana. But the penal colony also displays traits of disciplinary control similar to the penitentiary. The prisoners found themselves distanced and confined, effectively hidden from Metropolitan France. Disciplinary infractions were primarily punished with isolation. On at least some level, the *bagne* was expected to rehabilitate its *bagnards,* and they to rehabilitate themselves. And yet they were also deported and expected to spend their lives in a colony.

The frame before us wavers slightly: unlike the clear view from the center, the edge remains dim; unlike the consistent blueprint of the Panopticon, the penal colony blurs within its own form. The lines between empires, between geographic zones, between reform and repression cross and recross. The *bagne* is many things at once, always at a remove. It is punishment, yes, but it is also colonial, and its modern status remains shadowy and suspect. Like the fantastic machine in Kafka's short story, the French penal colony lost its claim to the very reason out of which it was born, becoming an impure, inefficient apparatus of torture and elimination. The sentences it wrote transformed; in place of ideal calls to moral and economic advancement, we find raw, physical marks of suffering.

CHAPTER 4

The Natural Prison

I was a Prisoner lock'd up with the Eternal Bars and Bolts
of the Ocean, in an Uninhabited Wilderness, without Redemption.

Daniel Defoe, Robinson Crusoe, *1719*

In the spring of 1895, the prison transport ship *St. Nazaire* deposited a
newly disgraced French army officer on a small and rocky tropical isle.
The captain's steps ashore—a minor encounter between foot and land
of the sort commonly erased from wider consciousness—would lead to
a potent symbolic moment within European history: the exile of Dreyfus on Devil's Island. Much has been written about the Dreyfus Affair,
his Kafkaesque trials and the subsequent upheaval of the French political landscape. Far less attention has been paid to Dreyfus's actual ordeal of exile; his period of punishment occurs in a dim realm offstage
while he awaits his return and eventual redemption.[1] Yet the notoriety
of the case, together with its theme of epochal injustice, underscores
that—wherever he was sent—he suffered, and suffered as an innocent
man. Thus while Dreyfus's deportation was far from typical of the experience of convicts in French Guiana, and the outrage it provoked was
not the first incidence of public outcries against the *bagne*, it nevertheless captures the essential mood pervading accounts of the later penal
colony: despair amid the floating terror of distant tropics. Therefore I
use it to mark the crucial slide of penal colony from a space of improvement to a space of punishment. Although the later penal colony
retained rhetorical trappings of moralization and development, its acknowledged purpose became more clearly punitive. The continued existence of this institution attracted an extraordinary measure of attention and sensationalization in France and beyond, particularly the

Figure 8.   Alfred Dreyfus, 1895

English-speaking world. Here I examine these sensational portrayals, with an eye for what they reveal about the topography of colonial anxieties. For we see in them another space opening behind that of development, a negative mirror of degeneration, death, and decay.

FROM PENAL COLONY TO DEVIL'S ISLAND, 1887–1946

The Harrow was not writing, it was only jabbing, and
the bed was not turning the body over but only bringing it up quivering against the needles.

Franz Kafka, "In the Penal Colony," 1919

First we should establish a few significant social facts. When the French reestablished the transportation of European convicts to French Guiana, they did so with full knowledge of its high dangers and death rates.

Indeed, the relatively low mortality of New Caledonia was now presented as a failing and a sign that the Pacific island was too easy a prison.[2] In the 1880s, Freemasons and certain factions of the French government, seeking a harder line on crime and recidivism, helped popularize the image of New Caledonia as a "paradise" for its prisoners. After all, the death rate there was only 2 to 3 percent a year, less than a third of the Guiana statistic.[3] In 1887 exclusive transportation of whites to New Caledonia ceased, and French Guiana again became the destination of white as well as colonial prisoners. Two years earlier the French state, now the Third Republic, had added another law to those of the Second Empire designed to deport recidivist petty criminals. Under this new legislation (known as *relégation*) persons between the ages of twenty-one and sixty convicted of a combination of offenses totaling more than seven, including two sentences longer than three months or fitting a number of other stipulations, could be classified as recidivists and transported to the colony for life.[4] Although not technically prisoners, they were nevertheless confined to the colonies, and the majority were assigned to labor camps strikingly similar to those of regular convicts.

Thus at the end of the nineteenth century, the penal colony in French Guiana entered a new administrative period. Transportation to New Caledonia ceased in 1897, and the Pacific *bagne* was subsequently phased out. But despite frequent outcries and sensational reports, the French Guiana penal establishment continued to exist through the end of World War II. Following continuing waves of bad publicity and the election of the Popular Front government in France, a decision was finally made in 1938 to cease transportation and let the Atlantic *bagne* atrophy. The intervention of the war and the occupation of France complicated and delayed closure until 1946, resulting in a final burst of suffering. Even in ending, this colonial machine remained imperfect and arbitrarily tragic, as the repatriation of convicts continued well after the war.[5]

IN THE *BAGNE*

For the last half century of its existence, the penal colony constituted a relatively stable social order. To balance its representation, I will quickly survey some of the social facts involved, using as dispassionate a tone as possible. Within the *bagne* the administration distinguished three classes of *bagnards: transportés*, convicted under common law;

déportés, convicted of political crimes; and *relégués,* recidivist criminals deported to the penal colony for life under the law of 1885. In addition the colony remained the home of *libérés,* those who had served out their sentence, and *relégués individuels,* recidivists who were exiled but not confined, and who shared a similar autonomy within the boundaries of Guiana and its economy. Whatever their classification, the *bagnards* were all transported to Guiana under similar conditions. After a waiting period on the Ile de Ré off La Rochelle in northern France, they were loaded onto an aging ship that made the journey once or twice a year. Locked into eight cages holding sixty to eighty people each, watched by guards, and threatened with jets of steam and "hot cells" over the boiler, they made the passage in fifteen to twenty days, depending on whether the ship stopped in Algeria.[6]

The largest prison camps in French Guiana, St. Laurent and St. Jean, were on the Maroni River by Suriname, and it was here that the ships deposited newcomers. Following their arrival, the convicts were sorted by type. Many of the *transportés* stayed in St. Laurent, which had a capacity of about twenty-five hundred, whereas the *relégués* were primarily sent upriver to work in St. Jean, which held about sixteen hundred. Those considered most "incorrigible," and those who broke disciplinary rules, were sent either to forest camps deep in the jungle, where they spent their time engaged in backbreaking cutting of wood, or to the Iles du Salut, just off the central coast. On Royale, the largest of the three islands, hard-core convicts lived an isolated yet relatively easy existence. Those who required additional punishment, as well as those who attempted to escape, found themselves in solitary confinement on St. Joseph. Forbidden to talk or smoke, they were allowed little exercise, sunlight, or food, beneath the constant gaze of guards. European *déportés*—of whom there were never very many—lived on the overly notorious Ile du Diable, or Devil's Island. Like Royale, life on Diable was relatively peaceful, the main punishment being restriction of movement in a highly isolated place. In addition to the Iles du Salut, a prison camp also operated onshore at Kourou, mainly housing convicts at work on Guiana's one and only road. Farther down the coast in the capital town of Cayenne, another contingent of convicts engaged in service labor. At various times there were also forest camps organized on the basis of racial segregation, a camp for those suffering from tuberculosis or other disabilities, and a leper colony near St. Laurent. Until 1903, the small number of women who were transported to Guiana lived in their own camp near St. Laurent, under the supervision of an order of nuns. For most of the twentieth century, however, the *bagne* was a thoroughly male affair.[7]

The convict population usually ranged between three thousand and seven thousand and hovered around 20 percent of the total population of French Guiana.[8] Despite the shipment of some seven hundred new arrivals per year, deaths and escapes kept the number of prisoners relatively constant. The average prisoner was Metropolitan, French, nominally Catholic, partly educated, between twenty and fifty years of age, single, and from the lower end of the urban social order. However, this profile masks considerable variation, and the colonies were also well represented, with *bagnards* from Algeria to Vietnam. The convicts were controlled by trustees and several hundred prison guards of mixed origin, including Corsicans, North Africans, and Guyanais, as well as about six hundred troops, including a detachment of Senegalese.[9]

Conditions of everyday existence ranged from fairly mild to quite severe. The colony was administered under rules established in Paris, often with extreme bureaucratic rigidity. Supplies were frequently stolen for sale on the black market, and petty graft, from bribery to the smuggling of exotic butterflies, constituted a way of life. Convicts were provided with minimal clothing: gray jumpers with red stripes for the *transportés* and blue ones for the *relégués,* two shirts, and a hat.[10] The diet was generally poor and frequently inadequate, and the guards, by all accounts, were free to mete out a good deal of physical punishment. For their part, the prisoners engaged in physical violence among themselves, contributing to an atmosphere of tension and domination common to mainland prisons. Rape and abusive homosexual relationships were common, and threats and murders not infrequent. The guards often looked the other way, though prisoners guilty of misconduct could be sentenced to a series of punishments from solitary confinement to the guillotine. Drinking and gambling provided the main source of entertainment. In a reverse hierarchy familiar to prisons, murderers and other violent criminals held higher status than thieves or *relégués,* and those who succeeded in escaping enjoyed the greatest renown of all. Several possible escape routes existed, the most common being to head northeast into what was then Dutch Guiana, either through the jungle or floating on a raft. Neither method of travel was easy, and many died in the attempt. After the Dutch adopted a policy of extradition the stakes grew even higher, as hopeful escapees had now to reach Brazil, British Guiana, Venezuela, or Trinidad. Still, some 150 a year did succeed.[11]

Upon the completion of their sentence (or the granting of *relégué individuel* status) the former convicts, known as *libérés,* were left completely on their own to find employment. They remained under a kind of parole known as *doublage,* which prevented them from leaving Guiana, either for a length of time equal to their original sentence or for life, and they were threatened with renewed sentences for any infractions. Many found the conditions of liberty as difficult as those of confinement, because employers preferred the free labor of convicts. Local laws forbade the ex-prisoners from selling drinks or working as restaurateurs or entrepreneurs of almost any sort, while at the same time requiring that they be employed. Only after a reformist decree in 1925 did this "reentry" become any easier, and many former convicts still either hovered barely above the threshold of subsistence or returned again to confinement.[12]

Thus equipped with a modicum of synthetic historical sociology, we can turn to consider representation and the lurid suffering that marked the penal colony, from Dreyfus onward. Kafka's story, as we shall see, was not an isolated nightmare.

AN ENGLISH DESCRIPTION OF 1878

"A Visit to One of the Prisons of Cayenne," published in the London religious journal *Good Words* in 1878, provides us with an entry prior to Dreyfus and foreshadows much of what would come.[13] Because of its historical location and its content, I will quote it at length. Opening with a historical and geographical sketch in luxuriant prose, it parlays this beginning into a form of social analysis, noting "the fatal malaria which lurks in the soil" and absence of Europeans, on the one hand, and the fact that neighboring colonies in British and Dutch Guiana are productive, on the other:

> The colony is going back in the world rather than forward. . . . The cloves, cinnamon and pepper of Cayenne were once a famous export. The liberation of the slaves killed this ancient prosperity. A few negroes still linger in the overgrown clearing of these large estates; here and there is a convict establishment, a Jesuit mission-church, a camp of gold prospectors; but the great body of the country belongs to the wild beast and the Indian. The people huddle in the town, which is falling into decay; and the finest French possession is still a mere convict settlement, while Demarara and Surinam [British and Dutch Guiana] are thriving colonies, with a large and prosperous white and coloured population. Cayenne is well fit to produce all the usual tropical vegetables—sugar cane, indigo, spices, tobacco, cacao and

cotten. The forests are rich in timber and the rocks in minerals. Only energy, skill, and capital are needed to make it another Demarara. (747)

Here we have the recurring theme of unfulfilled promise that runs through so much writing about French Guiana, and its awkward position between past and future. The author then goes on to describe his visit to Cayenne in 1875 aboard a telegraph ship charged with connecting the French outpost to the British by submarine cable. After proceeding over "repulsive-looking green seas" to the "savage outline" of the coast, he provides us with a meditation on the landscape before him, rife with romantic excess:

> There is a strange allurement in the appearance of these virgin forests of South America, so gloomy, so grand, so lonely. From the deck of the passing ship the voyager is never tired of gazing at the sombre wilds which he may never penetrate, but which hide under their sullen shade so much to excite the imagination. It is not the interest attaching to a land of ancient and faded glory he feels, but to one of brilliant promise; not to a dead land embalmed in the pages of history, but to a free and unknown wilderness fresh from the hands of Nature. Even these mountains of Guiana, all muffled as they were in fog, these dull shaggy forests soaking with wet, had some of the poetry of a savage wilderness for us. They had the peculiar aspect of secret possession which a tropical forest has above all others, and which is so suggestive of the wild denizens which lurk in its gloomy recesses—the jaguars which lair in its thickets, the deadly snakes which glide through its wet, glistening leaves, the wonderful orchids which bloom there unheeded, the gaudy birds which enliven its green foliage with the colours of the rainbow, and the red-brown Indians who rove under its dripping branches, or lie in hammocks under the shelter of their palm-leaf ajoupahs, and croon, through the long rainy day, some legendary chant of their tribe. Nor is the element of association entirely wanting. The golden city of Manoa, the El Dorado of Elizabethan times, was situated in the heart of this region. The names of Humboldt and Raleigh brood over it. (747–48)

The passage contains all the sexual imagery of a male explorer facing the well-imagined unknown. Exotic plants, animals, and humans fill a landscape of primitive beauty and freedom, unburdened by history, yet pregnant with the desires of past explorers. Whatever one might say about this description, it is far from neutral; the adjectives are evaluative, alive with feeling. Nature beckons with promise and distant dangers; the land is rich with dreams.

Yet the report follows these descriptions with an admission: "Our real experience was destined to be of a different kind." Instead of alluring wilds, they encounter the penal colony. Anchoring near the Iles du Salut, they (the gentlemen, we assume) are invited to visit by officers of the garrison and the chief doctor of the hospital. Leaving their sailors to mingle with a group of listless soldiers on the beach (suffering, we are told, from the climate), they meet with their hosts. Following instruction on general history of French Guiana and the *bagne* (presumably the source of anecdotes that sprinkle the narrative), they proceed on a tour of Ile Royale and Ile St. Joseph, the island then devoted to "maniac" and "convalescent" prisoners. The plight of convicts is described as follows:

> From the moment he sets foot in Guiana the individuality of each man is lost; he becomes a machine subject to the strictest discipline, suspicion and the severest of penalties. If he is unruly he is chained like a dog. If he is violent he is shot. He is known by his number, which is painted over his sleeping hammock and stamped on his clothes. A coarse sack hung on a nail over his bed contains all his worldly goods. (749)

Life is governed by routine; reveille at 5 A.M., breakfast, work between 6 and 10 A.M., 10:30 lunch, a siesta until 2 P.M. (partly spent fabricating "little curiosities" for sale), labor again from 2 to 6 P.M., and free time until 8. This routine blends into "monotonous years," often ending with a corpse fed to the encircling sharks. While noting all this with detached distaste, the author gives little sense of outrage, admiring the cleanliness of the hospital and the dedication of the Sisters of Charity who work there. Later, however, the group visits the cells of the "maniacs" on St. Joseph, and here the observations acquire a more critical undertone. Solitary confinement is the rule, chained to the wall in cells lacking light and ventilation. Kicking an Arab who shows "no sign of life," the attendant tells the party that the sooner this prisoner dies the better. A little later they meet a "victim of religious mania," who, in a "soft and resigned voice," claims to be greater than Jesus:

> "I am," he said, "a superior being sent to teach mankind; but I have been persecuted by the Jesuits. They have disemboweled me, they have turned my blood to water, and they have crucified me. But they cannot kill me. My inspiration keeps me alive. The sun has burned into my breast, and tried to scorch up my heart; but I will not give way to nature." (751)

Finally, after inspecting the cemetery, they have an encounter with a different sort of prisoner: "a young man of about thirty years of age, with finely chiseled features, and a look of refinement and distinction which marked him off strikingly from the other convicts we saw." His story arouses much sympathy, for he has remained there three years past his original five-year sentence for manslaughter, lacking sufficient funds to finance a voyage away from the islands. The author and his companions take up a collection on behalf of this young man, but the call of duty forces them to depart before securing his freedom (751–52).

This account is made all the more interesting in that it dates from a moment when the future of the French Guiana establishment was uncertain, after the redirection of new European prisoners to New Caledonia and before their reintroduction to Guyane and the new regulations of 1885. It attracted contemporary notice; a copy rests in a French archival dossier, surrounded by related papers and correspondence involving the French Ministry of the Navy and the Colonies. The article was brought to the attention of the ministry by a letter from William Tallach of the Howard Society, London.[14] A subsequent report from the governor of the colony to the minister, dated March 1, 1879, asserts that he has personally inspected the condition of the insane convicts and found sufficient light and air in the cells and rations that conform to the norms of transportation. He has prescribed several "slight improvements" in the sleeping arrangements but believes that the author of the article, while sincere, is comparing the treatment of the insane to that found in large institutions in France or England, rather than considering the particular circumstances and constraints of a penal colony. The report includes plans of the prison and asylum on the Ile St. Joseph, as well as the old barracks on the Ile Royale, where mentally ill convicts are to be transferred. A copy of this report apparently made its way to the interested parties in London, for in late April of that year, the secretary of the Howard Society composed a note thanking the ministry for its response, promising that they would "lay the vindication of the French authorities at the feet of the English public." The case of the *bagne* was—temporarily—closed.

The *Good Words* article raises three points for consideration. First, it provokes response on the part of its readership, a response that attracts the attention of the French administration. This marks early fascination with and concern about the penal colony on the part of non-French observers and notes its increasingly controversial place in French foreign relations. Second, the article contains essential elements of exotic description that will later be worked into patterns of sensational representation. The world of the penal colony is a mixture of strict regulation, a debilitating climate, exotic surroundings, and draining despair. Its administration balances between discipline and punishment, here tilting over the edge in cases of insanity and the refined prisoner trapped in savage exile. Third, while the article prefigures motifs found in accounts of the later penal colony, it does so without the same hyperbole. Race is noted, and class distinctions suggested, but moral outrage is limited to the treatment of those perceived to be at the edges of the enterprise: the insane at one end of the spectrum and the "refined" prisoner at the other. Though the name "Devil's Island" identifies a geographical feature, it does not play a central symbolic role in this English text—a minor point, but one that the excess of later representation infuses with significance.

THE SHADOW OF A NAME

Consider that name, "Devil's Island." Few later writers, especially those writing in English, would ignore it or its metaphorical possibilities. Again and again the words stretch imposingly across a title page to invoke damnation—a natural and recurring reference amid the litany of prisons. The allusion is too powerful for subtlety, as effortlessly, in the space of two words and a minimum of cultural associations, a prospective reader is transported to a dim red zone of suffering and retribution, heat and failed rebellion.

Looking up from books and across the waves, the actual referent is disarmingly modest: a small and narrow mound of rock and lush vegetation off the Guiana coast, the least of three Caribbean fragments lost in the equatorial Atlantic. Together with its two neighbors, this island presents a perfectly innocent profile, familiar in the late twentieth century from countless travel brochures of tropical islands. Indeed, its very insignificance becomes disturbing, a geographic footnote to the banality of evil. How, one wonders, could such a place come to represent damnation?

Historical investigation only complicates matters, for the name predates the prisoners. The triad of minor islands midway down the coast of French Guiana have no doubt borne many names, but since the late eighteenth century they have been marked in French as the Ile Royale (Royal Island), the Ile St. Joseph (St. Joseph's Island), and the Ile du Diable (Devil's Island). As an additional twist the group as a whole is now known as the Iles du Salut (Islands of Salvation). The most common and convincing explanation runs like this: once all three islands were known collectively as the Iles du Diable, but during the disastrous French attempt to colonize Kourou in 1763, settlers sought refuge from

mainland epidemics offshore. When they saw that they had not perished, the survivors renamed their refuge in honor of their salvation.[15]

The same Kourou expedition, coupled with later public accounts of
exiles in revolutionary France, gave the colony a reputation as a tropical European grave. Thus when the first administrators of Louis-
Napoleon's new overseas penal experiment disembarked their pioneering convicts on the islands, their choice of site was guided more by
caution and convenience than a desire to punish—that would come
more fully and fatefully amid fevers on the mainland. This set of historical and geographic facts presents us with a curious metaphorical assemblage: Hell is not simply where it's said to be, and its name is not
quite the same thing as its naming, particularly at a distance. Devil's Island never constituted the administrative heart of the penal colony. Nor
was it even the symbolic center of French references to colonial punishment—that dubious honor belonged to Cayenne, capital of the colony,
and to the term *bagne*, used to describe the overseas prison.[16] Yet
Devil's Island became a focus of attention for the world beyond the
French Empire, particularly in England and America. To understand
this phenomenon we must return to the scandal that briefly carried
French Guiana onto the map of European history.

DREYFUS IN EXILE

"In any case, if this man Dreyfus is innocent," the
Duchess broke in, "he hasn't done much to prove it.
What idiotic, raving letters he writes from the island."
> Marcel Proust,
> Remembrance of Things Past, *1913–1927*

So profound is my solitude that I often seem to be
lying in my tomb.
> Alfred Dreyfus,
> Five Years of My Life, *1895*

On October 15, 1894, a relatively obscure French artillery captain by
the name of Alfred Dreyfus was arrested under the charge of high treason. What began as a military and diplomatic issue mushroomed over
the ensuing decade into the most wrenching social and political drama
of fin-de-siècle France: currents of nationalism, republicanism, and
anti-Semitism, as well as tensions between church and state, army and
civil society, all came to focus on this man and the question of his guilt

or innocence. Dreyfus spent four and a half years in exile on Devil's Island before being brought back for a second trial in 1899 and final exoneration in 1906. The shadow of the "Dreyfus Affair" would linger on in France and Europe until World War II, when social rifts it had exposed widened into chasms. From the vantage point of the next fin de siècle, the passions of the Dreyfus Affair appear both distanced and prophetic: distanced in language and convention, prophetic in character and theme. Here we find a confrontation between nation and state expressed in direct and vivid terms, along with a struggle over the position of both individuals and minority groups between them. Dreyfus's combined status as a secular Jew, career military officer, and French citizen invited deeper accusations of treason than those committed to paper.[17]

Of all historically prominent figures, Alfred Dreyfus is certainly one of the most unlikely. Born in 1859 in Mulhouse, he was the youngest child of a large, close-knit, and prosperous Alsatian Jewish manufacturing family. Following the annexation of the Alsace by Prussia after 1870, Alfred's parents moved to Basel. He eventually continued his education in France, and after an erratic beginning succeeded in gaining admission to the prestigious Ecole Polytechnique for training as a military officer. Graduating in the middle of his class, he developed a reputation as a steady, cautious, and industrious junior officer, one of the more promising Jewish members of the French army, efficient and publicly impersonal, a prototypical technocrat more than a stereotypical Jew. In 1890 he married the daughter of a diamond merchant and seemed poised for a carefully successful career before suspicion fell on him in 1894. Someone had been leaking French military secrets to imperial Germany, and circumstantial clues pointed toward younger, privileged members of the officer corps. The evidence against Dreyfus was sketchy, however, and when he protested his innocence and refused to kill himself, the army wavered in his prosecution, until an anti-Semitic campaign made the matter a subject of public controversy. Convicted, degraded, and deported, he seemed without hope of redemption until the separate efforts of his brother Mathieu and a certain Colonel Picquart of counterintelligence raised support for a retrial, support that included the politician Clemenceau and the writer Zola in prominent roles. The plot thickened as new documents were forged to strengthen the case against Dreyfus, even as a more likely culprit named Esterhazy was found innocent. Dreyfus's second military trial in 1899 confirmed his conviction but also pardoned him; it was only seven years later that he received a medal in acknowledgment of his suffering. Throughout all this the captain cut a curious figure as either villain or martyr, described by observers on both sides as "humorless," or "emotionless," with a high-pitched voice and a distinct lack of charisma. Had fate not intervened, he would most likely have led a comfortable and thoroughly unremarkable life, representing an average rather than an extreme.[18]

As noted earlier, the details of Dreyfus's ordeal of exile have met with little examination. Still, the protagonist of the Dreyfus Affair spent more than four years on Devil's Island, suffering from heat, excessive surveillance measures, and his own fevered sense of martyrdom. During that time he read what materials were permitted and wrote as furiously as he was allowed, producing a constant stream of letters to his wife, all of which were carefully censored and many never delivered. His movements were restricted as well as his communication, and privileges concerning supplements in diet and other small pleasures were infrequently allowed. The terms of his imprisonment grew particularly severe amid increasing paranoia about the possibility of his escape in late 1896, when a new palisade was constructed to block his view of the sea and irons were placed on his limbs at night. All of this hysteria over the special prisoner affected his guards and the rest of the colony, which was alert to the arrival of Prussian ships and exposed to the heightened publicity surrounding the chosen site of his exile.[19]

The placement of Dreyfus's punishment was quite deliberate. At the time of his conviction the *bagne* in New Caledonia was still open and serving as the officially designated receptacle for political prisoners under the anti-Communard law of 1872. But by 1895 New Caledonia appeared too luxurious for a traitor; European common prisoners were again being sent to Guiana, after all, and thus a special law was enacted to redirect Dreyfus there as well. His confinement on the smallest of the Iles du Salut would represent both literal and symbolic isolation. Prior to the arrival of Dreyfus, the Ile du Diable had recently held the lepers of the penal colony, and during his imprisonment, he would be its only prisoner.[20]

Let us return to 1895 and review some essential facts as the prisoner steps ashore. Dreyfus is an Alsatian, a Frenchman, a Jew, a man between many borders. His occupation is that of a French soldier, an officer from a wealthy industrialist family, an assimilated technocrat. He is convicted of betraying secrets of his nation, republican France, to the enemy, imperial Germany. Dreyfus is not executed but rather exiled, confined by law in a "fortified place." He is shipped to a colony, across an ocean, with elaborate security. In the gathering storm his enemies are largely elements of the army, Catholics, aristocrats, and anti-Semitic nationalists who desire a "pure France." Some (though not all) of his defenders are republicans, leftists, intellectuals, and freethinkers. France is split around the question of his guilt, and Dreyfus becomes an example and a symbol, the focus of a question that implies many others: can a Jew be a true representative of France?

In the Dreyfus Affair we see numerous struggles waged over terms of identity. Not the least interesting among these is Dreyfus's own internal struggle in response to his fate. Certain of his own innocence, he nevertheless believes in the crime; between the two convictions his suffering is immense, as he agonizes that a real enemy of France has escaped notice. His account of exile is one of heat, fevers, doubt, and agony. He finds himself removed, not only geographically, but also socially— stripped of family, rank, and honor. His horizon is limited outside his hut by the sea and by the vast silence of exile; he receives little news under the palm trees. Letters are withheld from him, censored, and, when delivered, subject to a delay of three months. Amid the constant reminders of his status as political convict, Dreyfus fights to maintain his inner convictions, repeating them over and over to himself. In his journal and letters to his wife, as well as petitions to the authorities, he stresses his patriotism, his belief in family, duty, honor, and France. Certainty in the correctness of obligation constitutes his essential creed: "As an innocent man, my imperative duty is to go on to the end of my strength. So long as they do not kill me, I shall ever and simply perform my duty."[21]

However, he finds the challenge before him formidable. "Think of my perpetual tête-à-tête with myself," he writes. "I am more silent than a Trappist Monk, in my profound isolation, a prey to sad thoughts, upon a lonely rock, sustaining myself only by the force of duty. . . . My days, my hours, slip by monotonously, in this agonizing, enervating waiting for the discovery of the truth." But the days and nights grow infinite, and torture is "to have two eyes full of enmity leveled at you day and night, every instant and under every condition, and never to be able to escape or defy them!"[22] As time passes he grows more and more desperate.[23]

His experience on the "cursed" island is not only isolation but also a trial by nature: the climate, disease, and insects complete his misery. "Awful heat. . . . The hours are leaden. . . . Violent wind. . . . Impossible to go out. . . . The day is of terrible length! . . . Violent heart spasms . . . the climate . . . alone is enough to set fire to the brain." On May 7, 1896, he writes his wife that "you must expect that sufferings, the climate, the situation have done their work. I have left only my skin, my bones, and my moral energy." Education remains one of his bulwarks against the monotony; he studies English and reads books, including his favorite Shakespeare, especially *Hamlet* and *King Lear.* But even this pleasure is threatened by the climate: "My books were, after a little while, in a wretched condition. Insects laid their eggs in them and devoured them. Vermin hatched out everywhere in my hut." Over time the conditions of Dreyfus's punishment grow more severe: his guards are forbidden to speak with him; communication is completely suspended; his new hut is surrounded by a double stockade, further narrowing his perspective; surveillance becomes total; and he is locked in shackles at night. The prisoner's physical and mental health deteriorates in headaches, fever, and despair.[24]

Dreyfus the *déporté* provides an important image with which to survey Devil's Island. The immediate agony that the captain suffers is the terror of isolation. Like Napoleon he is cast away on an island, yet here the crime is not simply political transgression but a deeper treason. Dreyfus is dangerous precisely because he simultaneously represents everything the conservative forces arrayed against him love and hate: honor and patriotism on the one hand, secular reason and racial impurity on the other. Even as the Dreyfus Affair rages over the soul of France, Dreyfus fights for the soul of France within himself. On Bastille Day in 1895 he writes, "I have seen the tricolor flag aloft everywhere, the flag I have loyally served. My pen falls from my fingers. Some feelings cannot be expressed in words." And then on January 4, 1897: "My heart, you know, it has not changed. It is the heart of a soldier, indifferent to all physical suffering, who holds honor before all else; who has lived, who has resisted this fearful, this incredible, uprooting of everything that makes the Frenchman, the man, of all that makes it possible to live; who has borne it all because he is a father and because he must see to it that honor is restored to the name his children bear." For this particular prisoner, meaning, gender, and humanity—the very center of purpose—are to be found, painfully, hopefully, in the republican national flag.[25]

A quick reference to the broader outlines of historical context further positions our image of Dreyfus within the moral space of a national crisis. For all that he is Jewish, our deported captain nonetheless represents an upper portion of the social pyramid; France contains many others equally undesirable in terms of race and class. The French penal colony takes shape in a period marked by the internal extension of national standards throughout Metropolitan France, in addition to the external expansion of the French Empire. Metaphors of corruption are laterally applied to common criminals, recidivists, and colonial convicts, all those unworthy of the nation by social condition and behavior as well as heritage.[26] These metaphors are increasingly refined in neutralizing fields of technical knowledge, the scope of civilization calculated by an expanding social science and enforced in welfare planning. Evil becomes less a matter of sin than of disease, and moral problems are identified as social and biological in nature. The Dreyfus Affair marks not only the crucible of the public intellectual—an omniscient trumpet of justice such as Zola—but also the rise of what Foucault calls specific intellectuals—the specialized, anonymous technicians of modern norms.[27] As these norms are conceived, measured, and extended through and between nation and empire, the cataloging of natural and human exotica becomes the more rigorous occupation of new disciplines and museums. At the same time criminology begins to better identify and enumerate a recidivist population, the majority from urban areas.[28] Thus in a France defining and redefining both natural and urban environments, the use of geography as punishment realizes a new possibility of myth: not only could the underworld of the city be metaphorically compared to a jungle, but its natives could actually be transported to a living one, a place governed less by the new norms than by their perceived opposites. And Dreyfus, the Jewish army officer considered traitor, not only could be condemned in viscous broadsides as an agent of the Devil, but actually—by historical and administrative twists—then could be sent to the Devil's own tropical island.

A civilizing mission at home and a civilizing mission abroad meet in a specter of degeneration, the potential downward path from modern to primitive. Along the intersection between a modernizing Metropole and a colonizing empire we find the penal colony, and amid images of race, gender, and nature we find its representations, colonial shadows of the modern age. In this sense the laws of 1885, particularly those concerning recidivists, and the politically charged deportation of Dreyfus mark a redefinition of the penal colony. With these events the moral narrative of the project shifts, from that of advancing the colony while disciplining individuals through labor to that of cleansing the social and national body of its impurities. On the shores of Devil's Island, the French penal colony has become the land of exile.

SENSATIONALIST FICTION

Yet exile—the lonely suffering of a noble Frenchman far from home— is not the only threat of Devil's Island. Beyond the terror of isolation lies another terror, that of association. Not only does Dreyfus find himself cut off from his bourgeois milieu and his position as husband and father, but he also finds himself transported, away from Paris into a realm of heat and rain; as his sanity ebbs he is sharing his hut with insects. Meanwhile, common criminals labor ashore under a glaring sun. They too are not only isolated from cities and families but also associated, with each other and their new surroundings.[29] This association called upon sensational imagery, references, and metaphors as florid as the local environment and evoked a range of passions as exaggerated as those in the Dreyfus Affair. Many of these images had existed before. Visitors to French Guiana, both French and non-French, had made much of the penal colony as a site of interest and curiosity.[30] But as the century turned and decades progressed, the pattern gelled, and references reverberated into a sustained outcry. On the French side this resulted primarily from the work of a young investigative journalist named (appropriately enough) Albert Londres. On the foreign side this stemmed from a range of memoirs, reports, journalism, fiction, and films, largely in English and much of it presented for an American audience.[31]

The titles of works written or marketed in English give a sense of the language in play: *Horrors of Cayenne, Dry Guillotine, Hell on Trial, Devil's Island, Hell's Outpost, The Jungle and the Damned, Hell beyond the Seas, Flag on Devil's Island, Condemned to Devil's Island, The Man from Devil's Island, Isle of the Damned, Loose among Devils, Damned and Damned Again.*[32] For most of these books, the cover represents the contents quite accurately. The subtitles, when present, make reference to experience or "revelations." What these works promise is real terror, a narration that claims to be both terrible and true. The French line of this particular subgenre operates in much the same way and even employs many of the same metaphors of hell (*l'enfer*).[33] Yet it is the English appeal to "Devil's Island" that most clearly marks the crucial symbolic space, with geographic overtones but without geographical exactitude. Those discussed are "damned" and obvi-

ously exiled, but few readers are certain just where their suffering occurs. As well as reminding us that empires occupy conceptual fields beyond their physical boundaries, this slip between physical and symbolic
space reveals significant features of the surrounding colonial topography. To trace these, let us turn to a closer examination of some of the
works involved.

METAPHORS OF COLONIAL REVERSAL

You see it there on the Horizon, bleak and barren. A
windswept rock that rises out of the Atlantic. A spec-
tre. Desolate. That's one part of this Hell. You see it
again upon the broad Maroni river. A jungle pushed
back by wretches who were men. Here are Men in
Hell, who came from across the sea to die in loath-
some squalor, because they broke the laws of their fellow men. Devil's Island . . . Cauldron of a thousand
sinister fears; graveyard of many an unfortunate creature. What sorrows have been suffered here, what ago-
nies endured, what deaths died!

W. E. Allison-Booth, Devil's Island, 1931

We are on the opening page of a 1931 book, *Devil's Island: Revelations
of the French Penal Settlements in Guiana,* authored by one W. E. Allison-
Booth, sometime sailor, sensationalist writer, and amateur ethnographer. Fascinated by the penal colony of French Guiana, he subsequently
arranges to miss his ship in order to spend time there and get a closer
look. Shocked by the brutal conditions that he finds, he proceeds to
write a horrified account, decrying the suffering of these white "patri-
ots." Despite the deepening depression, his publisher claims that American readers pledge three hundred thousand dollars to help free one ancient, noble convict.[34]
    But what was the world that Allison-Booth abandoned ship to see,
the penal colony in action, circa 1931? *Devil's Island* offers a rather
hasty account of prisoners, "soldiers," Chinese merchants, and fallen
women, floating somewhere between sharks and snakes under a hot
sun. The narrative consists of anecdotes of prison life interspersed with
shocked observations and reflections built around one elderly Frenchman, sensitive, refined, and innocent, yet doomed to spend his years in
exile. While clear about his moral ground, Allison-Booth is vague

about its particular social and natural surroundings. We are left with an overall impression of something between a plantation, a jail, and a company town: a penal world within a colonial world—prison culture along the frontier.

Allison-Booth was far from the first to attempt an exposé of the penal colony, and quite certainly not the best. Albert Londres's searing account of 1923 set a standard for much of what would follow and moreover played a role in the eventual suppression of the institution. And it was the 1928 work of fellow American Blair Niles, *Condemned to Devil's Island,* that first aroused Allison-Booth's curiosity.[35] Indeed, Allison-Booth's contribution can claim little status as a literary, political, or historical masterpiece. By even the loosest of ethnographic standards its claim to authority is dubious, for despite the publisher's assurances and the first-person narrative, the text does little to affirm that the author ever actually set foot in French Guiana. Yet however that might be, in his very excess Allison-Booth clearly surveys that other entity, the symbolic space of Devil's Island. Partway through his work comes the following reflection:

> I fell to thinking of this paradox of modern civilization. One branch of the government goes to great expense to capture some wild animal for the national zoological collection. During its journey from the jungle to France the captive specimen receives the most careful of treatment, and everything possible is arranged for its comfort, and every care taken that it be brought back alive. At the same time another branch of this identical Government cages up men, human beings, takes them away from civilization with apparently no thought of their comfort, and takes them to a jungle to rot. It is as though they seek to re-populate the jungle with an inferior type of beast.[36]

Here Allison-Booth stumbles on a central horror of the French penal colony: the same jungle from which collectors extract beautiful butterflies and other exotic animals and plants receives its own specimens from civilization in return. Nature—no tamed garden here, but a wild and savage realm—takes its revenge. In the shadow of progress lies the threat of degeneration.

Indeed, the later penal colony presented the possibility of inversion, of a place where hierarchies could be turned and reordered, where a black man could be a guard and a white man his servant, where homosexuality could represent a norm. Through its slow unraveling along the margins of civilization and nature, the French *bagne* reveals an intersection between national and imperial imaginations, a colonial hell for secular sinners. To explicate what such a claim might mean, and what sensational titles might indicate about the system they describe, let us examine selected passages, following thematic loss of masculine purity, racial status, and finally humanity in the face of tropical wilderness.

THE MALE UNDERWORLD

I can no longer endure myself. The *bagne* has entered
in me. I no longer am a man, I am a *bagne*. . . . A convict cannot have been a small child.

> *Convict to Albert Londres,*[37]
> L'Homme qui s'evada/Au bagne, *1923*

If the essential condition of the penal colony was separation and reassociation, then the implied punishment of the *bagne* was that of a fall, the loss of one status and the realization of another. The first element of this process was quite literal; the modern prison ritual of registration, which identified the individual in the most minute terms, before removing all traces of individuality and replacing the name with a number.[38] Blair Niles's *Condemned to Devil's Island* describes the experience as one of scientific, dehumanizing classification:

> [T]he dreadful day when he had stood stripped in the office where the authorities registered finger prints and made inventories of men's bodies, recording every distinguishing mark, every wart or mole, every birth blotch and every tattooed design, making measurements, and adding these things to one's name and age and birthplace, and to the individual crime histories and sentences sent over by the French courts—all indexed and cross-indexed to facilitate emergency reference. . . . [P]art of a man seemed amputated and preserved in card catalogues; much as entomologists impale upon pins all that is mortal of once living insects, classifying as hymenoptera, lepidoptera, and so on and so forth, the brittle remains of creatures who had known life.[39]

Once across the divide between free and imprisoned, one could no longer depend on an identity or system of connections left behind. In dress and daily action, one became another being, stripped of most evidence of the past and always, categorically—even when in solitary confinement—a member of a group. In this way class position was redefined, for while one might have distant influence and money hidden in one's body, local influence was what mattered most.[40] The penal colony was, by all accounts, a violent place. To protect life and goods, the loyalty of other convicts and knowledge of guards who could be bribed usually outweighed one's former occupation or station of birth.

Furthermore, the dislocation inherent to an unfamiliar setting, coupled with the routines of group labor and an arcane language of prison slang, forced convicts to learn a new life. Though the regulations governing the *bagne* may have been exact to the point of pedantic, their application was never uniform, nor were they the only code governing behavior. Rules established between the convicts themselves were at least as important; as every account of the penal experience emphasizes, the price for informing was death.

Thus the loss of individuality was a social condition, experienced in common. Whether or not one came from the masses, here one became part of a new mass. The theme of noble prisoner, which we encountered earlier in the 1879 British account, crops up repeatedly in both writings by outsiders and first-person memoirs.[41] Amid the downtrodden general body of convicts, exceptions are provided who demand our sympathy—the man with a noble brow, the literate intellectual, the youth suffering for a crime of passion, or the innocent martyr. How, we are encouraged to ask, could such a figure end up in such a setting? The incongruity reflects anxiety over the possibility of failure, either of the penal system or of the larger order in which it is embedded. It also identifies the essential state of being in the penal colony: when in the *bagne,* one becomes a *bagnard.*

Loss of individuality entailed loss of masculinity and the certain comfort of one's sexual identity. Most works on the convicts, sensational to academic, note (and generally abhor) the prevalence of homosexuality in the *bagne.*[42] Indeed, one of its historians suggests that not to do so is to engage in misrepresentation: "It is not possible to write of the convict stations of Guiana and not mention the perversion of morals and the effect of the whole question on convict behavior. Not to mention homosexuality and the dramas it caused would be like describing a motor car without mentioning the motor, or writing a treatise on ballistics without mentioning combustion."[43] The slang of the penal colony records a prototypical relationship of involuntary domination, a *fort-à-bras* (strong arm) acquiring a *môme* (brat) as a passive partner. Much of the competition and violence between prisoners is ascribed to the contested establishment and maintenance of such relationships. Interspersed in these portrayals one finds scattered stories of devotion, lovers who sacrifice all for each other and close companions (sexual or no) who together face the world. The personal accounts contain frequent vignettes of rape and abuse, presented as both dehumanizing and emasculating.[44]

Neither the loss of social status and incorporation into a new, stig-
matized group nor the assertion of violent sexual norms between men
are phenomena unique to the French penal colony; they are generic to
accounts of most prisons. Rather, what made the *bagne* particularly
"hellish" to its observers were additional features attendant to its peculiar colonial status. Imprisonment here took place in a setting where
other significant norms could be (and were) upset, principally the racial
categories that prevailed throughout the rest of the French Empire.

RACIAL DEGENERATION

And on top of the strain and the pain
Comes the worst, the ultimate insult
The Arab guard barks at us, "Get moving white man!"
Day after day after day we suffer this
O sons of proud Gaul, is this what you have fallen to!
When even the strongest of you must hang down your
        heads for sheer shame.
Weep—weep for yourselves, you cowardly convicts:
You're not men anymore!
                                        Convict song "Oraput"[45]

In the *bagne* privilege of race did not hold. Many of the prison trustees
were from North Africa, some of the guards (and at least one director)
were black, and a contingent of troops protecting the colony were
from Senegal.[46] Although convicts came from throughout the empire
during the later period, the majority were white and from Metropolitan France. This created scenarios dramatically altered from the norms
of imperial relationships: the possibility of the "colonizer" being controlled by the "colonized." The implications of these scenarios were
not lost on the authors in question. René Belbenoit, a former French
convict turned American crusader, makes much of the penal colony's
role as a substitute for slavery, describing the history of Guyanais
labor as a racial sequence: "the black experiment, the yellow experiment, the white experiment." By coming last in the sequence, "the
white experiment" contradicts assumptions of racial superiority in European representations of slavery and imperialism. One photograph in
Devil's Island presents "a half-blind and half-starved white convict"
who sweeps the road, the caption emphasizing that he is under a "nig-
ger overseer," while another shows a Senegalese soldier outside his

barracks, reminding us that these troops (as well as Maroons and Amerindians) are used to round up escaped prisoners.[47] Englishman George Seaton remembers the Senegalese brought in to discipline the convicts during a riot as "a mob of black lunatics lusting to kill." At the same time he assures us that Arabs are likely to be trustees, whereas Allison-Booth notes that Chinese shopkeepers make trustworthy, if inscrutable, bankers.[48] The stereotypes are still in place, but the power relations are modified, even reversed, on a local, confined scale.

In addition, few writers, French or foreign, fail to note national differences or the particular irony that this notorious, primitive penal colony was run by refined, "civilized" France. The German Batzler-Heim and the Dane Krarup-Nielsen bitterly complain about their treatment (mistakenly in the second case) as "Bosche," while the Frenchmen Londres and Belbenoit base their crusade partly on concern for France's good name.[49] The American Blair Niles chooses to study the *bagne* precisely because of the peculiarities of its human geography:

> I selected the notorious Devil's Island Penal Colony as the place where I would make my investigation, because there the drama of the criminal is staged against a backdrop of tropical jungle, where descendants of escaped Negro slaves live the jungle life of Africa, dancing the African dances and worshipping the African gods. While, locked behind the bars of prison, are criminals sent from highly civilized France. The Devil's Island Colony thus offers a startling contrast between the primitive and the civilized. . . . And since the French possess to an extraordinary degree the gift of self-expression, it is my hope that through the French mind, we may come to understand better the condemned of all other nationalities.[50]

Throughout the texts we slide between categories of nation and race, as well as differing conceptions of civilization.

Racial inversion struck an especially strong chord among foreign observers, particularly those from North America, focused less on the divide between European and Arab and more on the divide between black and white, between the descendants of those who had most obviously been slaves and those who had not. In the penal colony, "[a]fter centuries the black man had at last his chance to revile the white."[51] A Canadian reporter en route to Africa saw the same stark racial threat as Allison-Booth:

> Over the whole of French Guiana the black vulture of death broods and breeds. . . . The country is patrolled by black soldiers from Senegal. Black

police sporting big black revolvers stalk the town. Black men run the bank. Black women issue moist-lipped invitation to come and enjoy their intimacies.[52]

After encountering "a negro with a white suit and a black revolver" at the customshouse, he witnesses two white men "cleaning a negro's outhouse." "What," he wonders, almost reflectively, "would the framers of America's Jim Crow laws think of this?"[53]

A particular source of outrage for these observers is the lot of the *libérés,* those prisoners who had served out their sentence but were fated to live out their lives in French Guiana under the provision of *doublage,* the regulation requiring a convict to remain in the penal colony after his term of confinement. Penniless, denied even the minimum care of the penal administration, they haunted the civil colony, searching for odd jobs and scrambling for cigarette butts. The "Avenue of Liberty" in Cayenne, our Canadian noted, was the "most misnamed street on earth." And as Krarup-Nielsen put it: "It is necessary to live among the 'liberated' prisoners of Guiana to realize their hopeless condition and understand the full irony of the word 'libéré.' As the convicts like to say, '*Le bagne commence à la libération* [the penal colony begins at the moment of liberation].'" The *libérés,* he thought, were the true pariahs, men "despised even by the poorest Negros whose forefathers in their day were brought to Guiana in chains, as slaves."[54] In addition to performing most of the menial labor in both the penal and civil colonies (such as emptying chamber pots) and acting as houseboys (*garçons de maison*), filling the roles of female as well as male servants, the *libérés* were reduced to fabricating trinkets for the souvenir trade—miniature, cigar-clipping guillotines proving particularly popular items. Thus even when they were freed, the *bagne* continued to set the terms of their identity. And French Guiana would claim them as well. In the forest that surrounded them and stymied their escape, convicts and *libérés* alike found one of their most reliable sources of income:

> In the ruined Colony of Guiana, men with pale faces and bodies wracked with malaria hunt butterflies grimly for a living. There, in that rain-soaked jungle which the condemned curse, God has put a brilliant thing, resplendent and fragile, to help miserable men conquer their freedom. . . . And these gorgeous butterflies, the only thing of real beauty in that infernal colony, wretched men must destroy for some food and money to hoard for escape from death.[55]

When pinned in turn and shipped to collectors, the tropics fed those it punished.

FEARS OF THE FOREST

The penal administration was never betrayed by nature—the bush, the swamps, the sea, the climate, the
sharks, the mosquitoes, the snakes, all were faithful,
honest servants.

> Memoir of a French forger, Francis
> Lagrange and William Murray,
> Flag on Devil's Island, 1961

Throughout these accounts runs an acute awareness of wild nature and its role in the enterprise of the *bagne*. Allison-Booth was far from alone in employing metaphors of wild animals when describing the convicts. George John Seaton, a wayward Englishman who spent twenty years as a *relégué,* writes in a similar tone: "Even I—the effete socialite—ac-quired a sinewy brutality. I was no longer the man-about-town; I was not even a man; I slid back a dozen centuries and obeyed the law that said, 'if all else dies, *I* shall survive.'" For Seaton the whole penal uni-verse becomes one of savage order, governing prisoners and guard alike: "[The guards] were, in a sense, just as imprisoned as we were. . . . They still had to endure the blistering heat and savage rains. They were just as likely to contract leprosy or tuberculosis. They were like animal trainers in the circus; they dared never relax."[56] Others also recognized the egalitarian side effects of shared local conditions, as well as the fear of living next to violence. The prisoners, abused as they were, repre-sented a constant source of threat: "There was a saying in the *bagne* to the effect that we were all—convicts, guards and functionaries—pris-oners: 'In the *bagne* one half watches the other half.'"[57]

As geography itself becomes a technique of isolation, the French penal experiment in Guiana threatens further ordeals implicit in sepa-ration from all that is civilized. Here, in an inversion of Rousseau, na-ture becomes part of the punishment, as the reputed primitive elements of society are returned to the reputed terrors of the jungle. Tropical wilderness itself serves as a menacing enclosure, between steamy cli-mate, exotic and dangerous animals in the swamps and forests, sharks in the sea, and rumors of cannibal Indians. In sensational accounts these tropics incessantly punish as they guard, turning everyday exis-tence into constant torment: "Fever and dysentery get every man!

Clouds of buzzing mosquitoes and fire ants sting your aching body
while you labor. Hordes of flies settle on your festering sores . . . [and]
at night the vampire bats come into the open barracks and bleed sleeping men white!"[58]

But to run from the human prison is only to face the real prison, to
go deeper into the equatorial nightmare of untracked jungle. The narrative of escape becomes that of a caged beast, driven mad by the sun,
fleeing from the wilderness and fighting to survive, far more than that
of a clever deviant outwitting a rational machine. Exotic nature itself is
the real enemy, full of hidden traps and unknown dangers:

> They still felt imprisoned, but prisoners now of this strange dumb forest,
> where in no direction could they look more than a few feet ahead, this for-
> est where thorns tore the flesh and clothing of men who would journey
> through it. In its uncanny half-light anything—beast or man-hunter—
> might be standing quite close, close enough to spring upon you, and in the
> mocking mosaic of sun and shadow you would never have the fraction of a
> warning.[59]

And even if a convict can elude his pursuers and avoid the savage plants,
the snakes, the sharks, and the constant threat of disease, another and
terrible possibility awaits: at any point he may lose his way. Land that is
uncivilized is also unmapped; both forest and ocean are vast and unmarked. As the commandant of the *bagne* would inform convicts on
their arrival, "The real guards here are the jungle and the sea."[60]

Many of the prisoners, after all, were from urban environments,
and even those from outside of the city had little experience with the
tropics or this specific locale. Ignorance attendant to the knowledge of
civilization became exposed. The question became starkly technical in
nature: "Could a Frenchman—lost—cut off from human kind—live in
the jungle alone?"[61] To be successful in the forest one must be familiar
with its ways, to be able to exist naturally within it. In the words of
one European who made his fortune in French Guiana during the era:
"I lived the life of my friend the tiger. The jungle that kills did not have
me, it spared me because I loved it fervently, because I owed it everything, because it taught me to be free."[62] But a "Parisian, naked,
climbing a jungle tree . . . really it seemed as if a man oughtn't to be
born as defenseless as he is."[63] Lost amid strange surroundings, lacking most rudimentary skills of survival and means of support, such a
prisoner was trapped more surely by his freedom than by his imprisonment. Listening to an animal howling at night, Blair Niles's protagonists realize their own limits beyond the world of men: "There was

freedom in it—wild freedom which knows no law but that of inevitable Nature. . . . They had fled from the tyranny of prison. Now
this incarnation of freedom terrified them, robbed them of speech and
movement."[64]

For all that the *bagnard* might have lived at the edge of civilization,
he was never a creature of wilderness, never a man beyond society.
Rather, transported, stripped of identity, subject to transposed norms
and reversed hierarchies, he represented a limit of degeneration. This
limit was made visible in the *bagne* but never crossed. The sensation
evoked in accounts of Devil's Island depended on empathy, an understanding that this underworld remained connected to the world that
created it:

> If you weren't afraid to come down among us, where we have to live, you'd
> see. As step by step you went lower into our pit you'd understand all along
> the way the causes. In the blackest depths you'd find you could see. It would
> be as if someone held a lantern to show every rung of the ladder that leads
> to us. But to you standing safe on the top, looking down, we are strange and
> horrible—we frighten you. Why? Is it because you see yourselves in us? . . .
> Yet our roots are up in your civilization. Don't forget that![65]

PLACING THE PENAL COLONY

You see, the world is made up of three things: heaven,
earth, and the *bagne*.
>   Director of the penal colony to Albert Londres,
>   Au bagne, 1923

As Michel Pierre notes, French Guiana represented such a distant and
mythic universe for many French people that when a young attorney
compared shipyard workers to the "convicts of Cayenne, under the terrible climate of the Pacific," no one expressed shock at his glaring error
in geography.[66] The colonial *bagne* existed in some vague unlocated
tropics, and one ocean was as good as another. What mattered was the
surreal sense of horror associated with the name—heat and disease, not
latitude and longitude.

At a higher level of abstraction, the very definition of a penal colony
complicates the spatial vocabulary of empire. Whether directly settled
or remotely administered, a colony represents an extremity or appendage: its essential geographic point of reference is only partially itself.
The goal of a colony is the transformation of a natural or unfamiliar
space into a recognizable or productive one. A nation, in contrast,

marks itself directly, whether or not its actual boundaries can be clearly drawn. The goal of nationalism is self-realization, the establishment and maintenance of appropriate frontiers (physical or symbolic) through which to define itself. While the spatial goals of colonialism and nationalism are not directly opposed, they are also not directly aligned: extending France into the world is not necessarily the same thing as demarcating its essence. The penal colony marks a boundary of the nation, a limit of its identity in both geographic and social terms. Like any colony it represents a physical extension of national influence, something between "home" and "abroad," a home abroad to be governed and transformed by a master home. Yet, unlike other colonies, it is specifically peopled by those decreed unfit to live within the nation, dangerous elements governed through colonial distance, former nationals now reborn in a lower order. Place thus becomes tremendously important, even as a geography of type overwhelms exact location. Exile is outside the nation but not beyond its greater borders of political and conceptual empire; rather, it occurs within the imperial framework of national identity as an intimate reversal.[67]

The historical sequence of the French penal colony indicates changing conceptions of race, gender, colony, and nation. During an era of high imperialism, offenders are removed from the shores of France to beyond those shores, from the national margin to the imperial rim. Convict labor first offers a potential substitute for slave labor, but then the particular colonial climate, read in racial terms, is deemed inappropriate for European convicts. Two decades later that which is harmful to Europeans becomes the appropriate universal punishment for all and, furthermore, the site of permanent exile for recidivists—those whose delinquent nature renders them unfit for France. At the same time, an effort to biologically and socially extend the nation by means of transporting women convicts and encouraging rehabilitation and reproduction through the formation of European families founders badly, failing to transform Guyane into a French Australia. Rather, the *bagne* lingers on as a male world of dubious sexual repute, a land of laboring criminals, delinquents, and political prisoners, those encouraged neither to return nor to reproduce. It receives those outside family and propriety, those destined for colonial existence—the fallen of a nation.

It is tempting to take Devil's Island as a literal metaphor and see the penal colony as a nationalist site of suffering, somewhere between civil purgatory and a form of colonial hell. The allusion of purgatory is a useful one, representing a "third place" within the symbolic geography of medieval Christendom, a purifying fire that becomes spatially fixed, a "Hell of limited duration," "God's prison."[68] Here a soul suffered but could still be affected by actions of the living and events in the present. The metaphor works rather well in the case of Dreyfus: an errant Jew accused of everything unspeakable by French ultra-nationalists and cast into torment could nevertheless hope for pardon and redemption. Purified by his suffering, he (a good bourgeois) could even ascend in another direction, briefly serving as a martyr for leftist intellectual circles and becoming a political symbol invoked long after his death.[69] For the ordinary *bagnard*, however, the comparison grows more troubling, as the paths to redemption grew less clear as the experiment continued. Individuals might be saved, but the group as a whole was damned.

In allowing a degree of significance to metaphors drawn from religion and filtered through commercial media, I would nonetheless keep in mind the technical apparatus to which they were applied. Throughout its existence the *bagne* remained an organization devoted to a principle of activity: the convicts worked, and when they did not work they received either medical treatment or punishment. The product of this labor was dubious at best; the penal colony produced little of material value and required massive subventions from the French government to continue its operations.[70] Original intent and promises notwithstanding, it did little to further the economic development of the region. Land was cleared, trees were cut, but no lasting agricultural presence emerged. What work was done, was done poorly, slowly, and incompletely. Albert Londres gives the most cutting statistic in his description of the road under construction by the penal administration, *route coloniale Numéro 1*, which the convicts call "Route Zero": "They've been working on it for over fifty years. . . . It's twenty-four kilometers long!"[71] Noting the severe conditions under which the construction takes place, he wonders if the purpose of the labor was to build a road or to kill convicts. In effect it accomplished both, one slowly and uselessly, and the other slowly and painfully. Thus while the penal colony functioned as a machine of sorts, it was a less than perfect one, poorly designed, badly maintained, and perpetually inefficient. Yet it remained in place, rusty and leaking, failing repeatedly but never dismantled. In it we have an important image for the tropics: the ruined machine at the margins of mechanization.

And around the ruined machine we have a ruined land. Even as the one decayed, the other spoiled, infected by its reputation. For those living in Guiana, the *bagne* had both a specific and immediate presence and a far-reaching and lingering symbolic impact. During the period of its operation, the convicts, whether actually serving a sentence or free, were deeply embedded in the life of the civil colony, working as servants, clerks, and technicians in addition to providing a manual labor pool. Including guards and army troops, the penal population accounted for a significant portion of French Guiana, and its administration represented a rival pole of authority. Governors came and went; the institutions of the *bagne* stayed. Furthermore, the penal colony supported a significant portion of commercial activities; its expenditures matched some 50 percent of the colony's total exports. Thus when calls came for its suppression, they met with considerable local resistance, and when the decision was finally taken in 1938 to suspend transportation, provisions were made to phase the *bagne* out gradually, easing the effects of the economic vacuum it would leave.[72]

Yet the symbolic weight of its reputation should not be underestimated. Even now, few discussions of French Guiana fail to mention its role as a penal colony, and during the period of its operation the reference was omnipresent. For those who grew up in the *terre de bagne,* it cast a shadow they could rarely escape: the need to always explain. The poet and politician Léon-Gontran Damas, as notable a literary figure as French Guiana has yet produced, was sent by his parents to Metropolitan France in 1926 for further schooling. He later recalled the moment the principal of the school asked him where he was from. When Damas replied "Guyane," the official could not help inquiring further: "'But this is the country of the convicts?' to which Damas answered: 'It is only the depository, the factory being elsewhere, in the Metropole.' With some blushing and hesitation the Principal pursued: 'But would your father be a convict?' Upon which Damas replied: 'If my father were a convict I would be as white as you, Sir.'"[73]

In 1938 Damas, working for what would become the Musée de l'Homme in Paris, published a report upon the effects of colonialism on Guiana entitled *Retour de Guyane.* Above all he attacked the "curse of the penal colony," which humiliated all Guyanais abroad and corrupted society within the country itself, questioning "what right France had to corrupt a colony in this manner" and reduce it to the level of a "cesspool" for the protection of the mother country. Calling for a renewed focus on gold mining in French Guiana on the grounds of both economics and "honor," Damas warned that the expiration of the colony might herald the "collapse of the French Empire."[74]

THE NATURAL UNDERWORLD

We arrive at kilometer twenty-four. It's the end of the
world. And for the first time, I see the *bagne!*

Albert Londres, Au bagne, *1923*

Out we go, our tools over our shoulders
Stumbling in and out among the gloomy trees
Like a row of drunken devils
For this is the real Hell, not Satan's.

Convict song "Oraput"

In the penal colony we find a state of nature, but a degenerate one.[75]
Rather than forget historical origins in alluding to mythical ones, the
bars of the *bagne* twist metaphors of the primitive into the very boundary of civilization, mixing temporal and geographic orders. The jungle
is mythically terrible, and imprisonment within this mythic space becomes a modern reality. Civilization, Enlightenment, modernity—all
these amorphous narrative bulwarks have their shadows, gaps, and
fears. The terror of Devil's Island takes shape amid metaphoric invoca-
tions of the jungle and of the savage, of associations between the beast
without and the beast within. Rather than provide an economic substitute for slavery, the penal colony becomes a zone representing the
threat of decivilization, a place where the codes of civilized life are suspended and held in abeyance, where white manly morals erode, and
where colonials command. If we follow Michael Taussig's vocabulary
for cultural dimensions of terror beyond physical brutality, then Devil's
Island should be understood as a space of death.[76] At its center stands
Kafka's machine, madly writing a sentence of suffering. If no longer internally coherent, the marks remain open for interpretation by different
audiences.

For those in Metropolitan France the penal colony served as a hidden punishment, a distant if graphic terror, retaining elements of torture out of public view. Yet it retained a veneer of reformation, for the
convicts were still told to "make a new life for themselves."[77] In addition, shipping convicts away from France in the name of colonization
cloaked their punishment in the robes of the "civilizing" mission: they
would be part of an effort to build a greater France, to develop Guiana,
and to integrate it into a Franco-world system. At the same time the
bagne underscored that resistance to the humane norms of France
could lead to decivilization and exile in the wilderness.

For those in Metropolitan nations outside France, the effect was equally distanced, while further removed; the punishment was not only hidden but also the product of another's justice. That this justice could itself appear unjust would only reinforce symbolic national borders and be incorporated within varying claims to civilization. Torture here is another's responsibility, hell over a different horizon, where it invokes righteous outrage and fear. We find such outrage in the British Empire, itself competing with France to civilize the world, where penal transportation was outdated policy. We also find it in the Americas (especially the United States), lands partway between colony and nation and uncomfortably close, in both geographic and symbolic terms, to the *bagne*. Within this outrage lingers a faint recognition of the possibility of colonial reversal and the evaporation of racial privilege, a small, distorted echo of the nightmare of plantation slavery.

For those sent to French Guiana, however, the penal colony served directly as a public display, a constant reminder of the operations of justice. The convicts were not merely confined but forced to labor on public works. Official executions were performed by that once-humane instrument, the guillotine, but before an audience of convicts and by a fellow convict, far beyond the gates of Paris. A slower execution, that of the "dry guillotine," the effects of the tropical climate, surrounded the entire process of deportation, reminding the convicts that this punishment could only happen *here* and not within Metropolitan boundaries. Theirs was a raw and primitive environment, one of torture and deprivation away from the public eye. Against the truth invoked in their conviction—justice—lay a suggested truth invoked in their punishment: no longer civilized, they were no longer human.

And for those already living in French Guiana, the penal colony also served as a public spectacle, if one not aimed directly at them or of their making. Not only did the proximity of prison life to their own lives parade the power of justice before them in an immediate fashion, but the constant importation of prisoners for this apparatus of punishment emphasized the particularly colonial nature of this power. Uncivilized elements were sent to them; their relation to France was that of a repository for human waste, and acts and punishments deemed unseemly for the homeland could still occur within their boundaries. In addition, the appropriation of the names "Guyane" and "Cayenne" in myths of the *bagne* and "Devil's Island" precluded other identities, while burdening the area with a symbolic brand and a historical chain to France. "The *bagne*," writes Ian Hammel, "left only a disastrous brand on Guiana."[78]

Brand here means "trademark" as well as "scar," indicating purpose, function, and maker. To be remembered as a penal colony is to be remembered not only as a prison, an exotic place of horror, but also as a colony, the object and product of another. In a metaphorical reworking of Foucault, the body in this case of spectacle might be the colony, punished before the world.

By the time Allison-Booth wrote his *Devil's Island,* the penal colony supported few claims for the marriage of rehabilitation and production. Despite improved medical technology, death rates in the *bagne* remained high; despite the ongoing labor of up to six thousand men, the organization depended heavily on state subsidies and accomplished almost nothing. A distant and rigorous punishment of little economic value, older forms of power existing along with modern ones, the exotic intermingled with the normal—many loose ends of colonial history lie buried in the *bagne.* Modernizing France, a convulsive patchwork of provinces, cities, farms, and factories, casts its shadow overseas. The logic of moralization embodied by the penal colony comes to function in reverse: rather than produce reform and development, the *bagne* institutionalizes failure at a distance. "It is as though they seek to repopulate the jungle with an inferior type of beast." Amid melodrama, the sensational account offers telling insight.

When Allison-Booth takes a farewell walk by the River Maroni, arm in arm with his favorite convict, he leaves us with a parting vision of the margins of nations and empires and the boundaries of nature and civilization. On the wide banks of a South American river, framed by the tropical heavens, two edges of France converge: the colonial frontier and the guillotine. But the beauty of the sky is deceptive, for the land below them is itself an executioner: the Dry Guillotine, the colonial blade of justice. Natural as they may be, these tropics represent the earthly work of humans, and our passage concludes with this reminder:

> Gazing across the river we could see the jungle of Dutch Guiana—a vast stretch of impenetrable undergrowth containing exaggerated beauty and horror, which alike were the creation of the same God. To our left, on the French side of the river, stood the guillotine shed, plainly visible against the background of a beautiful tropical sky. The stars twinkled brightly, like myriads of avenging angels gazing on this beauty of Nature, that had been transformed by man into hell on earth.[79]

Figure 9.   Tintin rocket, Kourou, 1994

PART 3

Modern Sky

"Distance is an empty word, distance does not exist!"
Jules Verne,
From the Earth to the Moon, *1865*

By and large, in discussions of modern life things float free. Amid uniform landscapes conjured from steel and concrete, coordinates of time and space become simultaneously universal and ephemeral. In the last century railroads and rifles appeared to travel the earth with impunity, and such contemporary cousins as television and missiles acknowledge even fewer boundaries. An enduring general assumption—however belied in practice—lingers when discussing modern machines: once sufficiently advanced and properly ordered, they will function in the same manner, no matter where they are. Is not material universality the facile magic of the modern, its most alluring and terrifying promise?

The case at hand involves the realization of natural space beyond the confines of our planet, the literal "outer space" of the Space Age, as well as shifting geometries on the human sphere below. Thus our discussion will revolve around twin meanings of the term *space,* one physical and the other human. This unavoidable wordplay reveals the historicity inherent in bringing the abstract expanse of the universe alive, recalling that before the launching of the first artificial satellite there was no active outer space to redefine the more immediate active one beneath it—in a sense, no modern sky above a modern ground. Technologies associated with the exploration and commercialization of this "outer" space have significantly transformed experiences of human space on a global scale, exemplified by the redefinition of the equator relative to rockets and satellite orbits. The case of Kourou and the Guiana Space Center both illustrates this point and describes its anthropological significance, serving as a reminder that technologies unfold between horizons of human history and geography and amid narratives of human temporal location embedded in expressions such as "Space Age." Technologies, in addition to acting on the world, play significant roles—literal *and* symbolic—in efforts to differentiate between groups of humans inhabiting it, past and present.

Thus we return to classic motions of anthropology, gyrations between situated and general, traditional and modern, natural and cultural. The challenge, however, is to take the modern as seriously as that which it has been positioned against, to respect the present and the past simultaneously, and to cease insisting on the absolute gravity of categories. In this way we can turn to the central question at the edge of modern place: what is our sense of "outer space," and how did it come to be?

CHAPTER 5

A Gate to the Heavens

Who gave us the sponge to wipe away the entire horizon?
What were we doing when we unchained this earth from its
sun? Whither is it moving now? Whither are we moving?
Away from all suns? Are we not plunging continually? Backward, sideward, forward, in all directions? Is there still any
up or down? Are we not straying as through an infinite nothing? Do we not feel the breath of empty space?
> Friedrich Nietzsche,
> The Gay Science, *1882*

Exerting himself to look out into space, man did not descry
something entirely different and alien; rather, what was held
out to him was a cosmic mirror of his own world, of its history and its potential.
> Hans Blumenberg,
> Genesis of the Copernican World, *1975*

In 1865, even as the American Civil War wound to a painful, bloody
close, a middle-aged Frenchman had a fantastic vision of its aftermath.
In a sardonic tone, betrayed only by a fondness for technical elaboration, he described how American masters of artillery, at a loss in retirement, would construct a giant cannon and shoot it at the moon. The
man, of course, was Jules Verne, a prolific former stockbroker who
helped to establish the popular genre now known as science fiction,
producing a remarkable stream of works filled with florid, masculine
adventure and the wonders of machinery. *From the Earth to the Moon*
was the third of his *Voyages extraordinaire* and, in a small, but precise
way, proved to be one of the world's more influential books.[1] Beyond
the pleasure and wonder it afforded Verne's contemporaries, it would
eventually inspire a small group of engineers to more practical dreams
of moon flight. Rarely has fiction translated more directly into fact.
Like a number of Verne's works, his moon voyage includes remarkably
prescient technical elements, from a Florida launch site to an ocean
landing. Even more eerily, the tale foreshadows a number of cultural
forces at play in reaching the moon, including the importance of excess
military expertise, public relations, and human cargo. And Verne, for

Figure 10.   Ariane launch, ca. 1988

all that he could not resist including a dashing French astronaut, was quite clear that this great feat of engineering would occur in the United States and not in France.

Over a century later, on Christmas Eve, 1979, a slim white rocket left the ground and slowly climbed skyward. Bearing the flags of a dozen nations and the French name for a figure from Greek myth, it represented the culmination of years of planning along with the dreams and toil of an army of engineers and support staff. Despite delays and disappointments leading up to it, this symbolic maiden flight would prove an auspicious turning point in European efforts to build an independent space launch vehicle. Over the ensuing decade the Ariane program more than fulfilled its promise, lifting communications, observation, and experimental satellites into orbit, while capturing half the world market for commercial launches. Its base, the Guiana Space Center (CSG), indeed lived up to its slogan, becoming "Europe's Spaceport," a center of high technology near the equator. Verne's compatriots had finally caught up to his prophetic vision. And the Space Age, it would seem, had at last arrived in the tropics.

The "final frontier" was not then very old. Even in the middle of the twentieth century, the sky was defined in a single direction; one looked up through it, not down from beyond. The Earth had but a single satellite, the moon, and the man on it was a figure of poetry, not technological triumph. What lay beyond the atmosphere remained the province of astronomic observation and literary speculation, not exploration or commercial development. Yet just as nineteenth-century Western imperial expansion began to unravel, ink drying on the last white areas of the disintegrating maps, a new and final frontier came into being above the emerging political boundaries of first, second, and third worlds. Frequently described in language of colonial conquest (the inexorable "progress of mankind" now carried beyond the confines of a single planet), this frontier reflects both a logical extension of modernist ambition and its limits. "Outer space" describes something undeniably distant from local place, a vastness stretching impossibly far from the familiar globe. To imagine this "beyond" as a frontier is to invite its exploration yet also simultaneously to reposition the surface already known. Once the heavens fill with human activity, the ground below shifts in meaning, drawing together into a globe. Divides and boundaries are recast, some growing obsolete, others deepening. And when the first Ariane headed skyward, its reflection, white and gleaming, headed down.

FROM SPUTNIK TO THE SPACE RACE

Go up a few miles and life as we know it ends. There,
we would no longer have an atmospheric blanket to
protect us. High temperatures exist but would not be
sensed. X rays and cosmic rays would penetrate our

bodies and dissociate our cells. The air pressure would
decrease below our blood pressure until our bodily
fluids began to boil. Time is always a relative concept.
Skyward all is darkness.

> *Erik Bergaust and William Beller,*
> *Satellite!* *1956*

"Today the dreams of the best sons of mankind have
come true. The assault on space has begun."

> *Sergey Korolev,*[2] *1957, quoted in James Oberg,*
> Red Star in Orbit, *1981*

The dawn of the Space Age came in the fall of 1957, in the form of a
faintly beeping metal ball. The Soviet satellite *Sputnik 1*, though modest in size and capability, cast a long political shadow, one stretching
through debates about science, technology, and education far beyond
the immediate purview of outer space.[3] To understand the significance
of the event and its representation, we must replay a small portion of
context surrounding this launch and the subsequent history of the
Space Race and satellite technology, sweeping quickly enough to blur
general patterns into view, yet finely enough to collect telling details.
The new configuration of technology and society described by the expression "Space Age" comes most clearly into focus when viewed
through extremes: a sudden break, an evolutionary leap, the cut in
Kubrick's film *2001* between bone tool and spaceship. In writing about
it one traffics between precision and expansive myth. To focus on only
one or the other loses the essence of their combination: a union of exact
instrumentality and abstract ends that opened the sky.

Let us first demystify the event. Although the launch of Sputnik was
a public surprise, it was far from unpredictable, or even unpredicted
among those paying attention to the possibilities of spaceflight. The
span of 1957–1958 had been designated the "International Geophysi-
cal Year," and both the United States and the Soviet Union broadly
hinted that a satellite launch would be an appropriate way to mark the
occasion. What better way to contemplate the Earth, after all, than
from beyond it? Both goliaths of the Cold War were engaged in experiments with nuclear warheads and working on another end of rocketry,
the missile. The basic technology for space launches had been available
for some time. And interest in the future and futuristic technology was
running high in certain quarters: science fiction boomed after World
War II, as it had after World War I. Thus while the launch of Sputnik

marks a watershed event, it was not one that, as it were, emerged from thin air.[4]

The tie to science fiction merits further stress, for it is a point to which we will return: not only were most of the major and minor figures of space technology deeply influenced by strains of futuristic literature, but the future that would transpire around them had been remarkably well envisioned beforehand. The case of Verne is in this sense exemplary more than exceptional. Well before the technical simulation of the Space Age we have another mode of anticipation: fantasies of the future. Dreams are made exact, legitimate, and even useful. Moreover, at certain points they are taken seriously. Thus it should come as no surprise that elaborate visions and mythic allusions wove deeply into outer space, for they ran through the very technologies that open it, as well as the cultural frame of the sky.[5]

The technical story of the rocket itself is appropriately global in scope. A device first made recognizable some thousand years ago in China traveled to Europe, where it remained a tool for signals and celebrations until enjoying brief popularity as a weapon of war in the early nineteenth century. Following improvements in artillery it fell again into obscurity, lingering marginally in the minds of Russian, German, and American enthusiasts of spaceflight until its dramatic return in World War II. The German device known as A-4, developed in secret and manufactured with forced labor, first flew successfully in October of 1942. Rechristened V-2, the missile began to rain from the skies only at the very end of the conflict. Nevertheless, it helped set the tone for much of the ensuing Cold War, for German scientists had dreamt grandiose plans around the A-4, including an orbiting space station. In the waning days of the Third Reich, a curious race occurred across Europe, one that foreshadowed the political standoff of coming decades, as American and Soviet agents both worked frantically to reach German V-2 sites and capture rockets, documents, and engineers. These trophies were then hauled away from Europe to the west and to the east, for testing and improvement on other continents. Technology born from the ashes of fascism would later rise phoenixlike amid a strategic and symbolic struggle between state capitalism and state socialism, in the form of both long-range nuclear missiles and space launch vehicles.[6]

Yet while there was much talk, research, and design throughout the 1950s, only after the launch of Sputnik did the Space Age come undeniably into view. Space became news. Space became strategy. Space defined the modern. As satellites and human vehicles proliferated above the Earth, each success or failure merited banner headlines, while the very possibility of such things and the terms used to describe them sank into everyday speech. Vast sums were invested in technology on either side, and each success or failure was quickly deployed by the United States and the Soviet Union in internal political struggles as well as in the propaganda war between them. Rhetorical appeals around each success or failure identified historical landmarks, a new world of which one was, or wasn't, a part. Beneath the shift from below to above the atmosphere ran a social transformation, extending the wartime arrangement between state policy and technical design into a lasting marriage. The two decades between the first Soviet satellite and the American moon landing, marked by a lonely hurtling transmitter at one end and a man's footprint in dust at the other, embrace a dramatic rise of an army of technicians. Even as new forms appeared in the heavens, techniques and social systems developed for space found additional application on earth.[7]

AMERICAN INFLUENCE AND FRENCH IMAGINATION

Amid the fireworks of American and Soviet competition for supremacy, the old center of Europe faded into the background. Although German engineers continued to play a role (particularly in the American program), they did so at a distance, and rockets rose from the empty edges of other continents—American marshland and Asian steppe—not the former heart of empires. Yet it would be a mistake to lose sight of Europe completely. The British and French did their best to acquire the remnants of the V-2 and develop something from it. The British played an important role in early satellite technology, and the French eventually became the third most significant space power, after the United States and the Soviet Union, and the driving force behind joint European ventures. This interest on their part was only natural. Beyond strong traditions of aeronautics and space enthusiasm, Britain had borne the brunt of early Nazi experiments in rocketry, and the first V-2 had left the ground aimed at Paris.[8]

An independent French presence in space fit within larger policies of technical modernization and diplomatic autonomy. The land of Verne focused on steering a separate course between the Eastern Bloc and the rest of its Western allies, as French governments of the Fifth Republic, under the firm hands of Charles de Gaulle and Georges Pompidou, strove to regain political prominence through technological independence, substituting tools for empire. When the strategic terms of international relations translated into nuclear warheads, rockets, and satellites, the French worked furiously to devise their own *force de frappe* and *fusée*. To work toward the latter end a national space agency was founded in 1962, the Centre National d'Etudes Spatiales (CNES). As its first president recalled, when other members of the administration questioned the decision on the basis of cost, de Gaulle confirmed the choice quickly when told the other option would be to rely on the United States. The French made good on their effort to field a launcher three years later, in November 1965, when they lifted a small satellite, *Asterix-1*, into orbit from Algeria on their own booster, Diamant.[9]

Yet for all their independence, the French remained simultaneously committed to cooperation. The Asterix launch had been racing against a second French satellite poised on a NASA rocket, while negotiations for a joint European rocket program were completed at the same time as the founding of CNES, inspired in part by the earlier creation of the European physics consortium, CERN. On March 29, 1962, a convention for an organization known as the European Launcher Development Organization (ELDO) was signed, with France, Britain, West Germany, Italy, Belgium, the Netherlands, and Australia as full members and Denmark and Switzerland as observers. ELDO would be matched by another cooperative institution, the European Space Research Organization (ESRO) to design experiments and satellites. The plan for the launcher was an ingenious bit of improvisation: the main stage would be comprised of Britain's Blue Streak rocket, an obsolete missile design redeployed for civilian ends, while France would build a second stage known as Coralie, and Germany would build a third stage, Astris. The completed ensemble would be known as "Europa." Australia's inclusion in the rocket program stemmed from its contribution of a desert launch site at Woomera, chosen by the British to test their captured V-2s on Commonwealth soil.[10]

The Europa program, however, went far less smoothly than French solo efforts. Although the Blue Streak base performed adequately, it was too modest to lift satellites into high orbit, and supplementary second and third stages fared less well. As the American and Soviet race continued, space technology advanced beyond the Europa design. The United States did not favor the European project and lent no aid. Funding was sparse and cost overruns endemic. But design changes (strongly promoted by the French) resulted in plans for Europa II, a more powerful model that could achieve the high orbit required by communications satellites. Under heavy French pressure, the European program also committed to another launch site, leaving Australia behind. Before continuing that story, however, we should consider the subject of satellites more closely and examine the ways in which they transformed the modern sky.

ARTIFICIAL SATELLITES AND THE NEW EQUATOR

The truth, of course, will be far stranger.
> Arthur C. Clarke,
> 2001: A Space Odyssey, 1968

Even as Allied forces raced for the V-2, a young English astronomer and future science fiction luminary was struck by accounts of German aerospace ambitions and toyed with the possibilities of communications using relay stations in space. Published in 1945, Arthur C. Clarke's article "Extra-Terrestrial Relays" combined bold proposals for applied rocket "astronautics" with a pragmatic observation that German developments moved them into the realm of possibility. Addressing the problem of atmospheric and topographic limits to long-distance communication, which would make comprehensive television transmission across even a small European country an expensive and technically complicated affair, Clarke proposed a set of three satellite stations in space to cover the entire globe. Prophetically he proclaimed that "a true broadcast service, giving constant field strength across the whole globe would be invaluable, not to say indispensable, in a world society."[11]

A decade would pass before Sputnik woke the world to the realities of the Space Age. However, Clarke's original title for his article, "The Future of World Communications," was soon to prove the better one. What he had grasped was the significance of a geosynchronous orbit, where the rotation of the body in question would coincide with that of the Earth. Rather than rise and set in the sky, such a body would remain constant relative to a chosen area of the globe and thus be in a position to provide it with continuous communication support. Signals could be sent from one location within that area and then transmitted to another. With a carefully positioned set of such space platforms, signals could even be relayed between them and thus from one side of the world to another. While initial outlays might be large, the overall expense of such a system would ultimately prove reasonable, given the small amount of hardware involved, relative to land-based systems. In a few startling pages Clarke outlined the basis for a practical approach to the heavens. His only major oversight was to assume that these communication satellites would be manned.[12]

What appeared a brash pronouncement at the end of World War II was taken quite seriously only fifteen years later. The beginning of the 1960s saw many significant milestones in space, including missions carrying humans beyond the atmosphere, beginning with Yuri Gagarin's 1961 flight. Yet while the Soviet Union won the symbolic races, sending up the first animal, man, and woman and landing pioneering probes on the moon, on Venus, and the like, it was the United States that began to put in place the basic practical infrastructure of space, launching the first weather satellite, the first navigational satellite, the first spy satellite, and—with a glorified balloon known as *Echo I*—the first communications satellite. The first active communications satellite, *Telstar,* was followed by the first in geosynchronous orbit, *Syncom II,* used to broadcast the Olympic Games in 1964.[13] Even more crucially, the United States created the Communication Satellite Corporation (COMSAT) to establish a worldwide system of communications satellites. This strange hybrid, partly state and partly corporate, prophetically identified the utility of outer space, opening it to commercial activity. The International Telecommunications Satellite Consortium (INTELSAT), largely controlled by COMSAT and American interests, began to establish the framework of space communications. Britain and France, dependent on American launchers, were forced to accept unequal roles within the organization. The Soviet Union, meanwhile, went its own way, claiming technical victory while in effect yielding much higher ground to the Western allies.[14]

In 1965 an orbiting bundle of mirrors and circuits named *Early Bird* became the first commercial realization of Clarke's proposal. Over the ensuing twenty years, satellite communications developed into both an industry standard and the primary focus of commercial activity in space. The artificial satellite became a naturalized part of the sky, greatly increasing both rate and volume of regular long-distance exchanges. The process of achieving geosynchronous orbit, however, redefined geography with a new practical physics. The period of any orbit is a function of altitude and velocity. At a velocity of approximately seventeen thousand miles (twenty-eight thousand kilometers) per hour an object can break free from the surface of the Earth; at an altitude of some twenty-two thousand miles (thirty-six thousand kilometers) it has a period of twenty-four hours and matches the rotation of the Earth. Satellites can only orbit the center of another body, and as the Earth spins, an orbit at any angle other than directly above the middle plane of rotation would not stay constant with the ground below. To maintain constant contact with a defined region on the globe a satellite must travel in synch with the midriff of the planet. Hence the equator, projected outward into space, becomes a key to communication. And rapid, long-distance communication, both national governments and international corporations slowly realized, represents a key organizing principle of contemporary economy and society. In this way the Space Age passed from a matter of dreams into reality, and from there into practicality.[15]

Although communications satellites dominated the commercial space market, they hardly exhausted its possibilities, let alone the practical aspects of artificial satellites. The very medium of space, let us not forget, offers an ideal field for scientific experimentation, a vast vacuum free of gravity. Moreover, a perch in space allows for constant and sweeping observations, both out to the stars and down on the Earth. If one focuses from sufficient distance, the movements of the world fit into a single frame. Global phenomena such as weather patterns, ocean levels, and even the shape of the Earth itself can be tracked and monitored in a systematic and continuous way. Remote-sensing—by broad definition "measurement from a distance"—comes most clearly into its own in the production of visual data: satellite photos that redefine maps, espionage, and all other forms of surveillance. The marketing of such images represents the development of a second significant commercial arena in space, begun with the American Landsat and continued in the French SPOT and other programs.[16]

With the exception of weather satellites that use a high, geosynchronous orbit over the equator to maintain contact with a particular region below, Earth observation satellites generally occupy low positions (six hundred to twelve hundred miles, or one thousand to two thousand kilometers) in near-polar orbits. By traveling across the rotation of the Earth rather than with it, and maintaining an orbital period of about one hundred minutes rather than twenty-four hours, their instruments can thus repeatedly sweep over the globe rather than fix on a particular region. By further following an orbit synchronized to the sun rather than to the Earth they can consistently monitor points on the globe at the same local time of day. Thus by the end of the 1960s we have two general groups of useful satellites, one engaged in communication and the other in observation, and two common and significant orbital paths, one turning slowly with the planet high above the equator and the other speeding low over the Earth around the poles.[17]

The widespread adoption of the artificial satellite presents us with an active, distinctly "modern" sky. The reorientation of the Earth in the Space Age is not solely a matter of cosmic contemplation or symbolic rivalry: there are significant technical consequences as well, for science, politics, and economics. The natural vacuum promises new scientific standards, a laboratory beyond the atmosphere. To a properly equipped eye in orbit, both stars above and land below grow sharper; earth, sky, and weather can all be monitored with lofty intimacy. Points on the globe need no longer be connected directly to each other but can instead acquire new significance through their relation to the zone above the atmosphere. In a sense, what has been a geometry of two dimensions becomes three, as connections are no longer restricted to the surface sphere of the planet. A platform in space offers both an imperial vantage point across continents and a potential beacon between them, circumventing geographical markers on the ground or altering their meaning. The world becomes more actively whole, open to inspection and connection from above, allowing a degree of uniformity never before possible.

Of course, the foregoing sketch abbreviates many stories. European conceptions of time and space shifted dramatically between the nineteenth and twentieth centuries, as witnessed by artistic movements under various banners of "modernism," while the establishment of universal time zones, news services, photography, telephones, and radio and television networks, not to mention aircraft, radically altered the rate and topography of everyday life.[18] Yet in order to evoke the meaning of the "Space Age," with all its powerful technological and representational possibilities, a certain degree of abstract distance is necessary. Although the airplane opened the sky and moved through it at dramatic elevations, and the radio tower filled the air with waves, bypassing ground connections, neither made the limits of the Earth entirely visible or transparent. Space technology closed the sky again, bounded it from above and sealed it whole. Only then could the sky become fully modern in an active, technological sense, and only then could what lay beyond it become meaningful as space, a vast sea of darkness surrounding a blue and green point of human place. At last the world was one.

The development of the artificial satellite represents the most realized transformation of the Space Age, as well as one of the best illustrations of placeless space: the constant and effortless spread of information across and knowledge about the globe. Yet it is crucial to note that the space of satellites is not placeless but *outer;* tightly bound in determined orbits, conforming to the geometry of the planet and matching its motion. The system of communication satellites that frees worldly connections, lifting news and advertisements across national boundaries and exchanging calls between time zones, does not itself float free.

HEAVEN'S GATE

A redefinition of the equator as a modern marker of the sky had technological consequences on the ground. After all, in order to have satellites in orbit, one must first get them there. While a large number of nations currently use satellite technology, relatively few possess the technology to launch payloads into space. By virtue of other factors of economic history, the industrial centers of the world, including the original giant twins of the Space Race, are located high in the Northern Hemisphere. In terms of achieving geosynchronous orbit, this position is less than ideal, because the further one is from the equator, the more fuel must be expended to place a satellite above the equator. The primary launch sites established by the United States and the former Soviet Union are both well north, the former (Cape Canaveral) at 28° latitude and the latter (Baikonur) at 45° latitude. The location of these sites was driven by other considerations than those of proximity to the equator, such as the need for sparsely populated land to increase military security and decrease the risk of accidental civilian death. The rockets and missiles of the Cold War could thus fall mistakenly without mishap, in preparation for their eventual planned trajectories. In the case of Cape Canaveral, eastward access to the ocean gave the added benefit of permitting a flight path over open water in the direction of the Earth's rotation, allowing rockets to use the planet's momentum to help reach escape velocity. An ideal launch site for communications and other geosynchronous satellites would combine such positive attributes found at Canaveral (a coastline with a large body of water and an open eastern horizon) with a location as near as possible to the equator. An open horizon toward the poles would add the additional benefit of facilitating launches of satellites into low orbit.

In more recent decades these facts of Space Age geography have not escaped the notice of certain states located deep in the tropics, and several of them (such as India, Brazil, and Papua New Guinea) have sought to capitalize on this newfound advantage of their geography.[19] In doing so they expose a technological irony of rocketry: the more remote a location, the better suited it is for explosive experiments. Thus when one is seeking to leave the globe, wasteland becomes valuable, and underdevelopment can appear a virtue. The same tropics that bore a sinister reputation of disease and disrepair could now beckon a key technology defining the future.

A MARGIN OF UTILITY

Courroux passe / colère finit / quand on oeuvre
(Wrath passes / anger ends / when one works)
> *Coat of arms for the city of Kourou,*
> *Anonymous,* Kourou: Ville en devenir, *1987*

At the moment of the French space agency's creation in 1962, the French army was using a rocket testing site named Hammaguir in the Saharan desert of Algeria. The Evian accords, however, signed on March 18 of that year—even as CNES came into being—committed France to seek another rocket range starting July 1967. Thus a search for a new launch site was on from the very inception of the French space program. Preferably, that site would equal or surpass Algeria in terms of location and availability of open land. Those responsible for the choice thought of French Guiana immediately, but they worried about the logistical difficulties (and potential political uncertainties) of establishing an operation at such a distance from the Metropole. Therefore the search continued in 1963 along two tracks, one focusing on possibilities within mainland France and the other concentrating on equatorial sites around the globe.[20]

Let us follow the equatorial search, via its summary analysis of sites. The following criteria were considered:

- polar and equatorial launching possibility
- proximity of the equator
- sufficient physical dimensions to ensure the security of launches
- existence of a deepwater port
- existence of an adequate airfield (with a runway of three thousand meters)
- shortest possible distance between the launch base and Europe

• stable political situation in order that the base's availability "is not linked to a change of local political regime"[21]

After numerous possibilities were dismissed out of hand, the report concentrated on a list of fourteen potential sites. The description and official evaluation of each ran as follows:

The archipelago of the Seychelles (4°37' South): not retained because of its restrictive dimensions, its tortured topography, and the impossibility of building a runway of sufficient length

The island of Trinidad (British West Indies, 10°05' to 10°50' North): a suitable site, but not retained because launching to the north is impossible and the political stability of the island is not guaranteed

The island of Nuku-Hiva (archipelago of Marquesas, French Polynesia, 8°55' South): a favorable site, but not retained because of the impossibility of building a runway of sufficient length

The archipelago of Tuamotu (French Polynesia, 15° South to 18°26' South): a favorable site, but not retained because of its distance from Europe (twenty thousand kilometers [twelve thousand miles]), the existence of cyclones, and the absence of fresh water

The island of Désirade (French West Indies, 16°20' North): a possible site, but not retained because of its hurricanes, insufficient dimensions, and absence of a port or airfield

The island of Marie-Galante (French West Indies, 15°33' North): not retained because of the impossibility of launching to the north (Guadeloupe being only forty kilometers [twenty-four miles] away) as well as the danger of hurricanes and the absence of a port and airport

Djibouti (French Somaliland [now independent], 11°35' North): a very favorable site, but not retained because of almost insoluble problems of security

Australia: Darwin (12°28' South) and Broome (17°57' South): attractive sites, but not retained because of their relative distance from the equator, their extreme distance from Europe, and the existence of cyclones

Trincomalee (Ceylon [now Sri Lanka], 8°35' North): a possible site, but not retained because of its distance from Europe, the existence of cyclones, the size of its population, and the uncertain political regime

Fort Dolphin (Malagasy Republic [Madagascar], 25°02′ South): a very suitable site, but not retained because of its distance from the equator, lack of a deepwater port, and need for airport improvements

Mogadishu (Republic of Somalia, 2°02′ North): a site with an excellent situation with respect to the equator, but not retained because of great political instability

Port Etienne ([Nouâdhibou] Islamic Republic of Mauritania, 20°55′ North): a very attractive site, but not retained because of its high latitude, the continuous presence of wind, and the difficulty in finding potable water

Belem (Brazil, Amazon delta, 1°27′ South): a very suitable site, but not retained because of a bad weather report, delicate security, linguistic difficulties created by the usage of Portuguese, and the risk of political instability

Cayenne (French Guiana, 4°50′ North): a very favorable site, whose sole important disadvantage is the weak capacity of the port of Cayenne, which could easily be circumvented by unloading on the Iles du Salut, approximately fifty kilometers [thirty miles] away, or by improving the port installations; ambient humidity necessitates serious precautions for the conservation of equipment but is not considered a major disadvantage

The terms of the presentation reveal a mixture of logics: an application of the desired geographical criteria (physical and social), as well as a bias against any political landscape threatening movement, and a preference for sites within the French sphere of influence, former colonies and continuing territories. The scope of the places under consideration parallels the list of potential penal colonies a century earlier; once again the search is for openings on the globe, margins to house an experiment.[22]

In February, 1964, the report was completed, establishing a classification by points "in function of selection criteria retained." The final ranking went as follows:

French Guiana	118
Australia	96
Brazil	90
Tuamotu	80
Trinidad	79

In the end, it was decided that French Guiana did indeed represent the best of possible worlds beyond the hexagon of France itself. At the same time, a comparison with the best European French site available (Languedoc-Roussillon) highlighted additional advantages, for despite the greater expense involved in building adequate facilities, French Guiana offered a better location, posed fewer social concerns, and promised greater potential "evolution." On March 21, 1964, General de Gaulle made an official visit to French Guiana and announced, in rather elliptical fashion, a coming "great work." On April 14, Georges Pompidou, the modernizing prime minister, personally decided in favor of building the base in Guyane.[23]

Within French Guiana the decision to locate the center at Kourou followed quickly, given the town's small population and its favorable geographical characteristics and location with respect to Cayenne and the airport (close enough for convenience, yet far enough for security). The space agency initially claimed land along the coast between Kourou and the neighboring town to the northwest, Sinnamary, some thirty kilometers by ten kilometers (nineteen by six miles) of savanna encompassing a smattering of agricultural sites and a hamlet known as Malmanoury. The social landscape was quiet and rural, and the number of people involved was quite small; in 1961 Kourou registered a population of 659, and Sinnamary had a population of 1,796, mostly Creole. On a Metropolitan scale the appropriation seemed a minor affair. Local opinion was more varied but less influential, and the transfer of authority was soon complete.[24]

BUILDING THE SPACE CENTER

For those persons coming to French Guiana for the
first time, we call attention to the fact that it is a country where they cannot expect to find an infrastructure
of services and facilities resembling those of the Metropole. And yet, if they only show interest and a certain
comprehension for Guyanais life and its difficulties
during this period of all-out evolution, they will be
welcomed with graciousness and amiability.

CNES brochure, 1970

Kourou's bucolic feel would not last long. Locating the launch site in French Guiana necessitated much work, both on the new center itself and on infrastructure in French Guiana to support it. The space center required a launchpad and a technical center, as well as a new town to serve those who would work there. In addition to the port and airport, the road connecting them to Kourou needed much improvement; in 1964 the trip between Cayenne and Kourou required the use of two ferries and took up to three hours to cover some sixty kilometers (thirty-six miles).[25] At the beginning of 1965, CNES established itself in Cayenne and set up an outpost in Kourou while plans were drawn and surveys conducted. The following year saw the beginning of construction, including the modernization of Rochambeau Airport and work on the port as well as buildings, and in 1967 a bridge over the Kourou River, a power plant, and meteorological sites also began to sprout. The major pieces began to fall into place the next year as the base itself became operational and the first supermarket and hotel opened. However, the initial phase of construction continued through 1970, with the completion of further sections of the town (including an air-conditioned cinema and pool), as well as installations for the Europa launch program.[26]

The rapid construction of the base and its attendant structures spurred an influx of workers from outside French Guiana, largely from Metropolitan France and neighboring areas of South America and the Caribbean. In 1966 CNES contracted Colombians to provide manual labor; they were supplemented by workers from elsewhere, particularly Brazil and Suriname. It should be stressed that the composition of this labor force of several thousand differed significantly from the smaller one that would operate the completed installation. The door of opportunity for those without specialized training swung open briefly and then shut.[27]

The first launch, that of a test rocket named Véronique, took place on April 9, 1968. Two years later the first French rocket of import, a Diamant, lifted off with a German satellite named *Wika*. But the initial optimism of the project dimmed even as the first wave of construction ended. Far from throwing wide the gates to space, the overall technical record of the first phase of the European space center was relatively meager. Although CSG could claim 354 "launches" between 1968 and 1978, 288 of these were test rockets, and another 57 were balloons; the total includes only nine satellite launch vehicles, eight Diamants, and a single Europa. The failure of the Europa II—which crashed into the sea after only two and a half minutes of flight—was an ominous sign, inspiring criticism of not only the rocket but also the organization that had sponsored it. Both now appeared disappointing: the launcher design could only manage an obsolete two-hundred-kilogram satellite, while ELDO itself reeled from crisis to crisis.[28] Thus at the beginning of the 1970s—less than a decade after its inception—the future of Kourou looked grim. The momentum of the project had flagged, and its sense of purpose wavered. This city of the stars, it seemed, was fated to fade like a comet.

THE SPACE CENTER AND DEVELOPMENT

Kourou is a city of the future.

    Anonymous, Kourou, *1987*

Effects of the establishment of the space center rippled through French Guiana, well beyond the immediate confines of Kourou. The spate of construction associated with the project, the substantial improvements in the general infrastructure of the department, and the sudden wave of migrant labor attracted to the area altered the local landscape. Even as Kourou transformed dramatically, French Guiana shifted around it, adjusting to the new conditions. And while the space center was not the only modernizing influence in French Guiana—the area's formal incorporation into the French state in 1946–1947 established much of the economic framework—it quickly came to represent everything, good or bad, that emerged alongside it.

The initial promises about the potential benefits in store for French Guiana from its involvement in the space program varied. De Gaulle had alluded to a "great work," the engineer in charge of the initial mission spoke of an "era of prosperity for Kourou, Cayenne and French Guiana as a whole," and one of the conservative political papers of the time predicted full-time employment for all. Opinion in French Guiana, however, was quite divided over the installation of a space base. Even before the official announcement was made, rumors circulated about what this new project might bring, and political debates already extant began to revolve around this new center of official gravity. Even as those in favor of assimilation welcomed the project, the local branch of the Socialist Party and other left groups[29] opposed it, raising concerns about Cold War politics and the launch site's potential role in nuclear conflict. Further, they were irritated by the "implantation" of the space center, pointing out that local officials had not been consulted and warning that the creation of such an artificial island in an underdeveloped country risked establishing a variety of "apartheid" similar to that of South Africa.[29]

In a press conference held in October 1964, the delegates of CNES maintained a measure of studied caution, albeit laced with progressive enthusiasm. Stressing that this was a purely civil affair, with no links to either the military or atomic testing, they explained the logic behind the selection of French Guiana to the assembled audience of local officials, suggesting that if the space project went forward successfully, this would be the only extant equatorial rocket base and hence "would certainly be the greatest launch site in the world."[30] France, they emphasized, had chosen to bypass the cheaper option of an installation at Roussillon, and this should be taken as a sign of commitment to its overseas department: "The government thinks that the supplementary cost will have, at least, the beneficial side effect of creating considerable activity in French Guiana, while Roussillon has other possibilities." For all that the primary motivation of building a space base was national and French, the technological development of the nation would here assist in the modernization of its outlying parts.

The stated goals were both strikingly egalitarian and relatively concrete:

> Perhaps you would now like to know what sort of human development we envisage with respect to this launch site? Well, we think that almost five hundred people will be necessary for it to function. To the extent to which you are able to provide us with half that figure, we would be happy to recruit them, either among those who live here or among those children of this land who have left and would like to return. In fact we can give 250 jobs easily enough to local people. The people arriving from the Metropole will be rocket technicians, space research technicians. We plan to establish similar conditions for everyone, those from Guiana as well as those who will come from the Metropole, in the region of *des Roches* or Kourou.

Space, then, was to be a cooperative affair, employment split fifty-fifty and equality guaranteed for all. French Guiana would provide land and muscle; France would provide a rocket and expertise. Together they would forge the future, while living in a model town. Yet the very sentence underlining the technical nature of the future Metropolitan immigrants, meant to reassure, also reveals the original tension of the project: unlike those already living there, these space technicians would be arriving in French Guiana with a purpose in mind. They would not be competing with local residents for labor positions because they were skilled, and yet their very skills would also set them apart. Egalitarian wishes aside, distinctions lay firmly at the base of the new vision, simultaneously exposed and hidden.

At a later point during a question and answer period, the issue of local effects came up again. A member of the city administration of Cayenne asked the president of CNES to elaborate on what the citizens of French Guiana might expect from the space project. After dwelling on images of direct flights between Paris and the new airport, the president returned to the issue of employment, suggesting a potential improvement in the "technical level" of Guyanais youth. Finally he considered what would happen if the project really took off and attracted the attention of other countries:

> That would have an absolutely major effect on the development of French Guiana, by bringing a lot of people, increasing the consumption of vegetables, food crops, and so forth. . . . Naturally this development, as all development, has to be considered carefully not to be harmful, for I think that you are all for the development of your country, but that you also wish it to be harmonious, preserving those characteristics you like. In this you can absolutely count on our cooperation, since it is one of the questions that preoccupies us. We do not want this development to be disorderly, or to produce shantytowns instead of cities, because what is necessary is that French Guiana profit as much as possible.

At once guarded and optimistic, the agenda is laid forth: unlike past ventures in French Guiana, this will be no pie-in-the-sky affair, but concrete, real, and carefully planned. The benefits beyond the initial promise of jobs begin to be detailed, including accurate prophecies about increased air traffic and a direct link to Paris and rosy hopes for future phalanxes of Guyanais engineers. But a mask of naiveté about development is shed; not all modernization leads to progress, we are warned, there are dangers of inequality, social chaos, and cultural discord.

However, the press conference would not close on such a doubtful note. Near the end of the affair the departmental director of the Service for Radio and Telephones asked whether or not the president of CNES thought the average American was proud of what was taking place at Cape Canaveral. Yes, was the reply. The exchange continued: would not the Guyanais also one day be proud of their launch site? "Well, Sir," the president replied, somewhat elliptically, "I think that we are proud enough of what we do, perhaps we are wrong, but after all when one does something well one is very proud." Hanging in the air was the prospect of technical assimilation: if the citizens of French Guiana identified with the space effort they could bask in its success, centuries of failure erased by a triumphant French rocket.

Such affirmations of technological pride notwithstanding, hostility to the space center continued in certain quarters. Even in the mid-1960s, opposition papers described the project as a "cancer," a "diabolical plan," that would produce a "white city" by chasing Guyanais from their land and redistributing it to Europeans. A more general survey of Creoles living in Kourou, the most affected segment of the population, indicated that in 1971 fewer than half of them considered the changes brought about by the base to have been positive.[31] A sample of remarks collected at the time reveals two poles of reaction: appreciation of material improvements in everyday life, countered by distress over social tension, heightened cost of living, and perceptions of racism. On the one hand, space brings practical comforts, symbols of progress, and increased possibilities of wage labor:

"Before, there was nothing in Kourou. Now you can find anything you want to buy."

"The base has brought us modernism [le modernisme]: I am for modernism. We have light all day long, drinkable water from the tap. With the fridge, everything preserves, and there's no more need to salt things. . . . Before, for entertainment, it was necessary to go to Cayenne. Now we have the movie theater and TV."

"By making their base in Kourou, the Whites have brought us evolution. The time of farming is past. It's necessary to be modern."

"The base has brought many people and a lot of work. We're no longer condemned to the abattis [agricultural plots]. You can choose the work you want to do, and when it doesn't pan out, you can always change."

On the other hand, the bonanza of the space base bears the blame for market fluctuations and a more rigid accounting of time, as well as a heightened sense of racial inequity over work prospects and distinctions in pay scales:

"I had a good job, but the company went away, and up till now, I haven't found anything else."

"Before, food for us was practically free[;] . . . now, you have to buy everything, and it is so expensive that you never have enough money to eat as well as before."

"The least of white workers earns three time as much as a Guyanais worker. He has allowances, advantages, solely because he's white."

"When I was on my habitation [agricultural site], I was free and happy with my farming and my breeding! I worked to my liking: I wasn't a prisoner of fixed schedules. . . . Now, I'm a slave of money, a slave of work!"[32]

Here, then, we have a split vote; an image of the Janus face of modern
good and modern bad, with references to capitalism, slavery, inflation,
and refrigerators, all encapsulated in the space center.

Like these personal views, the abstracted estimates of the space program's economic effects were mixed. The space center represented over
half of all investment in French Guiana at the time.[33] In concrete terms
the airport and port facilities found dramatic improvement, as did the
road between Kourou and Cayenne. In terms of jobs the picture remained less clear, for while some 19,500 people throughout the department were officially listed as working in 1974 (as opposed to 12,000 in
1962), the level of employment relative to both the total population
and the working population actually shrank slightly. Over the decade
between 1965 and 1975, Kourou went from representing 1.75 percent
of French Guiana's total population to 8.5 percent, even as that population grew from some forty thousand to close to sixty thousand. An
earlier trend toward population loss was thus now effectively countered; out-migration of young Guyanais Creoles to France was balanced by in-migration of foreigners into Guyane. Yet in this very solution to the long-standing demographic dilemma lay the seeds of new
and growing discord: French Guiana was becoming a more varied and
decidedly multiethnic society. All in all, at least some twenty-four hundred non-French foreigners (Brazilians, Surinamese, and Colombians)
participated in the construction of CSG.[34] Out of the thousand or so
people employed at the functioning space center, approximately 60 percent were "detached" from the Metropole. Following official estimates
of indirect effects, the functioning space program perhaps accounted
for some 15 percent of the employed workforce. But significant elements of that workforce—at both top and bottom ends—were not Creole. Metro technicians and immigrant laborers played increasingly
prominent roles.

Furthermore, the sudden bonanza of the space center and the visions
of manna it inspired proved relatively fleeting. After the initial phase of
construction was complete the need for unskilled labor fell drastically.
The collapse of the Europa program and the consequent growing lull in
space activity between 1972 and 1976 struck Kourou hard. Writing in
1975, the head of the local government warned that any further reductions would decimate not only the population of that town but also the
economy of the department as a whole. These reductions highlighted inherent difficulties in Kourou's role as a peculiar sort of company town:
"the support city of the European space effort," as a planning report

would later put it, inserted "into a Guyanais context." When push came to shove, the French space program had more to do with satellites and rockets than the setting of the launchpad. As an exasperated president of CNES wrote in 1974: "The organization that I direct has never had saving French Guiana for its mission."[35]

THE CITY OF SPACE:
A TOUR OF KOUROU'S NEW TOWN

But what was the urban space created around the space center? How does the physical layout of Kourou fit with its descriptions? In the enthusiastic memoirs of a former prefect, a political figure strongly in favor of closer ties with France, the early story of space can be summarized as follows:

> From a modest village of some hundred residents, Kourou has become a stylish city of five thousand souls, with a supermarket, a hospital, . . . two great hotels, a magnificent pool, where the Guyanais come to pass the weekend with their families or elegant company. Evidently researchers of CNES have the tendency to live in isolation, sticking with each other. But nevertheless they are consumers of remarkable purchasing power who affect the Guyanais market, and a number of new shops have been created in Cayenne to satisfy them. All Guyanais youth devoted to physics, mathematics, dataprocessing, and mechanics have been recruited by CNES. True, they are not numerous; most orient themselves toward letters, law, or medicine. But CNES has offered them other opportunities in their own department, and that they appreciate greatly. For jobs of lesser scale, a training center devoted to the various techniques of space has been opened in Kourou. Thus, as was easy to anticipate, the creation of CNES has been particularly beneficial to French Guiana. That has not, however, prevented the political situation from evolving in a different direction than it was logically permitted to hope.[36]

But such an outline allows no fine resolution; it provides only the most general of maps and vaguest of reservations ("evolving in a different direction than it was logically permitted to hope"). The French social scientist Marie-José Jolivet presents us with a more detailed, biting tour of the newly constructed Kourou, circa 1971. In Kourou, she suggests, "socio-professional hierarchy is found to be exactly inscribed on the ground." This thesis, simultaneously descriptive and analytic, merits extended attention.[37]

> Beginning the inventory by the Pointe des Roches, the granite promontory situated at the mouth of the river where one can still see "Dreyfus' Tower,"

the last preciously preserved vestige of the former buildings of the *bagne,* we successively distinguish:

• The *"des Roches"* quarter—Clearly at a distance from the rest of the town, this is the finest residential neighborhood. One finds there first of all a hundred-room luxury hotel, with bar, restaurant, and pool. Just beside it is a private club. Further on, by the sea, the two villas of the respective directors of CSG and ELDO, as well as six other houses reserved for their immediate deputies.

• The "executive" quarter—Further west, but always close to the sea, come then some one hundred identical villas set in rows, which principally house engineers and administrative personnel of the base.

• The city center—Italianate in style, its apartment blocks frame an internal plaza of sorts, prohibited to automobiles, adorned with flower beds and ornamental pools, and surrounded by arcades that open into shops. It is there that we find the supermarket . . . and the industrial bakery. . . . The residential buildings have two or three floors and include more than two hundred apartments, occupied by technicians, staff, and shopkeepers.

• The "Calypso" quarter—This consists of a group of three hundred prefabricated chalets, situated on the eastern side of the central plaza. These were the first lodgings built, originally to house the people who came for the installation of CSG, and later turned over to personnel of the construction companies. In 1971 their occupancy is more varied but still for the most part Metropolitan.

• The lower-income district—These low-rise, multiple-family dwellings stretch to the south and westward of the city center. In some 250 apartments Metropolitans and Creoles mix, mostly semiskilled workers, some teachers, and young civil service volunteers.

• The very low income district—This consists of high-rise blocks, built last at the entrance to town. This quarter includes two hundred apartments for the Creole workforce.

Such is the town of Kourou proper. Differentiation, one sees, comprises the primary element of its conception. But this phenomenon does not stop there: units forming the suburbs of the city only emphasize it. These are:

• The *"Cité Stade,"* or housing for the relocated—At the edge of town, this district was built to shelter those whose land was expropriated by the base. The structures are low-rise concrete blocks, the most economic possible, comprising sixty or so apartments that, in 1971, have already acquired a dilapidated look.

• The Maroon village—Well hidden behind the stadium and the empty lots that separate the housing for the relocated from the old town center, this village was built around a water standpipe by Saramakas and Bonis, with the help of recycled materials (old planks, beams) that were "generously" provided for them. In fact there are two distinct sections: Saramakas and

Bonis [Aluku] do not mix. As a whole it is composed of rows of rudimentary shacks that, far from resembling the charming villages along the Maroni, form nothing but a sad shantytown, despite the undeniable efforts by its residents to make the place more attractive.

- The Indian village—The Galibi [Kaliña] have changed location several times. Their villages were first formed of traditional huts: "carbets," entirely open [wood and] dried-leaf shelters. In 1971, they have just settled in a new village built in accordance with their wishes. This last is situated at the entrance to the town but near the edge of the sea and far back from the road. It is comprised of enclosed huts in Creole style, forms now preferred by those concerned themselves, who are weary of being the object (private life included) of tourist curiosity.
- The "Old Town"—Starting from the dock of the old ferryboat, the old town stretches along a main street perpendicular to the river. Formerly the national road, this street has become a cul-de-sac since the construction of the bridge spanning the Kourou River some kilometers upstream and the subsequent displacement of the road. Some houses in concrete have appeared here and there. But as an ensemble, with its old wooden houses, its quaint town hall, and its little church, the old town preserves the flavor of a rural Guyanese Creole settlement.

Having provided us with the elements, Jolivet then sums up the resulting social constellation:

For the Boni or Saramaka laborer: salvaged boards and a well-camouflaged shantytown (the landscape must not be disfigured!). For the relocated cultivator: cramped accommodations in a reserved housing development. For the Creole worker: a low-income apartment in a public housing project located at the entry of the city. For the skilled worker: an apartment in a standard public housing complex at the edge of the town's center, the only place where it is imagined that Creoles and White could mix. And then, the White town, with its hierarchical gradations also scrupulously respected. Such is the conception of the new city of Kourou! Can one have dreamed up a more vivid demonstration of the expertise of Whites to orchestrate the countless hierarchical encounters that allow them to maintain the ideological bases of their domination?

While Jolivet's tour is hardly dispassionate—relentless anger pressing between every line—it remains careful and spatially exact. The built environment, entrenched as is, lends empirical clarity to her claims: people in buildings are easy to locate, easy to count. Both the power and the weakness of a fortress, after all, lie in its fixed position and visibility.[38] The new town of Kourou, so exposed in its French Guiana setting, cannot hide the starkness of its form. In replacing the vernacular

Figure 11. Villas, Kourou, 1993

Figure 12. Apartments, Kourou, 1993

Figure 13. Shack, Kourou, 1993

dwellings of a Creole village and the decayed prison architecture of the penal colony, this wave of reorganization created another, rigid landscape. The vision is functional, beyond the resulting slabs of concrete: social groups are divided, and to each is given its due, that which it is thought to expect. Presented with open space and a relatively free horizon, the architects of outer space plan the most generic of postwar housing—the prefabricated villa, the apartment block—and allow another to emerge in a gap between them and the surrounding continent: the shantytown.

What we have in Kourou is a future archaeologist's dream. Structure speaks; society lies written on the ground. In one forgotten corner between river and the sea, a human epic is quickly rewritten, from first world to third world. Kourou, then, is a new colony (its imported elements "up to date"), but one that reproduces an old colonialism in its racial divides reinforced by social class. Taken more broadly, Jolivet's point carries further still. Social class here is reinforced by educational certification and technical expertise. The discrepancies of capitalism, wide verandah to tiny room, meet the gray uniformity of social welfare, row upon row of universal shelters; parts of France's space city would also be recognizable from the Sputnik side of the Cold War divide. Kourou in 1971, from every physical angle, is about as modern as things get.

At the moment of Jolivet's survey, Kourou was also entering a period of crisis, anticipated by the failure of the Europa program. Yet even as the space center lapses into inactivity and the buildings it inspired begin to decay (their futuristic touches aging especially badly), the structure of the urban layout remains. The requisite elements of a launch program are still in place, as is the general shape of the town next to it. Prophetically, Jolivet concludes her spatial review by wondering if the hierarchical structure of Kourou would not necessarily reproduce similar social patterns should the program expand again.[39] No matter what might come after, the foundations of the future had been laid.

ARIANESPACE, ESA, AND THE LATER SPACE CENTER

"Ariane is the posthumous child of the General
[de Gaulle]."

> Former French minister of science and
> industrial development, 1993[40]

In 1972 the future of the European Launcher Program appeared in as much doubt as that of the Space Age around it. The successful American moon landing left a vacuum of intensity and purpose, one that affected the Europeans at least as much as NASA. Britain, the driving force behind Europa I, left ELDO in 1970, and the Europa II program emerged stillborn. The shift in U.S. policy toward the space shuttle and toward greater cooperation in space cast the whole project of an independent European rocket into question on both technical and political grounds. The French, however, were not easily dissuaded. A working group at CNES sought a replacement for the planned Europa III, which was to be a two-stage rocket equivalent to the American Atlas Centaur, and came up with a three-stage design known as L3S. A "tough" European Space Conference in December of that year and an even more intense and interrupted meeting in Brussels during the summer of 1973 resulted in several momentous decisions. On the basis of these agreements, ELDO and ESRO were disbanded and then gradually reformulated over the next two years into a single entity, the European Space Agency (ESA), whose purview would include both space launches and space science. Furthermore, the conference endorsed the

L3S project, with the expectation that it would produce a working rocket within six years.[41] After arriving at the brink of extinction, the search for a European launch vehicle gathered new momentum.

ARIANE AND THE TECHNOLOGY OF SUCCESS

The European Space Agency proved a more resilient organization than its predecessors. Formally ratified in 1975, it grew to encompass thirteen member states (Austria, Belgium, Denmark, France, Germany, Ireland, Italy, the Netherlands, Norway, Spain, Sweden, Switzerland, and the United Kingdom) as well as an associate member (Finland) and a cooperative one (Canada).[42] The commitment to the new launcher, rechristened Ariane, proved in retrospect an excellent gamble. While the program was not free from hitches and awkward delays, it managed to squeeze under its original deadline, producing a rocket by the end of 1979. Despite subsequent setbacks, the program blossomed, filling a void created by NASA's overreliance on the expensive and problem-prone space shuttle. Largely designed around tested technologies, Ariane evolved into a reliable rocket, well suited to placing communications satellites into equatorial orbit.

The Europeans also proved prescient in another respect: the market for commercial space launches, particularly of communications satellites, expanded considerably in the 1980s. The final frontier became an arena of interest to corporations as well as nation-states, and networks of international communications grew rapidly. Again led by the French, the European venture was ready. At the beginning of the decade the space consortium established a new, semiprivate corporation to coordinate and market the Ariane rocket. Under the name Arianespace, it gradually expanded from its first commercial launch in 1984 to claim over half the satellite market, gaining a significant boost after the 1986 explosion of the space shuttle *Challenger* and the subsequent withdrawal of NASA from commercial launches. The first version of the rocket, Ariane 1, gave way to more powerful siblings, Ariane 2, 3, and finally the mature design, Ariane 4, which appeared in 1988. After its fiftieth flight in 1992, the Ariane program could claim forty-five successful launches (a 90 percent success rate) and eighty-five satellites placed into orbit.[43] At the same time, plans were under way for a new generation of rockets, the Ariane 5 series. Wider, heavier, and shorter, this model was designed to lift close to twice as much as its predecessor into equatorial orbit.[44] The adoption of such a powerful launcher would permit the European space program to accomplish two things: first, to accommodate the larger satellites anticipated in coming years or lift two satellites into orbit at once, and second, to launch a manned space vehicle known as Hermès, a smaller sibling of the American space shuttle.

The Ariane program initiated a second wave of construction in Kourou, at first picking up the slack left by the Europa cutbacks and then expanding the space center to unprecedented dimensions. The new launcher required a series of launchpads and other service facilities, and its success stimulated further urban growth. The number of active personnel required to run the operation remained roughly comparable to that of the earlier period, but the estimated factor of indirect employment related to the base grew.[45] In addition, the percentage of the workforce officially resident in Kourou expanded, surpassing 50 percent in 1985. At the beginning of the 1990s, the space program accounted for over half the department's production, supported a quarter of the population, and was involved in something on the order of two-thirds of all imports.[46] The postponement of the Hermès shuttle in 1991 dampened the expansive rhetoric of the space program, but the third wave of investment and publicity related to the Ariane 5 program, coupled with the continued general success of the Ariane 4 program, maintained CSG's high profile in and out of French Guiana. Given the hollow nature of the region's economy, the weight of the space program grew all the more obvious.

SOME NUTS AND BOLTS OF A LAUNCH

Let us examine an Ariane 4 launch "campaign" of the early nineties in detail, and through it the material culture of rockets and satellites. For all that a rocket may be a glorified firecracker, it is also a complicated one. Preparation of an Ariane takes about three years, including thirty months invested in the three stages and lesser periods invested in the other component parts. Because this is a joint European venture, the major contractors are large corporations spread throughout Europe, headed by the French firm Aerospatiale. Once together, the major elements of the rocket find their way to French Guiana by ship or plane, and after being unloaded near Cayenne, they are transported by road to Kourou. At this point the CSG launch campaign proper can begin, ideally lasting around a month. The preparation of the rocket takes place in the launch pad complex, first in an assembly area and then at the launch site a short distance away. The ground installations are expressly designed for the model of rocket in question. In order to accommodate the more powerful Ariane 4, CSG built a new launch complex to replace the initial Ensemble de Lancement Ariane (ELA). Functioning since 1986, ELA 2 is more flexible than its predecessor, having widely separated assembly and launch towers to permit simultaneous work on two rockets and facilitate a faster turnaround time.[47]

Over the first five days, the three stages are erected into a rocket. The first two stages represent one of the keys of Ariane's success: powered by liquid fuels, they draw on proven technologies for "simplicity and reliability." The third stage, however, represents technical progress, being cryogenic, or powered by oxygen and hydrogen at extremely low temperatures for extra thrust. Cryogenics, a technology over which the United States held a monopoly until the 1980s, is both "the key to power" and a matter of technical pride. French engineers were the second to successfully use cryogenics after the Americans, and the design of the next-generation Ariane 5 depends heavily on this approach.[48]

About thirteen days before the launch date the assembled rocket is transferred to the launch zone, while nine days before liftoff the first countdown rehearsals begin. At the same time a parallel preparation campaign for the satellite or satellites destined for orbit draws to a close in a highly sterile environment. Four days before launch the assembled and tested satellite finds a home in the bulbous cargo bay at the top of the thin rocket shaft. The completed object stands 58.4 meters tall (192 feet) and weighs some 339 to 470 metric tons (about 750,000 to 1,000,000 pounds), depending on the exact configuration. White, and painted with the logos of Arianespace and CNES and ESA, as well as the flags of participating nation-states, the completed launcher stands framed by the boosters attached to its base.[49] Though few onlookers consider it significant, many note at least one allusion embedded in the final form. Although all rockets may be vaguely phallic, Ariane 4—slim and shapely—is unmistakably so.

Final preparations include the filling of each stage with fuel, sending balloons aloft to measure the wind, and monitoring the equipment and other atmospheric conditions, particularly the threat of lightning. Sixteen hours and forty minutes before ignition (that point in time designated Ho), the countdown begins. At Ho minus six minutes a synchronized sequence begins, the internal power supplies activate, and the umbilical cords binding the rocket to its platform swing away. At Ho the first stage and booster engines fire, and 4.4 seconds later liftoff begins. The rocket climbs vertically for about another eight seconds, slowly gathering speed, before beginning to tilt on its journey away from the coast. At two and a half minutes into the flight the boosters fall away, followed in another minute by the first stage, freeing the remainder of their now-useless weight. The second stage ignites and burns for a little over two minutes before yielding to the third stage, which will accelerate the payload into orbit. Up to this point tracking stations in French Guiana have been monitoring Ariane's every move, but now a ground station in Brazil picks it up, followed in turn by one on Ascension Island, and then one in Gabon. About eighteen minutes into the flight the third stage expires, injecting the satellite into an elliptical transfer orbit from which it can achieve a geostationary position.[50]

The expense of this explosive venture is staggering. Beyond the cost of launch and the satellite itself, one must calculate appropriate insurance and frequently a spare satellite, should the first be lost. As one industry analyst likes to point out, satellites are worth far more than their weight in gold.[51] Yet if we consider the potential long-term return on initial investment, the economic logic of the industry emerges. Accepting a conservative total cost of two hundred million dollars to place and operate an individual communications satellite in geostationary orbit at the beginning of the 1990s, given eighteen thousand communication lines and an optimistic ten-year life span at full use, the long-term cost could translate into a figure as low as a fifth of a cent a minute.[52] Thus even while this branch of the transport business appears lumbering and slow in a world of high-speed mass production, it constitutes both a lucrative venture and a vital link in the vast network of international communication.

In sum, the technology before us consists of a few simple ideas and many complicated details. It is at once highly advanced and remarkably primitive, bending many fragile components into a raw exercise of power. It requires massive investments, risks all in the brief possibility of devastating explosion, and renders profits slowly at high volume. It is not—and could never be—the work of any single individual but requires the resources and skills of a large, competent organization.

HUMAN SYSTEMS AND ROCKET ENGINEERS

A technology, however advanced it be, does not in itself guarantee success. It must be applied by a rational organization.

Participant in a launching base conference, 1972[53]

To continue our consideration of the Guiana Space Center we need to establish a set of social facts delineating "Europe's Spaceport." At the point of our ethnographic present tense (the early 1990s), the CSG occupies approximately nine hundred square kilometers of coastal land, almost the same surface area as the island of Martinique, or 1 percent of the total area of French Guiana. As we have seen, the primary technical activities conducted at the center consist of final preparation and assembly of the three launcher stages and the payload, preparing and launching the assembled rocket, and monitoring its ensuing trajectory and performance. The CSG provides both facilities and logistical support for visiting teams in charge of particular payloads in different launch "campaigns," including testing and laboratory space as well as housing and social services. The program seeks to average eight to nine payloads a year using the Ariane 4 rocket, even while development continues apace on the Ariane 5 and the possible (if increasingly doubtful) future European space shuttle Hermès.[54]

The space operation consists of three separate, overlapping entities: CSG itself, a unit of CNES, the French national space agency, which is responsible for the launch facilities; Arianespace, a semiprivate corporation, which is responsible for the commercial aspects of the launch service; and ESA, an umbrella European space consortium, which is responsible for long-range planning and coordination of funding. Although united around common goals, this trio, sometimes jokingly referred to as a "trinity," do not always share specific interests. CSG seeks to forward French national aims and encounters the brunt of local pressure. Arianespace worries the most about commercial operations, competition, client services, and profitability. And ESA works to increase the European heterogeneity of the program, gradually diluting its French purity and maintaining its public face of European cooperation.

Both directly and through a complex network of arrangements with private companies, CSG itself engages approximately 850 persons and Arianespace another 250, while ESA maintains a tiny bureau of liaison agents. However much economic activity it may generate, the combined space industry only directly employs something on the order of 7 to 10 percent of Kourou's population and less than 1 percent of French Guiana's. Most of the technical and upper-administrative positions are filled by Europeans, and almost half of the center's workforce is still composed of Europeans on temporary overseas contracts. Kourou has the greatest overall number of workers within CNES, outranking the administrative headquarters in Paris and the satellite control center in

Toulouse. In 1987 the internal breakdown of CSG's labor force into official categories ran as follows: 30 percent engineers, 24 percent technicians, 17 percent secretaries, 15 percent laborers, and 14 percent administrators.[55] Outside of the administrative and secretarial categories, the workforce is predominantly male.

In addition to those directly employed in technical tasks, the presence of the center has created a need for a wide range of nontechnical support occupations around it. Such positions include midlevel bureaucratic posts within the town, largely filled by Guyanais Creoles, as well as manual labor and maintenance, largely performed by illegal immigrants. Security is also a concern, and security guards, units of the French army, and a detachment of the Foreign Legion are all deployed during launches. Along with the resident technical personnel, one must add rotating teams of engineers and other representatives of Arianespace and CSG's clients present to oversee the preparation of their satellites for launch. Numbering some two hundred to four hundred at any one time, these *missionnaires* stay an average of two months. The town has a number of expensive hotels and restaurants to cater to them, and a unit within CSG attends to their logistical needs and arranges entertainment, including nature tours.

The launch base in Kourou is at once pivotal and peripheral to French and European space activities. The success or failure of every satellite first rides on the crucial moment when the rocket carrying it rises through the sky. Thus the responsibility of overseeing the ground operations is great. Yet much of the work actually done at the space center is relatively repetitive and routine—in the realm of operation rather than of design—and hence many of the jobs are not glamorous. Broadly speaking, personnel at CSG fit one of two categories: mobile professionals who are passing through while rising in the ranks of CNES or Arianespace and subordinate technicians who are fixed in place and position. It would be a mistake to divide these realms too completely. Not only do they blur in the cases of certain individuals, but in this realm of technocratic France it must be stressed that the administrators in question are largely engineers, recipients of technical—if elite—education.[56] However, for our purposes the distinction helps underscore an essential difference between categories of people associated with the Guiana Space Center, separating those for whom it represents a temporary point within a career from those for whom it represents a steady job.

These two categories—the mobile and the fixed—fall loosely if imperfectly along ethnic lines; although a number of Europeans fill low-level posts, few workers born in French Guiana enter the career orbit. After all, such a career entails motion: to acquire the requisite experience one must migrate between different key points in the space world rather than remain fixed in Kourou. In this fact lie seeds of systematic resentment. For CSG will never—could never—exist wholly within Guyane. The support systems upon which it depends, from material production to trained staff and clientele, extend elsewhere on the globe, weaving most thickly over technological centers of Europe. Even if French Guiana were to become independent, in order to operate the space center it would need personnel equipped with both instrumental knowledge and international connections. On a crucial, institutional level, the work of the cosmos is irreducibly cosmopolitan.

DEFINING THE FUTURE

Engineers think like savages, my friend, as Lévi-Strauss
does not say. It's a matter of tinkering with what you
have on hand to get yourself out of terrible muddles:
what was only a stage becomes an infinite number of
stages, a real labyrinth.

Bruno Latour, Aramis, *1992*

However much the Guiana Space Center has changed between its first incarnation in the 1960s and 1970s and the Ariane era, it remains committed to a deep belief in progress, counterbalanced by a deep concern for reliability. Although outer space may have become an arena for commercial as well as national competition, it still represents an expanding domain, a seemingly endless horizon of human opportunity. The fundamental vision of the Space Age depends on improvement and expansion, a belief that the only thing standing between our species and the future is technical evolution. The essential optimism of Verne's nineteenth-century adventurers, cheerfully sailing out of their cannon to colonize the moon, remains very much alive. At the same time, however, rockets remain undeniably tricky and explosive. What is intended to be a transport vehicle can easily become a bomb. Thus every procedure must be standardized and routinized in an effort to achieve consistency. Yet however standardized things become, they remain imperfect and volatile at such a complex level of organization. The Ariane is a highly successful rocket, and still approximately one out of ten has failed. Defining the future remains a risky enterprise, as the ghost of NASA's *Challenger* reminds us.[57]

The tension between a progressive sensibility and a neurotic awareness of potential disaster has produced a fertile field of representation around CSG. This representational field, running through Europe, French Guiana, and the Ariane rocket, constitutes an essential dimension of the space enterprise. Examining it will allow us to excavate layers of meaning surrounding the space program and find fragments of cosmology and ritual in the culture of fantasy borne by Verne's descendants, proud authors of "French Guiana, Land of Space."

CHAPTER 6

The Margin of the Future

The future is more complicated than the past.

Satellite pioneer J. R. Pierce,
The Beginnings of Satellite
Communication, *1968*

A LAUNCH WITH GEORGES

In the words of a border patrolman watching on television in California: "I was there, I was part of it, I saw it happen." In the words of a foreign student vacationing at the Cape: "I am part of history, I have seen the launch."[1]

Comments on Apollo 11, 1969,
quoted in Dale Carter, The Final Frontier, *1988*

Near the end of 1992 I had the pleasure of receiving a formal invitation to an Ariane launch. Already present in French Guiana (rather than flying in on the charter plane from Paris) and a guest of the European Space Agency (rather than the launch company Arianespace), I was attached to the tour in a more marginal way than the main group of assembled journalists and dignitaries, spending my time in the company of the only other official ESA guest and, periodically, our liaison officer. My companion for the day, whom I shall call Georges, was an affable French businessman. Because of family connections, he had been invited to indulge his passion for space at this center of French technological pride, touring the site and watching the rocket rise. Expansive by nature (addressing me informally almost immediately), he kept up a running commentary throughout the day and evening. I will recount

Figure 14.   Control room, CSG, 1993

some of our public relations tour together, in part because it represents a common—and quite central—aspect of the space enterprise and in part because Georges lends a specific—and human—face to the pronouncements of space enthusiasts.

The morning began with a slide show, film, and briefing in three languages: French, English, and Japanese (the respective lingua francas of the space center, international technology, and this particular satellite). For over an hour we learned about the benefits of equatorial launches and how CSG has become "one of the world's most efficient launch pads and thus contributes to the worldwide reputation of Guiana, France and Europe." Simultaneous translation was available over headphones throughout much of the presentation. The audience, composed largely of middle-aged European men, along with a few women, a contingent of Japanese, and a smattering of Guyanais Creoles, listened politely without apparent passion.

Following the briefing, we were ushered outside into a group of air-conditioned buses marked by language, French or English. Georges and I climbed aboard a French bus, which left for a tour of the new Ariane 5 installations under construction. Along the way we passed rolled barbed wire and military guards. We inspected a test stand where the solid boosters of the future rocket would soon be put through their paces, a large trench gaping beyond it to receive the flames, and the cavernous hanger where the assembled rocket would take shape. To me it resembled nothing so much as a wide silo, or giant barn, lonely against the sky. From its gates, twin pairs of tracks stretched toward the horizon, awaiting the day when they would support the launch table bearing the future rocket to its launchpad. For now they ran empty, seemingly to nowhere, or to infinity. Georges was excited by everything and particularly impressed with the aesthetic combinations of beige, red, and white used in the design. All told, the completed Ariane 5 ground facilities would represent an investment of something over a billion dollars.[2]

Lunch was held at one of Kourou's newly added hotels and consisted of rum aperitifs followed by local fish, wine, and a dessert labeled *bavarois exotique*. As the dark-skinned staff maneuvered between the tables, the conversation around me turned to international cooperation, racism, and stereotypes. Cooperation, we all agreed, sounded like a fine principle; the question was how to encourage it in practice. Georges was convinced that international space ventures offered the best possibilities for a peaceful future, a position endorsed by the engineer sitting next to him. However, that man noted, much work remained to be done. Even with all the success of Kourou, few French people even knew where it was, assuming on a basis of the name and hazy colonial memory that the launch base was in Africa.

Inspired by another glass of wine, Georges went further. Space, he suggested, constitutes a new religion. Through its exploration, people can come together and find a common future. Soon, however, space-planes will replace rockets, taking off directly from Paris. Then the connection will be cleaner, more direct. When I asked him what he thought would happen at that point to French Guiana, he shrugged. "They're part of France," he said. "They have their vote, and anyway, we support them. A good part of these tours, you know, are to explain to us where our taxes are going." He added that he considered Guyane to be a rich but hardly "clean" country. Cayenne was the limit, its filth bordering on the third world; Kourou was better, cleaner, and more modern. But the people in the former colonies, he insisted, are, in the end, really like himself. "We French," he said grandly, "we colonized with religion."

Back on the bus, we headed for the ELA 2 launch complex, where the present rocket sat ready for flight. As heavy rain began to drum on the roof of the assembly facility, our young French guide told us how CSG experienced many problems with rust and hence was committed to a continual cycle of painting. The high humidity, he went on, also necessitated constant air-conditioning. As had happened a number of times in the different presentations, here he made reference to the space program in the United States, telling us that the climate at the Kennedy Space Center presented similar problems. At this point I noted that NASA represented the acknowledged industry standard, with Americans and (to a lesser extent) Japanese serving as the guarantors of value. American corporations, it was mentioned several times, believed in Ariane. We moved on to a set of control rooms where technicians monitored machines. Our troop watched them through glass. Amid the sea of light-skinned men in white shirts were a couple of women, and by the door stood two dark-skinned security guards.

Having inquired into my own interests, Georges proceeded to give me suggestions for further research. To understand the history behind CSG, he insisted, I must visit the White Sands missile base in New Mexico and, of course, the Kennedy Space Center in Florida. The Cold War, I must never forget, began with the race for the German V-2. Further, I must not underestimate the importance of the *bandes dessinées* (cartoon books), including *Tintin,* which he assured me had influenced an entire generation, particularly the episode where the hero visits the moon. The only problem with satellites and such, Georges went on, was the way they dramatically altered the scale of everyday life. Too much information flows through our brains now, all too quickly. He shook his head. Still, exploration, space, this was the path toward the future.

That evening Georges and I found each other again, in the parking lot where the invited guests waited to be herded onto buses, a much broader crowd this time, including many locals. After a long (and surprisingly cold) air-conditioned ride to the observation site, through guard posts and past long dark stretches of barren landscape, we sipped drinks and chatted until the countdown. As a voice intoned the descending numbers, a hush fell over the crowd, which collectively turned from the television screens and each other to face the horizon. Then the night was shattered as the rocket—at once distant but undeniably real—took to the sky. For a moment it wavered in the fragility of sheer power, and then, as if gaining confidence, gathered momentum. As its

light died away, followed by rolling thunder, the event grew abstract
again, a matter of charts and graphs on screen, graphical representations, and official announcements of the final success.

After the launch we returned to the Technical Center of CSG, to
enjoy an ample open-air buffet beside fire-fighting equipment: sipping
champagne and eating caviar sandwiches, spiced chicken, somosa-style
pastries, sweet tartlettes, and eclairs. An official of CSG and a representative of the Japanese communications corporation both made short
congratulatory speeches, but few people listened, moving quickly toward the food and talking to their neighbors. Later there would be a
poolside party at the Roches hotel, and the guest list would tighten, but
for now the crowd was fairly mixed, including a number of local residents not associated with the space business as well as employees and
clients of the center. An engineer told me he disliked being in the televised control room during the launch. "It's a sham," he said, pointing
out that the whole affair is automated and that most of the assembled
rows of space personnel are there for show, to present a face of authority. Seeing the rocket in open air, even at a distance, he thought felt
more real.

I drove back to Cayenne late that night on a largely deserted road.
Along the way I picked up a hitchhiker, a security guard originally from
Haiti. He spoke French quite well and told me that he had lived in
Guyane with his wife for about a dozen years. In a good month his security post might bring in seven thousand francs (some thirteen hundred dollars—far less, needless to say, than the salary of a European
space engineer), but the work was irregular and he did not enjoy it. He
would prefer to migrate north to the United States or Canada; he would
like to see his family in Haiti again; at the very least he would like to
find a new job, but for now he was stuck. I dropped him off in a poor
section of town and turned on the radio. A man's voice spoke in Creole-
accented French about independence. Foreign investment would be allowed in the new Guyane, he proclaimed, as long as the profits poured
back into the country to eliminate unemployment. Beneath the ground,
he suggested, lies the real wealth of the future, the precious mineral
keys to development.

The next day the tour continued, but neither Georges nor I took part
in it. As scheduled, the guests spent the day on the Iles du Salut, enjoying the atmosphere of a tropical island while exploring the ruins of the
penal colony. This trip constituted a regular feature of the public relations visit; a chance for the invited guests to experience a taste of "authentic" Guyane before boarding the return flight to Paris. In case of

rain, the backup event was a lunch composed of "typical" (that is to say, elegant and exotic) local foods in a traditional open wooden structure known as a "carbet," a tourist site at the edge of the forest that the space center had constructed for just this purpose. Both Georges and I had already visited the islands, and we had other engagements, in his case an adventure tour up the Maroni River. Several months later I received a letter from him that thanked me for photos I had sent. He had enjoyed his jungle trip, he wrote. It was an "adventure" that he would never forget, no more than the day we had spent together with Ariane. I could imagine his face bright red from sun, enthusiasm undampened by several days in a canoe.

Lest the tone of my narration mislead, I should stress that I liked Georges, however I might disagree with his political and historical assumptions or question his vision of the future. He was friendly to everyone he met and spoke freely. I also believe he was quite sincere in his faith in the Space Age. Thus I think of him while writing, and present him to you now, in order to give a sense of a sympathetic believer behind the rhetoric of the space enterprise. Although his statements about outer space may appear bombastic and empty, they contain a core of belief and affect. And, like the launch at their center, they are not simply false. Watching a rocket leave the ground, feeling its presence, can evoke a powerful sensation of reality. While some in the audience may pray for its safety and others may speculate about the thrill of explosion, a recognition of significant risk remains.[3] Although Ariane's rise is not exciting or magical to everyone—some complain how small, slow, and distant it appears—like the rhetoric around it the event contains a moment of literal power, an instrumental jolt between myth and fact. For humans and their tools have indeed left their planet. And that dream, made real, is not something to take too lightly. As Walter Mac-Dougall reminds us in describing the hyperbole of the moon landing: "President Nixon thought those days in July the greatest week since Creation—ridiculous perhaps, but also the most honest image of the hopes and fears of technocratic man: men as gods, creators in their own right with all the glory and tragedy of divinity."[4] Georges, I am sure, would more than agree.

SPACE FOR REPRESENTATION

A cultural system that can launch earth satellites can
dispense with gods entirely.

Leslie White, "Satellites and Gods," 1957

One of the metaphors which has occurred to me partly
through this experience of trying to share my experience of being an astronaut, is the idea of the space ship
as the Gothic Cathedral of our age.

> NASA astronaut Jeffrey Hoffman at ESA confer-
> ence, in Jean Schneider and Monique Léger-Orine,
> Frontiers and Space Conquest, 1987

The language woven around rockets has been far from modest. A complex field of representation, influenced by mythology and science fiction
as much as by technical description, underlies both the overall narrative
of the space effort and its composite elements. Not only is the "step" into
outer space described in cosmic terms, but the names of rockets and
satellites—particularly Western ones—carry mythic allusions. The American space program invoked Mercury, Gemini, and Apollo to watch over
the march to the moon and named its fiery chariots Atlas, Jupiter, and
Saturn. Not to be outdone, the Europeans stressed their connection
to classical civilization and the tradition of science, and when it came
time to choose a moniker for their new launch design, they recalled a
Cretan princess, whose precious thread allowed escape from the
labyrinth. Underlying this language we find a tireless claim to significance
(a "messianic zeal" one French space official called it), based on a mixture of national pride and a very general anthropology. For even as the
technological prowess of a particular nation-state rises or falls with its
rocket, the figure moving into the Space Age is Man, that aging, gen-
dered actor on the evolutionary stage.[5]

Let us examine the rhetoric of space, beginning with a brochure presenting the European Space Agency, its activities, and its aims. "Our Inheritance—Our Future: Space," the opening line reads, neatly collapsing
time into a geometry of human expansion. Concerns for knowledge, civilization, and competition mingle through the paragraphs that follow:

> From time immemorial, human beings have looked up at the Sun, the
> Moon and the planets and beyond them to the stars, and wondered. The
> Universe has drawn their mounting curiosity throughout the millennia.
> They have worshipped it, dreamed about it and tried, for many thousands
> of years, to learn more about it with the limited means at their disposal. Eu-
> rope has an invaluable heritage in this respect, built upon the work of the
> ancient Greeks and, nearer our time, of such famous astronomers as Coper-
> nicus . . . Kepler . . . Galileo . . . Newton . . . Halley . . . and so many, many
> more. With this inheritance behind them, it was clear that Europe could
> and would not be left behind when the "space era" was suddenly upon us
> with the almost unbelievable news that the Soviet Union had launched the
> world's very first artificial satellite, Sputnik 1, in October, 1957.[6]

Descent, it would seem, is destiny. Europe's very heritage must drive it forward, prevent it from being "left behind" (symbolically on a lower technological plateau, and literally on Earth). The goal of the presentation, we learn at the end of the overview, is to inspire pride in the reading public ("who are after all financing our endeavors")—the pride of having participated in this, "the greatest adventure of the twentieth century, if not all time."[7]

Here we have the major themes of space: religion and evolution. In the heavens, divinity and humanity can meet. The future is inevitable and fast approaching. It has always been overhead, beckoning, in the mysteries of the night skies. Now that destiny calls, one has to be on the rocket, or one is eliminated from this leap of destiny, bypassed and terrifyingly "left behind."[8] This is a race, a challenge of selectionary pressure, and once the gates of heaven are thrown open, one must leap through them to evolve. The combination of technocultural survival and progressive expansion is strikingly imperial in tone, recalling the rivalries of late-nineteenth-century European empires, where a focus on national expansion blended with ideologies of human progress. Not surprisingly, one of the frequent allusions in the Space Age is to an earthly adventurer, Christopher Columbus. Outer space is only the most modern of New Worlds.[9]

The choice of the name "Ariane" for Europe's resurrected launcher program is also instructive. The designation "L3S," while suitable for a hypothetical technical enterprise of a three-stage rocket, lacked the requisite "poetry" to represent Europe's future in space. CNES considered about two hundred suggestions, including "Ganymede" (the male lover of Zeus) and "Vega" (which was dropped when someone pointed out that it was the brand name of a Belgian beer). Two other proposals seriously considered were "Phoenix" (the mythical bird reborn in fire) and "Penelope" (the faithful wife of Odysseus). Delegates from France's partner countries eliminated both of these, the "still warm ashes" of the Europa project counting against the first, and connotations of an interminable wait eliminating the second. However, the French minister for industrial and scientific development, who was "very knowledgeable about Greek mythology," came up with "Ariane" (Ariadne), a name he would have given his daughter if he had one.[10] The allusion to Theseus's escape from the labyrinth appealed to everyone, though some wondered about giving a feminine name to so masculine a rocket. The gender of the machine, though treated as a topic of light humor, was actively considered. In the end, the choice was clear. "Ariane, part of a common heritage shared by all Europeans and pronounced in more or less the same way in all their languages, won the day."[11]

Not only was the naming of Europe's rocket conscious and carefully considered, but the resulting object quickly became anthropomorphized in both formal and informal presentations. Through the alchemy of feminine pronouns the metal and chemical tower transformed into a woman, powerful but fully in the service of Europe. This Ariane had a mission: to set Europe free from NASA and to demonstrate that old continent's unity and its future prowess following French leadership. Another example from promotional materials makes these links clearly: "The name Ariane harked back to the earliest of European mythology. It was Ariane who provided Theseus with the thread which he used to make his way out of the Minoan labyrinth. The modern Ariane takes satellites beyond the clutches of gravity, and Europe out of the labyrinth of dependency on others for launches."[12] In acquiring a name, the European launch vehicle also acquired the narrative around it. And as the program became successful, the designation "Ariane" could be read back into prophecy, developing new meaning. Europe, in the role of Theseus, had indeed escaped the Space Race labyrinth, avoiding the superpower Minotaurs. Ariadne's golden thread led from the Guiana Space Center up through the sky. Old culture, in the end, can learn new tricks.

In this abbreviated allusion, Ariadne, the "feminine" figure behind the scenes, moves to the front of the myth. The hoard of (mostly) male engineers, administrators, and technicians remain faceless, and in the absence of an astronaut, the rocket itself rules supreme. The personification contained in this promotional material continues, enumerating the design's progress: "All dynasties express themselves by numbers, and Ariane is no exception. Ariane 1 founded the family fortunes; its first test flight was in 1979. Since then the family has grown in statue [sic] and strength through Ariane 2 and 3 until today Ariane 4 ensures that, like all good leaders, the demands of the people—in this case the customers—are met."[13] The machine has become an actor, a ghost of monarchy, safely materialized and ruling through international corporation. Of course, this is all the coy and hopeful prose of publicity brochures. But within its focus on a humanized machine we find a key element of modern representation: the magic of scale.

Unlike many products of high technology, launch rockets are not items of mass production but very singular objects. Each represents a substantial investment of materials and hours upon hours of labor, unified and dramatically tested. In a world familiar with giant quantities,

rapid rates, and tiny fractions, rockets and satellites work in more modest numbers. The fiftieth Ariane launch took place in April 1992, over a
decade after the original launch. In 1993, a year marred by a launch failure, Arianespace could count seven launches, ten satellites placed in
orbit, and sixteen new contracts, small sums for sales of just under a billion dollars. But then, despite its grandeur, outer space remains a remarkably finite realm. The satellites now crowding some orbits hardly
match the congestion of traffic in small towns, and only a handful of humans have ever walked the moon.[14] Like minor deities of some pan-
theons, space missions and events are majestic in prowess but well within
the range of daily calculation. They are easy to imagine.

Yet space is transparent and obfuscating all at once. Even as rockets
and satellites represent clear and limited objects, the vast alignments of
technologies behind them are nominally acknowledged but effectively
hidden. At a great enough distance, the sea of humanity resolves into a
single being free from internal conflict, facing the horizon. Still, while
the apotheosis of the machine beyond the atmosphere may obscure the
actual technologies involved, it is the faceless army of designers who
hold the key card of defining function. Though the name matters, it is
not a technical issue: the rocket would fly, whether called Ariane or
L3S. Symbolism, while at the center of things, is constantly trivialized.
The mythic figures invoked in this technoculture are a matter of poetic
overlay rather than engineering; in the sense of divine efficacy, they are
effectively dead, disenchanted in their very resurrection. Moreover,
their symbolic fabric itself is thin, stretched to simplicity by rational
disbelief. The cosmology of space gyrates between grandiosity and simplicity; amid the passive, detailed jargon of technical description we
find flat mythologies—old ghosts now ordered by a straight arrow of
progress. In making their history, the prophets of space neutralize the
past, drawing on the machinery of the present and the endless gravity
of the future. Returning to old tales, they forget that heroes could be as
base as noble in conduct, open to opportunity even while directed by
fate, creatures of selfish desire and fickle interest. Theseus was no exception. When he sailed back to Athens, he left Ariadne behind.[15]

EUROPE, FRANCE, AND ARIANE

Hermes is not only a technical challenge, but also a
demonstration of Europe's determination to take an
active part in the further evolution of the human race.

ESA, "Hermes," 1991

Within the representational field of space, Ariane oscillates between overlapping demands of European cooperation and French national interest. On the one hand, the launcher program constitutes a multinational European enterprise. In this setting, as we have seen, common labor and the technical investment of an entire continent erase nationality, replacing it with an appeal to common humanity, professional identity, or greater cultural heritage. On the other hand, France has always been the driving force behind the resuscitated European launch program, remaining the largest investor in Ariane in symbolic as well as material terms. Here national pride takes central stage: Ariane is a shining example of French independence, ingenuity, and leadership. These twin influences affect both general representation of the program and particular concerns regarding the role of the Guiana Space Center.

By way of illustration let us glance at two advertisements, the first for a multinational corporation and the second for the French government. The figure of universal citizen of space takes clear shape in a Matra Marconi promotion that shows two figures, clad in sterile outfits, their backs turned, reaching over their heads to adjust a gleaming tangle of machinery. Around them the copy reads:

> Higher/Nearer: Who's French? Who's British? Who cares. They share a common language. They have a single culture—space. They belong to Matra Marconi Space, the first international space company. Across national boundaries. Without technological limits. Their goal: to bring higher technology nearer to users.[16]

It is amid this general, unified race of corporate technicians that ESA stresses its difference: peaceful cooperation before all. The context for French desire for particular national recognition becomes apparent in the following public relations release from the French Embassy:

> Throughout the world, France benefits from its image as the country of savoir-vivre—knowing how to live well. The French do not refute this image: they even work hard at defending it through painstaking efforts to ensure the quality of French wines, the refinement of French cuisine, and the charm of pedestrian promenades in their cities and towns, so rich in museums and historical monuments. But the American tourist visiting the Centre Georges Pompidou or discovering the Pyramide du Louvre might not be aware of another reality—that France is a country of technological prowess, capable of eminent and spectacular accomplishments known the world over—from the world's fastest train, to the Ariane rocket, to nuclear reactors, to advanced telecommunications systems.[17]

Echoing de Gaulle's desire that Frenchmen "marry their century," this passage serves as a reminder that official France sees itself as leading the way forward, not following behind.[18] Reason and refinement compose the tissue of French civilization not only in the sense of high culture but also in that of material efficiency. Ariane must exhibit not only the qualities of international cooperation but also those of national achievement. In this sense it is a piece of modern France's soul.

For the most part, French and European interests align, in keeping with strong French commitment to a united Europe. As a former French minister for science and research explains in the preface to a book about Ariane, the launcher combines market logic with the promise of common development: "It is easier, and more agreeable, to build Europe by constructing the future than by repairing the effects of past explosions."[19] Ariane promises the allure of a pure future, banishing historical darkness with a new and common technological day. However, at points the interests of Europe and France diverge, and one of the places they do so most concretely is with regard to the Guiana Space Center. ESA has worked to distribute contracts related to its projects to its member states in proportion to their financial commitment. As the Ariane program has grown to be more central and successful, and the level of its funding filtered through ESA has grown (particularly with the Ariane 5 program), that organization has sought to make the workforce at CSG less exclusively French and more representative of Europe. In contrast, the French agency CNES, which owns CSG, has no particular desire to yield slots within it to workers of other nationalities, and the French employees of the space center are in general less than enthusiastic about welcoming them. French Guiana, after all, is French territory, and the de facto work language of CSG is French, unlike ESA's official Anglo-Franco bilingualism. Addressing the fears of French workers, the head of the European delegation at CSG admitted that the process of "Europeanization" was "a little barbaric and very technocratic" and that it had prompted concern about a possible loss of "soul" as well as a job. By way of official response, the center points out that it counts only 106 "non-French Europeans" (largely Italians and Belgians) in the extended local space program and that knowledge of the French language is obligatory.[20]

The life of Europeans who live in Kourou is not always easy. Several non-French employees emphasized to me the degree to which the base is a French domain and the extent to which they feel alien. Even an official interview with an Italian couple in CSG's largely upbeat house magazine, *Latitude 5*, reveals strains of discord. Information, the Italians complain, was difficult to obtain prior to their departure and sometimes misleading. The woman of the couple—herself named Ariane, no less—notes that the personnel center of CSG did not even have an international phone line. She describes a deep sense of isolation, broken only by despairing calls to her mother from a phone booth. One of her friends from Spain, she adds, had it even worse, spending months in the company of no one other than her own husband. The Italian man interviewed—for all that he has been educated in Paris, is "perfectly francophone," and has "no regrets" about making the move—still doubts that CSG is ready for real European plurality. He suggests that space officials must first acknowledge the culture shock involved and the extent to which many French employees are invested in maintaining the status quo: "A [non-French] European who comes here is not a person like any other, only holding a different color passport. This is someone who's changing language, culture, climate, to a much greater degree than a Frenchman. . . . You know that many of those here on assignment from the Metropole are trying to recover 'their France' in Kourou."[21] For all that Ariane may represent the future of Europe, its foundation remains deeply French. Even the highest technology does not easily escape the gravity of culture, and common goals do not erase competing interests.[22]

THE CITY OF THE STARS

Living conditions in Kourou, whether in a villa or an
apartment, are extremely pleasant.
>   *Anonymous,* Kourou, *1987*

Kourou, ville maudite [Kourou, cursed town].
>   *Graffiti on wall near marketplace, 1992*

If relations between France and the rest of the European space force sometimes exhibit strain, such discord pales before the tensions between the French space program and the rest of French Guiana. As we have seen, the Guiana Space Center plays an uncomfortably prominent role in the local economy, and both the infrastructural developments surrounding it and the everyday life of its employees have served as a catalyst for dramatic social change. Efforts to represent the place of CSG in Guyane reflect such tension, and at times it is difficult to believe that all parties are describing a common subject. From the perspective of the space center and many of its employees, the Ariane program not only offers an opportunity for local employment but also conveys symbolic value by allowing French Guiana to participate in the future and erase its painful legacy in the triumph of common human technological progress. From the perspective of many of its local political foes, CSG remains an awkward implant, a French enterprise that uses Guyane's geography without contributing to its real development.

Ethnic terms near stereotype infuse everyday speech amid the order of society in much of French Guiana, and discussion of the space center is no exception. Kourou is sometimes called a "white" city: although Metros may only account for perhaps a quarter of its population, they dominate the upper echelons of the space enterprise and set most norms of behavior and consumption.[23] The "City of the Stars" is a place that evokes strong reaction in the rest of Guyane, much of it negative. The local left resents what they perceive as a legacy of colonialism, referring to CSG as CSE, the "Centre Spatial *Européen.*" Middle-class residents of Cayenne, Creole or otherwise, often dismiss it as a "town without a center," and reports in the local media identify it as a locus of crime. Rotating space personnel tend to either enjoy or hate Kourou, depending on whether they interpret their experience as adventure or exile. Yet I have met few people who live there for the town itself; it is not local enough for those seeking French Guiana, not global enough for those seeking France. Rather, it seems a place where lives muddle but rarely mingle, a suture between worlds.

Let us take another quick tour through Kourou, following its street map. The town has grown drastically in the decades that have passed since Jolivet's 1971 description, and its divides are less crude but no less visible. The luxury Hotel des Roches is still there, if a bit faded around the edges, as are the rows of villas beyond it. On the beach one finds a motley collection of sunbathers and volleyball players, mostly Metro, as well as the "Aloha Holiday Center," a thatch-sheltered bar framing the islands out to sea. A few men of indeterminate age, sporting tattoos, thick bodies, and cigarettes, mingle with bored teenagers at its counter, and nearby a group of Brazilians kick a soccer ball. The road fronting the shore, named for Félix Eboué (the colonial administrator, Free French hero, and one of Guyane's most famous sons), twists inland near the end of the beach and becomes the Avenue des Frères Kennedy (the Kennedy Brothers), nicely intersected by Christopher Columbus. Nearby a new set of green villas stand imposingly, with every entrance, even the garage, carefully barred. To the left one finds the central section of the New Town constructed in the first expansion, with squares named for Kepler, Newton, and Copernicus. The apartment blocks here have acquired a seedy air, but the open-air market attracts an ample array of vendors, many of whom sell local specialties for a premium price.

At the end of the Avenue des Frères Kennedy lies a major thoroughfare, the Avenue de France, which twists into the Street of the Jesuit Fathers. Across the street lies a modest quarter of low houses, schools, and a hospital, while to the right stretches another modest line of apartment buildings. Continuing in that direction, one encounters a remarkable constellation of the military, passing the yellow compound that houses the Third Regiment of the French Foreign Legion, behind which the Rue Alfred Dreyfus intersects with the Allée Bonaparte. Just beyond, the Village Indien matches this representational directness with the intersection between a street named for the Caribs and one named for the Galibi. At the end of the Avenue de France lies the traffic circle where it intersects with the Avenue Gaston Monnerville, another of Guyane's (and France's) former political luminaries. The road beyond leads out of town, past an artificial lake, a water ski center, two hotels (Atlantis and Mercury), and a residence named for Saint-Exupéry. Left and right lie newer districts that sport more imaginative architecture than that of earlier periods, including tiles and pastel colors that evoke southern France. The types of dwellings vary more quickly here as well, apartments and houses keeping less to themselves. In the area closer to the shore the street names follow the arts (Picasso, Dali, Matisse, Gauguin, van Gogh, Toulouse-Lautrec, Monet, Renoir, Seurat, and Cézanne), while on the other side we find representatives of the letters (including Sartre, de Beauvoir, Baudelaire, Mauriac, and Cendrars, and, a bit further out, Senghor), with a scientist (Pasteur) and a politician (Jaurès) thrown in for good measure.

Moving in this direction our first stop is the supermarket, which, along with the ubiquitous "Chinese" shops (small food stores predominantly owned and operated by Chinese proprietors), provides residents of the town with most of their staple items. Further on, the road divides around a small plaza that contains a covered fountain and is surrounded by small specialty shops of the sort common to any French town. Délices de la Ferme snuggles next to Déli-France, imported meat, baked goods, and mountain bikes are all available, and a small crowd at the corner bar surveys the scene. Continuing past another lake on the right, an ice cream parlor, and an ethnic arts store, we enter another field of names. A gallery of musicians lies to the left (Verdi, Mozart, Strauss,

Figure 15.   Cows, Kourou, 1992

Schubert, Liszt, Ravel, Vivaldi, and—over the Avenue Berlioz—Chopin, Mendelssohn, and Louis Armstrong), while a few scientists and playwrights cluster to the right (Einstein, Nobel, Beckett, and Camus). Keeping to this path (past Thomas Edison, Doctor Schweitzer, and the Brothers Lumière), one comes to another traffic circle, where a right turn leads out of town past the port and industrial zone.

Skirting the lake to the left instead, we move away from Mother Theresa and toward Martin Luther, passing a sports complex and municipal pool, en route back to the classic standby of modern French thoroughfares: Victor Hugo. Beyond some of the first temporary housing built for the space center lie the library and city hall, near the intersection with the older Avenue des Roches (named for a rocky spit at the juncture of river and sea). The road back to the Hotel des Roches runs past a hydroponic garden, as well as cul-de-sacs named for the Caribbean and the test rocket Véronique. Across the Avenue des Roches, the Rue du Suriname leads to the Village Saramaca, hardly changed from Jolivet's shantytown.[24] This crowded jumble of dwellings is officially allocated two roads, with the country of Suriname looping tightly back into the Maroni River. Following the Avenue des Roches away from the hotel leads one to the Old Town of Kourou, with its wooden houses fading slowly in the sun. Here stores may allude to everything from Montmartre to *Miami Vice,* but the street names return to local figures, with the exception of Choiseul (patron of the ill-fated 1763 expedition) and, grandly, unforgettably, stretching down the middle of things, the Avenue Général de Gaulle.

Throughout the tour the incongruity between reference and place is striking. The stars of civilization lend their names to shadeless streets, prefabricated buildings, and hot concrete. Air-conditioning and insects provide a background hum, broken by the sound of automobiles. The daily dramas reported in the news seem well removed from the themes of high art: a break-in here, a brawl there, a bike race, or yet another beauty contest. The villas sport security bars, and a number of shacks sprout satellite dishes. The composite landscape is undeniably modern, but its starker lines recall little of the grandeur of Mozart or the subtlety of Matisse. The allusions are present in name, but in name only.

THE ARCHITECTURE OF GRANDEUR

The location of the Space Centre and launch site in
Guiana, a French state located in South America, has
helped to transform this country [*sic*] its old unwhole-
some image—often called the Green Hell, Inferno, or
the land of jail—into a brilliant picture of the avant-
garde: "French Guiana, Land of Space."

> *Jean-Michel Desobeau,*
> *"CSG: Guiana Space Center," 1990*

Like all of the European space program, the Guiana Space Center invests quite heavily in public relations. A multitude of glossy brochures are available to describe its activities and overall mission, and visits by the public are encouraged. Beyond the ample welcome of the sort that Georges and I received, CSG runs regular tours of its facilities and features a space museum on its grounds. Although many visitors come from beyond French Guiana, the center has become a significant tourist attraction in relative local terms and invests energy in creating a positive local impression.[25] While its critics might complain about the tight control the base maintains, the charge cannot simply be one of lack of information or access. Rather, what emerges is an unbridgeable gap between grandiose statements of purpose and the conditions of everyday life. A similar representational gap infuses many plans of the local Guyanais government, and when the two combine forces the result is all the more extraordinary. To illustrate this divide I turn to a most remarkable brochure, prepared for the local agency in French Guiana responsible for road work.

Entitled "When the Sky Takes Root in the Ground of Guyane," the brochure's cover shows a number of humped cattle standing before a nebula. A bit further on the subject narrows to "The Milky Way and the City of the Stars," and subsequently we learn that the topic at hand is "The Milky Way, a project for the space of a road."[26] A remarkable flood of poetry follows, accompanied by equally remarkable illustrations, including another nebula with stars marked for "Monumentality," "Economy," "Culture," "Technology," "Urbanism," and "Health," and a river flowing from the tail of the Hermès space shuttle, on which three Amerindian children paddle a canoe. Only after nearing the end of the brochure does one realize that the "space of a road" in question was that running between Rochambeau Airport and Sinnamary, a singularly unremarkable stretch of two-lane highway. At the very end of the document we find that its call for research into practical and symbolic domains ("Functional, Technical, Aesthetic, Toponymic, Climatic, Ecological, Ethnological, Historical, Geographical, Touristic, Economic, and Mythic") is intended to lay the groundwork for a design competition. Given that all this symbolic interplay is to occur over a mere 131 kilometers of lightly traveled road, it would be a daring architect indeed who would undertake the Milky Way commission.

The space program does inspire practical as well as symbolic investment. New buildings rise, and new plans are made. Yet the results remain uneven, and with every new neighborhood built, the shantytown of the Cité Saramaca becomes all the more glaring.[27] The flights of rhetoric aloft, such as that along the Milky Way (which with the postponement of the Hermès program and the financial problems of French Guiana's local government has quietly faded from view), leave the red soil of the tropics far below. If the road through Kourou is indeed a mirror, it reflects a mobile reality more immediate and homely than Ariane. Still, however meaningless in technical terms, the space center furiously renews the symbolic landscape around it, continually struggling to redefine both present and past through the future.

REWRITING TIME

"History" means: yes, we know there were disagree-
ments, but that's in the background, that's over and
done with, let's forget it and deal with what is on the
table in front of us right now.
Stacia Zabusky on ESA personnel,
Launching Europe, *1995*

Time is of immediate interest to space personnel, whose experience of
French Guiana stretches between exotic fascination and desperate
boredom. Separation from "civilization" and experience of life in a
"third-world country" can cut both ways: the living is "free" but also
at times lacking in "culture," its rhythm more relaxed, a bit of "easy
California living," but without benefit of major urban centers.[28] For
those who long for elsewhere, the sojourn resembles that of a prisoner.
The most graphic story I heard along these lines was that of an engineer
who kept a calendar with vacation days marked in red and completed
days crossed off in blue. He then watched the white space between the
blue and red diminish, wistfully awaiting his next leave. In such a calendar we have a meticulous flag of exile, the colors of France infusing
the slow passage of time.

However, for many displaced Metros the sense of exile mingles with
one of adventure. The following comments from an interview in the internal magazine for CNES provide an intentionally representative example. The subjects, JL and C, are both thirty-five years old, have two
young children, and have lived in Kourou for two and a half years. He
works in the planning of satellite operations, while she is a secretary.

JL: The appeal of the money, whatever one thinks, was not my first motivation. I
wanted to change my surroundings [*me dépayser*], to go to a hot country. I spent
my childhood in Morocco, and here I found the heat that I missed.

C: The nature is fantastic here, but I'm waiting until the children are bigger to do
some jungle tours. French Guiana, it's a paradise for children. . . . The worst for
me are the mosquitoes and red ants; it's impossible to picnic.

JL: In the Metropole I would never do what I do here. . . . I have nevertheless been
disappointed not to find at CSG the same wealth of athletic and cultural activity
as at Toulouse [another CNES center].

C: Currently, because of having young children, I feel a bit cut off from others. I miss
that. Kourou is a closed city. You meet the same people at work and in town. People are only here in passing, they are tied to contracts with the space base. Above
all, I haven't yet made the effort. . . . Cayenne certainly offers greater interaction
with populations with deeper roots [*mieux enracinées*].

JL: When I return to the Metropole, I long to return to Kourou and this calm rhythm
      of life. I'll renew my contract to spend three more years here.[29]

Life is easy, even without picnics. Yet Kourou is closed, particularly for
a woman with small children. With less professional stake in staying in
French Guiana, C waxes less enthusiastic than her husband. She also
points out how transitory the space population is, much less involved
in its surroundings than the neighboring population of Cayenne.

This detachment on the part of *détachés,* those on assignment from
the Metropole, is not universal or always intentional. A few become actively involved in French Guiana, being stationed there for long periods
or at different points in their careers. Yet their involvement remains
fragmentary and subject to class interests well removed from the majority of the population. Witness an affable Belgian ESA official, whose
efforts included working to establish the department's first golf course.
He warns of the need for more balanced economic growth in the region, but his appeal remains a call for general progress: "The Land of
Prison has become the Land of Space, but Space must remain only a
prelude and a support in creating a real development of this region,
complete and balanced in all three sectors, primary, secondary, and ter-
tiary. . . . Europe and CSG have to continue to improve . . . and French
Guiana rejoin them."[30] Such a view finds consistent voice in pronouncements of most space officials: appreciation of local charm and a
desire for mutual growth. As a director of CSG commented on his assumption of the post:

> Guyane? I like Guyane very much! . . . The nature is extraordinary, it is still
> a place on the Earth where there are many things to do, which makes for liv-
> ing well, I believe, in all senses of the term. . . . The adventure of space is ex-
> citing, the adventure of developing a country such as Guyane is exciting too.
> It must be hoped that the space adventure helps French Guiana to develop,
> and conversely, that French Guiana equally helps the development of space
> on its ground.[31]

Yet even as such space officials express hopes for the development of
French Guiana, the greatest pleasures they find in life there lie not in experiences of modernity but rather in its absence. We find the virtues of
a calm life and an untouched landscape extolled repeatedly. In Guyane,
the "real" Guyane beyond the confines of Kourou, lie the promised
pleasures of authentic nature. The Belgian quoted previously remembered how the "Green Hell" he imagined he would find turned into
something else, as "the rivers and forest of Guyane would allow us to

live the adventure and the fascination of a virgin world." Amid his trips
he recalled "a memorable fricassee of toucans," some "ten thousand
francs in the pan" according to the estimate of a traveling companion
who was a breeder of parrots in Paris.[32] Such excursions constitute the
highlight of local tourism for many of the space personnel, as well as
their families and guests. Indeed, the arm of the space center in charge
of amusing visiting *missionnaires*, the employees of client satellite companies, regularly resorts to the natural surroundings as an entertainment resource.[33]

A trip made by the director of the space center reveals a particularly
curious mix of business and pleasure:

> In company of the secretary general of the prefecture and our spouses we
> spent three unforgettable days of Pentecost 1989 in a protected region on
> the Island of Twencke on the Upper Maroni, among the Wayana Indians. At
> the request of the secretary general I was to speak there about the space pro-
> gram. Therefore I had taken small models of Ariane and various satellites in
> my baggage. After my installation in a school *carbet*, curious Wayanas
> began to arrive little by little. There, in a hall that rapidly filled with about
> a hundred children and adults, I gave a presentation of our activities in
> Guiana (of which they had heard very summarily). And above all, I told in
> as simple as possible a manner the story of this rocket that takes off from the
> soil of French Guiana. I spoke slowly and I tried, as much as possible, to
> also demonstrate what I was telling thanks to my models. What was aston-
> ishing was the double translation practiced beside me. The instructor, an Al-
> satian who had lived for ten years in this village with his wife, translated my
> French into "standard" Wayana, and behind him, a young Wayana of
> twelve or thirteen years, apparently a very brilliant boy upon whose shoul-
> ders, I believe, rest many future hopes of the village, translated the "stan-
> dard" Wayana into colloquial Wayana in his turn. At the end, out of curios-
> ity, I asked how they had translated the Ariane rocket. In their language it
> was the "vessel of spirits." When I arrived in this village where we were to
> pass almost three complete days, I have to say that I had an immense mo-
> ment of doubt about the interest of this journey. I told myself, "But you are
> mad to have come here while you have so much to do in Kourou!" We were
> indeed on a small island where, outside of fishing in a canoe or participating
> in the simple life of Wayanas, there was nothing much to do. And then the
> magic took hold, I felt myself completely relax. We spent tremendous days
> there, living very simply. We went hunting and fishing with the Wayana, and
> there was also this little lecture and evenings together. These are powerful
> moments that I will never forget![34]

The account invokes several tropes common to descriptions of encounters between civilization and the nobler varieties of savagery, between the involved translation of Space Age technology to a Stone Age

audience, and the narrator's relief from modern stress in a simple life led along the river.[35] In this version, however, European and Amerindian meet peacefully and learn from each other. Both modern technology and indigenous virtue find affirmation: through the services of a schoolteacher and a star male pupil, Ariane reaches the inner forest, while an ambitious French professional learns to forage. Moreover, through his experience of weekend anthropology, our director of technology stumbles on echoes of religion, learning (ironically on a Christian holy day of the descending ghost) that his rocket is a vessel carrying spirits aloft.

For personnel of the space center, French Guiana—particularly its interior—represents a landscape of the past, alternately troubling and alluring. When venturing up rivers and into the forest, they are more likely to find a haunting paradise than the nightmare experienced by convicts half a century earlier. Yet what haunts them may be as much their own conceptions of worlds lost as the vanished lives of others. Like any true prophets of progress, they are acutely, if selectively, aware of history. Marking advancement, after all, requires rulers of measurement.

COMMEMORATION AT CSG

I was now come to the unhappy Anniversary of my
Landing. I cast up the Notches on my Post and found I
had been on Shore three hundred and sixty five Days. I
kept this Day as a Solemn Fast, setting it apart for Religious Exercise, prostrating myself on the Ground
with the most serious Humiliation, confessing my Sins
to God, and acknowledging his Righteous Judgments
upon me . . . and having not tasted the least Refresh-
ment for twelve Hours, even till the going down of the
Sun, I then ate a Bisket Cake, and a Bunch of Grapes,
and went to Bed, finishing the Day as I began it.

> *Daniel Defoe*, Robinson Crusoe, *1719*

Many families like to trace their ancestry, and the Ariane "clan" is no different.

> ESA, *"Reaching for the Skies," 1988*

In space, it seems, every day is an anniversary. Actions and events are constantly placed in reference to their precedents, as well as a greater temporal narrative. Launches function as historical markers ("Flight

36," someone might say, referring to a significant Ariane failure), and the progress of every year is carefully measured and framed with the past. The drama of space is indeed that of time; motion and progress signal significance. When facing the future, it seems, one can never remember too much, at least of the same thing.

Recent years have been kind to the Guiana Space Center in this commemorative regard: 1988 marked the twentieth anniversary of the first launch from French Guiana as well as the first launch of Ariane 4; 1989 was the twenty-fifth anniversary of the decision to found CSG and the tenth year since the first Ariane launch (not to mention the bicentennial of the French Revolution and the twentieth anniversary of the moon landing); 1992 brought the thirtieth birthday of CNES as well as the fiftieth launch of Ariane; 1993 marked the twentieth anniversary of the Ariane decision and the twenty-fifth operational year of CSG; and 1994 was the thirtieth anniversary of the base decision and the twenty-fifth anniversary of the moon launch. Each of these temporal landmarks (and more) have been carefully, and sometimes lavishly, observed. In 1989 a hot air balloon and a model rocket based on the one used by the cartoon hero Tintin graced the skies of Kourou. Less dramatically, but no less significantly, in 1992 (as in other commemorative years) the house magazines of CNES and CSG ran appropriate notices and interviews with employees who remembered earlier periods. Somewhere between entertainment and statements of official history, these interviews highlight human moments "then" and "now," reminding the reader that the frame of the space enterprise is inherently progressive.

To examine the phenomena more fully let us look at a particularly significant act of commemoration, the celebration of "twenty-five years in space" held in the summer of 1993. In honor of that occasion, CSG sponsored weather reports on the official television station, featuring a blast of music and a new slogan: "*De Véronique à Ariane, la passion des lancements depuis 25 ans*" (From Véronique to Ariane, the passion of launches for twenty-five years). As well as booming out nightly after the local news, this suggestive motto flashed boldly across numerous posters and other liberally distributed paraphernalia printed at the time.[36] The anniversary found its climax in an expansive soiree at the end of August, held in the new, enormous hotel built on the road near Sinnamary. Here, eerily separate from any larger settlement, in a blaze of light against the black expanse of the neighboring forest, a poolside gathering brought together the cream of French Guiana society. In addition to currently active space personnel and a number of pioneering figures who had been flown in for the event, the guest list featured prominent local political figures, including the elected representatives of the department and region. The food, a mixture of local ingredients and French sensibility, was served by dark-skinned women dressed in Creole costume. Ethnic dancers provided entertainment, as did a commemorative video documenting the space center's twenty-five years of achievements, accompanied by a rendering of "Que Sera Sera" performed on steel drums. The highlight of the event came just after dinner with a ceremony honoring the "Founding Fathers" who had been instrumental in the establishment of the space program. In an atmosphere of jovial solemnity, each was presented with an enormous wooden replica of the Ariane rocket. Similar to models carved from local woods by Maroon artists for the tourist trade, these measured some five feet in length, and as each aged male recipient held his upright before him, their shape left little to the imagination. After dances, drinks, and light conversation, the evening came to an end in a burst of fireworks.

For comparative purposes let us turn to another commemorative moment, one on a smaller scale but focused on a more significant historical event, the twenty-fifth anniversary of the moon landing one summer later. Here, amid general discussion of the significance of space and the importance of the decision thirty years before to found CSG, commemoration took a new twist as, in keeping with a tradition established five years earlier on the twentieth anniversary of the moon landing, a second Tintin rocket sat ready for launch from the CSG test rocket pad. Constructed by the model rocket club of Kourou, checkered red and white and in every respect a miniature of its cartoon prototype, the small machine basked in the admiration of an audience composed of several hundred people, a largely Metro family crowd. A speech by the club's president, the epitome of a tanned middle-aged engineer, expressed hope that activities like this would help youth make good use of their spare time and would inspire dreams of the future. The launch, he informed us, would be activated by a young woman born around the time of the moon landing. There followed a countdown, a quick pop, and then the rocket shot a short way up into the sky. At the apex of its flight it hesitated and then turned nose down. A parachute opened, and the little machine slowly drifted sideways to the ground in the neighboring savanna. Part of the audience ran to recover it and then paraded back, as if following a religious icon. The reception afterward featured chips and soft drinks. The accompanying press kit included statements by the club and the director of CSG, as well as a souvenir page of the 1989 rocket, nicely framed against a particularly bushy patch of forest. "From dream to reality," the logo read, "it's only a step."[37]

Between these two moments we find more in the way of similarity than difference. Both feature a degree of lavish excess—catered consumption on the one hand and an overpowered toy on the other—and both accompany rocket technology with allusions to "passion" and "dreams," simultaneous appeals to ancestors and coming generations, the achievement of the past, and the promise of the future. Both work to rewrite the present, with the failure of Europa becoming a temporary setback and the clarion call of the Space Race echoing on. The forest of Guyane is reborn in the shape of Ariane, and the American triumph on the moon is framed by the earlier exploits of a Francophone children's hero. Symbolic power returns momentarily to retired men, who grip their souvenir rockets, and is paraded before an audience of young people, who watch the exploits of youth. Thus, amid the repetitive everyday cycle of launches, the space program strives to make sense of itself. A commercial success, a French success, a European success, a human success—CSG succeeds only as long as its progress can be measured.

The historicizing impulse present in commemorative displays also finds expression in the space center's wider role as a protector of French Guiana's historical and natural heritage. In addition to maintaining its own history and historical sites (abandoned launchpads) through its museum, CSG works to curate all artifacts of value around it. Through an act of geography, the land grant bestowed on CNES for space activities includes the Iles du Salut, strategically positioned in the line of launch. Thus the space center is responsible for their upkeep and preservation, protecting both the natural habitat and the vestiges of the penal colony. In anticipation of the centennial of the Dreyfus Affair in 1994, CSG and the Regional Direction for Cultural Affairs (DRAC) combined forces to renovate the hut where the famous exile spent his days on Devil's Island. The operation involved helicopters and the expense of nearly two hundred thousand dollars, but in order to preserve the natural character of the setting, no means of public access was constructed.[38] History, once well defined, remains carefully sealed. As conceptions of national heritage (*patrimoine*) have widened, CSG has grown more catholic in its interests, proudly reporting rock carvings discovered on its territory and enumerating the species its estate protects. Like the Kennedy Space Center in Florida, the Guiana Space Center has found new meaning in an ecological age. Wilderness used as wilderness can remain wilderness; the open space around a rocket neatly translates back into a nature preserve.[39]

THE FUTURE OF NATURE

A few kilometers from Kourou lies the Amazonian
forest, with its rivers and creeks, flora and fauna, and
also men and women who live in perfect symbiosis
with the natural environment.

                            Anonymous, Kourou, *1987*

The last decade has presented the space program with new concerns,
stemming from the growth of environmental activism both in Europe
and in French Guiana itself. In the face of pressure to justify budgets,
and in keeping with its nonmilitary role, the European Space Agency
has increasingly focused on promoting its beneficial role with respect to
the environment, emphasizing the work of satellites that help to monitor a wide range of natural phenomena. At the same time, the Guiana
Space Center, challenged by charges that its rockets (and even more
their attendant technologies) threaten pollution, has gone out of its way
to stress that satellite launching is a relatively clean industry and that
CSG helps to maintain French Guiana as a wilderness preserve.

A connection between space and the environment is not entirely
new. In representational terms the most unforgettable image of the
Space Age is not of the infinite beyond but rather the finite below: our
own planet, blue, green, and white against the sea of darkness. Viewed
from beyond, the Earth becomes a whole and suddenly intimate place,
one that can fulfill the promise of Copernicus by traveling across another sky. Moreover—thanks to the compelling present tense of photography—it can be seen from a distance, recognized as a globe, and
widely reproduced as a potent symbol for reconceived relations to the
environment. Thus the tie between outer space and the fragile planet is
actually in some ways quite close.[40]

In environmental terms the direct impact of rocket activity is relatively light, barring a massive explosion of the launcher on takeoff or of
stored fuels. Although a launch itself does create some pollution, it is an
infrequent event and hence less relentless than the usual by-products of
industrial production. Tests related to the Ariane 5 program and its
plans for increased local production of propellants have raised additional concerns, but the key charge that local ecology groups level at
CSG is that it fosters the development of attendant technologies, consuming massive amounts of electrical power, and imports urban norms,
accustoming people to air-conditioning, automobile transportation,

and the like. While the space center may not bear complete responsibility for the transformation of French Guiana, it has undeniably served as the centerpiece of French activity in the department and acted as a catalyst for both legal and illegal immigration. Most prominently it has come to be associated with the large hydroelectric dam project at Petit Saut, a subject of much environmental controversy.

In response to these local concerns, as well as an increase in environmental discussion throughout Europe (as CSG's director proclaimed in 1991, "*Everybody's* preoccupied with the environment!"), the space center began to adopt a mantle of ecological concern in the early 1990s. Articles related to environmental issues appeared in the CNES and CSG magazines, and CSG even appointed a "Monsieur Environnement," an in-house ecologist who would oversee environmental matters for the space program, as well as conduct research.[41] The richness of Guyanais fauna and flora was extolled, including the red ibis, whose territory overlapped with that of Ariane. Archaeological remains also evoked concern. Satellite photos from the French SPOT system (itself launched by Ariane) were enlisted in the analysis of the environmental impact of the dam project. Trained back on the tropics below, these watchful eyes monitored the terrain, allowing French Guiana to "better know itself."

Here the representational cycle comes full circle and begins to turn inward. Humans, beings separated from nature by culture, develop civilization with the help of tools. The Space Age marks the technological triumph of these creatures as they complete their conquest of the planet, breaking the last links to nature. And yet, even as humanity's triumph is achieved, nature emerges to be rediscovered again. Humans, it turns out, are back on the ground. The future leads through the past, all the way to Eden.

SYMBOLIC MAPS

Those three have taken with them, out into space, all
the resources of art, of science, of industry. With such
resources, they can accomplish anything; you wait and
see, they will resolve this situation soon!
    Jules Verne, From the Earth to the Moon, *1865*

Launches, brochures, neutralized myth, and a mantle of misplaced names, such is the symbolic fabric surrounding the space center. It is a culture of

Figure 16.   Postcard of control panel, CSG, ca. 1987

triumph, filled with self-congratulation, but an anxious one, ever subor-
dinated to function, ever wary of failure. Another anxiety completes the
mix. The work of the Guiana Space Center has little to do with the initial
excitement of space exploration. The lineage of adventure lives on only in
name; commercial satellites are a normal part of global infrastructure, no
longer the stuff of dreams. In Ariane we have the great irony of modernization exposed: as the impossible becomes possible, it reduces the future
to the quotidian. Success brings its own narrative tensions, a need to defer
closure, to rejuvenate an aging tomorrow. In this sense Verne was wiser
than those who turned his fantasy to fact; in Verne's tale the protagonists
eventually circle the moon but never actually land.[42]

As we have seen, the presence of CSG has failed to acculturate the
bulk of Guyanais population to the Space Age; the devotion displayed
by my companion Georges remains an imported phenomenon. A symbolic line runs through Kourou, and in it we can distinguish the outlines of two symbolic maps of French Guiana. In one, CSG represents
the future, coastal Guyane the corrupt past, and the department's interior all the pristine qualities of origin. In the other, CSG represents a
continuing colonial legacy, coastal Guyane the deserving center of fu-

ture development, and the interior a reserve of nostalgia and resources. It would be too facile to describe the first of these maps as Metropolitan and the second as Creole, but in the complex circuitry of daily navigation they are often read that way.

SPACE AND PLACE REVISITED

What's up is like what's down, said Hermes. The goal
is to create the conditions for this truth.
                    Jean-Michel Desobeau, "CSG," 1990[43]

Consider this postcard: a blue machine sits in a vaguely defined room, surrounded by green panels and the glow of fluorescent light. The focus rests on the control panel at its center, a glowing bank of buttons, and as one's eye travels away from it the field of vision grows blurred, uncertain, sensing a roomful of motion. Nothing in the image itself conveys a sense of specific context, and only the legend on the reverse side securely locates it as an interior shot of the space center in Kourou, French Guiana. Unlike neighboring scenes along the rack of souvenirs— shots of exotic animals, people, and tourist landmarks—the card intentionally portrays something apart from conventional locality: a dynamic, artificial space, free from ties to the world. In this sense it is a veritable snapshot of modernity, a photo of a where that could be anywhere. And yet, significantly, the card marks a particular site on the globe and a set of human activities embedded in it. Indeed, the appeal of the image to its potential purchasers is partly based on this fact, for the room that could be in Houston or suburban Paris actually lies in northeastern South America, on the edge of a vast rain forest. What shouldn't be modern sometimes is; what is modern sometimes rests on what is not. Within the frame of a minor, banal artifact, the order of things modern is at once established and undermined; the nature of its subject locates a center of technology out on the margin.

I encountered the image in question on a hot and slow afternoon in the summer of 1990, during my initial visit to French Guiana. Few people were out in the streets of Cayenne, and most doors remained firmly shut from the noon siesta. Newly arrived on a flight from Paris, slightly jet lagged and uncertain of my surroundings, I felt strikingly out of place. Coming upon an open stationery store near the center of town, I stepped inside to escape the sun. Instantly, the surroundings became familiar: the constant climate of air-conditioning, the ordered racks of items displayed for sale, and the (comparatively dim) wash of fluorescent light. Momentarily revived by this commercial environment, I remembered a purpose and examined the postcard rack for a likely means of communication. Here the unhurried expanse of experience outside lay neatly and attractively packaged in well-chosen shots: carefully framed landscapes, tropical animals, elderly buildings, and traditional peoples. In this assembly of postcards, the world of French Guiana became manageable and consumable, simultaneously equal and present, ordered, separated, and—so to speak—clearly worth seeing. Then I noticed a rack with rockets and other machines, attractions of a different order, focused more on the future and less on the past. Amid them I found the postcard described, so remarkably placeless and empty of people and yet so appropriately available to represent and authenticate the immediate experience of my travels.

Beside the postcard with its glowing machine, let us now place a series of other snapshots, these taking their inspiration from ethnographic observation. While the specific notes from which they are drawn date primarily from late 1992 and the summer of 1993, I splice them here in an uninterrupted and flowing present, evoking an illusion of presence and omniscience of the kind suggested by film and providing a backdrop to the earlier description of my tour with Georges.

Before us we have an almost cool December night on the coastal savanna. Though the light has faded too far to distinguish distant forms, in one direction stretches a green ocean of rain forest, and in the other a sluggish brown sea. At the juncture where a slow river flows away from land lies a motley assortment of houses in Caribbean style, dimly lit by streetlights and serenaded by insects. People are out on the sidewalk, visiting, four older men play a domino game, and a woman lounges at a corner, perhaps waiting for a lover or a customer. All the signs are in place: this is the tropics, and the pace is slow. Yet the town does not end with this tranquil image. Moving further along the shore, one passes an uninviting huddle of shacks amid puddles, the scene displaying all the requisite symptoms of squalor. Further still and the scene changes dramatically; huts give way to concrete apartment blocks and then suburban houses, laid out with the methodical certainty of large-scale planning. Large, expensive automobiles of the sort designed for cooler climes are parked in driveways. Here and there a window flickers with the light of a television, and the streets are eerily empty.

Further inland, a crowd surrounds a number of air-conditioned buses in a large parking lot, talking in small groups. Both male and fe-

male, they are dressed in casual but expensive clothes, and while of varied ages, the majority are light-skinned. Boarding the buses with them,
one is lulled by the ride down the coast, passing a small colony of rather
nondescript buildings sprinkled amid the thick scrub. The architecture
could be that of postindustrial Belgium: glass, steel, and a few bright
colors amid spotlights. Far beyond these architectural outposts, out
amid the dark vegetation, a white pavilion casts its own pool of light.
The passengers climb off the bus and walk to the pavilion; equipped
with a round of drinks, they resume their conversations, occasionally
glancing up at a series of televisions that display shots of stern men sitting before machines or offer the view out along an open corridor toward a small, brightly lit object on the horizon, about the size of a
match. The atmosphere is of a garden party, at the edge of some immense golf course. As a voice intones a descending series of numbers in
French, the lights are lowered and the crowd falls silent, uniformly
turning to face the distant match. The concentration grows palpable as
the mood of the televised broadcast spreads beyond its screen. There is
a flare, then a flash of light as bright clouds billow around the base of
the sky. A new sunrise graces the night as slowly, ponderously, the
rocket rises above the ground. Then, as if gathering confidence, it
climbs faster, the light diminishing even as artificial thunder begins to
sound. Growing ever smaller the receding flare finally vanishes over the
ocean, amid general applause. The lights go up, the mood relaxes, and
drinks flow. A few minutes later more cheering erupts as the figures in
the control room smile and shake hands. Both humans and machines
have performed as expected.

Champagne is served to invited guests beneath the tropical stars,
toasting the newest addition to the heavens. Now that the rocket has
successfully risen and disappeared over the horizon, checkpoints
around the launch zone are reopened. At a lonely intersection a part-
time Haitian security guard prepares to leave his post. The last Chinese
store has closed, and an Amerindian checker at the Euro-supermarket
has departed to watch her television. In a crowded nearby shantytown,
a Saramaka Maroon turns the page of his calendar filled with rockets,
while in an empty villa a Brazilian maid puts an Italian child to sleep.
Somewhere above, marking the same equator but focused on another
sky, a Japanese satellite begins to broadcast. Europe's spaceport is
working.

Let us compare this little collage to the earlier postcard with its
glowing machine. Where the postcard features a technology of things,

we now find human shadows; the focus shifts outward, and the center grows blurred. Rather than a single universalizing object, we now have an amalgam of particular lives, imperfectly anchored around a technical event. Technology in action unravels along many lines, diffusing the object in question. By descending to the level of particular detail—even cursory detail—it becomes apparent that the launch of a satellite involves far more than a row of buttons or a single screen, that the machine at the center of the postcard is only one point in a vast array of worldwide connections. Kourou intersects with Japan, China, and Italy, as well as the neighboring rain forest. The lines attached to every launch run through many patient and impatient hands, to a cellular phone in a New York broker's convertible, to a glass of beer before a French legionnaire, and to a Brazilian mother's washing machine. Not all the links in these lines are equal in status, pay, or technical efficiency; some verge on the irrelevant. Yet separating them into neat categories ordered by criteria of causality becomes less certain the more one considers place. The control room is a placeless space of modern technology, the launch zone is a distinctive place redefined by modern technology, and the people who move between them—assembling, directing, cleaning, serving, and consuming—cross arrays of cultural and technical spaces negotiated between rhythms of a modern technology and the tropics. A rocket launch indeed represents the center of this motion, but it is a center that materializes and dissolves rather than holds steady, a center that can only take its literal and figurative meaning in motion. A rocket, after all, as its engineers like to point out, is a transport vehicle. Thus the clear vision of an empty control room, floating in some placeless, modern space, is at once strikingly accurate and perfectly misleading; its distortion lies not in an inverted choice of subject matter but in an inverted choice of focus. Back beyond the postcard, in the heat and bright sunlight, we again find a muddle of lives, clearly—if not simply—attached to the Earth.

Yet perhaps this ethnographic collage itself remains too smooth, too concentrated, too distant. Perhaps we should suspect it as well, for what, after all, does it lose of experience even by framing it? Then again, in focusing more closely, which particular stories shall we highlight? That of an engineer who wishes he were in Florida? That of a security guard who worries about his family in Haiti? That of a journalist who commutes from Cayenne for a Kourou dateline? Different experiences of CSG occur with different frequencies and only intersect momentarily. Behind the spectacular moment of the launch (a moment present for all, but officially witnessed by few) everyday interactions ebb and flow around the space center. The distance in the preceding description of Kourou is not simply an illusion. A placeless place in terms of most of its architecture, the new town divides people between long avenues and cul-de-sacs, with spatial units appropriate for different social classes.

Indeed, in a way the launch itself reflects the presence and absence of the space center in French Guiana: one need not be there to observe the event. Not only is a video feed transmitted by satellite to CNES, ESA, and Arianespace offices in Europe and elsewhere, but it is also broadcast live on local television.[44] And yet a chartered plane of invited guests arrives from Paris for almost every launch, while members of some circles in French Guiana fish for formal invitations. Physical presence, even when technically bypassed, remains a mark of social distinction. Even as the rocket rises, carrying its load, the signals of other satellites rain down; in enclaves of Brazilian immigrants one finds satellite dishes set to catch soap operas and soccer from further south, providing them with alternative spectacles. Negating absence maintains other cultural distinctions. But if it is Europeans who care most for the launches, it is also largely Europeans who travel to the interior in pursuit of the "real" jungle. What represents the local comes to be defined in global terms, and vice versa.

Just before leaving French Guiana in 1993, I had dinner with two young residents of Kourou, one a French citizen of Iranian descent who had grown up in the town and the other a Saramaka Maroon, a refugee from Suriname. The first was dressed well enough to attend any polite gathering in France—indeed he was now in university there. The second wore a less transportable array of clothing and sat quietly, because he spoke little French. The student gestured toward his companion and said to me, "Between us you have all of Kourou." He meant, he went on to say, that between them lay extremes of circumstances, opportunities, and histories, the one treated as a Metropolitan Frenchman, the other as an foreigner only recently emerged from the forest. The distinction between them was that between villa and shantytown: coexisting, interacting, ever-separate lifeworlds. What was unusual, the student noted—with insight and regret—was that the two of them should be not just next to each other but actually sharing a meal. Cultural twists and social divides are hardly unique to Kourou, of course; I could describe equivalents in both France and the United States. But in French Guiana they lie on the surface, concentrated and exposed.

With regard to human space, the "Land of Space" is a world of yawning divides collapsed into narrow fissures. Through its very existence the space center in French Guiana negotiates the boundary of physical worlds, providing means of transportation across them. At the same time, its geographic being in the world redefines other boundaries, superimposing advanced technology and an open horizon. Recall the transformation of French Guiana into a Space Age launch site that gave us a first point to consider: wilderness has its uses, even for high technology. In a more pointed reformulation, we might say that space technology did not erase wilderness but rather found parts of it useful when properly redefined. Unlike a factory or railroad, which might value uninhabited land only in terms of its potential for development (its transformation into a different kind of productive space, or a destination), the space center found value in the openness of the land itself, in its marginal status relative to human networks, and in its specific geographic position. Here, then, we have an example of a modern technology that acknowledges place.[45]

Yet the space program in French Guiana modified the local geography even as it used it. Social issues tied to development crept through the back door: CSG served as a catalyst for transformation. As a consequence of the space program—partly planned and partly unintended—the size and configuration of both Kourou and French Guiana shifted dramatically. Thus the analytic picture before us grows more complicated. A technology that sought a measure of continuing wilderness for its work, that required a well-positioned margin for experimentation, nevertheless transformed that margin in the act of making it useful. To use a place whose location mattered, additions were made, both to create a site adequate to the needs of the project (such as the construction of a series of launchpads) and to create a network of support structures for the technical personnel (such as living quarters and recreation areas). Further personnel not directly tied to the technical project were recruited to provide services approximating those of a culturally appropriate landscape for the technical personnel (such as restaurants and schools), and, as a result of the remarkable level of investment relative to the economy of the surrounding region, the project acquired another layer of unofficial personnel in marginal service categories (such as gardening and baby-sitting). In this way a site that was chosen for characteristics of place becomes increasingly an epitome of the placeless space of modernity, objects, and people that could—and have been—elsewhere. Like the Ariane rocket that it serves, the world of Kourou is an assemblage of imported parts. Unlike the rocket, however, it remains awkwardly earthbound.

Modern machines, then, can create a sense of universality, but at differing costs. The postcard described previously is an accurate illusion in yet another way: it appeals to the universality of technology. The central panel, empty, awaits command; it is free, available, open to any viewer. And yet not just anyone can be in front of any machine; modern technology requires modern technicians. The room that could be anywhere welcomes an inhabitant who could be anywhere, or rather an inhabitant who has been somewhere else and learned how to work within such glowing walls. Placeless space is not free from culture or social norms, for all that it may blur location. Rather, it depends on mastery of a set of cultural and social codes that allow for the possibility of universalized, mobile experience—the recognition of things one has never specifically seen before. The stationery store in Cayenne was, in this sense, familiar to me before I entered it.

To live a modern life is to live with such experience of dislocation, with neutralized environments and transported technologies. Engineers, while they may hunt for pleasure, can hardly be expected to hunt and gather on a daily basis. The last point runs deeper than irony, because in the Guiana Space Center we have the anthropological story in miniature: different ends of "development" collapse together, rain forest to rockets, "stone age to space age." As one visiting French executive pointed out, where else can you buy wooden arrows one day and watch a satellite launch the next?[46] Irony lies on the surface here, but it is an irony born of technique, local conditions, and global possibilities. Surrounded by languid tropical heat and rain, the Guiana Space Center tries to accommodate the rhythms of Paris, tries to be modern—at a distance. In this unlikely (but carefully chosen) point on the planet, global technology is revealed to be awkwardly local, and nature and culture are shown to be concepts in action rather than stable endpoints on an analytic grid. Concentrating on location, one encounters motion. Concentrating on space, one encounters place. Conceived in these terms, the vastness of modern heaven weighs heavily on the ground.

Figure 17.   Globe, CSG, 1994

PART 4

Worlds in Motion

"Geographies," said the Geographer, "are the books which, of all books, are most concerned with matters of conse- quence. They never become old-fashioned. It is very rarely that a mountain changes its position. It is very rarely that an ocean empties itself of its waters. We write of eternal things."

Antoine de Saint-Exupéry,
The Little Prince, *1943*

The first time I saw a live Ariane launch was on a battered black-and- white television in Cayenne. As fate or a programmer's joke would have it, the American film version of *Papillon* (dubbed back into French) was playing on the second of the two official channels then op- erating in French Guiana. Fascinated by this coincidence I switched back and forth as each story unfolded, the rows of concentrating men in light shirts under the fluorescent light of the present, the lines of marching men in striped clothing beneath the sun of the past. Tension grew in each narrative, but as the countdown neared and the men be- fore the terminals ceased their occasional asides and tightened their smiles, I stayed with the launch, watching the rocket slowly pull itself off the ground and up through the sky. Some twenty minutes (and not a few graphs) later, the satellite successfully separated from the last stage and headed for its lonely revolutions. The screen now filled with general applause and handshaking as the dignitaries and technicians stood up and began to clear off their consoles. As the live excitement died away, I turned to the other program, where a crowd of assembled convicts knelt in an open square before a guillotine. The condemned prisoner struggled; the blade fell. In a flash it sliced a head, spattering the camera with blood.

This fortuitous coincidence between the two poles of my subject— the simulated crossing of their central rituals within the space of one small screen—signifies nothing and yet reflects everything. Like the re- peated choice of Guyane as a land of experimentation, it is in essence arbitrary (the result of willful decision) and yet in practice echoes general principles (the logic of programming and historical construction of place). It is precisely in such a crossing between action and structure that the possibility of social science and modern thought is born. The arbitrary becomes normal and the random becomes essential; statistics bridge the gap between everyday affairs and significance, depriving fate and ritual of monopolies on meaning. Here the analysis will be qualitative rather than quantitative in form, but the movement will mimic the statistical operation of presenting inherently empty figures (like an average) as deeply revealing. The mimicry remains imperfect, of course, because the incident I have described was real—a product of experience rather than interpretation. Yet in the artifice of televised coexistence, we find a real act of representation, a revealing of structural meaning in the texture of a minor event. Between a machine's slow, calculated ascent skyward and the sudden, efficient fall of a human body lie rival impulses of modern life, and two alternative orders of displacement.

The following pages compare the penal colony and the space center on three levels. The first takes the task literally, noting structural similarities and differences between the two projects, as well as their respective relations to French Guiana. The second moves beyond each project to examine its relation to a different understanding of place, one caught between universal method and differentiated human profiles, the other between differentiated method and a universal sense of human nature. Finally, in the next chapter, the third level returns us to intersections between nature and technology in labor and the spatial implications of tropical development.

CHAPTER 7

Tropics of Nature

They still felt imprisoned, but prisoners now of this strange,
dumb forest, where in no direction could they look more
than a few feet ahead, this forest where thorns tore the flesh
and the clothing of men who would journey through it.
> *Blair Niles,* Condemned to Devil's Island, *1928*

The true wealth of Guyane is its nature—protect it.
> *Kris Wood, "Au delà du Spatial," 1995*

THE PENAL COLONY AND THE SPACE CENTER: A COMPARISON

We cannot help but to compare, *mutatis mutandis,* the
place and role of the penal administration in the
Guyanais economy a century ago to that of CSG [the
space center at present].

> *Serge Mam-Lam-Fouck,*
> Histoire de la Guyane contemporane, *1992*

From the perspective of the economic history of French Guiana, the
comparison of the penal colony and the space center appears inevitable.
Unlikely a pair as they may be, the two play similar roles as central
state projects, uneasily married to the rest of Guyanais society. As historian Serge Mam-Lam-Fouck points out, each created a settlement to
suit its needs, while contributing to the hollow nature of French
Guiana's economy.[1] Yet at the same time, there are significant differences in the practical administration of the penal colony and space center, and the rationale behind each project remains strikingly different.
Thus a comparison between the two gives us a frame within which to

Cayenne. — Forçats surpris par un Serpent boa.

Figure 18.   Convicts surprised by boa, ca. 1876

discuss shifting foci in French and European conceptions of modernization.

    To start with, let us briefly review the facts of each case. After a num-
ber of earlier trials, the penal colony begins operation in the middle of
the nineteenth century, partly as a substitute for a system of plantation
slavery. It conceives of French Guiana as open land for agricultural settlement, fertile ground for a tropical—and French—Australia, where
the action of moral reform can translate into a scheme of colonization.
Following a quest for the proper site within the colony, these early
hopes are belied by the high mortality of the convicts, particularly those
of European extraction. After an interlude where the flow of new bod-

ies is restricted to those of colonial origin, the operation resumes with an expanded mandate to rid France of its undesirable elements. Despite periodic calls for reform and increasing international discomfort, the *bagne* lasts through World War II. It leaves a deep mark on French Guiana, in both symbolic and material terms. As the movement of seventy thousand exiles progresses, the surrounding landscape shifts from a luxuriant field of dreams into a tableau of terror. At the same time, the colony as a whole grows accustomed to the presence of this artificial prison world within it, stumbling further down the road of economic dependence.

The space center begins operation in the second half of the twentieth century, in the midst of the Space Race and in the aftermath of the Algerian War. It conceives of French Guiana as open land for technical experiments and a gateway into equatorial orbit, an even more tropical—and French—Cape Canaveral. After an initial period of failure, a renewed pan-European launcher program produces a reliable rocket, and a regular stream of technicians and engineers arrives to assemble and guide it into space. The initial mandate to provide France with a launch site expands into a focus on commercial satellites, and although local opposition to the project continues, the effects of the enterprise on French Guiana in both symbolic and material terms only deepen. As the Ariane rocket gains importance, the surrounding landscape transforms from an orphan of history into a handmaiden of the future. At the same time, the department grows accustomed to an increased infusion of consumer goods, technical personnel, and immigrants, acquiring a new island with an artificial environment and a powerfully altered social profile.

At slightly closer range a number of striking structural similarities emerge. Not only do both projects found towns (St. Laurent on the one hand and the new Kourou on the other), but both operate as rival poles of influence and authority relative to the civil administration of French Guiana. Each involves the formation of a separate administrative body (the Administration Pénitentiare and the Centre Spatial Guyanais), with its own hierarchies, its own links to bureaucratic networks in Paris, and its own claims to significant national French interests. Each imports a population associated with its activities and exerts considerable influence over the surrounding economy. Most crucially, each controls and orders a separate territory within the larger political entity; each has a spatial presence, a direct impact on the landscape. And tied to this spatial strategy, each comes to serve as a symbolic nexus in collective Metropolitan imagination.

However, we can also point to strands of difference between the two projects, even within the outlines of their similarity. When the penal administration builds a new settlement at St. Laurent, it does so away from colonial settlements; when the space agency establishes a modern town at Kourou, it does so beside an existing hamlet. The penal colony operates opposite a colonial administration largely directed from Paris, whereas the space center operates opposite a more complex set of local as well as state political administrations. One employs leftover forces of law and order, whereas the other employs highly trained technical personnel; thus while both may have ties to the military, their strongest links lie at opposite ends of the chain of command. The penal colony imports the unwanted of France, whereas the space center imports the selected few. One, if anything, repels foreign immigration and is subject to international protest, whereas the other exerts a powerful attraction on neighboring populations and is subject to significant international cooperation. The penal administration controls a constellation of sites spread throughout French Guiana, whereas the space administration controls a more concentrated and defined domain. And the *bagne* reflects visions of an ancient underworld, whereas Ariane reflects visions of a new overworld.

One must also consider the difference in the general techniques involved. Penal transportation involves the direct use of human agents—the tools are bodies and populations. Rocket launching involves elaborate and expensive machinery as well as a skilled workforce—the tools are industrial materials ordered by knowledge. Each operation is predicated on a related but distinct spatial logic: the penal colony seeks open land to isolate and moralize convicts through labor, whereas the space center seeks open land to test rockets and maneuver satellites into orbit. Many of the specific additional attributes of a desirable site for penal colonization (distance from the Metropole, possibility of confinement and surveillance, and prevention of local disturbance) find echoes in the specific additional attributes of a desirable site for launching rockets (distance from the Metropole, adequate security, adequate possibility of transport, and political stability). But one final consideration in each case provides the crucial difference. For the penal colony, there remains the question of the appropriateness of climate for the new arrivals—a focus on qualities of place from the perspective of the ground—whereas for the space center, there remains the question of the proximity to the equator and possibility of both polar and equatorial launch—a focus on qualities of place from the perspective of the sky. This distinction warrants further elaboration, for the move between what I am calling earth and sky, empire and globe, describes a shift in relations between nature and technology and a sense of human position between locale and horizons. In this shift we find the edges of value sought by "development," the margins of a modernity that can endlessly transform, fracture, and yet continue, relentlessly consuming the future. To begin an elucidation of the processes at stake, let us first consider the matter of earthly place more closely.

EUROPEANS IN THE TROPICS

He is, or rather he believes himself to be, cosmopolitan; he dares to brave all the climates where other men can live, and his distant colonies constitute veritable experiments the results of which Science must study.

> *Paul Broca, cited in J. Orgeas,* La pathologie des races humaines et le problème de la colonisation, *1886*

In 1885 a French naval doctor by the name of J. Orgeas published a detailed monograph entitled *Contribution à l'étude du non-cosmopolitisme de l'homme: La Colonisation de la Guyane par la transportation: Etude historique et démographique* (Contribution to the study of the noncosmopolitanism of Man: The colonization of French Guiana by transportation: A historical and demographic study). The lengthy report—which had won the naval medicine prize three years earlier—examined mortality rates among convicts in the French Guiana penal colony, together with birth and infant mortality rates among the offspring of convict marriages. The conclusions to be drawn, Orgeas suggested, were clear and of import for all European efforts to settle in the tropics. The failure of Europeans to multiply in French Guiana was symptomatic of a wider, statistical, authenticated reality: "To pretend that Man is cosmopolitan, as seems to have been generally believed in the four centuries since the question was posed, is to pretend that he can live, work, cultivate the soil, and establish himself at all points on the globe; this thesis is not supportable, unless one categorically denies the authority of the most positive facts."[2]

Read a century later, Orgeas's statement is strikingly alien; not only does his conclusion fall flat in the face of contemporary international networks, but the very formulation of the problem verges on the absurd. How could humanity—Man, the conqueror of the Moon—be limited by as minor a factor as earthly geography? How could members of a species so dispersed, so mobile, so capable of transforming local environments, be confined by climate? And yet, in Orgeas's claim and our reaction to it we encounter a divide separating rival conceptions of nature and place and accompanying technologies for development. The rupture between a world in which the cosmopolitan possibilities of the human body could be in doubt and one in which they are taken for granted marks a significant threshold within the expansion of the modern world: the emergence of universal social space.

To better understand the distance between French Guiana's penal colony and its space center, one must focus on transformations in the experience of place for Europeans in each context. This shift is both physical and conceptual, the difference of living differently and of thinking differently. Against the image of the space engineer reflected in the tinted glass of an air-conditioned office, one must recall the colonial officer in full dress uniform beneath a midday sun. Against the ready assumptions of contemporary statistics and understandings of disease, one must remember the power of forgotten theories and the significance of former problems. Although the facts of the natural setting may not have altered in a drastic fashion, their human interpretation has, and the buffer of technology between the two (ambient temperature, say, and "heat") has been strikingly revised. The latter issue of the conceptual divide between nineteenth-century concerns and those of the present day is less intuitive than the transformation in material technology, and consequently I will treat it at length.

CONCEPTS OF CLIMATE AND RACE

Put a man into a close, warm place, and . . . he will
feel a great faintness. If, under this circumstance, you
propose a bold enterprise to him, I believe you will
find him very little disposed towards it; his present
weakness will throw him into despondency; he will be
afraid of everything, being in a state of incapacity. The
inhabitants of warm countries are, like old men, timo-
rous, the inhabitants of cold countries are, like young
men, brave.

> Baron Montesquieu,
> The Spirit of the Laws, 1748

To begin, let us revive Orgeas's problem, that of whether people and their customs have a natural habitat. Can one place human groups, or their ways of living, geographically? Are races or cultures directly tied to climates? These questions ring uneasily at present, burdened by the crude determinism they carry. But we should not forget that only a century ago they were taken quite seriously in scholarly circles; they constituted the frame for a real social problem, one subject to technical discussions. "Nature," in this sense, represented a different field, and in its relations to human life generated a more active geography. Travel over this map was not free or effortless; it involved great risk and dislocation. In colonizing, was not one leaving one's natural milieu and entering an unnatural natural environment?

Following the phrasing and emphasis of the era, the way we should ask the question is whether or not "The White Man" can live in "The Tropics." During the great period of European imperial expansion, we encounter strong doubts about the physical limits of European populations, about European bodies and their capacity to endure hot climates. How supple was the human form? Could anyone live anywhere? These questions, in and of themselves, were far from new.[3] However, with the advent of large-scale colonization, these concepts acquired technical importance; the issue of who can live where became a pragmatic as well as a speculative puzzle. Elaborate techniques developed to better acclimatize new arrivals, as well as to protect those already in place, while scientific debates over the effects of migration raged. Already in seventeenth-century New England a period of "seasoning" was identified, during which a debarking colonist required two years to adjust to the new milieu. By the nineteenth century the pith helmet became an essential article within the British colonial material repertoire, followed by the "spine pad," a quilted device to protect the delicate European nervous system from exposure to sunlight.[4] The colonial experience of place was further colored by geographical conceptions of illness. Many maladies prevalent in the tropics, including malaria, were associated with particular landscapes rather than with mosquitoes or other vectors of infection. In surveying and settling the ground, colonists designated locales as "healthy" or "unhealthy"; swampy lowlands were generally feared. The problem of inserting European settlers into a colony became one of finding a place for them to live—on top of a hill, say, or a location exposed to wholesome breezes. Statistics related to death rates found their interpretation in relation to sites; if a problem developed in a particular setting, the solution was to alter the characteristics of that setting—through draining or other improvements—or to move. When approaching the French Guiana case, we must remember this context: the very ability of Europeans to colonize the tropics was in question, even as Guyane came to represent a pernicious geographical extreme.

As described earlier, considerations of place played an important role in the early penal colony. Even after the selection of French Guiana as a general site of transportation, the issue of where best to establish actual penal settlements remained. When initial placement on the Iles du Salut proved successful, those islands were used as an acclimatization zone to season new arrivals. When the settlement at Montagne d'Argent proved deadly, it was relocated, and then other camps were opened and moved in turn, a process culminating in the creation of St. Laurent. Statistics played a key role in this process; the official reports are full of monthly mortality estimates and comparisons with annual averages. Any fluctuation that seemed favorable was quickly, eagerly reported.[5] However, the overall picture remained grim, and the Guiana penal colony's own statistics were turned against it in arguing for the redirection of European prisoners to New Caledonia. Two decades later, the same low death rate that had beckoned the Second Empire administration to choose New Caledonia as an alternative transportation site reversed significance amid the Third Republic's desire for retribution and urge to rid itself of undesirables. The emerging demographic language articulated old concerns: the fate of white settlers in specific alien environments. However, its evidence could be read in more than one way and used for more than one end.

Throughout the discussions of this period, race remained an essential category. Official tabulations carefully separated convicts on the basis of designated racial classifications and focused analytic attention on variations found between the resulting groups. The treatment of non-European convicts, especially those classified as black, differed from that of Europeans; by and large they received the more onerous labor assignments and were fed according to different dietary standards. In a setting where plantation slavery had been the norm, the laboring black body was taken to represent a certain standard, the tried and true equipment for hard work in hot climes. Unlike the sensitive European, a human of African descent was thought to be physically appropriate for the tropics and quite capable of subsisting on foods eaten by the surrounding population of former slaves (fish and manioc flour as opposed to meat and bread).

This focus on race in the administration of the penal colony has a lengthy genealogy, extending into concern over the fate of Europeans in French Guiana and on into more general accounts and justifications of Atlantic slavery, as well as into scientific debates about the mutability of species. As an entry into that wider frame and its relations to issues of place, let us recall the equivocating terms of that eighteenth-century master of climatic theory, Montesquieu:

There are countries where the heat enervates the body and renders men so slothful and dispirited that nothing but the fear of chastisement can oblige them to perform any laborious duty; slavery is there more reconcilable to reason, and the master being as lazy before his sovereign as his slave is with regard to him, this adds a political to a civil slavery. Aristotle endeavors to prove that there are natural slaves; but what he says is far from proving it. If there be any such, I believe they are those of whom I have been speaking. But, as all men are born equal, slavery must be accounted unnatural, though in some countries it be founded on natural reason; and a wide difference ought to be made between such countries, and those in which even natural reason rejects it, as in Europe where it has been so happily abolished.[6]

Here Montesquieu denies and affirms the logic of natural servitude in one and the same breath: "There are countries where the heat enervates the body . . . slavery is there more reconcilable to reason." Yet the key natural category invoked is environmental, not racial, because heat rather than descent per se produces the conditions of slavery. The distinction is important, for in it lies both ends of possibility leading to the penal colony. If the system of slavery in French Guiana is to be replaced, then it should be replaced by functional slaves. On the other hand, if convicts are to replace slaves, then they will—by virtue of the surrounding environment—become like slaves. In either case, Europeans play the role of Africans, and place rather than blood serves as the crucial factor. Humans may change (all are born equal), but for Montesquieu environments remain immutable.

A complex line of environmental reasoning can also be traced through the history of French biology, extending through Buffon and the crucial divide between Cuvier and Lamarck. It was under the influence of the last that the term *milieu* entered biological vocabulary in an active and plural way, dethroning static conceptions of climate and place. The relationship between organism and environment became decentered; space emerged between places, literally mi-lieu. The stage was set for the scientific investigation of the problem of "acclimatization."[7] French interests in biological acclimatization coalesced in the activities of a formal organization, the Société zoologique d'acclimatation, during the second half of the nineteenth century. More pragmatic than theoretical in inclination, the experiments of this society promoted interest in exotic animals and plants and helped to promote French colonial expansion, first informally and then formally. However, the activities of the acclimitization enthusiasts ran athwart the interests of a group of anthropologists, the Société d'anthropologie, and a fierce debate erupted in the early 1860s over the viability of acclimatization in a human setting. Led by Paul Broca and Jean Boudin,

the anthropologists favored the observation of measurable physical attributes (typified by Broca's craniometry) and took a more Cuvierian
line on racial determinism, maintaining that Europeans were incapable
of acclimating to the tropical colonies.[8] On the basis of figures taken
from European efforts to settle Algeria, Boudin argued in 1863 that
race crucially limited the range of human expansion. Far from being
"cosmopolitan," humans had a "limited faculty of acclimatization"
closely tied to race, a fact deserving of attention within the fields of
"medicine, public hygiene and political economy."[9] It is precisely this
debate into which we can place the work of our doctor Orgeas, while
keeping in mind that his writing takes shape one political generation
later, during the Third Republic, in the midst of a policy shift that
would produce the recidivist law of *relégation* and again send Europeans to French Guiana.

Before considering Orgeas's efforts more closely, let us summarize
and abstract the general principles involved. In the preceding passage
from Montesquieu we have one sense of nature—external forces conditioning the development of internal conditions and customs. In the act
of European colonial settlement we have a second understanding—external conditions transformable through the displacement of internal
forces. The process of acclimation represents a third, modified view, in
which internal mechanisms of an organism adjust over time to a new
terrain. Orgeas presents us with a fourth possibility—the incompatibil-
ity of particular internal conditions with particular external conditions.
In between these four natures we find the history of the penal colony.

ORGEAS AND THE NONCOSMOPOLITAN POSITION

Cosmopolitan: 3. Nat. Hist. Widely diffused over the
globe; found in all or many countries.
                    Oxford English Dictionary, *1989*[10]

Having established an initial context for Orgeas's *Contribution to the
Study of Noncosmopolitanism,* let us examine his argument more carefully. The first part of the work includes lengthy historical review of the
foundation of the penal experiment. In it Orgeas presents the terrible
statistics of the period of the 1850s, calculating that the life expectancy
of a convict on the Iles du Salut in 1855 was a meager one year, seven
months, and six days, and at Montagne d'Argent in 1856 a mere eight
months and fifteen days. Out of a total of 21,906 individuals transported to French Guiana between 1852 and the beginning of 1878 (a

figure including 399 women), a full 10,837 were dead, 10,306 from disease. The annual death rate attributed to natural afflictions in official documents fluctuated between 4.0 and 25.5 percent, as compared to New Caledonia's range of 0.8 to 5.61 percent.[11] Orgeas then proceeds through each penal installation within French Guiana, recounting aspects of its geography and history, before considering such general issues as diet and economic production.

In the second part of his *Contribution,* Orgeas presents a demographic study of this episode of penal colonization, beginning with marriage. He finds 418 cases of convict marriage, 371 between individuals of European descent.[12] Noting the tendency of convicts to marry members of their own race (which he attributes to a "law of ethnic affinity"), he proceeds to analyze the productivity of these marriages, finding that out of the 403 children born to them, 24 were dead at birth, 238 had expired afterward, 40 had left the colony, and only 101 were still alive and in place. He calculates the mortality rate for children between two and three years of age born at St. Laurent to be three times as high as in France. Thus the statistical evidence of the Guiana case, Orgeas argues, plainly indicates that Europeans fare poorly in such an environment. Male children in particular failed to survive, a pattern he believes to be general to the tropics. He closes with a reference to France's prime colonial rivals: "In India, the English government has attempted, in every way possible, to increase the marriages of its soldiers with English women; despite all these efforts, we know that it has never been possible, to follow the expression of Major-General Bagnold, to raise enough male children to recruit a fife and drum corps."[13]

In a second work published a year later, *La pathologie des races humaines et le problème de la colonisation: Etude anthropologique et économique faite à la Guyane française* (The pathology of human races and the problem of colonization: An anthropological and economic study conducted in French Guiana), Orgeas expanded his efforts, comparing the kinds and frequencies of diseases experienced by different racial groups in French Guiana. This time he also made the policy implications of his research clear: colonial efforts to establish settler colonies in the tropics were doomed to failure on scientific grounds. Persisting in this direction would only lead to a costly fiasco or the creation of a parasite colony forever dependent on the motherland, a place "where the metropolitan budget maintains all the officials, and where one is much less *exploiter* than *exploited.*"[14]

The general conclusions of *La pathologie* are worth repeating at length, for they clearly delineate the "noncosmopolitan position."

Orgeas lays them forth as ten principles, relating the physical character of human races, labor, and climate.

1. Similar to the vast majority of animals and vegetables, Man, the most complex of beings alive, is not cosmopolitan. He cannot change his latitude and climate with impunity.

2. A human collectivity, considered in its totality, cannot subsist without spending a certain sum of muscular activity and without exposing itself, to a certain extent, to the action of elements of the climate.

3. A European collectivity passing from temperate climates into torrid climates, by crossing the hot climate zone that represents an isothermic gap of ten degrees, is incapable of providing the sum of necessary muscular activity for its subsistence; it is incapable of confronting life by its own force, or of forming a social organism unto itself. Nature will cause Europeans living under these conditions to disappear rapidly. This fact is irrevocably attested to by experience.

4. Europeans living an artificial life in torrid climates, sheltered from the climatic elements, in the position of a privileged minority in the middle of indigenous races, can subsist for a longer or shorter period. But the anthropological character of these Europeans is not in harmony with this milieu, and the action of the climate on their organism is constant, worsening over time for each individual and from generation to generation in descent. Maintained indefinitely in torrid climates, the resistance of the white race would be limited to a very small number of generations, under the best conditions of artificial life. These are exceptional facts that should not be generalized.

5. The constant high temperature of the ambient milieu is the main pathological factor of the anemia that the European cannot escape in torrid climates and plays an immense role in general biological phenomena.

6. Muscular work is a secondary serious pathological factor of anemia. Consequently, muscular work has considerable influence over the progressive development of this physiological downfall and, as a result, on the duration of the resistance of the European race.

7. Negroes and races adapted to torrid climates escape anemia, thanks to anatomo-physiological particularities that are as much ethnic characteristics, and by a physiological mechanism that scientific analysis is not powerless to explain.

8. Races from torrid climates are protected by their pathological characters against the invasion of their habitat and the vital competition of races from temperate climates, better armed than they in the struggle for life. In the current state of the world, torrid climate races would be condemned to disappear if laws of nature did not preserve their existence.

9. Europeans will ever only be a tiny minority in the midst of indigenous races of torrid climates. The races of these climates cannot disappear, either before Europeans, or before their half-castes. The half-castes can dis-

appear. They would decrease rapidly if Europeans lost political domination (Haiti). They would disappear surely, by the rules of natural selection and vital competition, if all new contribution of European blood came to cease completely.

10. The physical characters of races from torrid climates, from which derive the pathological and physiological characters that are particular to these races, constitute conditions of adaptation to their milieu. The variation that the action of torrid climates imparts to Europeans and their descendants is only a pathological and fleeting variation, ending fatally with the extinction of the race, and not a physiological and permanent variation, deciding the adaptation of the race to the new climatic milieu. As far as the field of our observation spreads through the past of humanity, never has a race, by changing latitude of climate, presented a physiological and permanent variation due to the action of the milieu. Acclimatization does not exist: never has a race acclimatized and, in the current state of the world, never will a race acclimatize.[15]

Here we have a set of clear connections and oppositions between place and race: once adapted to a climatic milieu one is relatively limited. The organism cannot go through radical transformation; selection works relentlessly within a specified milieu. Acclimatization—and hence the possibility of cosmopolitan life, or settler colonization across climatic zones—is revealed as the philosopher's stone of biology.

EVALUATING ORGEAS

It would be easy to dismiss Orgeas's mammoth effort as an odd anachronism, a relic from an openly racist age. Certainly its claims serve to reinforce a European world hierarchy, suggesting that the imperial status quo of its day had all the inevitability of a natural arrangement. Within colonial settings the image of the tropically impotent European, requiring the labor of properly adapted others to survive, echoes arguments used to justify slavery. And yet we should not lose sight of the fact that this is a serious intellectual endeavor. The meticulous nature of Orgeas's evidence is impressive in both his tomes. His is a thorough, not a hurried, attempt to generalize. I emphasize this not to advocate his conclusions but rather to stress that the problem before him is real—that is to say, that the observed phenomena, however constructed, are not fabricated. Whether or not the official numbers he cites are perfectly accurate, there is little question that Europeans in French Guiana, and particularly those in the penal colony, died at impressive rates.

To better articulate the dilemma, let us take a sample set of statistics related to the French Guiana *bagne*, for the critical period between its founding in 1852 and the decision to send European convicts to New Caledonia in 1867. Here I will adopt the figures given in a document composed by a military officer in 1868, which correspond to those of Orgeas in most respects, differing primarily in that they include the small number of deaths designated as "accidental" as well as those attributed to disease.[16]

Glancing over the figures before us (table 1), we see the average population during a given year, the number of new arrivals, the number of officially recorded deaths, the total loss of population (including escapes and liberations), the official mortality rate, and Orgeas's mortality rate restricted to deaths by disease. Over the initial fifteen-year period, the penal colony produced an average annual death rate of 10.75 percent (Orgeas's restricted figure is 10.37 percent). Every year, approximately one out of ten convicts died.

TABLE 1   PENAL COLONY DEMOGRAPHICS, 1852–1866

	Average Population	New Arrivals	Deaths	Total Loss	Mortality in %	Mortality in Orgeas in %
1852	1,500	2,033	79	117	5.26	4.8
1853	2,703	1,017	522	561	19.31	19.2
1854	2,689	691	247	292	9.14	9.1
1855	2,954	1,224	769	849	26.06	25.5
1856	3,702	2,007	912	1,382	24.63	24.5
1857	4,139	1,040	348	516	8.41	8.4
1858	4,400	1,001	386	544	8.77	8.1
1859	5,177	1,245	537	795	10.37	9.9
1860	5,597	848	476	671	8.50	8.3
1861	6,376	1,501	535	770	8.39	8.0
1862	6,139	561	486	673	7.91	7.6
1863	6,233	1,069	394	857	6.32	5.7
1864	6,512	1,608	300	590	4.29	4.0
1865	7,595	1,152	428	741	5.63	5.2
1866	7,500	1,030	616	1,100	8.21	7.2
Total	—	18,027	7,035	10,458	—	—
Average	4,881				10.75	10.37

For comparison's sake, let us turn to other, independent sets of records. The period between 1834 and 1847, the last years of the slave colony, witnessed some accounting of death rates among both the free and slave populations. A summary of figures assembled by Serge Mam-Lam-Fouck runs as follows:[17]

TABLE 2   SLAVE AND FREE MORTALITY
IN FRENCH GUIANA, 1834–1847

	Slave Population	Slave Mortality in %	Free Population	Free Mortality in %
1834	17,136	3.15	4,947	3.42
1835	16,898	2.62	5,058	2.75
1836	16,592	3.15	5,056	3.70
1837	16,140	3.80	5,081	3.66
1838	15,751	3.22	5,189	4.99
1839	15,516	2.88	5,654	3.08
1840	15,285	3.11	5,697	3.12
1841	14,883	3.62	5,746	3.74
1842	14,560	3.41	5,805	3.05
1843	14,180	4.08	5,820	3.69
1844	13,988	2.62	5,902	2.69
1845	13,834	2.70	5,961	3.36
1846	13,375	2.79	6,171	2.75
1847	12,943	2.70	6,432	2.41
Average		3.13		3.32

Glancing over these figures several patterns immediately emerge. First of all, the recorded rates of death among the slave and free segments of the population are not remarkably different, although the average figure for the free population is higher (3.32 percent as opposed to 3.13 percent). Second, if we take the lowest mortality rate recorded for the early penal colony (4.0 percent), we find it exceeded only twice during the slave era, in 1838 among the free population (4.99 percent) and in 1843 among slaves (4.08 percent). The differences between the averages (10 percent against 3 percent) is even more striking. While one must treat all these statistics with caution, given the circumstances and interests involved, it seems that the death rates common to the *bagne* probably did represent a significant increase over the norms of slavery, and that earlier European immigrants to French Guiana were dying at a rate equivalent to or slightly higher than that of slaves.[18]

For another pole of comparison we have Philip Curtin's analysis of records of European troops stationed overseas in the early part of the nineteenth century. During the period between 1817 and 1838, mortality among these groups ranged from lows of 0.86 percent for the British in New Zealand and 0.95 percent for the French in Tahiti to highs of 16.46 percent for the French in Senegal, 17.0 percent for the Dutch in the Dutch East Indies, and an astonishing figure of 48.3 percent for the British in Sierra Leone.[19] The figures for the Caribbean region are as follows:[20]

TABLE 3   MORTALITY OF TROOPS IN THE
WEST INDIES, 1817–1836

	Nationality	Mortality in %
Jamaica	British	13.00
Windward and Leeward Islands	British	8.50
Guadeloupe	French	10.69
Martinique	French	11.22
French Guiana	French	3.22

Glancing over this initial comparative sample, the most surprising fact is that French Guiana—for all its evil reputation—displays the lowest rate of death, significantly below the equivalent figures for Martinique and Guadeloupe. While the dramatic variation in the mortality rates reported and further issues with the samples reported urge a measure of caution, it nevertheless seems clear that the average rate of 10 percent for the penal colony fits well within the range of early-nineteenth-century death rates for European troops in the Caribbean. An archival tabulation by Richard Price for Moravian missionaries in neighboring Suriname reinforces these findings, calculating an eighteenth-century death rate of 36 percent for arrivals "seasoned" on the coast and an astounding 80 percent for those fresh from Europe.[21] In general, then, it would appear that the penal colony, while deadly by the standards of the early-nineteenth-century slave colony on the same soil, was about par for the course by the standards of concentrated groups of European in the region (and throughout the tropics) during that period. The outlines of Orgeas's work appear to hold.

The noncosmopolitan claim also finds support in the general observation that French immigrants to the northern climes of Canada prospered and reproduced, unlike those arriving in French Guiana.[22] Similarly, the British penal colony in Australia, while perhaps not the "success" imagined by its French admirers, played a role in establishing an expanding immigrant population, whereas French efforts in Guyane utterly failed. Surveying the landscape of European colonial expansion, Alfred Crosby observes that large "neo-Europe" settler colonies only took root in temperate areas: North America, Australia, New Zealand, and South Africa.[23] Orgeas's opposition to acclimatization acquires a measure of empirical legitimacy.

And yet something has changed over the century separating us from the anthropology of our naval doctor. A variety of cosmopolitanism, the bane of Orgeas, has become an assumption, if not for all people in the world, then at least for most descendants of Europe, the very parties warned against it. Rather than represent a zone of danger and potential death, the tropics suggest vacations and escape for refugees of northern winters. The pith helmet has been replaced by the lawn chair, as sunlight soothes European nerves rather than destroys them. Properly equipped and inoculated, the modern tourist can go anywhere. In this banal observation lie the quiet ends of a vast spatial reconfiguration.

THE NEW TROPICS

To situate the place surrounding the space center, we must measure its distance from the place surrounding the penal colony. In one sense the two environments are very similar—in that they contain comparable elements—yet in another sense they are worlds apart. This becomes clearer if we continue our simpleminded demographic voyage and look at Philip Curtin's report on mortality rates among European troops overseas in the early twentieth century.[24] The difference is striking; the range falls between such lows as those of Americans in Hawaii (0.13 percent) and the British in Cyprus (0.17 percent) and such highs as those of the French in Morocco (2.20 percent) and Germans in Cameroon (4.11 percent), a significant recalibration from the early nineteenth century. The figures for the Caribbean are as follows:[25]

TABLE 4   MORTALITY OF TROOPS IN THE
WEST INDIES, 1909–1913

	Nationality	Mortality in %
Jamaica	British	0.78
French Antilles	French	0.49
Cuba and Puerto Rico	U.S.	0.36

Within this small sample we notice a remarkable decline in European death rates throughout the area. The mortality given for the French territories (0.49 percent) is a far cry from the figures recorded a century earlier (10.69 percent, 11.22 percent, and 3.22 percent); the frequency of tropical death has shrunk to as little as one-twentieth the former rate.

Between these two sets of statistics lies a crucial divide, one of the major gaps separating European empires of the eighteenth and twentieth centuries. The latter part of the nineteenth century saw numerous changes in the treatment of bodies and populations in the West. We can identify the advent of most modern forms of knowledge and the coalescing of contemporary professional and academic disciplines. Planning begins to reshape the urban landscape, public health measures begin to map and control illness, and numerous legal interventions extend the scope and purview of bureaucratic agencies concerned with welfare. Most crucially for us, Western medical regimes underwent a dramatic transformation, abandoning their long fixation with "climates" and "humors" for a germ theory of disease, even as nutritional norms changed alongside conceptions of proper environments. The emergence of tropical medicine and attention to social welfare in colonial settings created new bureaucratic structures and complex fields of representation within empire. In the process a significant frame of experience changed: general mortality declined, general hygienic conditions improved, and general population figures soared. The tropics had been domesticated.

Lest the picture grow too simple or triumphal, we should note that the impulses driving European modernization did not simply emanate from centers and fan out. The search for solutions to the great diseases threatening colonial populations itself affected medical history. Debates between those who attributed infection to contagion and those who attributed it to environmental conditions raged around such tropical standbys as malaria, cholera, and yellow fever, the first of which, we should not forget, was also endemic to parts of North America and Europe and the second of which could sweep back to Metropolitan centers with frightening speed. Research and experimental measures pursued in the colonies, usually under the direction of military physicians, provided a field against which new medical and public health practices could emerge. Elaborate technical measures developed, including such tactics as the removal of European populations to high elevations (such as hill stations), the draining of swamps, and the avoid-

ance of certain areas, on the one hand, and the isolation of infected pa-
tients, mosquito control, and the use of quinine, on the other. Between
environmental hygiene measures and the identification of mosquito
vectors, a new terrain of medical procedure suddenly came into focus,
with dramatic clinical success. Even if none of these afflictions were
eradicated (indeed, malaria remains a leading cause of death in the
tropical world), they had become subject to control. The tropics, once
domesticated, could now be administered. And this reconfiguration of
the medical landscape also altered the range of possible understandings
of the natural landscape, allowing that which had threatened to become newly alluring.[26]

The dramatic drop in tropical disease and death makes the context
of the later penal colony clearer. Although the mortality of convicts fit
easily with the death rates of European troops early in the nineteenth
century, it stood out in sharp relief against similar rates in the twentieth century. Even in the 1920s, the mortality rate in the *bagne* hovered
between 6 and 11 percent.[27] Thus the penal colony reflected an earlier
world of colonization, a ghostly domain in which anachronistic
norms held. When one lacked adequate nutrition or medical care and
worked in confined and oppressive conditions, the tropics could still
be deadly. In this small, circumscribed space, an evil climate prevailed,
and with it an archaic, biological hell, artificially maintained as a natural enclosure.

In contrast, the space center lies amid the new, modern tropics of the
twentieth century, warm climes of tourism and retirement. The heat and
light, the flora and fauna, and the temperature and humidity remain similar to those extant in the nineteenth century, but all are effectively neutralized. Beyond the generalized intervention of sanitation, refrigeration, and
mosquito control, an individual traveler has recourse to numerous personal technologies: dark glasses, individually prescribed medicines, and
common ointments to ward off insects or protect against sun. The particular landscape remains as exotic as ever to the European visitor, but the
sense of dread lies at a remove. After all, the mortality rate in French
Guiana clocked in at a mere 0.47 percent in 1991.[28] What was once deadly
is now a small thrill or a minor annoyance. The experience of place can—
if properly equipped—occur at a slight remove. Recalling the acclimatization debates confronting Orgeas, let us not forget the French term for air-
conditioning, *climatisation*. In the cool, refreshing waves of recirculated
air, Orgeas's impossible Cosmopolitan Man found a mobile home.

WILD ENVIRONMENT, HUMAN HERITAGE

The forest is a complex spatial ecosystem comparable
to a cathedral.

World Wildlife Fund, Panda, *1988*

Don't break the feeling you know, 100%.

English motto of a boat
on the Maroni River, 1994

To be sure, French Guiana represents an exception to some of the dominant themes of what here goes under the name of the "modern tropics." Relative to the massive resort systems dominating the Caribbean,
tourism in Guyane remains at an inconsequential level, and without the
compelling seashore or vistas available elsewhere, the terrain is unlikely
to draw the mass market. Rather, it appeals to those seeking a taste of
adventure, the wild edge of travel. For the most part these consumers
come from Europe, whether for a short tourist visit or a longer stay attached to family or professional occupation. By all accounts the vast
majority of those traveling into the interior (beyond those small populations, primarily Amerindian or Maroon, still significantly installed
there, and Brazilian and other gold miners) are Metros, not coastal
Guyanais. In my own informal survey of three tours I met one older
Creole gentleman on a weekend excursion, but he had lived in Paris for
some two decades and was married to a Parisian woman. Otherwise
the tourists were all authentically "Metro," being of European extraction *and* coming from urban areas. Given other accounts of wilderness
this pattern is not surprising; however, it merits further examination because it reflects a major shift in Western interactions with nature.[29]

Let us briefly explore two twentieth-century understandings of
place: that of the wilderness experience and that of the threatened environment. To call them "twentieth-century understandings" is not to
imply that they lack lineages extending well into the past; rather, it is to
roughly identify a moment of culmination, a point at which these view-
points achieve a currency that establishes a basic framework of debate.
The past hundred years have witnessed the emergence and spread of a
modern folk sense of ecology, alongside professional investigations
based on biological milieu. However partial, however incomplete, this
folk sense establishes the conceptual norms of official discussion. Public parks, national forests, hunting regulation, and environmental monitoring no longer represent the unexpected, and while their specific

Figure 19.   Tour boat, 1994

implementation may excite controversy, the possibility of their existence rarely does. A concern for nature has become natural.

This general term linking wilderness and environment—*nature*—has a
long and complicated history.[30] From a sense of birth or essence, the like-
ness of a thing, its meaning grew, moving to include the set of forces inherent in the world and widening to include everything in it. The
identification of an opposing category, *culture,* distinguished an abstract
figure of humanity (the one historically known as *Man*): a collective
being who is of nature and yet thinks nature, who lives in the world and
yet defines it. Along the tense outline of this human figure we find the
field of anthropology. In motion between nature and culture we find the
emergence of a self-consciously modern world, one in which life could be
lived outside of seasons, in which gardening could be a form of leisure, in
which landscape could become a focus of art and travel, in which bodies
and their functions could be clothed in intricate and distant rituals, in
which humans could imagine themselves separate from the universe they
imagine, and then finally in which humans could desire to free themselves
from the very bonds they themselves have created.

So what is wilderness to the adventurous modern? More specifically, what does tropical wilderness offer Europeans who have made their way to French Guiana? In the words of a tourist brochure, a "marvelous adventure," consisting of "beautiful and diverse landscapes" and "original populations."[31] The forest and the rivers leading into it promise an escape in the form of leisure coupled with a taste of another world. In addition to freelance operators and occasional group outings, a number of small companies (three in 1992–1994) provide a fairly regular service of organized tours from Cayenne and Kourou, ranging in length from day excursions to nearby sites to extended trips of a week or more to remote areas. The numbers involved are very small, at most a few thousand persons a year. Yet, other than alternative outdoor pleasures such as hunting or waterskiing and trips to the Iles du Salut and other coastal sites of interest, exploration of the interior represents one of the more significant leisure options available in French Guiana. It also carries with it the allure of authenticity: by going into the forest, by leaving civilization behind, one discovers the "real Guyane."

The place of nature within the field of consumption in contemporary French Guiana comes more sharply into focus when we return to the space center. In addition to other technical matters, CSG must consider the care of its *matériel humain,* particularly those employees "detached" from Europe, who, when not working, find themselves at loose ends far from the places they consider home. This limbo condition is even worse for the visiting *missionnaire* working for non-French organizations, who is, in a sense, effectively marooned on an island—far from a familiar language or expected services, languishing night after night in an efficiently dull hotel room. To attend to the needs of the *missionnaire,* CSG created an organization in 1985 known as Free Lance Service; the service offers translation, improvises solutions to unforeseen individual problems (for example, a change of sheets and towels during a hotel strike), and provides a "bungalow" (the classic colonial fortress) where visitors can relax and socialize.[32]

Free Lance Service also tries to provide entertainment to fill the stretches of "dead time" surrounding working hours. A key component of this enterprise involves excursions to places of local interest and the improvisation of outdoor activities, often involving "local" exotic cuisine and liberal consumption of alcohol. And it is precisely in this domain that the organization has discovered that cultural difference becomes significant and affects daily routine. Groups of visiting engineers and other clients from different countries have different attitudes toward the landscape and the possible pleasures it might provide. The

Japanese, in Free Lance's array of functional stereotypes, present a particular problem, because they require a constant stream of organized activities arranged for them, always in groups. In addition, they express a "horror" of the forest and insects and little interest in any cuisine other than their own, which eliminates a large part of the usual repertoire of distractions. By contrast the Americans are thought much easier to please, often improvising their own entertainment, be it floating down the Kourou River in truck tires or organizing a game of baseball. A group of Canadians, who "greatly resemble Americans," once even brought ice hockey equipment with them and played a modified game in a hotel parking lot. European space scientists (predictably compared to an absentminded professor in the Tintin cartoon series) love nothing better than to wander about the forest, threatening to blunder into disaster at every turn. Despite the differences between them, these visitors share a common condition: they are urban technicians, not "adventurers." They know little about the place where they are, and they often feel disoriented and uncertain. They require guidance of the sort that Free Lance Service provides in order to properly enjoy their stay and also "make the acquaintance" of Guyane. The act of coming to "know" Guyane, however, is also a crucial part of both short- and long-term activities associated with the space center. As mentioned earlier, the program of every launch visit includes either a trip to the islands or an afternoon in an "authentic" forest setting. For longer-term personnel and the friends and relatives who visit them, a trip to the interior constitutes a pilgrimage of sorts, an essential experience of place.[33]

One of the more popular trips to take—if not the most taxing or daring—is a voyage up or down the Maroni River. The river journey is usually taken in one direction only, with the return trip made via regional airline. On the river a large canoe provides transportation, ably maneuvered by Maroon boatmen, while a guide offers commentary and leads short trips into the encampments of Amerindians and Maroons living along the shore as well as into the primary forest beyond. The tourists are encouraged to buy local artifacts from people and discouraged from photographing anything other than the landscape. An appropriately exotic menu is served, liberally accompanied by alcohol.[34] The voyage forms a tableau of encounters between people in the boat and the natural surroundings and people in the boat and people out of the boat. A landscape that signifies wilderness mingles with a landscape that recalls third-world destitution, all around a vessel of first-world adventurers, who dutifully don life preservers for every set of rapids. Some of the cultural context and human relations grow bare in an evening scene: the inner circle of lighter faces engaged in avid discussion of world relations, the outer circle of darker faces listening in silence, *bananes flambées* in rum for dessert, blue flames rising from metal mess plates.

Tours such as these, including less formal excursions and hunting trips, constitute a significant symbol of "being there" for the Europeans in French Guiana. Along with practices like eating exotic game in restaurants or acquiring local artifacts (other popular pastimes), these actions testify to the accumulation of local knowledge, the process of becoming experienced in the local setting. For some they may also echo a deeper longing, a search for purity beyond the bounds of civilization. Certainly the history of the European exploration is far from over, even if maps can now be drawn from space. A number of unusual characters find their way into the nooks and crannies of Guyane's backcountry, living out their frontier dreams.[35] While many tourists view the river and forest merely as backdrops for aesthetic pleasure, a deeper identification with the natural environment and concern for its preservation has begun to emerge in French Guiana, both in areas of the public discourse and particularly within elements of the European population.

Reflecting increased environmental concerns elsewhere, the dominant language used to talk about nature in Guyane has shifted considerably over the past half century. The fierce jungle images of the penal colony have given way to descriptions of a fragile preserve under threat from every direction. The forest itself is now a treasure, part of the official *patrimoine* (heritage) of Guyane, of France, and of all humanity. It must be carefully studied, tended, and guarded for the future. Like tropical rain forests everywhere, it represents a reservoir of "biodiversity," a wealth of genetic material crying out for conservation. This reversal of view is most succinctly captured in the 1990 introductory issue of an activist environmental newsletter. Twisting the conflicting myths of French Guiana, it presents two maps of the department, one labeled *"L'Enfer Vert"* (Green Hell) and the other *"L'Eden Vert"* (Green Eden). The first depicts a landscape of pollution, hunting, gold mining, and roads, whereas the second offers an alternative vision of solar energy, rivers, and animal preserves. What was once valued becomes a curse; what was once cursed becomes valuable.[36]

The general ecological perspective finds fuller description in a 1988 special issue of a magazine published by the French branch of the international organization WWF (then the World Wildlife Fund and now the Worldwide Fund for Nature). The introductory editorial is by a prominent veterinarian, a leading member of one of the older and more established environmental organizations, who later became Guyane's first official representative in charge of environmental matters. In it he notes that French Guiana not only represents an "inestimable heritage [*patrimoine*]," but is perhaps the only tropical area that combines a high level of development with low population density and thus offers particularly favorable conditions for preservation. At the same time, however, it remains the only land without protected areas for wildlife or hunting restrictions, a place where forest concessions for logging are free or even subsidized, and where unpaved roads are built in hopes of luring more people to the interior. Arguing for an alternative vision of the future based on nature tourism, the author criticizes the short-sighted view of local politicians:

> What to think of a country, lacking mineral resources or significant agriculture, which squanders the only wealth in its possession without the slightest profit? What to think of those "responsible" officials, who recognize the interest of such an option in the socio-economic conditions of the country, but who continue to think that a vast, untouched forest is a sign of underdevelopment, a blemish to erase?[37]

When, he wonders, will the government explore "realistic and modern possibilities of development, well removed from poorly adapted classic schemes"? When will local officials explain to the populace that a standing tree or a living animal has far more value than some "boards" or "kilos of meat"? And why not "dream of the day when, these economic realities having been admitted, other values can be discussed as well"?

In the years following the publication of this editorial, the environmental movement in French Guiana has met with mixed success. On the one hand, it has managed to establish a degree of official recognition and to disseminate certain general ideas (not only are there annual "environment days," but even the space center hired an environmental consultant). On the other hand, the major patterns of behavior in the department remain relatively unchanged (emerging hunting regulations lack enforcement, and park plans are mired in controversy, while the population continues to soar), and any focus on ecology rather than development rouses strenuous opposition.[38] While Europeans do not exclusively compose the membership of the several environmental groups active in French Guiana, many of the prominent figures identified with ecological activism are Metro, and part of the impulse to preserve the forest of Guyane comes from Metropolitan France. At certain points, as we shall see, this European cast of ecology runs athwart the interests of Creoles who favor greater political autonomy and economic independence for Guyane.

Ecological activists also have an uneasy relationship with the most prominent pole of European presence in French Guiana, the space center. On the one hand, theirs is not a simple case of opposition, for while rockets and engine tests produce pollutants, and the fuel stockpiles of the base open the possibility of a widespread disaster, overall the Ariane program poses less of a direct environmental threat than most forms of industry. As witnessed earlier, a strain of environmental consciousness has entered the public presentation of the Guiana Space Center, and space officials make much of the work of satellites monitoring the environment. On the other hand, the indirect effects of the space center are significant and—from an ecological perspective— highly destabilizing. The space program bears much responsibility for Guyane's demographic explosion and fosters the spread of artificial environments and a culture of consumption. The entire space enterprise, large, bureaucratic, and perpetually removed from its locale, runs counter to ecological principles of rooting deeply and carefully in place.

The perspective of those concerned about the environment finds succinct expression in the following short review of the significance of space in French Guiana's history:

> Natural Guyane, barely threatened before the success of Ariane, is now a victim of this success. The population of 1964 has tripled in large part due to immigration, because of calls for a qualified workforce that did not exist in French Guiana and the rumor of well-paid jobs there. Demographic pressure increases the threat to the natural patrimony—roads, dams, rice paddies, allotments . . . hunting, harvesting, and garden plots by those who remain beyond the margins of the job market. The cultural patrimony has also suffered, because to ensure the social peace, in order that Ariane leaves on time, the French government, extolling equality, has weakened Creole, Amerindian, and Maroon cultural systems. . . . We consume and thus become consumers. . . . So this France, that in thirty years has conquered the space market with its wisdom and its feats of prowess, what does it do in Guyane to protect nature and its inhabitants? These ecosystems that are so well supervised on high by satellites—are they protected here on the ground? Not at all. Or hardly. . . . Reserves without guardians are not worth the paper on which they are delimited. What a contrast with space! . . . In French tourist lounges one speaks of protected areas, while species said to be protected are served on the tables of prestigious restaurants in Cayenne. Agreed, Ariane must depart on time . . . but the time to protect nature has also arrived. . . . We simply ask that the protection of the environment in Guyane is pursued with the same rigor, competence, and level of seriousness as the space program.[39]

Idealism and realism mix; while acknowledging the weight of the technology of the future, the article presses its hope for the future of nature.

It recognizes that the real law of this particular jungle is now that of space: "Ariane must depart on time." In following this law, humans built the space center and altered the landscape; in extending this law in new and unexpected ways, humans may save Guyane. Might not the modern genie, once out of the bottle, work more than one magic? Such is the hope of the article's author. The efficiency, the exactitude that finds expression in the space program should also be applied to the preservation of nature; the same power that extended human reach beyond the globe should now return and tend the garden, allowing it to grow again in peace.

Such ecological writing reflects a cosmopolitan sensibility that is planetary in scope. Within it, the refound Eden of French Guiana emerges as a particularly tender space of environmental longing: the great forest, the tropical sea of trees. Forests have a long history in the symbolic landscape of Europe, their branches sheltering dark possibilities of origin and wild voids that humans must cross to find the safety of each other's hearths.[40] The act of reshaping shadows beyond the firelight, of straightening paths of human action, forms a root metaphor of civilization. Witness the opening of one French history text:

> At the dawn of history our country bore large and dense forests. . . . Our ancestors' first struggle was against the forest. The profoundly man-made and variegated character of our soil is the result of an effort of conquest made upon the forest over thousands of years. . . . The land that nourishes us has been in a large part created by the hand of man. . . . Thus different regions were defined, tribes rooted themselves and local customs were born. Ancient frontiers were not lines but sterile areas or those difficult to penetrate. Those parts of primitive forest which took man longest to clear remained the real boundaries of province from province.[41]

European culture in the broadest sense—agriculture, an ordered sentiment of place—was built against the forest. Along the edge of the wild wood lies civilization and the limits of history. Through the trees we glimpse not only human reflections but also the possibilities of other worlds. Fear, hope, and nostalgia beckon, in amid the leaves.

And what of the tropical forest, the natural space of the equator, the exotic climate of certain difference? In a Guyanais schoolbook collection, originally published in 1915, we find a surprising description—neutral, accurate, yet nonetheless steeped in feeling for that other, earlier space, the vast expanse of the forest. For all the additional revolutions of the globe since its writing, for all the shifting of human horizons, the words remind us that wilderness too escapes simple confines of location:

When a painter of Europe wants to represent a virgin forest, he draws immense trees with knotty trunks, covered with parasites; lianas embrace these giants, like snakes in the group of Laocoön, or fall down their fronts, like untied hair. A bizarre vegetation covers a tormented ground, over which the gazelle plays, the snake slips, and the tiger crouches. On branches, monkeys, these perfected Léotards [acrobats], practice gymnastics. Parrots chat in the foliage. All this is most picturesque without a doubt, and offers varied resources to the drawing and its coloring. Too, each artist can, following his taste and imagination, create his own virgin forest. Nature, she has created only one, of the same grandiose monotony as that of the ocean. Imagine: on all sides, as far as the eye can see, spreads an innumerable army of gigantic trunks, smooth and straight as masts of a vessel, rushing up one hundred feet in the air. You walk for entire days, and you forever meet other trunks, so similar to the preceding ones that you cannot tell whether you have advanced a single step, or if you have gone in a circle, returning to your point of departure. Above your head, at a great height, a dome of greenery that never sheds its leaves and that is never pierced by a ray of sunlight; under your feet, a ground without vegetation and as clear as a park alley: here is the virgin forest, that which in Guyane we call the *Grand-Bois* [Great Wood]. Nothing opposes the step of the traveler who advances as through an endless colonnade. He walks and walks without ceasing, as if intoxicated by the continuity of sensations, and when he stops, alone, lost in this immense solitude, in the middle of this great silence, he experiences that feeling of sadness into which we are thrown by the thought of infinity.[42]

CHAPTER 8

The Nature of Work

"Do you see that?" said the Djinn. "That's your very own
humph that you've brought upon your very own self by not
working. To-day is Thursday, and you've done no work since
Monday, when the work began. Now you are going to
work."

"How can I," said the Camel, "with this humph on my
back?"

"That's made a-purpose," said the Djinn, "all because you
missed those three days. You will be able to work without
eating, because you can live on your humph; and don't you
ever say I never did anything for you."

Rudyard Kipling, Just So Stories, *1912*

THE MORALITY OF WORK, THE ART OF LAZINESS

"Adopt the colonial pace, my friend, and you'll get
along all right. . . . Never run if you can walk, never
walk if you can stand, never stand if you can sit, never
sit if you can lie down, and never do anything today
you can put off until tomorrow. That's the colonial
pace. Master it and things won't be so bad."

Advice to a convict, Francis Lagrange and
William Murray, Flag on Devil's Island, *1961*

Oh Laziness, mother of the arts and noble virtues, be
thou the balm of human anguish!

Paul Lafargue, The Right to Be Lazy, *1880*

Returning from nature to culture and the ever-expanding island of civilization amid the forest, we must consider the quality of human action
involved in transforming landscapes. The penal colony takes shape at
a crucial moment in European colonial understandings of place and

Figure 20.   Postcard of Kourou sawmill, ca. 1900

labor. Slavery had just been abolished in the French Empire, and an accompanying understanding of work in terms of race had far from expended its interpretive force. Not only were Africans thought more naturally suited to heavy labor in the tropics than Europeans, but the
landscape of the industrious colony was dependent on the vast exercise
of manual labor. Consider the following passage, written in 1845:

> The axe has lightened these formerly impenetrable forests. It has fashioned
> the trees that now support elegant structures; precious and useful planta-
> tions spread in the midst of these deserts obstructed with unproductive veg-
> etation. Convenient roads divide these newborn fields, dug by industrious
> hands; canals have received the excess waters and established internal com-
> munications; a working population displays its strength in these fertilized
> places; it fills the arms of the motherland with its trade and provides new
> food to its industry. Perhaps one day [this population] will be a great people
> when its Metropolis only offers a spectacle of ruins; and it will make way
> also, in the continuation of ages, to new nations that rise in their turn from
> its breast. Such is the work of colonization.[1]

Work represented the route to a better future, to the growth of new,
valuable lands. Who, then, would lend backs and hands to the enterprise? If slavery were at an end, then the crucial question facing the
colony was that of finding an alternative source of labor.

During the period of the early penal colony we see this search for new slaves, not only in French Guiana, but also throughout colonies built on the plantation model. Thousands of Asian Indians and Chinese found their way to new homes in different corners of the British Empire, serving as contract laborers on plantations. While the French were generally less successful at organizing intercontinental immigration, even in remote Guyane wave after wave of small groups arrived, in response to bureaucratic hopes that their bodies would prove industrious. The penal colony, of course, provided another long stream of captive travelers who were intended to serve both as plantation labor and as an army of industrious, rehabilitated peasants. Yet all these efforts and experiments failed in this particular margin; the plantations, which had been fading anyway, were not reborn, and a productive peasantry failed to materialize. French Guiana remained a land of tropical "deserts obstructed with unproductive vegetation."

The situation was complicated by the reluctance of the former slaves to stay on the plantations and continue to support the system of large-scale agricultural production for export. Indeed, the aversion of the newly freed population to any sort of agriculture or heavy labor beyond subsistence gardening is so striking that the historian Serge Mam-Lam-Fouck underlines it as an origin point for the stereotype of Creole "laziness" and "indolence" common in French Guiana. The fondness of the contemporary Creole population for bureaucratic positions, he argues, must be placed into a historical context, one in which "from the origins of colonial history until departmentalization, slavery, the utilization of overexploited immigrant labor as well as that of convicts, contributed to the devalorization of working the earth, in the eyes of the Creole. It represented, in effect, beyond the humiliation of the slave, the exploitation of the coolie and the downfall of the convict."[2] The emerging Creole cultural traditions valued freelance gold mining over heavy agriculture and prized administrative positions when the gold rush faded. Even commercial possibilities, such as running a small store, failed to attract many Creoles, which opened the way for Chinese domination of the small-scale retail market.[3] Instead, Creoles in Guyane developed a reputation for idleness and lack of ambition, a stereotype alive among the contemporary Metropolitan population. While the details of this stereotype are particular to Guyane, its general outline conforms to a widespread colonial trope of the "lazy native" and to writings about tropical idleness. This theme, quite popular in its day, merits exploration, because it places that other pole of our concerns—nature—within the field of labor.[4]

CLIMATE, TECHNOLOGY,
AND THEORIES OF INDUSTRY

Whatever may be the cause, it is generally agreed that
the native races within the tropics are dull in thought
and slow in action.

> *Ellsworth Huntington,*
> Civilization and Climate, *1915*

"These uniforms are too heavy for the tropics, surely,"
said the explorer.

> *Franz Kafka, "In the Penal Colony," 1919*

In addressing climatic theories of action, my purpose is not to revive
old prejudices but rather to understand their connection to shifting
conceptions of place and development. The worldview expressed in a
division of the planet into natural zones of greater and lesser industry is
not only an artifact of the politics of imperialism, it is also a statement
about the "noncosmopolitanism" of humanity. In this view the social
and cultural species would be just as limited as the biological species of
our good doctor Orgeas; the human spirit would be held just as captive
as the human body by place and milieu.

As an entry into these debates let us look more closely at an American classic of the genre, Ellsworth Huntington's *Civilization and Climate,* originally published in 1915.[5] Huntington opens his work by
comparing races to varieties of trees, each of which brings forth different fruits of civilization. While one does not expect any given species to
suddenly produce the fruit of another (a pear on a cherry branch), the
quality of the fruit nonetheless depends on factors of the environment.
From this point he moves logically to ask whether one can separate the
effects of climate from those of race and whether the effects of climate
were not more significant than some of his contemporaries thought.
Granting strong "racial" differences in levels of ability (and a particularly strong line between white and black—this is America in 1915, ripe
with prejudice), he nevertheless suspects that physical environment
may be crucial and asks what "five hundred or a thousand years of life
in Egypt would do for either Teutons or Negroes if no new blood were
introduced?"[6]

Huntington then proceeds to investigate a wide range of topics asso-
ciated with his environmental position, including "The Effect of the
Seasons," "Work and Weather," and, of course, "The White Man in the
Tropics." Evaluating climates on the basis of different criteria of work

and health, he suggests that the ideal environment would have a mean temperature rarely falling below the "mental optimum" of 38° F (3.3° C) and rarely rising above the "physical optimum" of 64° F (17.8° C).[7] In a remarkable act of speculative cartography, he maps the state of "civilization" in the world (largely centered in Northern Europe and parts of North America), noticing a strong correlation with the distribution of "health" and with the climatic conditions that he believes favor vitality. Expanding his model into the past, he suggests that shifting centers of civilization in different periods of history are linked to shifting climatic patterns. Ultimately, he concludes that climate is the major force opposing human progress: "The climate of many countries seems to be one of the great reasons why idleness, immorality, stupidity, and weakness of will prevail. If we can conquer climate, the whole world will become stronger and nobler."[8]

Although both the methods and the conclusions of Huntington's work merit the most strenuous skepticism, revealing as they do more about the geography of his own biases than of comparative human vitality, nevertheless we should not lose sight of the fact that his is a modified racism, an environmental strain as full of weather as blood.[9] Here again we have a cautionary tale for white men entering the tropics, but this time the caution is more universal than that of our medical guide Orgeas: *anyone* entering the tropics will lose mental and physical vitality. Evolution recedes in the direction of a refined Montesquieu: the climate of a country dictates the general spirit of its inhabitants, and that spirit shifts over time—rather literally—with changes in the wind. The problem of development becomes one of challenging nature at a deeper level than the soil, of remaking the very air around human beings.

Huntington's call for the conquest of climate found echoes in later arguments linking human energy to the environment. In one of these, S. F. Markham's 1944 work *Climate and the Energy of Nations,* the point is further refined, fixing the crucial environmental variable on climatic *control* rather than climate itself.[10] The goal is to achieve an optimum set of atmospheric conditions, but this, the author sensibly points out, can be achieved in a variety of ways, through combinations of clothing and technologies of heating or cooling. The history of relative human energy is then a history of human ability to regulate temperature and humidity, or a general history of "air-conditioning."[11]

Markham notes that the principle of "conditioning" air appears far earlier than 1907, when the term was first employed, and should include heating and ventilation as well as cooling. Indeed, he imagines a prehistoric man "conditioning" his cave with fire, leading to the impressive heating work of Roman engineers. Reducing air temperature, however, proved to be a more difficult undertaking than increasing it, and the practice only emerged in modern history. In northern climes stores of ice could preserve into the summer months when well packed, and by the late eighteenth century, ice had become a commodity of note. During the same period, experiments in cooling commenced, and by the late nineteenth century the principles of compression and ammonia absorption were well established. Starting around 1880, the development of refrigeration in ships and railroad cars allowed perishable goods to be transported over much greater distances. Meanwhile, some manufacturing plants had adapted techniques previously developed in India to cool air by means of wet matting. A mechanized version of this practice, focused on controlling humidity, would be christened "air-conditioning" in the American South. The first large "scientific" cooling system, developed for the British Houses of Parliament in 1836, had met with mixed success. But in the 1920s, movie theaters in North America and Europe adopted improved varieties of air-conditioning to regulate both temperature and humidity, and on the eve of World War II, individual units were available. A revolution in climate was in the making.[12]

Yet amid this clear triumph of technical space over place, Markham also reminds us that it comes at a price and cautions against assuming too sudden or complete a world transformation: "It should not be forgotten that air conditioning depends almost exclusively at present upon electricity for its motive power, and it is therefore obvious that it will be restricted for many years to those countries which have adequate and economic supplies of electricity."[13] Control requires power—a point we shall return to in due course. But what about those areas lacking the necessary conditions for the adoption of large-scale artificial cooling? If we accept for the moment Huntington's thesis that a cool climate promotes industry and social growth, and a warm, humid climate sloth and social stagnation, what, we might ask, are the actual techniques of laziness? What do lazy people do? To explore this topic let us return to the penal colony and the issue of its failure to remake the landscape of Guyane.

THE PENAL COLONY AND THE "SYSTÈME D"

débrouiller, se. Beyond a shadow of a doubt, the first
word you should learn in French, since without it, you
cannot understand the French and their outlook on

life. *Se débrouiller* and the justly famous *Système D (le système de la débrouillardise)* express a whole concept, essentially individualistic, which is only very feebly translated by "to manage," "to get along," "to muddle through," "to make out for oneself." If you call someone *très débrouillard(e),* you are paying him one of the highest compliments that the list of French adjectives allows for: it means a compound of *astucieux, énergetic, indépendent,* and *volontaire,* not to mention *imaginatif,* in short, resourceful.

> Michel Levieux and Eleanor Levieux,
> Cassell's Colloquial French, *1980*

One night an English lord came to the hotel and the waiters were in despair, for the lord had asked for peaches, and there were none in stock; it was late at night, and the shops would be shut. "Leave it to me," said the German. He went out, and in ten minutes he was back with four peaches. He had gone into a neighboring restaurant and stolen them. That is what is meant by a *débrouillard.* The English lord paid for the peaches at twenty francs each.

> George Orwell,
> Down and Out in London and Paris, *1933*

As we noted earlier, it appears that in the first moments of the French system of transportation a degree of enthusiasm reigned. Inmates of the Metropolitan *bagnes* volunteered to ship to French Guiana, and the initial clearing and construction was accomplished with alacrity. Although the ominous iron sign over another camp lay far in the future, the phrase was already in the air: work could make you free. Released from dreary port confinement and given promises of liberty and small holdings, some of the convicts seem to have briefly embraced the words of penal reformers. However, as disease and despair took their toll, the work ethic rapidly disappeared. The envisioned industrious settlements failed to materialize, and complaints grew over the lack of productivity. By the time of Dreyfus, the meaning of official work had clearly changed, moving further from industry and closer to punishment.

Rather than labor for civil redemption and eventual liberty, the central enterprise of life within the bagne had become a matter of survival, of finding small pleasures in the midst of oppression. In the later penal colony, the principal preoccupation of every convict was to get by, to *se débrouiller:*

> Whoever does not work the system [*se débrouille*] is an imbecile. Even for those who aren't adept with their hands and who don't have a position or job, there is always a way for them to get a hold of a bit of money. They wash laundry for others, replace them in the soup line, help the dealers of the penal colony cut wood, wash containers, go and fetch water. In sum, everybody keeps busy, everybody finds ways to improve the meager fare of the penal colony.[14]

The record is full of examples of minor craft production, petty graft, gambling, and small favors. In and of themselves the examples are sometimes striking—the collecting of butterflies or the carving of miniature guillotines, for example—but not particularly unusual or unexpected. Accounts of prison life in many settings contain parallels.[15] Yet taken together as a part of an entire system, these minor acts acquire wider significance.

The fixation with "getting by" was by no means limited to convicts in the penal colony. The streets of St. Laurent, we are repeatedly told, were among the cleanest in the world: not a single cigarette butt could escape the keen eyes of the *libéré*, the only creature alive more desperate than the *bagnard*. The guards, too, often played their own games, extorting money or accepting bribes to look the other way, while beyond the penal colony many in Guyane made money supplying its needs, trimming corners all along the way. In an age of growing industry, of mass, standardized production, this small corner of France thrived on improvisation. Amid the slow heat of tropical days, an impure "Système D" came into being.

In most respects the "Système D" represents a perfect reversal of visions of development. Rather than being productive it is reactive; rather than being planned it is improvised. Here individual action does not build social cohesion or lead to progressive enhancement of life but instead manages to patch things together, to get through one crisis and on to the next. The horizon shrinks to that of immediate situations, retreating from general principles to the day at hand. The nineteenth-century colonial image of the industrious farmer and his teams of laboring servants gives way to that of the traveling tinker and his troop of itinerant handymen. Moreover, the story of the official and the story of the unofficial plainly separate; everyone comes to know that real business takes place in darkness or the shadows of late afternoon, not the full light of day. Rather than simply follow or oppose the system in place, the social actors work around it. Their field becomes, in Michel de Certeau's distinction, one of time and tactics, not space and strategy—the art of the weak, not the architecture of the powerful.[16] On the map of the world, then, with its grids of geographic position and homogenous human spaces, we must add latitudes of accommodation. Writing about a stylized North African in France, de Certeau describes immigrant experience as a superimposition of worlds and a consequent formation of new spaces in language and culture. In this way displacement can inspire creativity; it leads to improvised compromises rather than simple conformity through an "art of being in between."[17] In the penal colony the only hope for a convict lay in between, in between the other convicts and the guards and in between the walls of the official structure and the order of its day. And the composite world of the *bagne* itself grew in between, poised between Metropolitan and colonial policies, at the edge of civilization.

The ethos of the "Système D" allows us to reverse our thinking about industry and its absence to consider laziness and its absence, to understand the action of inactivity so stereotypically associated with the tropics. All the accounts agree that while tedious inefficiency lay at the center of the penal colony, between the cracks a great deal took place. Rather than control their surroundings, a possibility largely denied to them, the convicts adapted, finding corners to shave and moments to seize. They negotiated, as only those in a position of structural weakness can. Here we must remember that our construction of the "tropics"—for all that the region may occupy the midriff of the globe—positions it at the side of human affairs. The act of its colonization involved the importation of tools and systems designed elsewhere and left a space between them and their new locale. This gap between a standard structure and a particular milieu creates an area open to negotiation, indeed, an area requiring it. The arts of laziness, then, can be understood as an alternative to the arts of control, as well as another reaction to displacement. Alongside the engineers and architects of colonial policy, we should place the *bricoleurs* of colonial experience, nimble-fingered amateurs, muddling and adjusting and always making do.

THE MODERN TROPICS, A NEW DEVELOPMENT

In addition it is often said that the French have
colonies but no colonists; that even if they had
colonists, they would not know how to colonize.

They apply to the jungle the meticulous care of metropolitan bureaucracy. They export nothing into their
overseas dominions except damaged officials; and they
import nothing from them except the same officials,
worse damaged.

> *Albert Guérard*, France, 1946

Turning to face the space center, we confront a modified conceptual topography. Kourou is a neutralized, controlled corner of the tropics,
with much of its cultural fabric simply imported. Amid the restricted
space of artificially cooled buildings and automobiles, in zones free of
carrier mosquitoes and amply supplied with wine and cheese airlifted
from France, the distance between Paris and Cayenne shortens; the effects of translation between them grow less clear. If the island mimics
the mainland successfully, if Crusoe builds a little England—or
France—is his task done? What does development mean in this context? To answer this question, let us return to a crucial turning point of
Guyane's history: the aftermath of World War II and the period of formal empire. It was during this era that the natural, political, and moral
space of French Guiana was neutralized through a combination of
DDT spraying, departmentalization, and the final closing of the penal
colony.

In 1949, a former teacher at the Lycée Schoelcher in Martinique
published an overview of the new overseas departments and territories.
His description of French Guiana includes a call to arms for its development, a development still conceived in terms of a need for immigrants, agriculture, and industry:

> French Guiana is the most extensive of our possessions in America. It ap-
> pears the most forsaken, but also the richest in interesting possibilities, in la-
> tent resources. . . . The moment appears favorable. The departure of the
> *bagne* liberates the country from a heavy moral mortgage, compensated, it
> is true, by the disappearance of a labor force that, being penal, accomplished
> a good part of the most irksome works. Before us is a country practically
> empty of men, since most of those who are established there live in the town
> or in large villages and do not always have qualities that would suit pio-
> neers. While respecting the legitimate interests of this population, interests
> that it knows how to defend with a remarkable energy, it is desirable that
> the work of reconquest begin, following a methodical plan, rational and
> above all complete. It would be useless to import the most modern and ex-
> pensive equipment without at the same time having the specialized person-
> nel to operate it and roads that are indispensable for supply and exploita-
> tion. But such personnel, in the current state of things, must inevitably come

from the outside. To remain in flourishing health, its members must be able to support the fatigue of the equatorial climate and accept the rough discipline necessary in such conditions. Until proven otherwise, most men of the white race are unsuited to prolonged heavy labor under tropical conditions, albeit that a minimum of exercise appears indispensable. The "laborers" have to be sought elsewhere, among the blacks or the yellows. But Africa already lacks enough people for its own development. It does not appear easy, at the present conjuncture, to get Indochinese or Hindus to come. Antilleans only settle in Guiana to get their start or to seek gold. The problem is therefore to find men, and when they are found, to train them, to bring them to concentrate their efforts on a chosen sector, and so avoid the lamentable failures of the past. Gold mines aside, it seems that the method of painstaking labor is the only one really applicable at present. Incontestably, there is magnificent work to accomplish there, such as should tempt young men fond of broad horizons and adventure.[18]

The appeal is for an army of Crusoes, advancing ashore to improve their collective island. The questions of race and level of expertise filter through patterns of history and perceived practicality. But the call remains, the call of a wilderness inviting domestication.

Yet even as this schoolteacher's vision takes shape, it has a certain tint of anachronism. For all that these words would find an echo in the official Plan Vert of the mid-1970s, the 1940s were already bringing French Guiana a new kind of immigrant: the specialist bureaucrat. While the presence of these specialists did not completely overwhelm the local population or prevent the arrival of general immigrants (indeed, it would eventually encourage them), it did represent a new element in the administration of things: specificity of purpose. It is this final sharpening of technique that separates different impulses within development and projects of modernization.

The term *impulses* works better than *periods* because the watershed of departmentalization constitutes something less than a straight divide. The colonial administration was full of officials, and the penal colony represented a specialized use of the land. But in degree of specialization and training, the officeholders of the postwar era represent a body more actively engaged in the technical process of governing populations; they are Foucault's "specific intellectuals," detailed practitioners of discrete programs. Let us not forget that one of the first acts of those administering the newly created overseas department was to mount a public health campaign specifically targeting endemic diseases and demographic decline. Similarly, the actual function of the space center is related to the location of French Guiana more intimately than that of the penal colony ever was; the coordinates of rocket launching are more exacting than those of agriculture or settlement. At the same time, however, climate and local conditions recede behind latitude and issues of general stability, natural and social. The human technical system that produced the space center is thus more focused, but so focused in fact that everything outside its technical field of vision fades into generic gestures. In design and in function, local considerations serve as afterthoughts. Place is to be controlled and then used, as hermetically as possible.

In the examples before us we find reflections of two edges of modernization. Writing about urban planning in late-nineteenth- and early-twentieth-century French colonial settings, Paul Rabinow distinguishes between two modern moments: the locally sensitive "techno-cosmopolitanism," which seeks to administer to the needs of situated groups of humans, and the socially generalizing "middling modernism," which seeks to satisfy the needs of universal human forms.[19] The structure of the penal colony was neither fully middling nor fully modern. Even in principle, penal colonization is itself a hybrid form bred between punishment and discipline. The material on which the *bagne* sought to work remained categorically differentiated in administration; the techniques of race balanced those of humanity. Hints of universalism appear in the effort to build an Australia on the equator, but these hints soon vanish into the tropics. Unhealthy spaces and forms consume the debris of Metropolitan modernization, and the impulse is lost in an inversion of progress, a negative techno-cosmopolitanism of spoiled history and spoiled nature, and a noncosmopolitan experience of death. Development collapses into an archaic, stable space of suffering.

In contrast, the architecture of Kourou is both intensely middling and modernist. From the blank concrete of its housing blocks to its list of luminary street names, Kourou is designed for a universal human form, not for a situated group of humans. The space center's representation of purpose is one of relentless purification and transcendence; the gateway created belongs to those who would walk among the stars, leaving the tropics far behind. Indeed, the Space Age can be read as the highest expression of middling modernism, with visions of future colonization of other worlds and galaxies representing the extension of universal human space throughout the universe. From the language of its mission to the gestures of its celebration, the Guiana Space Center enthusiastically embraces such a future, claiming action in the name of science and humanity. Even in its environmental moments, the appeals to heritage are global and universal in scope. Here development shoots skyward, moving beyond earthly divides to a free horizon of future possibility. Between the penal colony and the space center we glimpse the shifting space of the modern tropics: a dark, humid isolation cell, a vast, cold sea between the stars.

THE RHYTHM OF SPACE

At the space center an ethos of efficiency outweighs that of "getting by." By virtue of its leading position in an international market of importance and its role as a central symbol of French technical prowess, the complex around Ariane assumes a northern work ethic. The system of launch campaigns prevents strict temporal regularization, with activity building over months to the sudden crescendo and dissipation of each launch, and the staggering of responsibilities and projects between different teams and departments keeps tension from being permanently centered. This rhythm is at odds with the leisurely cycle of most local practice, in which an ample siesta dominates the center of the day. But in order to be the leading and "most modern" launch complex in the world, the CSG must operate in synch with many world clocks. The large backlog of satellites awaiting launch accumulated during the late 1980s and early 1990s further increased pressure on the facility to produce quick and regular launches.

Rocket technology as a whole dictates in favor of repeated testing and standardization and against improvisation. Launches are volatile moments; even after a decade of regular launches, the success rate of Ariane—a reliable rocket—hovers just above 90 percent. Every failure represents not only the loss of merchandise but also a costly delay, because the reasons for the malfunction must be determined before operations resume.[20] The possibility of a major disaster (such as an explosion on the launchpad), while remote, hovers unpleasantly in the background, and obsessions over safety are matched by fears about sabotage and industrial espionage. This inherent conservatism and focus on control marks space transport as a strangely static technology, wedded to regulation and structure in an effort to corral its necessary experiments with explosive power.

However, the space center and the engineers who work in it cannot completely escape the tropics. The relative atmospheric stability of Guyane facilitates launching (even if CSG had lost its claim never to have delayed a rocket because of weather). But the local climate, while stable, exhibits different characteristics from that for which much of the equipment of the center was designed, not to mention the expectations of its personnel. The launch complex wages a constant battle against heat, humidity, and dust, conditioning the air throughout the varied workplace, screening out contaminants from satellite assembly areas, and repainting structures to combat rust induced by heavy rainfall. Just as the new town of Kourou serves to support human agents of space, a myriad complex of secondary technologies serve to support Ariane and its cargo, constructing and maintaining a climatic fortress around them.

The social environment surrounding the space center also creates tensions within its operations. Although European space personnel publicly praise the relaxed sensibility of working in "Mediterranean" Guyane and compare it favorably to European conditions, in private some complain about the lax work habits of Guyanais employees. Beyond the threat of strikes and other protests, which periodically disrupt space activities, they sense a lack of professional commitment to labor, an unwillingness to disrupt patterns of life to achieve greater success. One engineer told me an anecdote about a local automated car wash, which displayed a sign announcing that its hours of operation were limited to the morning. "That," he said, "sums up Guyane."

A focus piece on secretaries in the CSG house journal provides a further window into work relations at the space center. Both the content and the form of the article help position the official symbolic location of the local setting relative to the international norms of the project. Tension exists on both sides; against a space official's private complaints about lapsed work ethic, we must place a secretary's complaint about calculating stress. As one such employee commented: "Sometimes CSG makes me think of a jungle where the reason of the strongest is always the best." A more extended example is found in the story of someone whom, we are told, "many of you know" and her struggles with her immediate superior:

> A number of years ago, I had a boss who wouldn't stop persecuting me. He was constantly really unpleasant to me, causing the worst problems, spending his time making unpleasant remarks to me in front of everybody. This went on for a long time, and I'd truly lost all taste for coming to work. Being able to stand it no longer, I went to consult a clairvoyant, and she told me that a very simple method existed to neutralize evil people: I had to obtain some large salt and to sprinkle it on the ground under my boss's seat and everywhere where he was in the habit of passing by, and immediately he would become as sweet as a lamb. Starting the next day, I flooded the place

with salt, putting as much as I could without being noticeable. Believe it or not, but that worked. Coincidence or no, from that day on his attitude toward me changed, and our relationship became much better.[21]

Placing the anecdote into an interpretive frame, the article concludes with the following comment: "To cast a spell? A very local manner to settle problems with a hierarchical superior. Yes indeed, CSG is also Guyane!" The underlying conflict, already solved in the narrative, is solved again; the action described translates through exoticism into humor. Magic has entered the cathedral of reason, and tradition returns in new and unexpected forms. Its power, however, becomes muted in the presentation; salt is quaintly archaic—even if it reportedly works.

Yet Creole secretaries have no monopoly on tradition or ritual behavior; as we have seen, mythic themes and commemorations weigh heavily in space. Another article, commemorating the tenth anniversary of Ariane's crucial first launch, the moment of the rocket's symbolic and material birth on Christmas Eve of 1979, provides counterbalancing material. An official describes how, once everything "humanly possible" had been done to ensure success, space personnel deposited some eighty ritual candles at the church in Kourou. He continues to claim that this tradition continued for at least the first seventeen launches, with the exception of the second and fifth, both of which were failures. From the sixth launch on, the lighting of a candle became an established protocol. The point is driven home by an accompanying cartoon, which shows a security officer sneaking through the forest to place his candle on an altar, only to arrive and find many already there, grouped around a model Ariane. Here again official publication turns the limits of reason into a joke, though this time without implicating Guyane. Instead, the account covers the tension of imperfection running beneath standardization, the reminder that engineering can fail, and that even a reliable rocket can blow up.[22] Salt or candles, the actions cover similar anxieties over the limits of control, even if one is read down into local superstition and the other out into general humor.

The same founding moment of the initial Ariane provides other interesting details. Because the launch had been delayed into the holiday season, a plane brought relatives from France to join the hardworking rocket crew, a "Charter des Femmes" (charter of wives) to provide solace. Families reconstituted, the pioneers finally delivered. Immediately after the successful launch, we are told, senior officials in the space program engaged in the first snowball fight ever staged in French Guiana, using a frozen pile created by the liquid oxygen of the departed rocket.

An accompanying photograph shows a small group of laughing men playing around their "normal" December find: men become boys with the help of their most magnificent machine. A rocket in the sky, a White Christmas with family on the ground—the sense of triumph was complete. The tropics had never been more modern. Yet a final story completes the scene, even as the snow quickly melted on the ground. An earlier abortive launch attempt had left the bottom of the rocket blackened, and efforts to clean it had only made matters worse. Worried about appearances but informed that a regular coat of primer would take an additional twenty-four hours to dry, the official in charge decided to improvise (on se débrouillera), skip that stage, and slap white paint on immediately. The gimmick worked, and Ariane gleamed clean enough for the publicity photos. At the birth of European technical triumph, then, just below the skin of elaborate design, we find a tiny act of "making do." White snow, white paint, and a white rocket seize the day, but their triumph is less than pure.[23]

In similar fashion, for all the modern rhythms of the space center, everyday life in French Guiana, even in Kourou, remains a matter of partial improvisation amid the structure of grander plans. The barriers defending controlled climates require constant maintenance and power. Heavy rains and steady heat often reveal flaws in buildings designed for other conditions, and some electronic equipment suffers quickly from exposure. Minor crises require bricolage—fiddling, fixing, and making do with the materials at hand. While an impressive and ever-increasing array of consumer goods can be found in French Guiana (mountain bikes, fax machines, Norman cheese, and Algerian wine), not all of them can be found at once, and few are made with the tropics in mind. The world system delivers, but erratically and without guarantees. Similarly, while services up to and including dog grooming are available, they are not cheap, and few operate around the clock. Overall, the pace of life remains relatively slow, as replete with pause as with action. Lacking a landscape reworked by industry, a protective urban cocoon, the urgent line of cars commuting to and fro between the space center and Kourou remains distinctly incongruous.

Deep tensions also lie beneath the surface of imported norms and the translation of modern France to Guyane. An issue of a radical newspaper from 1994 sums up one of these in an article entitled "Il n'y a pas d'été en Guyane" (There is no summer in Guyane). Pointing out that the tropics experience only two seasons, dry and wet, rather than the

four of Metropolitan France, the piece decries the structure of the
school year on the French calendar and the creeping cultural assimilation infecting Creole society. The best way to keep Guyane French, the
article suggests, is to ensure that Guyanais "physically" feel French. But
this is unnatural, and nature must not be subverted: "To be in accord
with our environment, let us conform to our geography: There is no
summer in Guyane."[24] The piece is typical in that the fundamental
cleavage identified in French Guiana runs down the Atlantic, pitting
"Guyanais" (in this case synonymous with Creole) against "French."
Not all of the tensions of recent modernization, however, break so simply along a single ethnic line. For all that colonial history lies just below
the surface of French Guiana, and issues of race just above it, faith in
things modern does not merely emanate from Europe. Rather, influences
weave back and forth: gold miners cross the river from Brazil, even as
ecologists decry air-conditioning from France. A technological complex
like the space center itself determines nothing. But its mass distorts social gravity, and amid the many tendrils of all it represents, claims of
moral purity shift from work to conservation and back again, compli-
cating clearer divides of class and race. For a richer picture of this web
of conflicting elements in French Guiana, let us turn to an ethnographic
moment and the major disputes within it.

A TALE OF TWO ROADS (AND A DAM)

"A road is like the tongue of men; one never knows
what it will carry."

> Town official of St. Georges,
> France-Antilles, September 2, 1994

In the summer of 1994, different threads related to development came
together in a set of controversies related to the opening of a dam, the
construction of one section of road, and the closing of another.
Conflicts over nature, technology, and autonomy that surfaced in debates over the projects illustrate major storm systems blowing through
the modern tropics, to and from the rest of the world. In the partial, in-
conclusive drama of these events we can glimpse the complex ecology
of enterprise involved in a technical center like CSG and the manner in
which "work" and "development" implicate more than individual action and economic organization.

TROUBLED WATERS AT PETIT SAUT

"Never in the world have so many precautions been
taken to master the impact of a development project
on the environment."
                    Official description of Petit Saut Dam, 1994[25]

Between a demographic explosion and striking shifts in the material
habits of its residents, French Guiana confronted an energy dilemma in
the mid-1980s. Not only had its population roughly doubled over the
preceding decade, but the consumption of energy had risen at an even
faster rate and continued to grow at 10 to 12 percent a year. The two
largest consumers of power were the system of telecommunications relays operated by TDF (Télé Diffusion France) and the space center,
which together accounted for some 30 percent of the total use. CSG required significant energy for both launch operations and general air-
conditioning, and ambitious plans for the Ariane 5 rocket projected
even higher rates of use. But the majority of electricity flowing through
Guyane powered smaller enterprises and households replete with a
growing range of personnel technologies, including refrigeration and
climate control. The result was heavy dependence on imported fossil
fuels and ever-rising energy bills.[26]
      To diminish the need for fuel imports and to establish a foundation
for future growth, the French state utilities company (EDF) decided to
invest in a large-scale hydroelectric project. Taking advantage of
Guyane's plentiful water, such an installation would simultaneously
reduce the cost of electricity production and provide an independent
renewable source of energy for the future. The possibility of a dam had
been discussed since the 1950s, and an inventory of potential sites
begun. After further research in 1987, the final decision was taken to
construct a dam across the Sinnamary River at a site known as Petit
Saut (Small Rapids). The arguments in favor of this location focused
on the relative geography of the department and the relative degree of
environmental impact of the project. While a major river such as the
Oyapock might generate more in the way of potential power,
damming it would also present greater technical problems and, because of its border location, require extensive political negotiation.
Petit Saut, in contrast, lay near the center of the department, not far
from the coastal areas that consumed the most electricity (Cayenne,
Kourou, and St. Laurent). Thus it would be clearly within the jurisdic-

tion of French Guiana and require less in the way of additional infrastructure to reach consumers. Relative to other potential sites on the
Mana and Approuague rivers, Petit Saut seemed to offer the best conditions in terms of surface area to be inundated relative to the amount
of power produced. It was, we should also note, quite close to the
space center.[27]

Once the decision had been reached, the dam at Petit Saut materialized quickly. A five-year project of construction began in 1989, employing an average of four hundred workers at a time. In addition to an
access road, they cleared the site and built the dam—the largest in
"France." The total cost of the effort ran in the order of 540 million
dollars, a significant sum within the context of Guyane.[28] Of this figure,
approximately 3.5 percent was directed into a study of the environmental impact of the dam. Experience with major hydroelectric projects in other countries cautioned that flooding a large section of forest
could wreck ecological havoc as well as create significant health problems, particularly in malarial areas. However, EDF maintained that the
Afobaka Dam constructed in the early 1960s in neighboring Suriname,
while causing significant short-term damage, had eventually stabilized
in ecological terms and proved greatly beneficial in promoting energy
independence.[29] The anticipated impact of Petit Saut was smaller, and
EDF promised to support extensive environmental research, including
use of SPOT satellite photography. High above, the proud eye of
France would watch its hand below.

However, despite these precautions, controversy surrounding the
project grew. From a European viewpoint, the impending flood threatened numerous exotic and colorful animals, as well as a segment of
tropical rain forest. Perceptions within Guyane were mixed, though they
usually took local energy demands more seriously than those positioned
at a remove: "Of course, in a Parisian or New York editorial office, it
was easy to perceive the subject in quite a different manner, notably
from the perspective of the environment—so Amazonian, and above all,
so photogenic."[30] With criticism mounting, the utility company began a
rescue operation to save animals within the affected area and heightened
its public relations campaign, pointing out that all the activity would actually increase ecological research in the area. In addition to extensively
surveying the threatened flora and fauna and working to ensure water
quality, EDF sponsored a major archaeological salvage operation, recovering artifacts associated with Amerindian occupations, gold mining, and the camp of Indochinese political prisoners at Saut Tigre.

Before the threatened waters of the future, researchers worked fever-
ishly to catalogue traces of the past.[31]

Environmental activists were not convinced; they continued to express their dismay with Petit Saut, if not actually impede its construction.[32] Support among the Creole population also began to thin, particularly as fears grew over the possibility of accidents, ecological
destruction, and decreased water quality. Labor activists organized
work stoppages at the site, and political groups favoring increased autonomy for Guyane increasingly identified the project as an imposition
of the French state and argued that it had primarily been designed to
serve the needs of the space center. By the summer of 1994, with the
dam nearly operational, Petit Saut had become a symbol at the center
of a range of fault lines in Guyanais politics, a physical reminder of the
problems of power in tropical France.

THE FIRST ROAD: CLOSING THE SPACE ROUTE

This reflection led me to put French colonial power
into relief. In effect, in the name of colonization, it
does what it wants for the development of Guyane,
and for that has no limits to its actions, lies, manip-
ulations, repressions, and demagogy.

Reader of a radical paper
on the space center, 1994[33]

Even as tension over the dam increased, another source of conflict
emerged, this one directly involving the space center. A segment of the
major coastal road (named "Route Nationale 1," or "RN 1," in honor
of its original status as the descendent of the ill-fated penal colony project), crossed directly through the territory of CSG on its way from
Kourou to Sinnamary, passing between the major technical installations. Since the success of the Ariane program, concern over security
and safety had grown, and particularly with the advent of the Ariane 5
rocket, space officials sought to limit access to their domain. Toward
this end they sponsored the construction of a deviation road swinging
in a large loop around the space center and neatly hooking up with the
access road to Petit Saut. The opening of this alternative route in 1991
facilitated the closing of the crucial segment of RN 1 during launches,
as traffic could now be diverted throughout the critical day without
major inconvenience. It also allowed CSG to press for complete closure

of the old road, turning it into a self-contained "Route de l'Espace" (Space Road).

The public at large, however, resenting the additional length of the new deviation and lack of facilities along it, continued to use the old road whenever possible. Despite an interchange design encouraging the use of the deviation, a steady stream of cars headed straight through the space center on every day it was open. Space officials maneuvered for total closure, urging the state to decommission the road and transfer jurisdiction to them. A number of local politicians had opposed the project since its initiation in 1987, and now a group of the most prominent elected officials staged a preemptive strike. Holding a press conference in early July 1994, they denounced the space center's intentions, warned of increasing estrangement between Guyane and the space program, and called CSG a "state within a state." Guyane's conservative deputy cautioned that continued strife might lead to a "divorce," while the socialist president of the regional council proclaimed: "It is unthinkable that a prosperous, rich, and regular activity of such high technology develops, and that less than ten kilometers away there exists the most complete destitution, lacking a minimum of comfort, security, or hygiene."[34] Reaction was swift. The prefect called a meeting between space officials and the political representatives of Guyane, and on July 13—the eve of the French national holiday—he announced that although the road would close, a new initiative would seek to foster the development of Guyane alongside that of the space program.

Yet the matter was far from closed. A political organization known as "Mouvement de décolonisation et d'émancipation sociale" (Movement for Decolonization and Social Emancipation, or MDES) took up the ball, accusing the space center and the state of colonial practices and the elected officials of betrayal. MDES demanded that the matter be put to a referendum and set about gathering signatures of support. A night rally held in Cayenne drew a crowd of several hundred, with music and speakers who shouted slogans in both Creole and French, decrying the loss of road and the demise of culture and tradition in general. While activists encouraged passing drivers to sign their petition, one woman pointed out that for all the advanced satellites riding up into the sky from Kourou, towns in the interior of Guyane lacked reliable television and phone service. "What use is the space center to us?" she asked, generating applause. Another man reminded the audience that the road had existed prior to CSG's arrival and suggested that it would also exist after the center's departure. "What do we get?" he asked rhetorically. "Color TV, but they still think we're savages."

Meanwhile, the space center went on a counteroffensive. Television news crews from both the state network and its recently legalized competition were given elaborate tours and shown the large stocks of dangerous materials. Space officials granted numerous interviews, citing concerns for public safety and categorically denying any desire on their part to segregate themselves from the rest of French Guiana. Rumors of plans for a separate port and airport were unfounded, they suggested, or misunderstandings of plans for the suspended Hermès spaceplane project. They claimed that the design of the deviation was the best possible, given constraints of safety and the need to meet the access road to Petit Saut. As a gesture of goodwill they even offered to cede land south of the deviation road back to general state control.

The controversy continued, with the Guyanais Socialist Party (PSG) responding angrily to accusations from MDES and Walwari (another relatively radical organization) that they were selling their heritage down the river. While occasionally decrying the racism of the space center, MDES sought to forestall the suggestion that their own crusade smacked of ethnic chauvinism, proclaiming that their movement welcomed members of all groups, not only Creoles but also "Metros and Chinese" who were opposed to CSG. The essential issue, they stressed, was one of popular sovereignty; a decision enforced from outside and above was inherently "colonialist." In the charged atmosphere of French Guiana, these claims struck a responsive chord, and by August MDES announced they had gathered ten thousand signatures. A letter to the editor of one activist paper decried the actions of the "CSE [Centre Spatial Européen]" and compared the social atmosphere in Kourou to that of a South African town under apartheid, suggesting that it was equally difficult to be black in either place.[35] But by that point, the space section of RN 1 was not the only road to controversy.

THE SECOND ROAD: BUILDING TO BRAZIL

The angel would like to stay, awaken the dead, and
make whole what is smashed. But a storm is blowing
from Paradise; it has got caught in his wings with such
violence that the angel can no longer close them.

Walter Benjamin, Illuminations, *1969*

"By itself, French Guiana cannot compensate for the
destruction of the Brazilian Forest."
                              Statement of business organization,
                              France Guyane, *August 2, 1994*

Even as the storm over the space road broke, clouds gathered over another end of the coastal route begun by the convicts. A second section
of roadway extending south and east of Cayenne and designated "RN
2" ended at the town of Régina, well before reaching St. Georges and
the Brazilian border. Despite repeated plans and promises, construction
had long showed little signs of life, but in the summer of 1994 crews
began clearing the way for further work. On July 19 a group of activists
associated with the ecological group WWF decided to block the project, protesting destruction of the forest. In a press release they decried
the expenditure of nearly one hundred million dollars and the elimination of an estimated 450,000 trees, all to allow the passage of what they
argued would amount to a mere five to ten cars a day. A further petition to French president François Mitterand reminded him that this
was a French department and part of the "last primary forest of the Atlantic" and "natural Amazonian heritage"; the expanse of Guyane represented the only "tropical forest of importance" under the administration of a "rich country." Surely while advising third-world countries to
attend to their environmental responsibilities, France could hardly ignore its own.[36]
    The response was swift and vitriolic, as the ranks of local opinion
joined. The syndicate of Socio-Professionals of Guyane (headed by the
primary contractor for the road) accused the WWF of being a "tiny
group of French ecological fundamentalists" engaged in "neocolonial
practices" under the cover of ecology. Ecology came naturally to the
Guyanais, the syndicate argued, and they were in no need of schooling,
particularly by outsiders: "All the communities of French Guiana have
always lived in symbiosis with their environment, from which they
draw essential resources indispensable for their subsistence, except for
the European community. . . . The great majority of the Guyanais people do not want Guyane to be transformed into a nature reserve for
pseudo-scientists and French researchers of all sorts."[37] In any event,
they suggested, international opinion was clear that ecology and development concerns could be joined in "eco-development," and Guyane
had so little in the way of roads (420 kilometers in four hundred years,
went the slogan) that the whole debate was ridiculous.

The PSG also broadcast a protest against the WWF action, albeit a shorter one expressed in less extreme terms. The conservative deputy of French Guiana sent a letter to the conservative French prime minister, Edouard Balladour, further denouncing the ecologists, suggesting that the WWF's real motives were political and subversive and that their tactics were those of misinformation. Why, he wanted to know, had the WWF not protested when the space center built the fifty kilometers of deviation road? Finally, an article in a radical paper tied to the most outspoken workers' organization attacked one of the leading ecologists personally, insinuating that he was an outsider with a European plot and that the real disappearing species was that of the "Guyanais." Without development, the local population would grow extinct. Furthermore, the real ecological problem lay elsewhere: where local hunters had always shot only enough to feed their families, now French gendarmes staged trophy hunts, depleting the fauna. The article closed with a call for the ecologist to calm himself and allow the Guyanais to develop in peace, because they had a more intimate link to the landscape than he ever could: "He can teach us nothing about Nature, for we are a part of it."[38]

The second rejoinder of the business community was cool and cutting, charging the WWF of assuming "nature" to be a simple good and of waging a campaign in the name of ecology that was both superficial and self-serving. Key to their misapprehension was the long French tradition of tending gardens:

> Since André Le Notre, the French have cultivated the art of beautiful gardens; we link the idea of a successful landscape intimately with the pleasurable frame of agreeable life. It has even become a social necessity. When discussing the policy of a town, better living, or the environment, the creation of parks and gardens is inseparable from our quest for well-being. But going from there to make a reserve of ninety thousand square kilometers out of Guyane is a limit not to be crossed. . . . In Guyane it is still only the period of the "conquest." . . . To transform it into an immense reserve would perhaps provide a clear conscience to France, its forest, and its ecologists, but the choice of whether to construct a road to lessen the isolation of a region only concerns the Guyanais, who will never be able to accept that this department is "only a preferential field of experimentation" for scientists badly in need of a thesis. . . . Those who wish a national petition to save this forest of Guyane when 90 percent of the French only know this department for the penal colony, Ariane, and butterflies and would not, for the most part, be capable of finding Guyane on a globe, leave us a bit skeptical.[39]

Rather, the business association suggested, environmentalists should stop sipping cocktails at fancy conferences, pretending nature was "paradise" and blocking the interests of local populations. They should turn to their real task: working to educate the population and to lighten the impact of development on the environment.

Faced with this wave of reaction, the WWF rallied their ecological allies and sought to retrieve the moral high ground. After all, business interests, not ecologists, they protested, are more likely to be found at hotel conferences. However, the statement they issued was more conciliatory in tone. They were not against development, not against the road if it should prove absolutely necessary. Rather, they sought only to focus attention on the project and to call for the highest possible level of environmental monitoring and care for any species threatened by the advance of the coastal route.[40]

As the summer faded the different conflicts simmered down; in October the state finally closed the space road without inciting riots, while the route to Brazil crept uncertainly eastward. CNES, the parent of CSG, launched a public relations campaign focusing on French astronauts to generate goodwill, while the activist ecology publication included a letter from a reader defending the Brazilian road. However, the acrimony of the disputes was not quick to dissipate, and together they struck an unsettling chord, reverberating against conflicts past and hinting of more to come.[41]

In the gap between the penal colony and the space center we have more than a contrast between failure and success, between active laziness and displaced industry. The work of high technology is partly a matter of bodies, training, and organization. But it is also a spatial disturbance, a reconfiguration of a greater ecology of enterprise. A web of artifice extends into the environment, and natural elements take on new roles in social relations and cultural representation. Between poles of power and vectors of motion lie the internal divides of modern French Guiana. At one pole lies the space center, limiting motion on the ground to ensure it above the sky. At another pole lies the new dam, built to free the department from imported fuel, while powering rockets, refrigerators, and a cooler climate for all. Movements of people and things cross over each other, producing new assemblages of natural and cultural elements. Slowly, rising waters close over the remains of a penal camp for Southeast Asian nationalists, photographed all the while by satellite. Elsewhere on the ground machines carve a path toward the southern border, a project descended from the penal colony and now opposed by inheritors of Columbus. Development and nature ring through the air, while splintered groups of new and old moderns face both forward and backward. Storms of progress blow, but the angels of history no longer fly in a single line.

LOCAL MEETS GLOBAL

At the beginning of August 1994, a remarkable debate took place on French Guiana's third (and just recently legalized) television channel. Between strikingly awkward camera angles and poorly positioned microphones, one of the major figures favoring the completion of the road to Brazil faced off against a prominent local ecologist opposing the project. By most rhetorical standards the exchange was a mess; the positions expressed quickly lost any semblance of subtlety; the participants interrupted each other, and members of the tiny audience intervened. Yet amid the chaotic hyperbole, there emerge complex social and political tensions stretching between tangled issues of development and the environment in French Guiana. In the world of Ariane we are far from our opening vision of ax-wielding industry and tropical sloth, and yet we are still within its shadow; the debate contains traces of old prejudices as new terms of value, and reversed projections of progress and tradition. Here I offer a partial and loosely translated transcription of selected portions of the argument, closing this narrative on the edge of an uncertain present, one much larger than French Guiana.[42] The two protagonists are Monsieur D, a Creole road contractor, and Monsieur F, a Metro ecologist. Rather than offer direct commentary, I will let their words dangle free, like a live wire.

> D: To start with, this is not an internal debate in Guyane, but a case of Guyane against outsiders, ideological fundamentalist ecologists.
>
> F: I feel Guyanais. Monsieur D is originally from Martinique; I'm from Champagne. We're both from other *French* departments. Furthermore I represent a world organization [WWF] as well as a local coalition of environmental groups [SEPANGUY, Pou d'Agouti, Ibis Vert]. My credentials are not what you make them; I'm Guyanais, and can show you my identity card. But this is an issue of human inheritance [*patrimoine*], a global issue.
>
> D: The Antilles [Martinique, Guadeloupe] share a fundamental culture, a Guyane-Antilles culture. The French are from *outside*. This is a foreign, world group, not a local interest. Why did you not protest against important French projects, like the deviation road around the space center, or that to Petit Saut Dam?
>
> F: Other groups did go on record against the dam, but here we're discussing this road—
>
> D: You can consider yourself what you want—a Brazilian even—but this is a business for those it concerns, not for outsiders. Under cover of ecology, you're forwarding a political agenda [of dependence]. . . .

We need roads, need to redistribute the population, need to have links with our neighbors, with Brazil, yes, even to Venezuela, to end this artificial tie to France.

MAN FROM AUDIENCE: In Guyane we're all ecologists, and put trash into cans. We've lived four hundred years without development. What has France brought us? The penal colony, the space center. The space center pays no taxes. You pay taxes Monsieur F (I assume you do), I pay taxes, but they—

F: What about the two hundred million francs for the road?

D: The European community is paying the largest share—

F: Do you want roads everywhere, even to Saül [a town in the interior]?

MAN FROM AUDIENCE: Yes . . . we need to protect things, but also need to get places. Everyone talks about tourism, but what kind of tourism can you have without access—[cacophony]—This road only represents 0.001 percent of French Guiana's forest!

F: The road itself—the line through the forest—is not the real problem. But it leads to much more, devastation on either side of the road, deforestation, immigration—

D: I visited the United States recently—do you know the U.S.?—and I went to Yellowstone Park, a beautiful park—with many roads. And that is in the U.S., a country with serious environmental legislation [not like here].

F: No, no, France actually has the most restrictive environmental codes—

D: The road network in the U.S. is fantastic. And the great ecologists come from the U.S.—the WWF is originally an Anglo-Saxon group, isn't it? Yes, well, remember that all the important currents of ecology flow out of Anglo-Saxon logic.

F: There are many things in the U.S.—

D: What do we want? We want to establish the means of development, and it's not for outsiders to tell us what to do—

F: But you're not president of Guyane—

D: Look, there are slaves and slave owners. Modern supporters of slavery work under the guise of ecology. The problem with this country is that there's no infrastructure. We need to open up the land and redistribute the population. Saül has the best soil in Guyane, perfect for agriculture. If we want to encourage local production we need to have means of transport. And we must industrialize—France doesn't want us to, so that we'll remain dependent. We're in favor of ecology . . . the Amerindians, the Saramaka [Maroons] know how to live in harmony with nature. What we have here is a colonialist attitude: Grandfather comes in and says, "No, no, stop this." We think we're old enough to make our own decisions.

MODERATOR: Why not regulate hunting and build the road?

F: These things go together; we must not separate them. I'm not an evil Metro colonialist; I have been here, working for ecology for twenty-two years. I was one of the first [audience interruption]. Once, yes, you could find populations here in harmony with the environment, but we have to use the past tense. Why build a road to Maripasoula [an interior town] when there is a river? This forest is the heritage of the entire world [*patrimoine mondial*]. This is the least populated country on the planet; that in itself is priceless. Why populate it?

D: Someone has to pay for it. Brazilians need something to eat.

F: You were talking of national parks. . . . Yes, other countries have problems, but it's not for French Guiana to solve all the problems of Brazil or Haiti.

D: You speak only in your name.

F: I represent several groups in Guyane, and besides, you have private interests in this matter, I believe. How many Guyanais work in the construction crew?

D: There are Saramakas [Maroons, with a homeland in Suriname], and young Guyanais [Creole] interns. It's not your role to determine what should be done here. You're from the national territory—I'm from the one under domination.

F: I am speaking for other organizations—

D: Look, I won't play the role of the victim; I have respect for what you did for the turtles—

F: Thank you.

D: But your work here should be to train young Guyanais, then to go back to France. No need for Grandfather . . .

F: I have worked with the turtles because they're specifically Guyanais, and I employ Galibi [Amerindians]—

D: You're the chief.

F: It's not so simple, I'm a scientist . . . besides, you're also the boss [of your crew].

D: Guyane is artificially part of the North. As in other parts of the North, people from poorer neighbors, Brazil and so forth, are attracted by its wealth. What we must do is stabilize the border. How to do this? By building the road. Yes, and establishing a frontier trade zone [*zone d'activité*] that will attract serious investment. That way Brazilians can come to the border and work. People in St. Georges want to stay Guyanais, not to become Brazilian. With a stable, working border they can do so—

F: They worked hard to have *French TV* and not Brazilian . . . a bit of imperialism, no?

D: Guyane will turn to Europe, not France. The policy of decreasing isolation [*désenclavement*] will help us develop. Yes, you have technical knowledge, but leave it to Guyanais to develop the method.

F: I'm a professional ecologist—

D: You're an agitator. No, I'm not against you, I'm against the role you play.

F: Immigration isn't so simple. How can you limit—

D: Some of my friends are ecologists—real ecologists—Americans. You sound like the frontier police, not an ecologist. Ecology is to the left, not on the side of the gendarmes. Guyanais don't condemn the Brazilians, it's the French who do that. You're in charge of this place. Could you do such a thing in Brazil, in Suriname? Brazilians come here to try and eat. Immigration is a problem throughout the North, all the rich countries have problems. Look at the U.S. and Mexico, even Brazil—yes at places in Brazil Peruvians and Bolivians cross the border [to work there]. Any time one neighbor is richer and the other poorer, well, then you have migration. Both Guyanais and Brazilians can benefit from a trade zone.

F: I knew Guyane when it had a population of fifty thousand. People lived in wood houses—nice Creole, wooden houses. They had a quality life. Now, twenty years later with immigration, people live a stressful life, with air-conditioning. An artificial life, excuse me, but as stupid as certain Metropolitans; people imitate Metropolitans. I feel Guyanais, but I'm told I'm not Guyanais by someone who lives like a European. There is a Guyanais identity that has utterly forgotten Creole life. Let's take roads. I don't know if you've seen those nice signs they've put up by the roadsides, but since January—just since January—they're thirteen dead and three hundred injured. What will your road do? Add another ninety or so. It's a Pan-American project, it will link Belém to Caracas—

D: When I was little, people used to hide from whites, the *vieux blancs,* the *bagnards* [from the penal colony]. . . . Yes, perhaps things were better before. But it was the French who destabilized things by their behavior.

F: The forest belongs to humanity.

D: It's the business of those who live there. This concern is a bit—excuse the expression—co-lo-ni-a-list.

F: What do you want for the Guyane of the future? Roads to Maripasoula and everywhere else? Harmony with nature is past, people have changed how they live. This is a part of a global heritage, not only Guyanais. More population will lead to problems like Brazil and Haiti. What does development mean?

D: We must link ecology with development. Remember, [the dam at] Petit Saut eliminated four hundred square kilometers [of forest].

F: That's EDF [the utility company]; we opposed it. People say Petit Saut is all for the space center, but that's not true. CSG only uses 25 percent of the total energy. The rest is Guyane, especially all the *air-conditioning!*

D: Europe is bigger than France. You want us to return to trees and live like monkeys. Well, we don't want to; we won't. Against these fundamentalists [*integretistes*], this tiny outside group—

F: Your "Guyanais" are the elected officials and companies—

D: Not ecology for ecology's sake—ecology and development!

F: Agreed, but . . . we want to redo the ecological impact report, be more careful. . . . Remember, this is one of the last primary forests *in the world*. Not in Guyane, not in South America, *in the world*. It's a richness for all humanity, as well as Guyane—

[general interruptions and chaos]

D: Economic development is for now and for the future. We need to use the space of our territory. The Saramaka, the Amerindians know how to live in harmony with the forest, they don't need lessons from Grandpa.

MODERATOR: Yes or No to Development, Monsieur F?

F: You can't put it that way. But no to this version of the road.

MODERATOR: Yes or No to Ecology, Monsieur D?

D: Oh yes. I'm an ecologist.

CHAPTER 9

The Imperfect Equator

Space and the tropics are both utopian topical figures in
western imaginations, and their opposed properties dialecti-
cally signify origins and ends for the creature whose mundane life is outside both: civilized man. Space and the tropics
are "allotopic"; i.e. they are "elsewhere," the place to which
the traveler goes to find something dangerous and sacred.
Donna Haraway, Primate Visions, *1989*

FIRST IMPRESSIONS

Some of the most memorable photographs are those not taken. If I were
to choose an emblematic image to accompany the contrasts I seek to
capture, it would be one I do not possess, of Rochambeau Airport in
the summer of 1990. Lacking the clear, unsettling detail of film, I can
only shape the scene from memories of sensations, some singular, some
repeated: an airplane, direct from Paris, crosses a flat and muddy edge
of the Atlantic, then banks and circles over the low green sea of forest
just beyond it, down between rising houses and scattered trees until
wheels touch tarmac. At the end of the runway the plane slows, turns,
and finally stops before a small, but brightly painted terminal. Leaving
the air-conditioned cabin, the passengers step into a world of light,
heat, and humidity, a sudden transit to the tropics. And yet, even while
registering this most abrupt and unlikely change of environment, their
attention moves down the runway to a neighboring plane, beak-nosed
and silent. Etched against that thick, undisciplined greenery most commonly associated in English with the word *jungle,* under a strong midday equatorial sun, stands the unmistakable profile of a Concorde, that
supersonic pride of Franco-British aviation. The impressions are both
simultaneous and startling, and they lead in quite opposite directions:
associations with nature, the uninhabited, and the wild, on the one
hand, and with technology, the controlled, and the civilized, on the
other. Cool, stale air from an airplane cabin, warm pungent air of the

Figure 21.   Path of the Stars, Kourou, 1993

exterior, a futuristic aircraft, and an archaic landscape, all quite suddenly filling the same moment.

Within the anthropological tradition known as ethnography, arrival
scenes have often played a privileged and crucial role, even as first encounters cast a seductive allure over the history of colonialism. What,
after all, more surely represents a crossed boundary than a foot meeting shore, the initial and passing wonder of contact? Because the focus
of this work is on boundaries, their techniques, and their representation, I have returned here, with an account of my own first arrival in
French Guiana. Despite the rhetorical burden of such initial experiences and their fetishization, I am reluctant to abandon the rhetorical
power of their sensation, that fleeting yet certain confirmation that life
is in motion. Sometimes, by chance and the turmoil of interruption, one
can absorb past knowing, even as a child or a stranger uncertainly
grasps the raw wholeness of things. Only later, in scattered bits and
pieces, would I arrive at the knowledge through which to interpret the
image and enlarge it with explanation: that an important satellite
launch had taken place the day before at the nearby space center, one

made particularly significant by a previous failure, that because of this significant event important French officials had arrived on a supersonic flight to witness the performance of Europe's rocket (and would depart again shortly), that the large contingent of male passengers with shaven heads were arriving to begin their stint of obligatory military service, that this airport, rather oddly positioned relative to the urbanized region it serves, had first been built by American forces during World War II, and that what I took to be jungle was actually the heavy scrub of secondary rain forest, the product of human habitation and clearing of the land. Yet even without such explanation the image bears a certain witness, the plane gleaming white beneath the colors of France, the tangled backdrop green and impenetrable. Here we have Culture against Nature, imperial technology against wilderness, a contrast of extremes or an extreme of contrast. What startles is not the existence of either element in question, plane or landscape, but rather their combination in the same scene. This was most certainly not where a Concorde *should* land, and yet, undeniably, there it was. The edge of such contrast forms the center of this work: connecting things that seem not to fit and yet undeniably do, by virtue of their coexistence.

In its pursuit of the Fridays of this world, anthropology has sought knowledge in depth to establish clear, locally ordered patterns of belief and practice. With enough time, the transitory and the incongruent could be filtered out of analysis, and the authentic distilled, revealing the inner heart of society and culture. When reversing the direction of inquiry, however, and bringing anthropology "home from the tropics" to address modern life, it is precisely the incongruent and transitory that become significant. "Science" and "technology" describe vast, busy networks, obviously incomplete at any local scale. The truth of modern power lies in change, in open practice. Surfaces matter, for in them we detect movement and distant links. To include the Crusoes of the world in anthropology, we must not lose sight of the exterior of their islands or the work of their hands in an accounting of their words and thoughts. This is especially clear when looking at the tropics and the structures they left behind.[1]

Although the European Metropoles did not simply acquire empires through technical superiority, an expanding set of imported problems and solutions played a central role in maintaining and transforming those empires. Colonialism reworked nature overseas even as industry did at home, only at a distance and less perfectly. Most crucially, it introduced a magic of scale, one that reworked space in ways simultaneously symbolic and practical. Even the smallest of metropolitan artifacts recalled an associated universe of material culture. To fit in a new setting, the artifact would need either to have that universe reconstructed around it or to be incorporated into an altered local milieu. Otherwise it would remain out of place. Here a distinction between technical and nontechnical material culture becomes important: while passive objects might appear incongruous or appropriate depending on cultural perspective, active objects are not simple commodities, in the sense that their consumption involves performance and secondary effects.[2] When the element in question constitutes part of a technical system, being out of place multiplies the risk of malfunction and poor performance in the absence of parts, supplies, or expertise. This in turn provokes two sorts of responses: increased extralocal importation of additional elements of the system, or increased localized reliance on improvised repairs and bricolage. Thus a car can grow into a network of roads or shrink into a hodgepodge of parts, a rocket can beget a city of commodities, and a penal colony can amass a ruin of corruption.[3] In this magic of scale we have one of the key dilemmas of technology and development. To understand its human costs we must pause to consider issues of independence and mastery, returning to our guiding myth of Robinson Crusoe.

WORKING MASTERS, PORTABLE ISLANDS

In a little Time I began to speak to him and teach him
to speak to me; and first, I made him know his Name
should be Friday, which was the Day I sav'd his Life; I
called him so for the Memory of the Time; I likewise
taught him to say Master, and then let him know, that
was to be my Name.

> Daniel Defoe, Robinson Crusoe, 1719

Defoe's castaway defines a lonely individual, and yet he acquires an important shadow, the man he rescues from cannibalism and renames after a day of the week. Friday proves a perfect servant; unshakably loyal in his devotion, he provides his master with the subservient companionship of which he had dreamed. Despite the fact that Friday is native to the region, Crusoe reforms him to fit his improved island, teaching him to abhor cannibal feasts and labor productively. In our colonial myth, then, the displaced hero crosses a middle plane between exile and home, as he transforms from piteous castaway into governor. In that middle plane he becomes a character and a half: a man with a dependent, the truncated family of master and servant, joined forever by the thunder of a gun.

Long before our present story but somewhat after Defoe, a German scholar gave a famous analysis of servitude amid a grand account of the emergence of consciousness. At a crucial point in Georg Hegel's *Phenomenology*, a recognition of strength and weakness gives birth to the overpowering lord and overpowered bondsman. Hegel's dense description of the aftermath of conquest provides a complex fable of social change. Forced to work by the master, the slave comes to know the world and control it, achieving independent consciousness. At the same time, by forcing the slave to work the master becomes dependent on the service performed and hence is weakened. Servitude is thus inherently unstable, for craft and control of nature provide a remedy for the threat of death. Labor, in this tradition, describes a key to power and eventual freedom.[4]

This moment of the master and slave resonates through much subsequent writing about domination and world history, surfacing memorably in Marxist visions of struggling classes and postcolonial accounts of mutually constituting colonizer and colonized. It is the latter echo that concerns us here, for in it we encounter less perfect masters and slaves.[5] Hegel's power figures live symmetrically in abstraction, unmarked by location or heritage, beyond a vaguely classical agrarian past. The darker shadows of empirical record around Defoe's novel tell less certain stories. More is at stake than violent rule and labor when the Atlantic slave trade leaves a painful vocabulary of color and when the end of European empire witnesses new systems of inequality. As the Martiniquan psychiatrist Franz Fanon notes, the master and slave in a colonial system defined by race are not the same as those in Hegel's dialectic:

> For Hegel there is reciprocity; here the master laughs at the consciousness of the slave. What he wants from the slave is not recognition but work. In the same way the slave here is in no way identifiable with the slave who loses himself in the object and finds in his work the source of his liberation. . . . In Hegel the slave turns away from the master and turns towards the object. Here the slave turns towards the master and abandons the object.[6]

The dynamic of liberation promised in Hegel is thus lost in the colonies; race distorts the opposition of domination, eliminating its symmetry and deferring the reversal of power. The colonial slave works, but without mastering nature or learning craft. In this setting, labor does not produce independent consciousness, but only a complex of dependency.

Fanon leaves us here, but *Robinson Crusoe* contains a second, related clue, one that will take us deeper into a consideration of the technical fault lines in colonial space. Crusoe, the displaced man, is a ruler who knows nature for himself and refashions the world around him. He has already labored as his own slave and mastered mechanical arts. Despite his gun, he is not simply a warrior; despite his merchant past, he is not simply bourgeois. He is a working, well-equipped master, corrupted by experience and bolstered by far-flung ties. Thus the opposition between lord and bondsman on this tropical island is not between pure command and service but between different, unequal identities within a common project of practice. The field of power between independence and labor is offset not only by race but also by a technical landscape.

How might the work of a master and the work of a slave characterize themselves? Further provocation comes from another citizen of the German language, this one writing not long after Sputnik. In *The Human Condition* Hannah Arendt distinguishes between three forms of activity: labor (that which is necessary for life), work (that which leaves an imprint on the world), and action (that which changes political conditions). Arendt's larger aim is to chronicle a perceived decline of action and the eventual glorification of labor in modern existence, and as with Hegel, her narrative world contains but a single history, and her terms remain abstract. Here I am not seeking to adopt Arendt's firm and idiosyncratic definitions as given. But her etymologically based distinction between labor and work touches on relevant lines between toil and skill, expended energy and design. Thus Arendt's vocabulary has its uses for this argument, demarcating processes that further living and reproduction (at a minimum, "getting by") from those that produce objects and transform the world (at a maximum, "technology"). In Crusoe we find both labor, his struggle to adapt to an alien land, and work, his eventual domination of an "improved" island. Only after he has domesticated nature does Defoe's protagonist become a master in the world of human affairs, rescuing other men in violent acts of mercy. This point is crucial: he is not a passive owner of his island but an active governor, the lord of an extended household, manipulator of a modified environment.[7]

It would be a mistake to think of the place that Crusoe washes ashore and the place where Friday lands as the same ground. Between these two narrative points, Defoe's hero has reworked the fabric of the landscape around him, recovering fragments of the ship, fashioning tools, domesticating animals, farming, practicing crafts, and building shelters. He has actively developed systems to cope with the challenges of an unfamiliar environment, ease his labor, and extend his reach. He has also struggled with melancholy and self-doubt, established codes of conduct, and created a record of his occupation. His island includes guns, Bibles, and goats in a pen—an order of life in which a European can feel natural amid the tropics, more natural, in fact, than a Carib. Shaped by his hands, the island has become his through artifice as well as through conquest; it is now an archipelago of things, interventions, and small solutions. Such a place cannot be remade by labor but only by work that crafts new objects and forges new ties. We should also not forget that the space Crusoe inhabits contains active bits of elsewhere, and it is mobile. When a ship arrives, he can come and go, precious stocks of powder, shot, and ink can be resupplied, and the island can be charted for inclusion on maps of the world. His place is already a world space. Once in it, Friday also sails the world, as servant and apprentice. Facing both a new language of command and a technical action, he adapts to Crusoe's life as well as to the island. He gets by.

Our fictional guidebook can only take us so far. Amid the range of imperial experience, few islands were so uninhabited, few landings so uncontested, few servants so willing, and few masters so industrious. But set against Hegel and Arendt, *Robinson Crusoe* suggests an important principle: in the tropical expanse of empire, universal theory is forced to confront an exposed space of imperfection. Because the colonial lord and bondsman emerge on a frontier between different alignments of nature and technology, their relation is defined in spatial terms. The rule of the latter by the former rests on an imposed order of life, one referenced to elsewhere. The division between them returns to a distinction between work and labor, with expertise reserved for a mastery of the horizon rather than local toil and improvisation. The colonial bondsman thus cannot master nature and play off the lord's dependence, for nature has been reworked in the master's conquest, a conquest born of a voyage as well as violence, of dislocation as well as production. In the colonial drama, action extends ever offstage. So too do plans, techniques, and criteria of improvement. The reasonable story of theory, so clear within a single dimension, becomes an uncertain line across a larger domain of history, ever shifting, flawed, and incomplete. Within this domain, some islands are not only larger than others but also more portable.

FRENCH GUIANA AND THE AFTERLIFE OF ISLANDS

Fancy has depicted men without reflection, others
without shadow! But here reality, by the neutralization
of attractive forces, produced men in whom nothing
had any weight, and who weighed nothing themselves!

Jules Verne, Around the Moon, *1870*

Even in Defoe's day, the world around Crusoe's island could be thought
to compose a vast, interacting system, knit together by trade and communication across land and sea. At the scale of centuries, this system
only accelerates and tightens. Yet within it lie different moments, different configurations of space, time, and power. Returning to French
Guiana, we can summarize the projects before us in terms of two such
technical regimes of space. The penal colony lies at an intersection of imperial history and racial geography. A shadow of the prison, it operates
crudely, in place. The space center lies at an intersection of multinational
history and global geography. A shadow of space exploration, it operates efficiently, between places. Neither the penal colony nor the space
center is really of Guyane, but both make use of it from the outside. Between the two we shift from a slow, fixed engine of dislocated moral retribution to an active, mobile network of technical service. A comparison
between them could include the following opposed constellations of
terms, under the imperfect rubrics "Empire" and "Globe":

Empire	*Globe*
penal colony	space center
punishment	communication
improvement	development
French Empire	multistate and corporate networks
territories	connections
maps	planet
civilization	technology
race	certified skills
natural and unnatural men	neutral men
place overseas	place from space
natural order	technical norms
natural threats	fragile nature
ground	sky

The line dividing these rival lists is at once stark and uneven: while clear
at a distance it blurs under close inspection. Improvement and develop-

ment are cognates within different structural settings; territories connect and the ghosts of race haunt regimes of certification. Conditions change, the world hurtles on, and yet the Globe carries a stamp of Empire. For in the end, we both are and are not talking about the same place. What was, in effect, a realm of two dimensions has become a space of three: the ground remains, but above it arcs a new and altering sky. Parts of the older order linger in and amid the new but no longer constitute a central axis of definition.[8]

Whatever names we might give these successive historical orders and however much the divide between them wavers, an anthropological shadow emerges along the divide. Here at last is a universal subject in both material and ideal terms: a being who can go anywhere without regard to local conditions, a being who could conceive of the entire planet as a home, a vast, dispersed ecosystem. In Devil's Island the contradictions of European colonialism came together, with racial categories of whiteness painfully exposed. A sense of nature lies at the center of both experience and understanding. At the Guiana Space Center, whiteness recedes behind the extended artifice of a technological network. A sense of nature remains, but as coordinates of geometry; life itself has moved to different registers of technical consideration, namely the management of exotic flora and fauna. Our second metaphorical island features light men in the tropics, and although their northern lives may cast heavy shadows, what matters is their ability to circulate and function without regard to place. They are "there" but not "really there," their surroundings distanced enough to be thought of as "nature." A form of placeless practice can be detected behind the old myth of Man. With sufficient technical insulation the species can indeed become cosmopolitan: scattering plans and buildings across the future, leaving footprints on moondust as well as Caribbean sand.[9]

But in imagining the lineage of Defoe's island through eras of empire and globe, we must remember the shadow of Robinson's servant. Friday hovers always at the edge of Crusoe's story, a reminder that few lands were empty, however far-flung or small. In the language of Empire the divisions are tense and clear (if imperfectly maintained), both colonizer and colonized emerging from colonization, along with a grammar of human typology. Although the penal colony partially inverted relations, a geography of race still runs through its rolls. Alongside fallen Europeans we find groups of colonials, North Africans, West Indians, and Indochinese, laboring with even less sense of work or redemption. Their mutual saga is one of survival more than resistance, of making do and getting by as long as possible with the means at hand.

Amid the reworked coordinates of an active globe, vocabulary grows less secure. *Guyanais* implies local identity against Metropolitan connections, but between Creoles, Maroons, and Amerindians the term is sometimes unstable. An analysis of class must acknowledge the meaning of citizenship and French education, together with a shifting matrix of origin transformed by migration. There are many possible Fridays in our story now, and often more than one Crusoe. Distinctions of planning and improvisation remain, along with harsh inequalities of life. But behind them patterns of understanding and dream weave differently, sometimes wandering across each other. Modern dreams disrupt other ones and set things in uncertain, glancing motion. Ultimately, they can ricochet and disrupt themselves.

WEDNESDAY, SEPTEMBER 30, 1992

"Crusoe," he said sternly, "take heed of what I say. Beware of purity. It is the acid of the soul."

> *Michel Tournier, Friday, 1967*

In the heat of late morning, back sweating against the seat, I am driving toward the town of Kourou from Cayenne. The two-lane highway slowly curves along the coast, the red and green land empty to either side. Occasionally the pavement crosses the remains of the old road beside it, partly overgrown and even narrower. Traffic is surprisingly dense, with luxury automobiles impatiently weaving between slower, aging machines and heavy trucks. Along the way, billboards caution drivers about the extraordinary accident rate, while traffic signs remind them—should any doubt remain—that this is indeed the main road. The car I am driving, a product of the same Yugoslavia that, by late 1992, has disintegrated in civil war, whines shrilly. Beside me sits a Brazilian hitchhiker, a short wiry man with dark skin and hair. In a mixture of imperfect French and the remnants of my childhood Portuguese we improvise a conversation. Though I picked him up on the outskirts of Cayenne partly as an act of impulsive, surface ethnography, he surprises me with the readiness with which he tells his story, anticipating questions to present a version of his life.

This life, he says, is hard; he left Salvador years ago when he lost his job as a truck driver, and he cannot find work in Brazil, where the "Mafioso" rule. He claims to have been in French Guiana for just two months (which seems unlikely), currently picking melons in Cayenne and living with other Brazilians doing odd jobs in Kourou. He worries about being caught and deported, even though he says his papers are in order (which also seems unlikely). During the week he rises before dawn to travel the sixty kilometers to where he works, but weekends he marks with a big Brazilian beer, a visit with a prostitute, and the promise of a soccer game. Perhaps I would like to meet some of his women friends? He knows some nice women, he says, not the ones who go with legionnaires. I do not respond, trying to think of a way to deflect the offer with a joke. Perhaps I would like a beer? He has two Heinekens, the Dutch product of choice, and I accept one, though I do not open it, mindful of the local accident rate. The can is grimy and only slightly cool. He snaps his open and takes a deep drink. Perhaps, he suggests with a slight glint in his eye, we can make a regular arrangement—do I travel to Kourou every afternoon? I tell him that this is a rental car, that I only have it for a few days, that I can't afford such transportation. Though all this is true, he does not quite believe me, particularly about the last point. I have told him that I'm not French (a fact also amply clear from my speech), yet he sometimes includes me with the proprietors of the land, the masters of cars, in a plural "you." Why, after all, would I be in this situation? Surely I am after something, surely we can make a deal. A regular ride, I slowly calculate as he talks, could save him many times the inflated local price of a Heineken.

As I realize this he finishes his beer and casually tosses the can out the window. The action shocks me—I have been living in urban northern California, a most ecologically minded milieu, and the wanton act of littering is unthinkable. I open my mouth, but ethnographic conscience stills my tongue. Given the vast expanse around us, the weight of the action is far greater in symbolic than material terms, and anyway, in this setting from what position do I speak? The thought echoes in my head while he continues with his story. We arrive in Kourou, a sudden suburban expanse amid empty land, and he directs me to his destination, all the while pointing out what he says are houses of prostitution, and the places that he and other Brazilians frequent. "Just ask for Paulo," he offers as I let him out, "I'll show you a good time." We wave and go on with our days.

ROMANTIC ROBINSONS, MODERN FRIDAYS

Crusoe thinks he can distinguish between force and
reason. As the only being on his island, he weeps from
loneliness, while Friday finds himself among rivals,

allies, traitors, friends, confidants, a whole mass of
brothers and chums, of whom only one carries the
name of man.

> Bruno Latour,
> The Pasteurization of France, 1984

Amid the many divides cut through French Guiana, the central one in
human affairs lies between the rental cars and taxis that serve the airport and the collective taxis (*taxis collectifs*) that run along the dusty
roads, giving rides without questions or receipts. This line marks where
the world of credit cards ends and the world of collected change and
wadded bills begins. In the tropics neither system functions smoothly,
and both frequently require improvisation and argument to operate.[10]
But a crucial difference remains in the degree of improvisation necessary for survival.

Neither Paulo nor I was in any sense native to the setting of our interaction; both of us arrived in Guyane from elsewhere and lived our
lives in relation to frontiers. I never met him again, but statistics on the
borders of French Guiana suggest that he was most likely deported only
to reappear again a few weeks later. I myself left and returned again
several times, under less strained conditions. We represented different
migrations: travel born of professional curiosity and travel born of economic need. For me "getting by" was an intellectual experience; for
him it was a way of life. Yet we also expressed different understandings
of the place and purpose of material culture, different modernities, if
you will. Where I gave him a ride, he presented me with a drink and an
ethical quandary. In this brief male encounter, references to prostitution
and alcohol—nineteenth-century sins, classic colonial vices—failed to
startle. But his minor and casual act of littering woke my dormant sense
of civilization. The naturalness of this material and symbolic pollution
of what I considered to be a natural landscape jarred my moral sensibilities. I felt simultaneously more and less modern than he was. Although both our universes may have contained the same elements, the
different ordering of them was suddenly and unmistakably revealed.
The material objects between us may have had the same outline, but we
felt their edges in unlike ways. We both traveled, both inhabited islands, but we fashioned on them disparate structures, finding dissimilar
names for hope and despair. Between us lay a shifting sea of meaning
and different conceptual wreckage of industry and civilization.

In a 1967 rewriting of Defoe, the French novelist Michel Tournier imagines an alternative to Crusoe's island, relocated to the Pacific of the historical castaway Selkirk and transported forward in time to the eighteenth century. As indicated by the work's title, *Vendredi* (Friday), the weight of the experience shifts from Robinson to the man who joins him on his island. In Tournier's version the master still seeks to impose his will on land and servant, but this time the free laughter of his companion emerges triumphant. Robinson loses his hoard of salvaged order, finds love in the soil of the island, and slowly turns to the open sky. When a British ship finally lands on their isolated shore, the world it represents so repulses this Robinson that he decides to remain behind, allowing Friday to depart and taste the life of other shores.[11] Elegant and thoughtful, Tournier's *Robinsonade* gives us another human figure to consider: a universal subject who, freed from a desire to control space, learns to live in place. Here the very device that brought this Crusoe overseas—the ship—loses its magic hold on him. He denies his civilization at its edge and falls into another nature. His island, in the end, is the one he learns through exile and Friday, not the one he sought to rule. And when this Friday leaves to travel the world, he does so without his master.

Given Tournier's Crusoe and this other island, the image of the universal subject before us grows less sure. Robinson, it turns out, can become a romantic rather than calculating castaway, and Friday, once allowed to speak in something other than fractured English, may displace himself and sail away on other adventures. While Tournier's reworked island still lacks women, it transforms into a land of desire: a place where Robinson consummates his "immense compassion for all living things."[12] Nature is no longer a wild force to be held at bay but a wild companion to be sought out, admired, and loved. Rather than carve the image of himself on the land, this Robinson unearths the image of the island buried within his soul.

In the reversal of Defoe's tale, the purity rubs off Crusoe, off colonialism, off his island, and also off Friday. This version of the myth depends both on the original and on another displacement between historical precedents and the world of Tournier's present. Rather than one master and servant, one colonizer and colonized, we have a sense of motion over centuries and between categories. Appeals to universality, boundary crossings, and dreams of the future come from several directions. Our universal subject is washed by the waves, and its image blurs and runs. Yet an outline lingers, diffused but persistent. The deep cuts of history resist the tide.

AFTER THE SPACE AGE

The West is now everywhere, within the West and outside; in structures and in minds.

Ashis Nandy, The Intimate Enemy, *1983*

When acknowledging a mobile world and impure forms, we must not forget the inertia of inequality or the historical gravity of power. Not all directions were equal in colonial systems, and in the aftermath of empire, residual masses continue to exert attractions. Colonies and empires reinscribe time in space and space in time, defining some places as older and more significant and others as newer, reborn through contact and hence derivative. Progress thus becomes a matter of both geography and history, with implicit comparison to other places as well as eras. The axis between culture and nature plays a particularly acute role in such comparisons, for it runs through economic structure and moral sensibility, separating future and past. Here we should recall that human relations do not occur in a vacuum but across an active landscape and through an ever-shifting field of artifice. Colonialism is not only about domination; it is also about creating and solving problems, modifying the conditions under which life could be lived. The work of modern science and technology continually reinscribes this axis in graphic terms: technical systems extend the landscape of the machine forward, and scientific investigations push the boundary of nature further back. Hence the chronology of ages so prominent in media attempts to define the present, where a moving horizon of technology defines the material and symbolic present around new parameters of possibility.

An "age" revolves around a paradox of identifying change. Surely humans who inhabit the same sphere and who—within the ordered difference of time zones—experience the same year all live in the present. And yet, when certain statements are made about the conditions of that present, it is equally evident that they do not apply to everyone. Even as it claims universality, the modern defines itself against what it thinks it has left behind. Nowhere is this clearer or more poignant than in the term *development:* an area and its inhabitants are defined in terms of their relation to a shifting body of material culture and patterns of exchange known as "technology" and "economy," being categorized as "developed," "underdeveloped," or, most hopefully, "developing." Vast

agencies and networks of exchange operate under the aegis of promoting world "development," and despite several decades of scholarly skepticism about the success of such efforts, not to mention continuing, ever
more acutely defined disparity of average life conditions in different
parts of the world, the term has slid easily out of postwar bureaucratic
reports to become a fixture of everyday speech. For those lagging behind
the age—third world, East, or South—a frame for the future has been
set before arrival.[13]

At the end of the century, the age built around outer space is itself
aging. The glory of initial exploration now fades into more practical
forms of commercial exploitation as new horizons open on a smaller
scale of microcircuitry and microbiology. Cultural sensibilities in elite
settings within developed centers have shifted away from bolder forms
of universal function; the architecture of the future now attends to difference and local variation. Yet the final frontier is less "finished" than
reduced to the level of function, for human space now extends into
outer space, with the planet itself woven into a vast technical system of
satellites. In the Space Age one limit of modernist ambition has been
achieved: an island encompassing the globe. The scale of connection
opens new possibilities for migration and transmission of information
beyond metropolitan networks; it has the potential to produce alternative localities and other kinds of motion. And still patterns of inclusion
and exclusion persist. Like trade, knowledge circulates most frequently
through centers; like a mobile fortress, technology reinforces the order
of political economy. To be of an age it is not simply enough to live during it. One must also inhabit its landscape. Even at a low, quotidian
level, with a welter of unintended consequences and secondary systems,
the ecology of artifice has reinvented nature. Although experience of
this new geography may remain multiple, not all positions are equal.[14]
And around earthly networks, developed and undeveloped alike, there
now hovers a frame of the fragile planet, a practical representation
measuring the extent of all tomorrows.

THE EDGE OF THINGS

Like the man whom it shelters and nourishes, each
    land has its proper vocation.
There are deserts of sand and fire, deserts of ice and
    snow, both equally hostile to Man.
There are temperate plains with fertile soil, which,
    with Man's labor, sprout in abundance.

There are softly enchanting places, which one says are
   created for his pleasure.
But there are places of grief, where the suffering of
   Man, rejected by his fellows and overwhelmed by
   nature, cries out to heaven; places of expiation,
   places of mercy; a small portion of the earth sym-
   bolizing the entire world of men.
Are you not that, oh my dear Guyane?
Beautiful country!
Untouchable!
                        History of a religious order, circa 1978[15]

In Jules Verne's classic lunar fantasy, *From the Earth to the Moon,*
members of the Baltimore Gun Club shake off post–Civil War lethargy
by constructing a giant cannon to lob a projectile toward the Earth's
natural satellite. However, they briefly pause to consider another project, carried away by the inspirational speech of the dashing French
would-be passenger of their cannonball. Why not, he suggests, use a
massive explosion to right the Earth's axis, producing a world without
seasons?[16] The vision is breathtaking, mad, and thoroughly modern. It
extends the principle of climate control beyond buildings to a planetary
scale, creating zones of steady temperature from which humanity can
pick and choose. The elimination of the natural cycle of time with one
massive technical intervention promises perfection, nineteenth-
century style; the hand of Man, in the form of artillery, will correct the
work of God. Yet cosmology and practice do not always flow in even
lines. In its very triumph, this rash vision of engineering would subtly
expand the most somnolent of natural geographies. For the tropics—already seasonless, if not weatherless—would hardly be affected. Rather
than represent an aberration of stability, they would constitute just another band of that modified planet, hotter than most but thoroughly
normal. In effect, modernization elsewhere would render them modern,
without internal change. Verne's enthusiastic cannoneers, focused beyond their world, overlook the real edges of its present.
   Amid the giddy early days of the Space Age, a new view of the Earth
took shape. Even as outer space framed the globe, capturing its spherical unity and its conceptual perfection, satellites measured its dimensions and found it physically uneven. The world indeed appears one
and round, but it is roughly shaped, more pear than orange. The North

Pole of our pear protrudes, while the South Pole sits in a slight indentation. In form, if not scale, the planet matches the imperfect social geography of development—a minor revision unremarked by the general public and most of the academy, but one worth noting amid the profusion of global metaphors.[17] The large truth of European exploration, a practical geometry charted by tiny ships over heaving seas, finds itself qualified not only by less heroic accounts of conquest but also by smaller truths of improved instruments and their harvest of destabilizing detail. Although our world may have no edge, it remains circled by a line. From a distance this imaginary line can be drawn exactly by an armada of satellites; up close it fades amid bright light, heat, and dust. Moving back and forth above the tropics, we glimpse the globe and lose it again among dense foliage. But visible or invisible, ideal or useful, the equator divides imperfectly, separating uneven spheres on every level.

Such is also the case with modern categories: examination reveals that the lines defining them fall unevenly, and imperfect oppositions leave historical shadows and scattered anomalies at their side. Here we have followed a series of shadow histories: the penal colony behind the prison, Devil's Island behind Australia, commercial space behind the Space Race, and the Guiana Space Center behind Ariane. Among these shadows we find other lines of tension extending through and beyond empire: local against global, nature against technology, and improvisation against design. These are not restricted phenomena, unique to French Guiana. Rather, they constitute an imperfect framework of history and geography for modern life, around all its replicating, alternating forms. But in French Guiana they are especially apparent, in the absence of larger norms and amid the remnants of old dreams. It is there, only partly by chance, that outer space crosses tropical empire.

In regions where deposition is light, debris rests near the surface and archaeology requires less toil. French Guiana is a particularly good site to search for material and symbolic relics, minor ruins of future and past. Often one hardly has to dig. As every Ariane rises, it passes over Devil's Island. In such contrast lies the heart of motion and "a small portion of the earth symbolizing the entire world of men. Are you not that, oh my dear Guyane?" Modern life becomes most apparent along its horizon, the great, shifting frontier of nature, technology, and small things left behind. A dark roadway, broken trees, an empty can. The West grows sharpest in the evening, against a distant, setting sun.

Notes

Unless otherwise noted, all translations of French works are mine. In general, I have favored literal renderings over stylized ones.

CHAPTER 1. ROBINSON CRUSOE, ANTHROPOLOGY, AND THE HORIZON OF TECHNOLOGY

1. Page references here are to the World's Classics Edition by Oxford University Press (Defoe 1972), based on the first issue. See also the Norton Critical Edition (Defoe 1975) for additional critical and contextual material. In best eighteenth-century fashion, the full title page of the work summarizes key elements: The Life and Strange Surprizing Adventures of Robinson Crusoe, of York, Mariner: Who lived Eight and Twenty Years, all alone on an uninhabited Island on the Coast of America, near the Mouth of the great River Oroonoque; Having been cast on Shore by Shipwreck, wherein all the Men perished but himself. With An Account how he was at last as strangely deliver'd by PYRATES. Written by Himself. The first of the sequels (Defoe 1903a) takes him around the world, and the second (Defoe 1903b) offers meditations on his condition.

2. Green (1990) gives a thorough account of the many reworkings of the Crusoe motif across centuries, including a long line of French variants, from Rousseau's *Emile* through Verne's *Mysterious Island* to Tournier's *Friday*.

3. For analysis of Verne, see A. Martin (1990: 22), and for Verne's influence on spaceflight pioneers, see McDougall (1985a: 22).

4. For a sampling of criticism, see Defoe (1975) as well as Bloom (1988), McKeon (1987), and Watt (1963), which remains the quintessential materialist rendering of Crusoe. Ray (1990) gives further background on the work's place relative to French and English traditions of the novel, Bender (1987) links the

novel form to the rise of the penitentiary, Schonhorn (1991) examines Defoe's often neglected conservative streak, amid his general Lockean vision, and Green (1979) places the work within a wider context of imperialist fiction. Here I rely strongly on the reading of Hulme (1986), who places Crusoe back into the Caribbean and the writing of the New World.

5. Defoe (1972: 4).

6. Robinson sails the world, not a regional sea, and whereas Odysseus lends his name to a state of travel, Crusoe gives his to an island. In *Dialectic of Enlightenment*, Horkheimer and Adorno engage in an extended analysis of the character of Odysseus as he navigates between myth and enlightenment, making a comparison with Crusoe: "The wily solitary is already *homo oeconomicus*, for whom all reasonable things are alike: hence the Odyssey is already a *Robinsonade*. Both Odysseus and Crusoe, the two shipwrecked mariners, make their weakness (that of the individual who parts from the collectivity) their social strength. Delivered up to the mercy of the waves, helplessly isolated, their very isolation forces them to recklessly pursue an atomistic interest. . . . Odysseus and Crusoe are both concerned with totality: the former measures whereas the latter produces it. Both realize totality only in complete alienation from all other men, who meet the two protagonists only in an alienated form—as enemies or as points of support, but always as tools, as things" (Horkheimer and Adorno 1987: 61–62). In addition to distinguishing between measuring and producing reality, one might also note a distinction between the axis of gender and desire in each work: whereas Odysseus encounters numerous temptations in the form of women and always seeks escape to return to hearth and wife, Crusoe inhabits a world with women firmly at the margin, in which his real marriage is to his island. Tournier's (1969) rewriting of the Defoe myth plays on an elaboration of this subtheme, which resonates with some feminist accounts of knowledge, desire, and nature (for example, Merchant 1990).

7. Defoe (1972: 70).

8. Ibid.: 66, 137.

9. Indeed the spontaneous appearance of barley leads him to proclaim a miracle and find meaning in his suffering (ibid.: 78).

10. Witness the remarkably brief paragraph in which he weds, has three children, and sees his wife expire (ibid.: 305).

11. Ibid.: 277, 305–6.

12. Ibid.: 47.

13. Hulme (1986: 214).

14. Ibid.: 176.

15. Disciplinary doctrine in North America calls for a division into four "subdisciplines": social or cultural anthropology, archaeology, physical or biological anthropology, and linguistic anthropology, in descending order of numerical representation and influence. This doctrine is frequently ignored in practice. Neither of the two institutions that have granted degrees to me in the subject adhered to the sacred even number, one counting three formal subfields (social anthropology, archaeology, and biological anthropology), and the other five (sociocultural anthropology, archaeology, physical anthropology, medical anthropology, and linguistic anthropology), with a quiet sixth (folklore). Nor is this confusion recent; even a cursory glance along the lines of descent show a

rather fluid vocabulary belying official tradition (see Boas 1948 and Stocking 1979). Beneath convention lie more painful ties between practitioners differently grounded in a common dilemma of defining the "human."

16. See Boas (1962), Malinowski (1944), and Kroeber (1963), to name a few forefathers who confronted contemporary existence. The comparative sensibility of foremothers Margaret Mead (1928) and Ruth Benedict (1959 [1934])—the best known of all to wider audiences, if institutionally marginized—also should not be forgotten.

17. On the importance of Europe to any postcolonial project, see D. Scott (1995). Here the focus on the edge of Europe seeks to recall the possibility of multiple modernities within the West, as well as the emergence of modern formations between colony and metropole (Cooper and Stoler 1997).

18. For the outlines of some of this literature, see Clifford and Marcus (1986), as well as Behar and Gordon (1995), Fox (1991), Geertz (1988), Kondo (1986), Marcus and Fischer (1986), Narayan (1993), Rabinow (1977), Stocking (1983), and Visweswaran (1994).

19. Asad (1973) and Said (1979) represent two sources of criticism; Stocking (1992) provides a more detailed and historically nuanced account. Appadurai (1996) and Gupta and Ferguson (1997a, 1997b) render the spatial logic transparent, while Fardon (1990) sketches a number of different area genealogies. Dening (1980) provides a lyrical study of islands and beaches in a Pacific branch of the discipline.

20. For anthropologically inclined commentary, see Fox (1991), Geertz (1983), Latour (1993), Marcus (1986), and Rosaldo (1989).

21. Here some differences in national traditions must be noted. While similar remarks might be made about the British tradition and (perhaps more weakly) about the French, other "native" anthropology traditions (such as the Mexican or Brazilian) concentrate less on a displacement of language or culture and more on an internal displacement of class, remaining within national boundaries. A more complete consideration of such issues lies outside the scope of this work, but historical legacies of the formation of academic traditions within differing contexts of national identity and imperial relations should be kept in mind.

22. See Geertz (1973: 5–6), Nader (1972), and Rabinow (1989, 1996a), as well as Gupta and Ferguson (1997a).

23. For an overview of such work, see Cooper and Stoler (1997) and Pels (1997). For a small sample, see Cohn (1987), Comaroff and Comaroff (1992), Dirks (1992), R. Price (1983, 1990), Rabinow (1989), Prakash (1995), Taussig (1987), and N. Thomas (1994). The more historical ends of postcolonial studies and varied interdisciplinary influences (for example, B. Anderson 1991, Guha and Spivak 1988, and Said 1993) have also weighed heavily in shaping the historical focus on modern empire.

24. For an overview of globalization in the context of anthropology, see Appadurai (1996), Featherstone (1990), Fardon (1995), Hannerz (1989), Kearney (1995), and Marcus (1995). A focus on consumption and commodities (for survey, see Miller 1995) constitutes another effort to integrate local material culture within wider systems of exchange. Wolf (1982) and Mintz (1985) remain the most influential introductions of world systems thought into anthropology, introductions that came, I would underline, through the greater Caribbean. The

description of post-Fordist systems of production and accumulation summarized by Harvey (1989) identifies a significant shift behind global realignments in the language of Marxian political economy, while the different works of Giddens (1993) seek to provide a general context for its social analysis. Another line questions the primary bureaucratic discourse of political economy, "development." Inspired by Foucault, Ferguson (1990) and Escobar (1995) make explicit and detailed criticisms of development discourse from within anthropology, whereas Pigg (1992) offers a clear and concise illustration.

25. Latour and Woolgar (1986) and Traweek (1988) are two particularly influential laboratory ethnographies. For more recent experiments within anthropology, see Gusterson (1996), E. Martin (1994), and Rabinow (1996, 1999). Downey and Dumit (1997) and Marcus (1995) collect a range of studies, Nader (1996) provides a tie with anthropology's heritage, and Hess (1992) and Franklin (1995) offer an overview. Many of the more provocative and controversial elements of science studies literature influencing this ethnographic detour can be found in Biagioli (1999). Bruno Latour's (1988, 1993, 1999) irreverent philosophical histories and Donna Haraway's (1989, 1997) transgressive explorations of cyborgs and related creatures between fields of science and fiction remain key interdisciplinary influences, as does critical attention to gender (such as Keller 1985).

26. For a provocative discussion of the possibilities of localization as a key concept in anthropological practice, see Gupta and Ferguson (1997).

27. I would also suggest that the internalist impulse displayed in many studies of science and technology only underscores this tendency, as the inner workings of a particular machine or logic come to represent a period and quickly unfold to hide its historical horizon. One of the aims of this work is to talk about technology's attachment to the world in a way that allows offshoots, secondary systems, and reverberations into view, while using a marginal vantage point to emphasize the plural character of historical space. Periodization has, of course, long been a preoccupation in branches of the humanities, but the conceit of cultural production to represent universal time (for example, the "Renaissance") plays out rather differently than that of material culture, whose effects quietly litter and transform environments. Prehistoric archaeology, with its necessary methodological conflation of time and culture in the form of artifacts, illustrates an extreme of periodization, ruptured only by silence (for historical description of the "three age system" of prehistory and its significance in relative dating, see Trigger 1989).

28. Ortner (1995) draws a useful distinction between "ethnography" and the "ethnographic stance," the latter allowing for a broader legacy of cultural sensibility beyond presentist monographs. Rabinow (1997: ix–x) proposes the term *dia-ethnographic* to describe studies traversing cultural fields. Here I am shifting focus from center to edge in "culture" to concentrate on key elements of social framing in modern spatial practices, but with a very literal eye on geography. For a classic example of geography in the ethnographic tradition, see Evans-Pritchard (1940).

29. See Bilby (1990).

30. The play on Clifford and Marcus (1986) would be "Writing Place before Writing Culture." Lest this allusion be misunderstood, I underline that the

distinction lies in technique and emphasis rather than subject categories. For a sketch of possible approaches to accommodating the rival impulses of ethnography and the world system, see also Marcus (1995). The concerns of professional geographers, particularly those in the cultural tradition, have long constituted an interesting, equally factious parallel to anthropology (for an overview, see Livingstone 1992). The approach here is a focus on a key site, coupled with historical comparison and emphasis on problem solving between planning and improvisation. With reference to a recent intersection of geography and anthropology in political ecology (see Peet and Watts 1996), it might also be described as a colonial ecology of technology.

31. Lévi-Strauss (1966: 21–22). Rabinow (1996) follows an earlier definition of "incidental movement" for bricolage; here I adopt the more literal usage in colloquial French for improvised problem solving, endemic in French Guiana.

32. Between 1990 and 1994 I went on four research trips to French Guiana and two to France, totaling approximately fourteen months, split between each site.

33. The opposition of space and place has a lengthy lineage in and out of academe; for informative discussions, see Certeau (1984), Heidegger (1977), and Tuan (1977).

34. For etymology of the term, see *The Oxford English Dictionary* (see the 1989 edition, 3: 494–96). The French cognates are essentially the same; indeed the terms *coloniser* and *colonisation* may derive from their English equivalents (see *Le Grand Robert de la Langue Française*, 1985, 2: 711–12).

35. For discussion of such distinctions, see Salomon (1990).

36. See Chalifoux (1987) as well as Price and Price (1992).

37. This definition would not deny that people with strong attachment to locale can also live with reference to elsewhere. I would, however, draw a distinction between those who consider themselves (and are considered by others) to be "in" place and those who consider themselves (and are considered by others) to be "out" of place, in addition to noting varying rates, scales, and qualities of circulation.

CHAPTER 2. HISTORY ON THE WILD COAST

1. Such disturbances have occurred intermittently through Guyanais history; for an account of a 1983 riot, see Bilby (1990).

2. See Ralegh (1928).

3. Whitehead (1995) offers some suggestive evidence about the historical roots of Manoa. For an earlier effort to support Ralegh's account in face of his skeptics, see Van Heuvel (1844).

4. V. T. Harlow in Ralegh (1928: cvi). For context and interpretation of Ralegh's career, as well as textual analysis related to the exploratory era of Europe's encounter with the New World, see essays in Greenblatt (1993).

5. The term *Cayenne* may have similar origins, although one etymology would give it a European lineage (see Huyghues-Belrose 1990). Grenand in Hurault (1989: xviii) provides demographics.

6. See A. Henry (1989) and Bilby (1990). In 1704 the tabulated population included 264 whites, 83 Amerindian slaves, and 1,132 or 1,137 black

slaves; in 1787 the totals were 1,299 whites, 1,279 Amerindians, 483 free blacks, and 10,430 slaves (Marchand-Thébault 1986: 58).

7. Jolivet (1982).

8. A quick comparative census illustrates Guyane's marginal role in the plantation system. Whereas the slave population of Saint-Domingue stood at 80,000 in 1730, that of Martinique at 36,000 in 1720, and that of Dutch Guiana at 50,000 in 1738, French Guiana only counted 6,996 slaves as late as 1763 (Bilby 1990).

9. Marchand-Thébault (1986: 11–17, 56). See also Bruleaux, Calmont, and Mam-Lam-Fouck (1986) and Mam-Lam-Fouck (1987: 13–27)

10. Until the beginning of the twentieth century, French claims extended south to the Amazon, a largely theoretical reign ended by the arbitration of the tsar of Russia and the Swiss government. Had the parties involved ruled in France's favor rather than that of Brazil, French Guiana would be approximately three times larger than its current size (A. Henry 1989: 177–86).

11. The number of immigrants varies between eight thousand and sixteen thousand in different sources (Bruleaux 1992: 157). Jacques Michel (1989) provides the most documented figure of 11,082, while Chaïa (1958: 60), who gives us the most exhaustive effort at post facto diagnosis, believes that 10,446 arrived and 6,500 died, based on figures of three thousand who returned to France and nine hundred who stayed. Given the range of records involved, I will adopt a commonly repeated estimate of twelve thousand. The point is that the Kourou expedition represented a large and sudden influx of European immigrants—about equal to the total number of persons involved in the plantation colony (12,549, including 10,748 slaves, according to Chaïa 1958: xxi)—and that a shocking number of them died.

12. See Damas (1938: 24–25). Damas takes the account from Pitou (1807).

13. Lowenthal (1960a).

14. See Archives Départmentales (1989) and A. Henry (1989: 144). For an account of a revolutionary exile, see Pitou (1807).

15. Bilby (1990) and Mam-Lam-Fouck (1987: 29–48).

16. The British also blocked French efforts to recruit in India in 1877 (Mam-Lam-Fouck 1992: 31).

17. Estimates for the number of miners working the fields hover around ten thousand for the period between 1890 and 1930, with a peak of some twenty-five thousand in 1901 (Bilby 1990; Jolivet 1982: 121–22). Given the nature of the terrain and activities involved this accounting is understandably loose; however, it is probably safe to state that throughout the gold rush period, the population of miners roughly equaled that of convicts.

18. Mam-Lam-Fouck (1987: 85–151). Also see Strobel (1998) for a lyrical portrayal of the fading world of Creole miners.

19. Bilby (1990). The Inini was also the scene of one of the more poignant footnotes of the penal colony in 1931, when some five hundred political prisoners from Vietnam were transported to special camps along the edge of this interior territory (A. Henry 1989: 201; Mam-Lam-Fouck 1987: 146).

20. The period brought Guyane a small whiff of international significance: an American newsreel from 1940 expressed concern that Axis powers would

use the territory as a beachhead from which to strike into the Western Hemisphere (*March of Time* 200 MT, 6–13, Reel 2, 1940). On the closing of the *bagne*, see Donet-Vincent (1992).

21. A. Henry (1989: 211); Mam-Lam-Fouck (1992: 44); and Alexandre (1988: 138–40). The airstrip at Rochambeau, which was built partly with Puerto Rican labor, subsequently developed into Cayenne's current airport.

22. For a general description of France's DOM-TOM system, see Aldrich and Connell (1992). The policy—an aberration in the history of decolonization—stems partly from the assimilationist thread within French colonization (Girardet 1972; Lewis 1962). It should be noted that, at the time, French Guiana possessed two political figures of clear national stature: Félix Eboué, who had rallied Free French forces while governor in Chad, and Gaston Monnerville, who served as president of what became the French Senate between 1947 and 1968 (Mam-Lam-Fouck 1992: 65, 415).

23. The report is quoted in Cooper (1970: 70). The context of the quotation is Senegal and general efforts of the French legislature to redirect colonialism through development.

24. Mam-Lam-Fouck (1992: 21–22, 36).

25. Ibid.: 86–109.

26. Electricity use rose 506 percent between 1949 and 1953 and 111 percent between 1953 and 1958. The number of cars in the colony tripled between 1952 and 1960, despite the lack of roads. At the same time the relative value of exports (largely gold, rum, and wood) to imports fell from 21.26 percent in 1949 to 10.4 percent in 1956. (Mam-Lam-Fouck 1992: 110–50.)

27. Bilby (1990) and Mam-Lam-Fouck (1992: 181–205).

28. Bilby (1990); Mam-Lam-Fouck (1992: 260–80); and Schwartzbeck (1986).

29. Sécretariat d'Etat aux DOM-TOM (1976).

30. For a discussion of the efforts of American magnate Daniel Ludwig to build an enormous paper plant in the Amazon jungle in the 1960s and 1970s, see Miles (1990).

31. Mam-Lam-Fouck (1992: 272–73).

32. The estimated surface area of French Guiana varies between 83,534 square kilometers and 91,000 square kilometers, depending on the source. For our purposes the common round figure of 90,000 square kilometers will serve.

33. See CNRS/ORSTOM (1979). Also see Groene (1990) and Croyere (1984).

34. CNRS/ORSTOM (1979); ONF (1992); and Saga (1988).

35. Estimated numbers are something on the order of twelve hundred vertebrates, seven thousand to ten thousand plants, and four hundred thousand insects (ONF 1992: 10–12).

36. Trade with France, Metropolitan and otherwise, accounted for 67.08 percent of imports in 1992 (total value 3,811,659,000 ff, or approximately 762,331,800 U.S. dollars) and 84.74 percent of exports (total value 541,971,000 ff, or approximately 108,394,200 U.S. dollars). Here I am following figures provided by the French Guiana Chamber of Commerce, CCIG (1994: 6); the national statistics institute, INSEE (1993: 15), gives slightly different figures, with exports only covering about an eighth of imports. The

neighboring French overseas departments of Martinique and Guadeloupe exhibit similar imbalances.

37. INSEE (1993) and CCIG (1993, 1994).

38. The department is subdivided administratively into two districts (*arrondissements*), one governed from Cayenne and the other from St. Laurent. The legislative body of the department is composed by a general council (*Conseil Général*) with nineteen members, each elected to represent a canton for six years. Since 1975 French Guiana has also been a region (*région*), a larger political grouping normally uniting several departments in the Metropole. The decentralization policy of 1982 also established a regional council (*Conseil Régional*) with thirty-one members also elected every six years. In effect this placed another sovereign into the same realm, and the separation of powers between general council and regional council is not always simple. On a more local level there exist twenty-two communes (the most recent created in 1993), each with a municipal council and a mayor. On a national level French Guiana has two deputies, one senator, and an economic and social advisor (Bilby 1990; CCIG 1993: 7–8; and CCIG 1994: 9).

39. Bilby (1990).

40. Ibid., and Hurault (1989).

41. For more on the Aluku, see the comprehensive dissertation of Ken Bilby (1990). For the Ndjuka, see Vernon (1992). For the Saramaka, consult the numerous works of Richard and Sally Price (for example, R. Price 1983; S. Price 1984).

42. Chérubini (1988: 13); Price and Price (1992: 24); INSEE (1993: 14, 27); and CCIG (1994: 9).

43. The official birthrate was 31.7 per thousand in 1991, and the death rate was 4.7 per thousand. In addition to the number of people presently living in French Guiana, one can add those born in French Guiana who now live in Metropolitan France, a total of 12,198 in 1990 (INSEE 1993).

44. For more on tensions within the ethnic landscape of French Guiana, see Bilby (1990), Chalifoux (1987), Chérubini (1988), Jolivet (1982), Mam-Lam-Fouck (1987, 1992), and Price and Price (1992).

45. For an initial point of comparison, see Lowenthal (1960b).

46. Hulme and Whitehead (1992).

47. Trouillot (1992).

48. For example, Mintz (1985), Price (1990), and Wolf (1982).

49. Ralegh (1928: 73).

CHAPTER 3. BOTANY BAY TO DEVIL'S ISLAND

1. "In der Strafkolonie." See Thiher (1990: 51). As Hayman (1982: 187) points out, Kafka was perhaps influenced by early reports of trench warfare and would surely have heard of Devil's Island from the Dreyfus Affair and German war propaganda.

2. The work was first published in French as *Surveiller et Punir* (Foucault 1975 and 1979). Foucault locates the central motif of mechanisms of discipline in Jeremy Bentham's plans for the Panopticon, a model penitentiary where inmates would live under the constant gaze of a central tower and each other. The

effect is to "induce in the inmate a state of conscious and permanent visibility that assures the automatic functioning of power" (Foucault 1979: 201). Here the deterrent presence of surveillance and guards becomes further refined into the deterrent possibility of their existence. Thus in modern societies, ultimately it is individuals who learn to guard themselves.

3. For a sampling of the reception of Foucault among French historians of the modern prison, see Perrot (1980), Petit (1984), and Petit et. al (1991). For more conventional narratives of French prison history in English, see O'Brien (1982) and Gordon Wright (1983). Ignatieff (1978) offers an account of English prison reform that strongly overlaps yet remains differently positioned than Foucault's. Garland (1990) surveys the place of punishment in social theory from a less threatening perspective. Semple (1993) provides an exhaustive study of Bentham's Panopticon project. Beyond debates over chronology and the role of class, some of the reaction to Foucault's metahistorical account, I would suggest, stems from theoretical discomfort with his ambivalent portrayal of the Enlightenment legacy of reform or simple misreading, such as that of those who assume he claims that torture has vanished from all of the contemporary world.

4. Foucault (1979: 272, 279). See also interviews in Foucault (1980a), especially pages 63–77, 146–65, and 224–25. T. Mitchell (1991: 35) and Kaplan (1995) contain discussions of Panopticon prototypes in colonial contexts, and Stoler (1995) gives a wider reinterpretation of Foucault's thesis on sexuality in light of imperial dynamics of race.

5. The most common etymology given for *bagne* (*bagnio*, in English) links it with a bathhouse, or more likely, simply a building in which prisoners were housed during the period of hostilities between Mediterranean Europe and the Ottoman Empire (Le Clère 1973: 16–17, 27; Petit et al. 1991: 169).

6. See Ignatieff (1978) and Gordon Wright (1983). Another line of descent would lie in Russia, where links between exile and the settlement of Siberia strengthened in the eighteenth and nineteenth centuries (Petit 1984). Because the Russian experience represents an alternative version of empire one step removed from the intercontinental ventures of England and France, and because references to Siberia appear far less frequently than Botany Bay in the French documents that concern us, I leave this thread to one side.

7. For a more detailed description and chronology of the Australian adventure, see Shaw (1966), Hirst (1983), Carter (1988), and especially R. Hughes (1986), the most readable and comprehensive account, from which these figures are largely drawn (R. Hughes 1986: 161–62).

8. Ignatieff (1978: 47). Lest the complexity of genealogies be lost, it should be noted that Howard's views owed much to Dutch prisons, and other British reformers were aware of earlier experiments in France and elsewhere.

9. See Bentham (1962), Ignatieff (1978: 75), and Jackson (1987: 2).

10. Jackson (1988: 45).

11. Cited in Jackson (1987: 12). This is a draft passage apparently intended for his Finance Committee report. For further detail on Bentham's Panopticon scheme and his opposition to Australian transportation, see Everett (1966), Hume (1973, 1974), Jackson (1987, 1988), and Semple (1993), in addition to Bentham (1962, 1977).

12. Hirst (1983: 21–27) and R. Hughes (1986: 162).

13. From Vidal de Lingendes, "De la colonisation pénale," 1845, p. 11. CAOM H bagne 1.

14. Forster (1996) provides a focused survey of French interest in Botany Bay and Australia during the period. When asked in 1851 to prepare a report on prior French projects of penal transport, the head of the French archives traced the tradition back to the era of the initial settlement of Canada and a 1540 patent letter given to Jean Françoise de la Rouge that allowed him to recruit sailors from among those facing the death sentence (CAOM H bagne 3). Experiments in Louisiana between 1718 and 1722, however, foundered (Gordon Wright 1983: 31). See also Pierre (1982: 10–12).

15. Gordon Wright (1983: 31, 44).

16. Cited in Devèze (1965: 28, see also 25–26).

17. See Gordon Wright (1983: 45–46), Devèze (1965: 51), and Pierre (1982: 15).

18. Gordon Wright (1983: 48–53).

19. "Memoire sur le choix d'un lieu de déportation," signed Forestier, dated 1816, in CAOM H bagne 1. Colin Forster reviews this same text, noting that Forestier was Councilor of State of the Committee of the Navy and Colonies (1996: 15–18).

20. T. Ginouvier, *Le Botany-Bay Français, ou colonisation des condamnées aux peines afflictives* [sic] *et infamants et des forçats libérés*, printed in Paris, 1856. CAOM H bagne 3. See also Forster (1996:28).

21. CAOM H bagne 1. Another dated 1830 makes an argument based on what will be a familiar racial logic of labor: "French Guiana indeed is not in the least way proper to this end[;] . . . experience of several centuries has proved that all labor in the air of these climates is mortal to whites." CAOM H bagne 2.

22. CAOM Guyane L1 (01), Lettre du Gouverneur de la Guyane française à direction, 11 September 1828.

23. Gordon Wright (1983: 70–81).

24. Documents dated July 1848, in Bodereau des pièces communiqués à la Commision présidée par M. Amiral de Mackau, Mars 1851. CAOM H bagne 1. For Marquesas reference, see Devèze (1965: 90) and Gordon Wright (1983: 92).

25. Cited in Clair (1990: 41) and Pierre (1982: 17). Louis-Napoleon was himself fascinated with Australia (Miles 1988: 21).

26. Gordon Wright (1983: 93, 295–96).

27. Devèze (1965: 119–29); Merle (1995: 40); Pierre (1982: 18–19); and Gordon Wright (1983: 93–94).

28. From *L'Univers* (Union Catholique), 16 January 1857. CAOM H bagne 1.

29. Witness a tract on penal deportation written in 1828 by a navy officer and later reprinted in 1840. The author criticizes British transportation for allowing prisoners excessive freedom and failing to encourage rehabilitation, stating that the real purpose of transportation must be "moral" health: "The goal of deportation is not only to distance from society those men that it has branded but also to return them to honest sentiments and to rehabilitate them in their own regard, by distancing them from places where the memory of the

offense of which they have proven guilty exposes them to the ceaseless contempt of their fellow men; contempt that follows them, brushing repentance aside, that excites them to revenge and leads them into new crimes." "Mémoire sur la Déportation des Forçats présenté en 1828, a Son Excellence le Ministre de la Marine et des Colonies par M**** lieutenant de vaisseau," printed in Le Havre, 1840. CAOM H bagne 3.

30. CAOM H bagne 1.

31. Vidal de Lingendes, "De la colonisation pénale," 1845, p. 14. CAOM H bagne 1. The passage concludes by considering the opposite extreme: "On the other hand, to exile the inhabitants of southern countries amid frozen deserts like those of Siberia would expose them to most excruciating suffering, and perhaps also to death."

32. The same governor sought to encourage convicts to marry prostitutes from Martinique, but his plans met with little success, and he was quickly removed from office (Devèze 1965: 129; also Clair 1990: 19).

33. Cited in Devèze (1965: 130), who notes that the clearing of Ile Royale took only fifteen days. See also Clair (1990: 20).

34. *Journal de Debats Politiques et Littéraires,* 30 July 1852. CAOM H bagne 1.

35. *Les Antilles,* no. 20, 10 March 1852. CAOM H bagne 1.

36. Devèze (1965: 133) and Miles (1988: 25–27).

37. CAOM H bagne 4.

38. Letter of 21 December 1854. CAOM H bagne 14.

39. Devèze (1965: 135).

40. "Extrait du rapport de M. le Médecin en chef de Cayenne," 1854. CAOM H bagne 14.

41. Letter of 15 February 1857. CAOM H bagne 14. On diet, see *Notice sur la transportation à la Guyane Française et à la Nouvelle Calédonie, 1868–1870,* p. 59, and Clair (1990: 49).

42. Pierre (1982: 24–27).

43. Another thousand or so women would be sent to New Caledonia; the majority in each case were sentenced under the recidivist laws of 1885 (Clair 1990: 39). Mortality among them was remarkably high: 23–54 percent in New Caledonia and 44–69 percent in French Guiana. For a statistical breakdown, see Krakovitch (1990b: 283–95), Clair (1990: 36–39), and Devèze (1965: 136), as well as the exhaustive early studies of Orgeas (1885, 1886).

44. Clair (1990: 23).

45. Devèze (1965: 142).

46. "La Verité sur les pénitenciers de la Guyane," *L'Economiste Française* 21 (25 October 1882): 292–93, together with a lengthy rebuttal letter from the governor to the minister, 14 December 1862. CAOM H bagne 4.

47. 10 September 1856. CAOM H bagne 14.

48. From Bollot, "Un Pénitencier doit être une véritable maison de santé morale," 1868. CAOM H bagne 4.

49. Gordon Wright (1983: 95). The shipment of about fifty Metropolitan women to French Guiana during the suspension of European arrivals (1867–1885) represents an interesting exception (Clair 1990: 36). Isabelle Merle (1995: 63) suggests that this redirection of convicts of European extraction to

New Caledonia can also be read as another effort to establish a "white" colony. For further discussion of the Pacific *bagne* and its colonial context (here convict settlement occurred alongside campaigns of indigenous pacification rather than in the aftermath of plantation slavery), see Merle (1995) and Bullard (1997).

50. Merle de Beaufont to minister, 21 December 1864, pp. 88, 102–3. CAOM H bagne 4.

51. Bollot, "Un Pénitencier doit être une véritable maison de santé morale," 1868. CAOM H bagne 4.

52. "Etude sur la transportation à la Guyane." CAOM Guyane L1 (08). Although undated, the draft copy (with many sections amended or crossed out, and footnotes added) makes references to the thirty-year history of the overseas *bagne*, which would place it in the early 1880s. Judging from content and style, it appears to be a draft of Orgeas's extended demographic study (1885 and 1886).

53. From Eribon (1991: 237), quoting a 1975 *Le Monde* interview with Foucault.

54. In this sense the penal colony serves as an example of an alternative modernity constructed around institutionalized failure, a place where governmental norms are suggested but not applied.

CHAPTER 4. THE NATURAL PRISON

1. Marie-Antoinette Menier's article, "La Détention du Capitaine Dreyfus à l'île du Diable, d'après les archives de l'Administration pénitentiaire," represents a significant exception (Menier 1977).

2. As the new venture in French Guiana gathered steam, the *bagnes* of Metropolitan France closed; Toulon, the last, shut down in 1873 (Le Clère 1973: 22; Pierre 1981: 77).

3. Pierre (1982: 35). Official death rates for the *bagne* in Guyane fluctuated between 4.5 percent and 26 percent (Pierre 1982: 311–12). As we shall see in chapter 7, 10 percent can be taken as a rough average for the time period involved.

4. The transportation of recidivists was a proposal of the First Republic, in part inspired by the British example of Botany Bay (Devèze 1965: 25–29). The terms of the 1885 debate were scarcely changed; one senator pointed to the success of transportation in Australia as justification for the new policy (Gordon Wright 1983: 143–45). For text of the law, see Pierre (1982: 309–10). For additional intellectual context, see Pick (1989: 182–83).

5. A number of efforts toward its abolition were made within as well as without the French government (Gordon Wright 1983: 150–51), but the eventual suppression occurred only with shifts in the political climate. The most famous campaign against the *bagne* was that of the journalist Albert Londres between 1923 and 1927 (Londres 1975). The efforts of prominent Guyanais, including M. G. Monnerville and L.-G. Damas, also played a significant role in abolishing transportation (see Donet-Vincent 1992, 1993). Though the final European shipment was in 1954, the last Indochinese prisoners of the interior

camps returned in 1963, while a few *bagnards* stayed behind, a handful of whom were still living in Guyane in the 1980s and 19990s (Clair et al. 1990: 45, 82). For interviews with survivors, see Michelet (1981) and Miles (1988).

6. Alexakis (1979:111–12) and Pierre (1981: 78–79).

7. Pierre (1981: 78). Also see Le Clère (1973: 68–71). For a thorough study of women in both the Guiana and New Caledonia Penal Colonies, see Krakovitch (1990b).

8. Mam-Lam-Fouck (1987: 141). It should be noted that the civil population contained a much smaller percentage of Europeans than the convict population (Mam-Lam-Fouck 1987: 163–227).

9. Michel Pierre provides a relative breakdown of the *bagnard* population (63 percent European, 25 percent Arab, 7 percent black, and 5 percent Asian) but without specifying total figures (Pierre 1982: 41). A sample from 1907 (a low year) shows 2,605 Europeans to 998 Arabs, 361 Africans, and 130 Indochinese (Le Clère 1973: 61). For further statistics, see Devèze (1965: 165–68), Krakovitch (1990b: 260–61), and Pierre (1982: 307–15). For a character profile of the petty French underworld, see the life of Arthur Rocques as reconstructed from documents by Claude Barousse (1989).

Born July 1852 (the same year as the *bagne*) of unknown father in Montpellier, Arthur Rocques was probably brought up as an orphan before leaving school at twelve. After spending his teens as a cabin boy, he left the navy in 1869 and was first arrested for theft in Tours. In 1870 he received a month in prison for rebellion and two more for vagabondage (his later memory was selective, recalling only the humiliation of France at the hands of the Prussians). Part of the army fighting against the Paris Commune, he deserted (which he also neglected to mention later), and received a ten-year sentence, probably spent in a disciplinary battalion in North Africa, although no record of his presence there remains. During this period he somehow learned grammar, arithmetic, geography, history, a good *"dose d'anglais,"* a little Spanish, and some literature, art, biology, and accounting. Books became his irreplaceable companions. Released, he wandered back through France and into petty crime. In 1886–1887 we find him in Sèle, engaged to work for a woman who had a small horse and buggy enterprise. Marie Vors, a widow, had two daughters—one drove coaches and the other was apprenticed as a milliner. After two years of wages, some drink, and gambling, Rocques married Marie, who was fourteen years his senior. When trams arrived in town, their business folded, so in 1891 they moved to Montpellier. He started to take "business trips," gamble, and swindle, and then was arrested for posing as a police official in order to get into people's houses. Sentenced to five years, he escaped from police. By this point he had acquired a mistress—his stepdaughter Julie, the milliner. It is unclear how long the affair had been going on, but she was by then expecting his child. He moved to Vichy under a false name, then to Marseilles, and began passing counterfeit money. In 1900 and 1901 his two daughters were born; the couple left one with Marie near Bordeaux and gave the other to a wet nurse. Arthur and Julie were arrested in La Rochelle on November 16, 1901, for trying to use false two-franc pieces. He was sentenced to hard labor for life but gave an impassioned speech accepting blame and clearing Julie. This succeeded in saving her, but he was deported to Guyane in 1903. Once there, Rocques complained about horrible food, oppressive heat, and having no money. He wrote many letters to officials about conditions in the *bagne* and tried to run his family from afar, seeking to guide his daughters' education by sending them long letters, drawings, and exercises. However, his family grew estranged, and he died in 1920, a lonely and bitter man.

Aside from his striking autodidactic ability and tabloid personality, Arthur Rocques's life describes a fairly representative trajectory through the more marginal classes of France, bobbing above and below the line of criminality. Richard Price (1998) unearths a striking colonial corollary in the case of Médard Aribot, a Martiniquan carver exiled as a *relégué*. While even more remarkably idiosyncratic, Médard's life puts the *bagne* into regional context, and Price's reconstruction of the colonial order in Martinique provides an exceptionally nuanced panorama of the contemporary French Empire in its "old" colonies.

10. Clair et al. (1990: 27) describe white uniforms with red stripes without specifying *relégué* dress. Whatever the exact hues fading in the sun, accounts usually portray the clothing as poorly made, ill-fitted, and subject to wear and theft.

11. Clair (1990: 23–35) and Pierre (1981: 79–82). Reported successful escapes ranged from a low of three in 1935 to a high of 250 in 1906. An estimate for the years up until 1921 suggests that about one in six prisoners eventually escaped or disappeared in the attempt (Pierre 1982: 311–12).

12. Miles (1988: 155–66) and Pierre (1981: 82).

13. J. Munroe, "A Visit to One of the Prisons of Cayenne," *Good Works* (October/November? 1878): 746–752. Copy contained in CAOM, H54. Hereafter, this work is cited parenthetically in the chapter text.

14. Tallach wrote: "At the Prison Congress in Stockholm I listened with much interest to your eloquent speeches in defense of transportation. . . . Pardon me, dear sir, for the liberty I now take in inviting your official consideration of the article in question." The French administration did consider it, because the article is underlined and annotated. The letter, addressed to E. Michaux, Directeur des Colonies au Ministère de Marine et des Colonies, is dated November 12, 1878. This and all other documents related to the minor affair reside in CAOM, H54. The mention of the Sisters of Charity receives a "*très bon,*" and those related to the mentally ill contain many lines and crosses.

15. As an addendum, it is sometimes noted that the strong currents surrounding the remotest island may well have inspired thoughts that the Devil lurked nearby, grounding the choice of name in nature and locating the threat of damnation surrounding salvation. Support for the Kourou narrative can be found in early maps that refer to the entire group as "Diable." See Adélaïde-Merlande (1986: 195), Bouyer (1990: 68), and Huyghues-Belrose and Bruleaux (1988). The convict forger Flag offers an interesting variant, suggesting that the name derives from flocks of black birds that would descend on the island—resolving the issue again to nature, though here in living form (Lagrange and Murray 1961: 9).

16. Despite the fact that in French its name was most frequently associated with the *bagne*, Cayenne, like Devil's Island, only played a minor role in the

penal empire. Its encampment during this period was occupied by the best-behaved prisoners and its streets by a surfeit of *libérés* (Miles 1988: 34–36).

17. Bredin (1986); Halasz (1955); and Gordon Wright (1987).

18. Following his rehabilitation, Dreyfus retired into a highly private and quiet life, suffering from occasional attacks of fever and a lingering aura of notoriety. In 1908, while attending the ceremonial induction of Zola's ashes into the Pantheon, he was slightly wounded by a gunman. With the outbreak of World War I he was mobilized in the reserve artillery command for the defense of Paris, and he later served in the battles of Chemin des Dames and Verdun, before finally rising to the rank of colonel in the reserves. The war claimed the lives of his nephew and son-in-law. While carefully collecting and classifying materials relating to his case (and apparently suffering from repeated nightmares), Dreyfus would rarely speak of his ordeal. In July 1935, at the age of seventy-five, he died quietly in bed (Burns 1991). Among the frequent complaints about his lack of public flair, we can note that even his champion Clemenceau is said to have described him as "looking like a pencil salesman" (Bredin 1986: 490).

19. Menier (1977).

20. Devèze (1965: 104–5) and Gordon Wright (1983: 149–50; 1987: 249–51).

21. Dreyfus (1901: 200). As Jean-Denis Bredin points out, religion—otherwise at the center of things—plays no role in Dreyfus's writing (Dreyfus 1899, 1901); his journal mentions God only twice (in reference to Schopenhauer) and Judaism not at all. Rather, his religion is that of the patriotic soldier, honor and country above all (Bredin 1986: 130).

22. Dreyfus (1899: 119, 137; 1901: 191, 226–67).

23. Dreyfus writes:

> My suffering is at times so strong that I would tear my skin from my flesh, to forget in physical pain this too violent torture of the soul. I arise in the morning with the dread of the long hours of the day, alone, for so long, with the horrors of my brain; I lie down at night with the fear of sleepless hours. . . . My body is broken, my nerves are sick, my brain is crushed, say, simply, that I still hold myself erect in the absolute sense of the word only because I resolved to, so as to see with you and our children the day when honor shall be returned to us.
>
> Ibid.: 47

24. Quotations from Dreyfus (1901: 173–74, 261, 226–27; 1899: 150). See also Bredin (1986: 132–33).

25. Quotations from (Dreyfus 1901: 154; 1899: 176); also Bredin (1986: 127).

26. E. Weber (1976) and Girardet (1972). For a discussion of race, class, and national identity in a later parallel to French Guiana, see B. Williams (1991).

27. See the essay "Truth and Power" in Foucault (1980b, esp. 126–33). Also see Rabinow (1989: 16, 251) for the distinction in a relevant context. "The Affair" continues to serve as a defining moment of the "engaged" intellectual in action. Ironically, Dreyfus would qualify for the specific category as an efficient military technician, concerned more with precision than passion. In this sense he was very much a figure linked to Kafka's world.

28. O'Brien (1982: 288–89).

29. In an extreme conflation of race and climate, 525 political prisoners from Indochina settled the interior Inini territory in 1930 under the worst of conditions (Clair et al. 1990: 45).

30. For example, Bouyer (1990).

31. There was also British, German, and South American fascination with and outrage over the *bagne*. Here I focus on the American strand, which would prove the most significant. Donet-Vincent (1992); Londres (1975); and Miles (1988).

32. See Batzler-Heim (1930), Belbenoit (1938, 1940), Allison-Booth (1931a, 1931b), Davis (1952), Krarup-Nielsen (1938), Lagrange and Murray (1961), Niles (1928), Rickards (1968), Seaton (1951), Sinclair (1935), and Willis (1959). For titles not directly referenced, as well as additional reading in English and French, see Miles (1988: 197–204). In addition to these written accounts, one could also add film: between 1925 and 1955 a number of Hollywood works found their setting in the French Guiana *bagne*, a tradition that would be recalled most successfully in the film version of *Papillon* in 1973. French cinema has also produced a range of works on the penal colony, one of the more recent of which, *Seznec*, resulted in the partial restoration of the prison ruins in St. Laurent (Miles 1988: 110–15).

33. For example, Roussenq (1957). At this point the most familiar reference to both English and French speakers is the account of the petty pimp Henri Charrière, known as "Papillon" for his butterfly tattoo. Charrière turned his own (and other people's) experiences into a runaway best-seller in 1969, later released as a Hollywood blockbuster (Charrière 1970). For more sober evaluations of the authenticity of his narrative (particularly his claims to innocence and prowess), see Ménager (1970) and Villiers (1970).

34. Allison-Booth (1931a: vi). This figure can be taken as a measure of the dubious hyperbole infusing the work.

35. On exposé literature, see Londres (1975: 13–197) and Donet-Vincent (1992, 1993). Another version of *Devil's Island* was published under the title *Hell's Outpost*, and in the preface to that edition the editor makes the connection to Blair Niles (Allison-Booth 1931b).

36. Allison-Booth (1931a: 59).

37. The convict is Roussenq, a figure legendary for his extraordinary incorrigibility and time spent in solitary punishment.

38. All convicts in Guyane received a number based on their "matriculation," or sequential order of entry. The man born Henri Charrière, for example, may have been called Papillon, but upon arriving in the *bagne* he was officially known as No. 51367 (Clair et al. 1990: 56).

39. Niles (1928: 44). Here choice of metaphor echoes the manner in which this particular removal from civilized society involved natural order.

40. One of the more frequently noted items of convict material culture was the *plan*, a small screw container for precious items that was inserted into the body through the rectum (for illustration, see Miles 1988).

41. Papillon is far from the only convict to claim innocence. One favored motif on the part of foreign-born authors is to claim that they were tricked into joining the French Foreign Legion and then falsely judged by its rules (see Batzler-Heim 1930 and Krarup-Nielsen 1938).

42. Allison-Booth, whom I have chosen as a guide, is in this respect an interesting exception; rather than homosexuality he focuses on the presence of "fallen women" to entertain the guards, leaving only an ambiguous chapter title "Men Must Have Women" as a hint about the rest. This aspect of his account fits with its general omission of detail and suspiciously vague portrayal of everyday experience in the colony. For a period medical view of homosexuality among the convicts, see L. Rousseau (1930), and for further historical discussion, see Donet-Vincent (1992: 62).

43. Bourdet-Pléville (1960: 179).

44. None of the narrators admit to homosexual encounters themselves; rather, it is constantly spoken of in general or eyewitnessed terms. The sexual activity of choice for the narrator occurs either in the jungle with remarkably willing Indian women or in town with Creole women turned prostitute. A reassertion of heterosexuality and masculinity becomes necessary as a prisoner's autobiographical narrative makes the transition from "a jungle hell" to an overcoming, a survival. The hero must suffer, but in order to speak, to claim his identity as a man, he must remain unfallen. (For example, see Charrière 1970: 158–86, and Milani 1977: 207–9). In light of what follows, the tension of sexual conquest can also be read as an effort to reassert the imperial order of race.

45. "Oraput" was the name of a timber camp for incorrigibles. The song appears in several versions in different sources, not all of which include the slang reference to Arab command. Here I follow the rendition of a former prisoner, René Belbenoit (1938: 60) and adopt his free translation. The French: "De douleur, de dégoût nôtre coeur se soulève / Car la voix d'un arabe a crié: Roumi rö! / Ce supplice sans nom chaque jour se repète: Enfants des vieux gaulois, qu'êtes vous donc devenus? / le plus forts d'entre nous marchent en courbant la tête / Pleuvez, pleuvez foçats, vos coeurs ne battent plus! [your hearts beat no more]."

46. Herménégilde Tell, the father-in-law of Félix Eboué, became director of the penal administration in 1919 (Weinstein 1972: 72).

47. Belbenoit (1940: 18–19) and Allison-Booth (1931a: 71, 102). See also Batzler-Heim (1930: 95–96).

48. Seaton (1951: 60, 115) and Allison-Booth (1931a: 30–31).

49. See Batzler-Heim (1930), Krarup-Nielsen (1938), Londres (1975), and Belbenoit (1938, 1940).

50. Niles (1928: xiii).

51. Ibid.: 216.

52. Sinclair (1935: 20).

53. Ibid.: 22–24.

54. Ibid.: 23; Krarup-Nielsen (1938: 255).

55. Belbenoit (1940: 246–47). Mounted under glass and handsomely framed, butterflies remain a staple item in contemporary Cayenne tourist shops.

56. Seaton (1951: 25, 50).

57. Lagrange and Murray (1961:174). See also Niles (1928: 366–67).

58. Belbenoit (1940: 37)

59. Niles (1928: 190). Another breathless example: "Before we know it we're surrounded by huge trees, ninety feet high, palisanders and mahogany

with orchids growing on them and other dead trees leaning on them. We walk cautiously to avoid invisible dangers, like this slime in which I sink up to my knees. Once out of that trap I'm caught in a web of minuscule lianas, sharp as steel wire, real nooses that wrap themselves around my ankles" (Milani and Grin 1977: 119).

60. Miles (1988: 51).

61. Niles (1928: 206–7).

62. Cendrars (1958: 61). Jean Galmot, whose letter is cited here, was a Frenchman of many trades (gold seeker, rum merchant, writer, and politician), whose death (most likely by assassination) following an electoral victory sparked one of the worst periods of rioting in French Guiana's history (A. Henry 1989: 193–99).

63. Niles (1928: 251).

64. Ibid.: 199–200.

65. Ibid.: 133.

66. Pierre (1981: 76; 1982: 305).

67. Ann Stoler has questioned simple categories of "colonizer" and "colonized," examining European moral narratives as conceived in gender and race. She concludes that "sex in the colonies was about sexual access and reproduction, class distinctions and racial demarcations, nationalism and European identity—in different measure and not all at the same time" (Stoler 1991: 87; see also Stoler 1989, 1995). In the case of Devil's Island a similar formulation would seem to hold, though here the moral questions were inverted: rather than methods to prevent degeneration and guard European prestige in the colonies, we find mechanisms to contain Metropolitan degeneration and transport it into a distant and rigorous colonial spectacle.

68. The comparison of nationalism to religion is an old reflex (see, for example, Hayes 1960). For a discussion of the development of purgatory within the context of medieval theology and social history, see Le Goff, who suggests that "the mobile frontier turned out to be the one between Purgatory and Hell" (1984: 226). Although terminology in play derives from the historical legacy of Christianity, conceptions of worldly and otherworldly place in relation to death can be found elsewhere, such as in Malinowski's description of *baloma* in the Trobriands, where the main spirit form of the dead person goes to a particular neighboring island (1954: 150). We should also note that the rise in transportation can be placed alongside a decline in the enforcement of the death penalty. "The new humanitarian system was still killing prisoners but in new ways and in remote places" (O'Brien 1982: 285). Thus another way of casting prison history would be to describe a vast expansion of the moment of execution.

69. See Burns (1991: 295, 328). When writing his memoirs, Dreyfus described the project to a friend as differing from that of Robinson Crusoe in that he (Dreyfus) had no goal to live on his island but rather must write to fulfill a particular duty: that of telling the story of "the five years I was cut off from the world of the living" (Dreyfus 1901: 294).

70. Mam-Lam-Fouck (1987: 139) and Pierre (1982: 285).

71. Londres (1975: 68). The "fifty years" would appear a rhetorical exaggeration, because construction only began in earnest in 1906–1907, less than

two decades before his visit (Miles 1988: 84; Bilby 1990). If so, it is an easy one to excuse. See also Pierre (1982: 111).

72. Mam-Lam-Fouck (1987: 142); Pierre (1982: 284); and Donet-Vincent (1992).

73. Quoted in Racine (1988: 49). Damas's experience was far from unique; Gaston Monnerville, the Guyanais politician instrumental in orchestrating the final closure of the penal colony and who eventually became president of the French Senate, worried equally about the land's reputation. See also Miles (1988: 194) and Weinstein (1972: 128). Forty years earlier, Clovis Savoie, an earnest historian of New Caledonia, concluded his work with the following appeal:

> French Readers! Tell your friends that *New Caledonia is no longer a penal colony.*
> That since 1896 no more convicts have come to New Caledonia. That since 1896 the
> penitentiary has slowly passed away, by the constant reduction of its personnel of
> convicts and *relégues.* That the sale of the furniture and of the equipment of the pen-
> itentiary depot on the Ile Nou is today finished [1922]. That *New Caledonia,* this land
> blessed with beautiful sunshine and a good climate, has become *free soil* like any
> department of France. Make the legend that detracts from the good reputation of our
> magnificent island disappear. Tell all this to your friends. Thank you!
>
> Savoie 1922: endpage

74. Kesteloot (1974: 232) and Damas (1938: 202).

75. Belbenoit (1938: 60): "*Chacun pour le tavail s'arme d'une bricole / Et dans le forêt sombre advance trébuchant / L'on direant des démons, la sara-bande folle / Car l'enfer est au bagne, en non pas chez Satan!*"

76. In *Shamanism, Colonialism, and the Wild Man: A Study in Terror and Healing,* Taussig seeks to rework colonial history along the lines of "mythic subversion of myth," exploring the colonial reality of the New World in a more than realist fashion. "The formulation is sharp and important," he writes, "to penetrate the veil while retaining its hallucinatory quality" (Taussig 1987: 10). Twin concepts that mark a point of entry to this veil are those of the "culture of terror" and the "space of death." Understood as a social as well as physiological state, terror becomes the "mediator *par excellence* of colonial hegemony." The space of death, populated by the social imagination with "images of evil and the underworld," becomes the place where "the Indian, African and white gave birth to a New World" (ibid.: 5). Taussig then proceeds to read accounts of torture in Colombian rubber plantations for keys into their universe of terror and death. As he notes, "two interlacing motifs stand out in these stories: horror of the jungle and horror of savagery" (ibid.: 75).

77. Seaton (1951: 21).

78. Hammel (1979: 44). See also Petit et al. (1991: 258).

79. Allison-Booth (1931a: 227).

CHAPTER 5. A GATE TO THE HEAVENS

1. Verne was well read by all three of the major figures usually mentioned in connection to the development of the rocket: the Russian Tsiolkovsky, the American Goddard, and the German Oberth (Winter 1990: 1–27). Ironically, his main technical flaw was to choose a cannon over a rocket as a means of propulsion into space. See Verne (1958, 1966a, 1966b, 1995).

2. Sergey Korolev was the chief engineer of the Soviet space program after Sputnik's successful launch.

3. As W. W. Rostow wrote in 1960:

> There is no clear analogy in American history to the crisis triggered by the launching of the Soviet satellite on October 4, 1957. This intrinsically harmless act of science and engineering was also, of course, both a demonstration of foreseeable Soviet capability to launch an ICBM and a powerful act of psychological warfare. It immediately set in motion forces in American political life which radically reversed the Nation's ruling conception of its military problem, of the appropriate level of the budget, and of the role of science in its affairs. The reaction reached even deeper, opening a fundamental reconsideration not only of the organization of the Department of Defense but also of the values and content of the American educational system and of the balance of values and objectives in contemporary American society as a whole.
>
> Quoted in Bulkeley 1991: viii

4. Popular science accounts of the coming Space Age were also in evidence; see Bergaust and Beller (1956). Also see McDougall (1985a: 60–119).

5. See McCurdy (1997).

6. See D. Carter (1988), McDougall (1985a: 43), Neufeld (1995), and Winter (1990).

7. Historian Walter McDougall makes the technocratic argument most strongly: "The advent of spaceflight in our time, therefore, is not just a tale of the gumption of Russian, German or American rocketeers, but also of the progress of the idea of command technology as a tool and a symbol of the modern scientific state" (McDougall 1985a: 19). The fact that W. W. Rostow, a player in the Kennedy and Johnson administrations' space policy, was also the author of a central work of development theory should not be too quickly overlooked. For more on the history of rockets, see Winter (1990). McDougall's volume, *The Heavens and the Earth* (1985a), stands out as the single most comprehensive and literate history of the Space Age. Wolfe (1979) captures the essence of the Space Age within popular culture, while Arendt (1978) and Blumenberg (1987) offer skeptical counterpoints about its significance in human history. Leslie (1993) and Galison and Hevly (1992) provide additional context to situate the growth of the American space program amid general trends of Cold War research.

8. Collins (1990) and Naddeo-Souriau (1986).

9. See interview with Pierre Auger, "Le CNES a 30 ans," *CNESQUISE-PASSE?* (April 1992): 26. Auger, a specialist in cosmic rays who had been instrumental in the earlier creation of CERN (the European Center for Nuclear Research), went on to play key roles in the creation of CNES and cooperative European space programs. See also Pestre and Krige (1992), Collins (1990), and McDougall (1985b). Hecht's (1998) account of the French nuclear program nicely illustrates the marriage of technology and politics in postwar efforts to reinvent France as a technological power. See also Bess (1995).

10. Collins (1990: 9–10); McDougall (1985b); and Morton (1989). Other test sites considered were in Canada, South Africa, Australia, New Zealand, and the Bahamas (Morton 1989: 10).

11. A. Clarke (1968: 37).

12. Pierce (1968).

13. Ackroyd (1990:1–2).

14. McDougall (1985a: 357–59). Because of its high latitude, the Soviet Union's early communications satellites used an odd elliptical orbit rather than a geostationary one. Given the curvature of the Earth, equatorial orbit serves areas near the poles less well than those in temperate or tropical zones, a factor that comes into play in developing systems of mobile satellite communication (Williamson 1990: 296). However, for the majority of the globe and the systems that seek to encircle it, geostationary orbit is the position of choice.

15. Blonstein (1987: 1–9); King-Hele (1992); and Pool (1990).

16. Pease (1991:11); Lambright (1994); and Mack (1990). SPOT is an acronym for Système Pour l'Observation de la Terre (System for Earth Observation).

17. Pease (1991: 1–27). Orbits are tricky things, and their fine points require more calculation than here described. For our purposes the most significant point is that maintaining position aloft and performing designated functions requires energy; even when well placed in the initial launch, satellites have a limited life span. For more on communication satellites, see Ackroyd (1990), Blonstein (1987), L.J. Carter (1962), and Williamson (1990). For more on geostationary orbits, see Soop (1994). For observation satellites, see Mack (1990) and Pease (1991). For orbits, the shape of the Earth, and the early history of satellite theory, see King-Hele (1992).

18. Kern (1983) and Read (1992).

19. Shifting plans for the establishment of tropical launch centers can be followed in general and industry news stories (most consistently and specifically in *Launchspace* and *International Space Industry Report,* or more generally in *Aviation Week and Space Technology*). The journal of the Guiana Space Center itself, *Latitude 5,* regularly monitors active launch competition in the United States and Russia, as well as the potential threats in China, India, and Japan, and development of rival launch sites in places such as Brazil. For historical grounding, see the collection in CNES (1972); the most interesting alternative to a tropical land base remains a floating platform, once contemplated by the United States, built for test rockets by Italy and recently introduced for commercial launches by a Norwegian-Ukrainian-Boeing consortium known as Sea Launch (Reuters 1994). For a discussion of space technology relative to development, see Wise (1990). I would also like to thank John Leedom for providing me with regular clippings and local perspectives on the New Guinea situation.

20. The chapter text's subsequent description of the choice of a launch site appears in a 1994 CNES/CSG press release on the occasion of the space center's thirtieth anniversary (CNES 1994). The press release (also printed in *Antilla* 582 [29 April 1994]: 21–22) consists of excerpts from both an official history of CNES (*l'Histoire du CNES,* in preparation by Claude Carlier) and a 1964 CNES report by Raymond Debomy ("Recherche de sites de lancement"). Studies aside, it should be noted that both French and later European choices of Kourou have more than a whiff of political destiny about them.

21. Other criteria not explicitly mentioned in this document but often noted in later discussions of the location of CSG are stability of the physical (as

well as political) climate, lack of seismic activity, and "good conditions for communications and investment, and quality of life for the future technicians" (Desobeau 1990: 4).

22. Indeed the space survey matches the penal colony survey in its relative disregard for the issue of whether the territories in question were under active control, and either could have been accomplished with a reasonable atlas.

23. CNES (1994).

24. Jolivet (1982: 443–49) and Mam-Lam-Fouck (1992: 293).

25. See interviews in *Latitude 5* 21 (July 1993): 11–13.

26. Desobeau (1990: 7).

27. Out of 1,016 workers employed in the construction in 1967, 206 were European, and 330 were from elsewhere in South America. In 1968 the operation employed 3,502 persons. The official ethnic breakdown was as follows: 26 percent European, 11 percent Guyanais Creole, 20 percent Maroons (primarily Aluku and Saramaka) and Amerindians, 3 percent French Antillean, 4 percent from English and other Caribbean islands, 6 percent Surinamese Creoles, and 30 percent Colombians and Brazilians. In 1971, after the end of the first phase of construction, the labor force had shrunk to 1,599 persons, 52 percent of whom were European, 16 percent Guyanais Creoles, and 8 percent French Antillean. (Figures taken from Mam-Lam-Fouck 1992: 301 and Jolivet 1982: 445.) Like all statistics in this context they may represent as much of a distortion as a record; oral evidence suggests that the number of Maroons was much higher than the figure given (R. Price, personal communication, 1995).

28. CNES (1987, 1990); Collins (1990); and ESA (1992a).

29. Mam-Lam-Fouck (1992: 296).

30. See the "Conférence d'Information, Jeudi Oct. 1, 1964," published in Guyane's *Radio Presse,* 6–8 October 1964.

31. Figures vary between 30 and 40 percent. Mam-Lam-Fouck (1992: 297) and Jolivet (1982: 469).

32. All these comments (and a few more besides) are to be found in Jolivet (1982: 470–74). I have reordered their presentation slightly from the sequence she gives; however, all date from 1971.

33. According to a 1987 report commissioned by CNES, some 5,292 million French francs flowed through the space center between 1965 and 1974, 3,156 million in the form of investment (Rémondière and Colmenero-Cruz 1987). Figures are given in 1985 French francs equivalent. Given a rough currency exchange of five to one prevalent in the early 1990s, five billion francs would be about one billion dollars (somewhat less in 1985).

34. Mam-Lam-Fouck (1992: 302).

35. Ibid.: 299, 304, 306.

36. Vignon (1985: 365).

37. The following passage is to be found in Jolivet (1982: 446–47); sections of it are also translated in Bilby (1990) and Price and Price (1992: 42–44).

38. Certeau (1984: 34–39).

39. Jolivet (1982: 447).

40. From J. Charbonnel, quoted in *CNESQUISEPASSE?* 74 (July 1993): 36–37.

41. ESA (1992a).

42. Austria, Norway, and Finland only joined in 1987. It would be a mistake to consider all these separate entities equal in terms of weight within the organization, and it is no accident that ESA's headquarters are in Paris (ESA 1987). France has always been particularly interested and invested in Ariane, providing over half its budget, as well as its launch site.

43. Desobeau (1990) and ESA (1992a). A 90 percent success rate is considered an essential benchmark in designating a rocket "reliable." After one hundred launches the Ariane family was at 93 percent.

44. That is to say, about seven thousand kilograms as opposed to about four thousand kilograms. Like the earlier series, however, it uses a transfer orbit to boost the satellite rather than reaching high orbit directly (ESA 1992a). The Ariane 5 story lies outside the main body of this work, because it only became (disastrously) operational in 1996. In its various configurations, the Ariane 4 has been the main workhorse of CSG during the 1990s. At the end of 1998 the mature design of the Ariane 4 clocked in at 96.4 percent (three failures in eighty-six attempts). The Ariane 5, with one failure in three tries, posted a less stellar 66.7 percent and has a long climb back to its promise of increased reliability. See *International Space Industry Report* 3, no. 1 (4 January 1999): 22.

45. The factor for indirect employment increases for the period between 1975 and 1985, from 1.9 to 2.3, and francs spent on the project increasingly stayed within the department (Rémondière and Colmenero-Cruz, 1987).

46. Mam-Lam-Fouck 1992; Rémondière and Colmenero-Cruz 1987; CNES 1988; and INSEE 1995. With the dramatic demographic expansion of the department, the new projects related to the space center were estimated in 1987 to represent a smaller percentage of the total investment, falling by half to around 27 percent. More recent estimates of the economic weight of the space program made in 1995 by the French bureau of statistics, however, suggest that it accounts for a startling amount of all formal economic activity in French Guiana: 49.8–57.2 percent of production, 28.3–33.7 percent of added value, 28.3–35.4 percent of revenue, 26.7–33.7 percent of employment, 19.9–25.7 percent of the population supported, 59.1–72.9 percent of imports, 20.3–27.7 percent of customs revenues paid, and 41–49.8 percent of local taxes (INSEE 1995: 107–9).

47. The Ariane 5 program has given birth to an even larger assemblage known as ELA 3.

48. The third stage of Ariane 4 has also proved the trickiest, being implicated in a number of launch failures. Ariane 5 has a cryogenic main stage powered by liquid oxygen and hydrogen and two large solid fuel boosters strapped to each side (Arianespace 1993; ESA 1992a).

49. Isakowitz (1991). Different arrangements of boosters, either liquid or solid fuel, are added for extra thrust depending on the weight of the particular load.

50. ESA (1988; 1992a); Isakowitz (1991); and Soop (1994).

51. The gold standard comes from A. Miles in the summer of 1993, as based on a price of gold at roughly 360 dollars per ounce versus a two-thousand-kilogram Hughes 601 satellite at about two hundred million dollars (or over nine thousand dollars per ounce), a factor of around twenty-five. For general estimates, see Blonstein (1987).

52. CNES, Palais de la Découvert, and SEP (1991).

53. From M. J. Jamet in CNES (1972: 333). Translation as given in abstract.

54. CNES (1988); CSG (1994); and ESA (1991).

55. CNES (1990). Compared to a similar breakdown for CNES as a whole, this distribution displays a lower proportion of engineers to technicians and laborers, as well as a surprisingly high proportion of administrators and secretaries.

56. The majority of influential administrators of the space center come out of the elite *grande école* system of postsecondary education. This fits with a wider French educational and employment pattern. As the French embassy explains in an official publication: "In France, engineers occupy the greatest number of top management posts, competing with other specialists, such as economists and business school graduates, for the highest positions in government and industry. Prestige and salary put the French engineer near the top of the social ladder. The vast majority of French engineers are trained in prestigious institutions called *grandes écoles,* often separate and independent from the university system, sometimes with administrative ties, but always jealous of their autonomy" (Embassy of France 1989). Alfred Dreyfus, we should not forget, was himself a graduate of the most prestigious of the technical *grandes écoles,* the Ecole Polytechnique. For a profile of an exceptional local space technician, see "Paul Henri: Un Amerindien dans le siecle," *Latitude 5* 18 (October 1992): 29–31.

57. On the *Challenger* accident, see Jensen (1996) and Vaughan (1996).

CHAPTER 6. THE MARGIN OF THE FUTURE

1. The charisma of rockets is perhaps best encapsulated in the story of a "conversion by launch" of a black activist at Cape Canaveral, who arrived to protest *Apollo 11* and left a believer (McDougall 1985a: 412).

2. CNES and ESA (1994a).

3. See D. Carter (1988: 177).

4. McDougall (1985a: 413).

5. See interview with J.-D. Levi in *CNESQUISEPASSE?* 67 (October 1991): 4–7. Mailer (1970), Pynchon (1973), and Wolfe (1979) offer literary—and often insightful—versions of the Space Age. The collected presentations in ANAE (1992) and Schneider and Léger-Orine (1987) provide a relevant sampling of lofty views on European Space.

6. ESA (1989b).

7. Like most ESA documentation, this brochure is available in both English and French, the two official languages of the organization; I am quoting directly from the official English version, as I have done whenever possible.

8. Wolfe (1979).

9. For example, we have the following passage on the technical importance of "the vast natural laboratory" of space (ESA 1989a): "Scientists have two main reasons for wanting to get their instruments into space. First, they very naturally want to explore virgin territory accessible to their space vehicles in the same way that Christopher Columbus wanted to explore the new world. . . . The second main reason for getting into space is to escape the obscuring effects of the Earth's atmosphere and to look at the stars in all their glory." See

also Schneider and Léger-Orine (1987: 3, 117, 129, 139) as well as the discussion of "Frontiers of the Twenty-First Century" in ANAE (1992: 192–93). NASA (n.d.) contains a remarkable conceptual slide between Columbus's encounter with "dusky skinned hunters" and "our leap toward the stars."

10. This account of the naming appears in an ESA publication (1992a) and can thus be taken as an official memory of sorts, however inflected.

11. ESA (1992a). As a quip of questionable—but representative—taste had it, the feminine name was appropriate because both rockets and women "require lengthy preparation and deliver brief pleasure." For several variants and embellishments of the christening, see CNESQUISEPASSE? 51 (May 1988): 3–4. Although there is no mention of why Ganymede lost favor, one can imagine the complications a rocket recalling male homosexual desire would pose for an organization like ESA.

12. ESA (1988).

13. Ibid.

14. For Arianespace figures, see Arianespace (1994). All told, six Apollo flights (11, 12, 14, 15 and 17) made the voyage between 1969 and 1979, and a dozen astronauts (white male explorers all) bounded about the lunar surface. In discussing a possible return to the moon, the French weekly Le Point compares this brief romp to that of an undisciplined baboon (Ponchelet 1992: 79). A 1991 map distributed by the Hughes Corporation reveals the degree of crowding along some segments of the geosynchronous orbit, namely those that serve North America, Europe, and Asia.

15. Ariadne remains on Naxos, either dead, pregnant, or simply abandoned. In some versions she marries Dionysus, and in others she dies (Graves 1960: 339–48).

16. Private collection of author.

17. Embassy of France (1989).

18. Gordon Wright (1987: 442).

19. Hubert Curien in Naddeo-Souriau (1986: 7).

20. See M. Hauzeur, "L'Europeanisation du CSG," Latitude 5 16 (April 1992): 4–5. Francophone anxiety runs deep within CNES as a whole, because English is by far the dominant technical language of space. See the call for the use of French in scientific settings in "La Langue Française et les réunions scientifiques internationales," CNESQUISEPASSE? 74 (July 1993): 34–35. For the numbers of non-French European employees, see R. Borel, "CSG: L'Europe avant l'heure," Latitude 5 16 (April 1992): 6–8. The count specifies fifty-four Italians, twenty-four Belgians, eighteen Germans, eight Spaniards, five Britons, one Irish citizen, and one Swiss, adding up to 111 rather than the 106 total given.

21. "Nous ne sommes pas prets pour l'Europe," Latitude 5 17 (July 1992): 8.

22. In an ethnography of ESTEC, the ESA science center in the Netherlands, Stacia Zabusky (1995) describes the intricate choreography of space scientists and engineers negotiating nationality, expertise, and common goals. Although many of their dilemmas echo at CSG, the context of Kourou is far more French.

23. An estimate of the ethnic demographics of Kourou in 1991 ran as follows: 3,500 Metros, 6,500 Creoles (both Guyanais and from the French

Antilles), and 4,000 immigrants (Brazilians, Haitians, and Surinamese). The last figure must be adjusted upward to include "a good number" of illegal immigrants. *CNESQUISEPASSE?* 65 (April 1991): 12.

24. For additional flavor of Kourou and French Guiana as experienced by Maroons, see Bilby (1990) and Price and Price (1992).

25. In 1993 some twenty thousand members of the general public visited the base, as well as sixteen hundred schoolchildren in 160 classes. See *CNESQUISEPASSE?* 78 (July 1994): 31. Given that CNES also owns the Iles du Salut, and that many visitors to French Guiana are drawn by friends and relatives working at CSG, the space program constitutes a significant actor in the local tourist industry (CCIG 1993).

26. "*Quand le ciel s'enracine dans la terre Guyane . . . La voie lactée et la cité des étoiles / La voie lactée, un projet pour l'espace d'une route.*" Printed in France for the Direction Départementale de l'Equipement. No date given, but its subject matter would place it between the late 1980s and the beginning of the 1990s.

27. In 1990 an ambitious seven-year project, Le Plan Phèdre, called for over one hundred million dollars of investment in the region, of which nearly half would come from CNES. An article in *CNESQUISEPASSE?* describes Kourou with the help of two photos, one of the "lively and pleasing" new Quartier Monnerville, with its resplendent fountains, and the other of the Village Saramaca—"that little African village of certain charm"—soon to be renovated and sanitized (*CNESQUISEPASSE?* 65 [April 1991]: 13). In the mid-1990s, new housing for the village Saramaca was finally under construction.

28. These comments stem from both fieldnotes and materials produced internally by the space center, such as in *Latitude 5* 17 (July 1992): 8. Because of the repetition involved I present them as an anonymous, self-reinforcing cultural voice.

29. "Un paradis pour les Enfants," *CNESQUISEPASSE?* 65 (April 1991): 14.

30. M. Hauzeur in *Latitude 5* 21 (July 1993): 3–5.

31. Interview with M. Mignot, *Latitude 5* 15 (January 1992): 5–8.

32. M. Hauzeur in *Latitude 5* 21 (July 1993): 3–5.

33. The organization "Freelance" both shelters clients from inconvenience and seeks to make their stay pleasurable. See also chapter 7, as well as *CNESQUISEPASSE?* 60 (March 1990): 38–40.

34. Interview with A. Rémondière, director of CSG between 1986 and 1991, "Emotions Guyanaises," *CNESQUISEPASSE?* 69 (April 1992): 31–32.

35. A cartoon published in the CSG employee magazine, *Latitude 5,* nicely parodies the director's encounter: A European man lost in the jungle asks three Amerindians: "Do you know the place where the White Man shoots the big stick that spits fire?" One of them replies: "Ah! Yes! No doubt you mean the Guiana Space Center. As well as our launcher Ariane IV. After our hunt, allow us to take you there. We have to go back to work there in a few hours to participate in the last controls before the launch." Meanwhile, one of the other Amerindians thinks: "Another one fresh off the boat!" *Latitude 5* 5 (July 1989): 29.

36. The primary local newspaper of recent years, *France Guyane,* the product of a conservative chain, contained a special commemorative insert.

37. CSG and CLAMFUK (Club de Mini Fusées de Kourou) 1994. Lancement de la Fusée RG, 21 July 1994, Site Fusées Sondes.

38. See *Latitude 5* 25 (July 1994): 21–22 and *France Guyane* (12 August 1994): 6. For additional discussion of the islands relative to CSG, see *Latitude 5* 10 (October 1990): 10–12, and 14 (October 1991): 19–21. The anniversary grew even more surreal when Charles Dreyfus, Alfred's grandson, arrived on Devil's Island in the spring of 1995—his way paid by the space center (Miles 1995; also CBC interview on "As It Happens," 2 May 1995).

39. "In fact there are more endangered and threatened species at the Kennedy Space Center than at any other refuge in the continental United States" (NASA 1992: 46). See also NASA (n.d.). The Kennedy Space Center hosts a large museum and tour operation and displays striking parallels (if on a different scale) with the Guiana Space Center in terms of practices of commemoration as well as landscape.

40. See Blumenberg (1987), Cosgrove (1994), and Ingold (1993).

41. See *CNESQUISEPASSE?* 65 (April 1991): 15–18 and *Latitude 5* 15 (January 1992): 21–23.

42. Verne left his readers in suspense, before returning with a sequel, *Autour de la lune* (Around the moon), several years later, in 1870 (like the first volume it was first published in the periodical *Journal des Débats*). See Verne (1958, 1966a, 1995).

43. Only the English version of Desobeau (1990) contains the line used here.

44. For a description of a launch viewed from ESA's main research and technology center in the Netherlands (it is broadcast at all centers of the European and French space worlds), see Zabusky (1995: 4). In French Guiana one has several options for observing Ariane live, including a general public observation site, any location near the coast with a clear horizon, and the television broadcast.

45. I do not mean to suggest that a launch site is the only example of modern technology involving place, or incorporating an open horizon. Nuclear test sites present interesting inverse parallels. See Gusterson (1996).

46. The quip works more richly in French, because one of the terms used for a rocket launch, *tir,* also describes the shooting of an arrow. While the artifacts in question are of the souvenir variety, primarily intended to authenticate a jungle experience, hunting with guns and the consumption of exotic game animals remain popular and controversial activities in French Guiana.

CHAPTER 7. TROPICS OF NATURE

1. Mam-Lam-Fouck (1992: 306–7).

2. Orgeas (1885: 5)

3. As Clarence Glacken (1967) meticulously documents, concepts of the environment have had a long history in Western thought, maneuvering between philosophy and science. A concern for climate runs through the lineage of medical thought from ancient Greece to the emergence of disease theory.

4. See Kupperman (1984: 215), Kennedy (1981: 51), Curtin (1989), and W. Anderson (1992, 1996a, 1996b).

5. An example: On the fifteenth of March 1855, the governor writes to the minister reporting that out of a total of 492 convicts at Montagne d'Argent during the month of February, fifty-three were sick and ten had died, an improvement of 19.92 percent over the number ill during the same month the year before and 0.02 percent over the previous death rate. CAOM H bagne 14. For different views on the emergence and use of statistical reason, see Hacking (1990), Poovey (1998), and Porter (1995).

6. Montesquieu (1900: book 15, section 7: 240).

7. See W. Anderson (1996a) and Rabinow (1989: 129–34). It should be noted that French science came late and grudgingly to Darwinian versions of evolution, and that the story described here is presented in crude and summary form. For a richer account of nineteenth-century evolutionary debates, see Bowler (1989). For a more nuanced presentation of acclimation and opposition to it in French science, see Osborne (1994). For a theoretical frame through which to interpret the emergence of milieu, see Rabinow (1989) and Canguilhem (1989).

8. Osborne (1994: 83–97). Also see Gould (1981).

9. Cited in Osborne (1994: 94).

10. Examples given in the OED for cosmopolitan date to 1860 (Gosse) and 1875 (Lyell). Orgeas's use of the term, while archaic to the ear of contemporary cultural studies, is quite in keeping with the tradition of natural history. See also the Tresor de la langue française, 6: 254 (Paris, 1978), which provides the following gem from Teilhard de Chardin's 1955 Le Phénomène humain: "Zoologiquement considérée, l'Humanité nous présente le spectacle unique d'une 'espèce' capable de réaliser ce à quoi avait échoué toute autre espèce avant elle: non pas simplement être cosmopolite,—mais couvrir, sans se rompre, la Terre d'une seule membrane organisée [From a zoological perspective, humanity presents us with the spectacle of a 'species' capable of realizing that which has eluded all others before it: not simply being cosmopolitan—but covering the Earth with a single, unbroken organized membrane]."

11. Orgeas (1885: 20–27).

12. Ibid.: 63.

13. Ibid.: 122.

14. Orgeas (1886: 416).

15. Ibid.: 416–18.

16. From Bollot, "Un Pénitencier doit être une veritable maison de santé morale," in CAOM H bagne 4. His statistics are drawn from the Notice Officiel and the paper Toulonnais. Because the other death rates for French Guiana do not factor out accidental deaths, I prefer to use these; however, it should be stressed that although the rates given in different sources vary slightly, depending on whether the official numbers are modified for accidents or compared to naval physicians' reports, they vary only slightly (see also Devèze 1965: 142; Orgeas 1885: 26). For uniformity between nineteenth- and twentieth-century sources, as well as the comfort of the average reader, I have translated later demographic statistics based on a unit of one thousand into simple percentages.

17. Based on statistics found in Mam-Lam-Fouck (1987: 31–32) as adopted from the Almanach de la Guyane française. Figures in the original are

calculated per thousand, rather than the percentages to which I have converted them here.

18. The figures available for the 1834–1847 period only differentiate the population by civil status, slave versus free, rather than by racial category. During the earlier period of 1807–1828, freed slaves outnumbered white colonists, eventually by as much as two to one; thus it is likely that free blacks represent the larger statistical mass in the figures for nonslaves between 1834 and 1847. The number of white colonists recorded for 1842—the one year available—is 1,215, virtually unchanged from the 1,280 present in 1828, and only about a fifth of the total free population (Mam-Lam-Fouck 1987: 32).

19. Curtin (1989: 7–8).

20. Figures are drawn from Curtin (1989: 8), where original calculations are per thousand.

21. R. Price (1990: 300), original rates given per thousand.

22. Orgeas (1886: 311).

23. Crosby (1986).

24. Curtin (1989: 9–10)

25. Figures from Curtin (1989: 10).

26. "With the yellow fever danger gone, Jamaica began to encourage tourism to exploit the comfort of its winter climate and its new reputation for healthfulness" (Curtin 1989: 132). For a cogent summary of disease, race, and empire, see W. Anderson (1996a) and M. Harrison (1996). Also see Headrick (1981) for technical shifts associated with late-nineteenth-century European imperialism, and Rabinow (1989) on colonial planning and administration. For more on malaria, see Desowitz (1991) and Humphreys (1996), and for more on yellow fever, see Delaporte (1991). Needless to say, the story presented here is highly abbreviated.

27. L. Rousseau (1930: 355) gives the following death rates for hard labor convicts: 1924—7.77 percent; 1925—6.14 percent; 1926—7.54 percent; 1927—8.15 percent; 1928—10.30 percent; and reports that the rate for those sentenced under the recidivist laws was over 10 percent every year, rising to 11.45 percent in 1927.

28. (INSEE 1993: 30–31). The range in the official INSEE 1993 book of statistics is between 0.56 percent in 1987 and 0.41 percent in 1992. All original figures are given per thousand.

29. For an overview of interest in wilderness in the United States and historical patterns relative to urbanization, see R. Nash (1982).

30. As the late critic Raymond Williams writes, *nature* "is perhaps the most complex word in the language" (R. Williams 1983: 219). See also Arnold (1996), Evernden (1992: 18–35), Glacken (1967), Oelschlaeger (1991), K. Thomas (1983), R. Nash (1982), and Merchant (1990). Bess (1995) provides a survey of recent French attitudes about nature precisely in relation to high technology.

31. Guyane Excursions, "Le Maroni–Le Tapanahony (Descriptif)," collected 1994. Touristic fascination with the "original" peoples of French Guiana, the Amerindians and Maroons, can be read as reflecting a general Western obsession with romanticized origins (see, among others, Fabian 1983 on anthropology's role in this project).

32. The specific examples and phrases used in this discussion are taken from an article in the CNES magazine by Anne Paradis, "SOS Missionaires," *CNESQUISEPASSE?* 60 (March 1990): 38–40.

33. Recall the visit of the director among the Wayana described in chapter 6. For more on tourism, see MacCannell (1989) and Graburn and Jafari (1991).

34. A tour group I accompanied in the summer of 1994 (fewer than a dozen people) managed to consume some seven liters of rum and twenty liters of wine over four relatively exertion-free days. Amid new conditions of controlled adventure, echoes of colonial degeneration remain.

35. For a classic example, see Cognat (1977); for a more recent sketch, see Bilby (1990). Lezy (1989) provides a history of exploration in the area as well as an account of his own attempts to replicate such efforts in the mid-1980s. For another survey of the typical tourist itinerary in French Guiana, see Doucet (1981). For more on art collecting and river trips in French Guiana, see Price and Price (1992).

36. See *Le Pou d'Agouti* 1 (June 1990): 8–9; also see ONF (1992).

37. Sanite (1988).

38. The periodical *Le Pou d'Agouti*, published by the organization of the same name, offers the most lively overview of environmental issues in French Guiana. Named for a local biting insect, the *Pou* does its best to serve as an ecological gadfly. Together with the WWF, it comprises the most vocal element of environmental politics in French Guiana; organizations such as SEPANGUY (Société D'Etude de Protection et d'Aménagement de la Nature en Guyane) and the LPO (Ligue pour la Protection des Oiseaux) tend to be a tad more sedate. In 1994 another publication appeared, *Le Tamouchi*, with views more in keeping with official accounts linking architecture, urbanism, and the environment.

39. Wood (1995).

40. R. Harrison (1992). In *Tristes Tropiques,* Lévi-Strauss (1973: 91) finds the alterity of the New World amid trees: "This forest is different from Western forests because of the contrast between foliage and trunk. The foliage is darker, its shades of green suggesting the mineral rather than the vegetable kingdom."

41. Romier (1962: 11–12).

42. Laporte (1983: 175).

CHAPTER 8. THE NATURE OF WORK

1. Vidal de Lingendes, "De la colonisation pénale," 1845. CAOM H bagne 1.

2. Mam-Lam-Fouck (1987: 215).

3. This ethnic hegemony is such to have been coded into speech: in Guyane *le chinois* also means a corner market. The number of these establishments is quite remarkable, particularly in Cayenne.

4. For background on the position of climatic debates within the history of professional geography, see Livingstone (1992: 216–59). S. Hussein Alatas (1977) discusses the "lazy native" in the context of Southeast Asia; see also Certeau (1984), Ong (1987), and J. Scott (1990) on patterns of resistance to enforced labor. Sherry Ortner (1995: 173–93) provides cogent criticism of easy

assumptions of "resistance" as a category. Here the focus rests on "getting by." While some convict behavior could be described as "resistance" (certainly the repeated violation of rules displayed by the most "incorrigible" would fall into such a category), I am less interested here in defiance than in survival. Because the literature on "resistance" has grown extensive and generated heated response, it is important to underscore the significance of less functional oppositions to power in their own right, ways around rather than struggle against. For eloquent testimony on ways that survival itself can comprise achievement, see Carolyn Steedman (1987).

5. Ellsworth Huntington (1876–1947) was a Yale geographer who both advocated restrictive immigration policies and served as president of the American Eugenics Society between 1934 and 1938. He was also involved in early work in human ecology (see Kingsland 1993). *Civilization and Climate* went through many printings; the 1924 version cited here is the third edition.

6. Huntington (1924: 30).

7. Ibid.: 220.

8. Ibid.: 411.

9. Huntington composed his map of civilization on the basis of evaluations provided by a number of "well-informed persons"—distinguished scholars and experienced travelers. He sent a total of 213 inquiries to twenty-seven countries and received 138 responses, of which fifty-four satisfied his requirements sufficiently to represent a contribution. In the end his contribution list included twenty-five Americans, eight Britons, eight "Teutonic Europeans," six "Latin Europeans," six "Asiatics," one "Non-Teutonic and Non-Latin European" (a Russian), and no Latin Americans. Given the distribution, the resulting maps are rather predictable: England and the North Atlantic states score a perfect one hundred, closely followed by Germany and northern France at ninety-nine, whereas central Italy (outside of Florence) receives an eighty-five, Greece a seventy-two, central China a sixty-six, the United Provinces of India a fifty-three, New Guinea a fifteen, and the poor Kalahari Desert a mere twelve. The Guianas, French, British, and Dutch, together rate a collective thirty-four (ibid.: 240–74, 415–32). Among the Americans who participated we find the names of two anthropologists of note: Aleš Hrdlička and Edward Sapir. Two others declined the invitation to contribute to his larger project. Alfred Kroeber wrote that he had to "frankly confess that I believe you will obtain misleading results." Franz Boas put it even more strongly:

> I feel . . . quite unable to comply with your request, for several reasons. . . . It has been my endeavor, in my anthropological studies, to follow . . . the same principles that are laid down for the natural sciences; and the first condition of progress is therefore to eliminate the element of subjective value; not that I wish to deny that there are values, but it seems to me necessary to eliminate the peculiar combination of the development of cultural forms and the intrusion of the idea of our estimate of their value, which has nothing to do with these forms. It seems to my mind that in doing so these obtain subjective values, which in themselves may be subject of interesting studies, but which do not give any answer to the question you are trying to solve.
> Livingstone 1992: 226; Huntington 1924: 249, 415

10. Markham (1944: 20).

11. For a more recent and detailed history of air-conditioning in the United States, see Cooper (1998), who notes that early systems developed in industrial settings were intended to dehumidify as much as lower temperature (a significant point when considering the operation of delicate bits of technology as well as more massive forms of industrial production). Arsenault (1990) considers the cultural implications of the technology in the American South, as windows closed and porches emptied.

12. Markham (1944: 200–6). Cooper (1998) distinguishes between systems incorporated into building design (important to institutions and manufacture) and commercial mass production, also noting a strong countercurrent of open-air enthusiasm. Because the focus here is on the possibility of control rather than the history of the technology per se, I am simply following Markham's broader progressive account.

13. Markham (1994: 206).

14. Roussenq (1957: 55–57).

15. For an example from a very different climatic zone, see Solzhenitsyn (1963).

16. Certeau (1984: 34–39).

17. Ibid.: 30.

18. Revert (1949: 269–71).

19. See Rabinow (1989: 12–13; also 1994; 1996: 59–79). In "techno-cosmopolitanism" planners recognize history and nature; consequently, their designs—while modern and technical—retain a flavor of local specificity. In "middling modernism" planners abandon ties to a historical and natural milieu in favor of a social and technical one; consequently, their designs—also modern and technical—are pure and universal, designed for an abstract human subject. The essential difference between the two planning moments thus emerges in clear anthropological terms: a concern for particular groups as opposed to a concern for humankind. Rabinow's schema provides us with an additional vocabulary for development, particularly the norms of modernization. While the structures of "developing" society are less clearly drawn than those of the built environment, the generalized condition of "underdevelopment" and general efforts to act on the third world certainly replace history and nature with society and science. In this sense institutionalized development represents the final colonization of local conditions by universal principles, producing a new empire of experts. "Middling modernism's project was more audacious, seeking to create New Men freed, purified and liberated to pursue new forms of sociality which would inevitably arise from healthy spaces and forms" (Rabinow 1994: 403). For the emergence of such "New Men" worldwide, the space requiring redesign becomes the globe.

20. After the hundredth launch in 1997 the Ariane program (excluding the next-generation Ariane 5 rocket) had seven failures, giving it an overall success rate of 93 percent. Failed launches were 02, 05, 15, 18, 36, 63, and 70 (Reuters, Cayenne, personal communication).

21. Paradis (1993).

22. See the collection of anecdotes gathered by Joëlle Brami, in Brami (1989).

23. Ibid.

24. *Ròt Kozé* 45 (July/August 1994): 4.

25. Quoted in *Le Pou d'Agouti* 12 (March-April-May 1994): 29.

26. See A. Calmont (1987), EDF and CNEH (1993), and Jules (1994). In 1988, EDF reported a consumer base of some thirty thousand clients, drawing a total of forty-five megawatts. By 1992 that total had grown to seventy megawatts, and estimates for 1995 predicted a demand for one hundred megawatts. Operations surrounding Ariane 4 required twelve megawatts, a figure expected to increase to seventeen megawatts with the advent of Ariane 5. (EDF and CNEH 1993: 7). In relative terms, the growing energy use in French Guiana remains well below North American standards, if well above those of Africa (CCIG 1994: 53).

27. EDF and CNEH (1993) and Jules (1994: 29).

28. Some 2,700 million French francs. The dam design called for the use of rolled, compact concrete, a total length of 750 meters, and a reservoir of 315 square kilometers at 35 meters. The resulting structure can produce 116 megawatts, a relatively high 368 kilowatts per square kilometer of submerged surface (EDF 1993; Jules 1994: 35).

29. Jules (1994: 34–35). For comparison, see Hennigsgaard (1981) and Wali (1989).

30. Ayangma (1990: 4).

31. EDF (1992).

32. For example, the cover of one issue of the activist periodical *Le Pou d'Agouti* (no. 12, March/April 1994), transforms the initials EDF into "Enterprise de Destruction de la Forêt [Forest Destruction, Inc.]."

33. From *Ròt Kozé* 45 (July 1994): 2.

34. Quoted in B. Villeneuve, "La Dot du spatial," *France Guyane* (16 July 1994).

35. *Ròt Kozé* 45 (July 1994): 2. Material for this and the following synopsis stems from direct observation as well as reports on local TV (RFO and ACG) and in *France Guyane* during the months of July and August 1994. Special acknowledgment must be given to the Reuter Bureau of Cayenne, which followed the road stories assiduously and shared public information most generously.

36. WWF Communiqué de Presse, Operation "Acajou," dateline Versailles, 19 July 1994.

37. Intersyndicale des Socio-Professionels de Guyane. Communiqué de Presse, 21 July 1994.

38. See Parti Socialiste Guyanais Communiqué, 21 July 1994, and letter by L. Bertrand published in *France Guyane* (2 August 1994), as well as *Ròt Kozé* 45 (July 1994).

39. "SEDTP et intersyndicale répondent au WWF," *France Guyane* (2 August 1994).

40. *Le Pou d'Agouti* 13 (July, August, September 1994): 19.

41. Despite all the fuss, state permission had only been granted for the first twenty-three kilometers of deforestation, and the eagerness of the French government to facilitate the flow of persons over the Brazilian border was far from clear. As the paper in Martinique reported, even some local officials had private reservations about the benefits of the road, and those with interests in the local

airline and shipping business displayed no particular concern for its swift completion (*France-Antilles*, 2 September 1994). Most people I queried, although they favored the road, were amply skeptical about its ability to transform St. Georges into a booming metropolis. Like many issues in French Guiana, this saga of the roads appears a conflict over symbols as much as anything else. In 1996 and 1997 the most violent disturbances since the 1970s occurred in Cayenne, initially over chronic underemployment and subsequently over a series of arrests by the authorities.

42. The "Debate Route Regina–St. Georges" was broadcast on ACG the evening of August 1, 1994. I both watched it live and later repeatedly reviewed a video recording. However, since a number of comments were inaudible (at some points several people were talking at once), and others repetitious, I have condensed sections and spliced once or twice, trying to trim excess while retaining adequate detail and an accurate portrayal of each position, as reflected in written statements made by each side.

CHAPTER 9. THE IMPERFECT EQUATOR

1. See Latour (1993: 100–3). Here I am suggesting a slightly different symmetry of analysis than that Latour calls for, because the focus rests on the divide between "home" and "tropics" rather than on a repatriated discipline per se.

2. The strategy of incorporating the human and nonhuman symmetrically into studies of science and technology (as in Callon 1999, Latour 1993, and Haraway 1997) is an instructive balance to the Marxist legacy of focusing on production (see Harvey 1989 and Lefebvre 1991 for relevant discussions with spatial sensibility). With respect to concerns about mystification, I would recall the equal error of veiling the active presence of machines, animals, plants, dust, and wind behind terms such as "social relations." Neither nature nor artifice is simply a passive prop in a human drama, even less so when the categorical distinctions between them grow increasingly blurred.

3. This is not to imply that yielding to design equals success and persisting in improvisation equals failure. Bricolage is ultimately the most functional of approaches in that it seeks practical solutions to immediate problems. But as Lévi-Strauss (1966: 17) indicated, it operates within a closed universe, whereas planning, however disastrous, projects itself outward.

4. The crucial line of Hegel: "Through this rediscovery of himself by himself, the bondsman realizes that it is precisely in his work wherein he seemed to have only an alienated existence that he acquires a mind of his own" (1977: 118–19). Alexandre Kojève summarizes the importance of craft to the Hegelian slave by describing work as a kind of *bildung*: "Therefore—once more—thanks to his Work, the Slave *can* change and become other than he is, that is, he can—finally—cease to be a Slave. . . . Thanks to his work, *he* can become other; and, thanks to his work, the *World* can become other" (Kojève 1969: 52, 41–55). See also Winner (1977: 188). Here we have the kernel of the Marxist tradition of liberatory labor, pitting the materially engaged worker against abstract capital. Unfortunately, the dynamics of high technology do not appear to

conform to those of this fable, still less when one considers their spatial dimensions.

5. On colonial domination, see Fanon (1967, 1968), Memmi (1965), Mannoni (1990), and Nandy (1983). Fanon's (1968: 39–41) description of a divided Algeria, settler and native, provides a stark and powerful vision of Settler and Native against Marxist tradition.

6. Fanon (1967: 220–21).

7. See Arendt (1959). In Arendt's terms, Crusoe's realm is a private matter as much as a public one and can only become truly political once he is no longer alone. Thus his career on the island moves across each of her categories in turn, as Crusoe survives, builds, and finally governs.

8. Frederick Cooper and Ann Stoler (1997: 33–34) sound an appropriate cautionary note about not taking colonial categories and archives simply on their own word, or ignoring the dynamics of empire in attempting to distinguish the fluid, hybrid nature of the present. Here the image I would evoke is less that of a break than a layering, a further folding of a system over itself and subsequent rearrangements.

9. Even without an isolating shipwreck, the traveling expert inherits aspects of Crusoe's condition: restricted mastery and a habit of improvement. Not unlike the virtuous gentlemanly witness of science in seventeenth-century England (Shapin 1994), the twentieth-century international expert defines a kind of limitless neutrality within limited social terms. While the mobile space of travel opens to anyone with sufficient funds, authorizations, and inoculations, the status of natural modern (a transcendent success in biological and social mobility) remains restricted, marked primarily by neutral expertise and sensibilities of design and unmarked in formal terms by gender, race, or even a shred of culture. The very neutrality involved opens a door of universal possibility while obscuring the steps necessary for actors located within different fields of probability to cross the threshold. Members of historically marked groups, struggling against greater social gravity in the form of disparities in wealth and education, acceptance of appearance, psychology, and culture, must work harder to become neutral. They must also detach themselves from local expectations. The essence of a "career" remains motion and the ability to imagine a life alone, at home on standardized islands amid shifting landscapes. Thus while knowledge may always be locally constituted and applied at its end points in the world, its incorporation into professional expertise depends on abstraction and mobility.

10. Since the adoption of a microchip system in French credit card technology, cards from elsewhere in the world can pose problems and arouse suspicions. Early versions of the chips reportedly suffered in high humidity, and—as everywhere in the world—the equipment to read them sometimes fails to function. And yet, many a ride in a *taxi collectif* involves negotiation between a driver demanding a standard fare and a passenger seeking alternatives. Conflict only increases in encounters between official and unofficial realms: I once witnessed a long and painful interaction between a Maroon with a fantastically crumpled American hundred dollar bill and two skeptical Creole postal clerks reluctant to exchange it for French francs.

11. Tournier (1969, 1972).

12. Tournier (1969: 120).

13. For relevant criticism of development discourse, see Ferguson (1990) and Escobar (1995). The discussion of ages here can be extended further into the academic vocabulary of geography, periodization, and formal history and anthropology. In addition to Fabian (1983) and Said (1979), see Bentley (1996), Chakrabarty (1992), Cooper (1994), Coronil (1995), and Prakash (1995).

14. For sometimes hopeful renderings of the possibilities of a mobile present, see Appadurai (1996) and Haraway (1997). Gupta (1998) provides additional testimony that repeated failure itself can constitute an alternative modern tradition.

15. From Soeurs de Saint-Paul de Chartres, *250 ans en Guyane*, STI Roma (no date but from contents circa 1978). The sisters of Saint Paul de Chatres ministered in the penal colony. The work opens on the third page with these lines.

16. Verne (1966b: 248). Verne would later expand this idea in a 1889 work *Sans dessus dessous* (see A. Martin 1990: 179–91; Verne 1995: 109).

17. The combined polar difference amounts to about forty-five meters. See King-Hele (1992: 178–81) for illustration and explanation, and Fischer (1995) for the human context of early work in geodesy. Thurston Clarke (1988: 14) provides a romantic summary of the essential facts:

> But since the earth is an imperfect sphere, rotating around the poles and bulging in the middle, the equator, like a river, desert or mountain range, can only be exactly where it is: equidistant from the poles and perpendicular to the earth's axis, at 24,901.55 miles the longest circle that can be thrown around the earth. It divides the world into climatic and vegetative mirror images. On the equator at sea level, gravity is weakest, barometric pressure is lowest, and the earth spins fastest. To its north, winds circulate clockwise around zones of high pressure; to its south, counterclockwise. Where it crosses oceans, placid seas spin unpredictable hurricanes into the hemispheres; where it crosses land, predictable temperature and rainfall nurture life in sensational abundance and variety.

Bibliography

Beyond the items listed here, I have consulted additional documents at the Centre des Archives d'Outre-mer (CAOM) in Aix-en-Provence, France, at the Archives Départmentales in Cayenne, French Guiana, at the European Space Agency (ESA) library in Paris, at the Bibliothèque Franconie, at the library of the Chambre de Commerce et Industrie de la Guyane (CCIG), at the Reuters Bureau in Cayenne, and in private collections. In addition, I have benefited greatly from the receipt of materials generously provided by the Centre Spatial Guyanais (CSG), Arianespace, the Centre National d'Etudes Spatial (CNES), and ESA. Where relevant I have cited additional sources in notes. General sources consulted include issues of the 1960s newspaper Le Radio-Presse, *the current local paper* France Guyane, *the ecology publication* Le Pou d'Agouti, *local news broadcasts on the television stations RFO and (in 1994) ACG, and finally the in-house CSG/CNES publications* Latitude 5 *and* CNESQUISE-PASSE?, *not to mention numerous brochures from the various space agencies.*

Abonnenc, E., and M. Abonnenc. 1981. "Le bagne de la Guyane française durant les années 1856 à 1872: Un manuscrit révélateur." *Bulletin de la Société de Pathologie Exotique* 74, no. 2 (March/April): 235–252.

Ackroyd, Brian. 1990. *World Satellite Communications and Earth Station Design.* Boca Raton, Fla.: CRC Press.

Adas, Michael. 1989. *Machines as the Measure of Men: Science, Technology, and Ideologies of Western Dominance.* Ithaca, N.Y.: Cornell University Press.

Adélaïde-Merlande, Jacques, ed. 1986. *Histoire des communes, Antilles-Guyane.* Vols. 2–3. N.p.: Pressplay.

Alatas, Hussein, Syed. 1977. *The Myth of the Lazy Native: A Study of the Image of the Malays, Filipinos, and Javanese from the Sixteenth to the Twentieth Century and Its Function in the Ideology of Colonial Capitalism*. London: F. Cass.

Aldrich, Robert, and John Connell. 1992. *France's Overseas Frontier: Départments et Territoires d'Outre-Mer*. Cambridge: Cambridge University Press.

Alexakis, Chantal. 1979. *Les bagnes*. Paris: Editions Pygmalion, Collection en marge de l'histoire.

Alexandre, Rodolphe. 1988. *La Guyane sous Vichy*. Paris: Editions Caribéennes.

Allison-Booth, W. E. 1931a. *Devil's Island: Revelations of the French Penal Settlements*. London: Putnam.

———. 1931b. *Hell's Outpost: The True Story of Devil's Island by a Man Who Exiled Himself There*. New York: Minton, Balch.

ANAE (Académie Nationale de l'Air et de l'Espace). 1992. *Les apports de la conquête spatiale à l'humanité/Contributions of Space Conquest on Mankind's Welfare*. International Workshop, Paris, June 11–12, 1991. Toulouse: Cépaduès-Editions.

Anderson, Benedict. 1991 [1983]. *Imagined Communities: Reflections on the Origin and Spread of Nationalism*. London: Verso.

Anderson, Warwick. 1992. "'Where Every Prospect Pleases and Only Man Is Vile': Laboratory Medicine as Colonial Discourse." *Critical Inquiry* 18 (spring): 506–529.

———. 1996a. "Disease, Race, and Empire." *Bulletin of the History of Medicine* 70, no. 1 (spring): 62–67.

———. 1996b. "Immunities of Empire: Race, Disease, and the New Tropical Medicine, 1900–1920." *Bulletin of the History of Medicine* 70, no. 1 (spring): 94–118.

Anonymous. 1987. *Kourou: Ville en devenir*. Barcelona: Delroisse. Space souvenir book.

Anonymous. 1994. "La Guyane dans l'Union Européenne." Luxembourg: OPOCE. Informational brochure.

Appadurai, Arjun. 1996. *Modernity at Large: Cultural Dimensions of Globalization*. Minneapolis: University of Minnesota Press.

Aravamudan, Srinivas. 1993. "Tropicalizing the Enlightenment." *Diacritics* (fall): 48–63.

Archives Départmentales. 1989. *Cayenne 89: Expositions organisées dans le cadre de la commémoration du Bicentinaire de la Révolution française*. Cayenne: Archives départmentales.

Ardener, Edwin. 1987. "'Remote Areas': Some Theoretical Considerations." In *Anthropology at Home*, ed. Anthony Jackson. London: Tavistock.

Arendt, Hannah. 1959. *The Human Condition*. Garden City, N.Y.: Doubleday.

———. 1978 [1968]. "The Conquest of Space and the Stature of Man." In *Between Past and Future: Eight Exercises in Political Thought*. Middlesex, U.K.: Penguin Books.

Arianespace. 1993. "Les missions du lanceur européen." Informational brochure.

———. 1994. "Exercice1993/Annual Report." Corporate brochure.

Armengaud, Jean. 1990. "Introduction." *Bois et Forets des Tropiques* 219 (March special on Guyane): 3–6.

Armstrong, Nancy, and Leonard Tennenhouse. 1989. *The Representation of Violence: Literature and the History of Violence.* London: Routledge.

Arnold, David. 1996. *The Problem of Nature.* Oxford: Blackwell Publishers.

Arsenault, Raymond. 1990. "The End of a Long Hot Summer: The Air Conditioner and Southern Culture." In *Searching for the Sunbelt: Historical Perspectives on a Region,* ed. Raymond A. Mohl. Knoxville: University of Tennessee Press.

Asad, Talal. 1973. *Anthropology and the Colonial Encounter.* New York: Humanities Press.

Augé, Marc. 1986. *Un ethnologue dans le métro.* Paris: Hachette.

Ayangma, Fred. 1990. "Petit-Saut: Innévitables incidences." *Version Guyane* 6 (October): 4–8.

Baccini, H. 1991. "Le CSG et la protection de l'environnement." *Latitude 5* 12: 8.

Bachelard, Gaston. 1994 [1958]. *The Poetics of Space.* Boston: Beacon Press.

Bainbridge, William S. 1976. *The Spaceflight Revolution.* New York: John Wiley and Sons.

Barousse, Claude. 1989. *Parole de forçat: Le dossier Arthur Rocques.* Arles: Actes Sud.

Basalla, George. 1988. *The Evolution of Technology.* Cambridge: Cambridge University Press.

Batzler-Heim, Georg. 1930. *The Horrors of Cayenne: The Experiences of a German as a French Bagno-Convict.* Ed. and introduction by Karl Bartz. London: Constable and Hall.

Baudry, Patrick, and Alain Souchier. 1986. *Ariane.* Paris: Flammarion.

Behar, Ruth, and Deborah A. Gordon, eds. 1995. *Women Writing Culture.* Berkeley: University of California Press.

Belbenoit, René. 1938. *Dry Guillotine.* New York: E. P. Dutton.

———. 1940. *Hell on Trial.* New York: E. P. Dutton.

Bender, John. 1987. *Imagining the Penitentiary: Fiction and the Architecture of Mind in Eighteenth-Century England.* Chicago: University of Chicago Press.

Benedict, Ruth. 1959 [1934]. *Patterns of Culture.* Boston: Houghton Mifflin.

Benjamin, Walter. 1969 [1955]. *Illuminations: Essays and Reflections.* Ed. Hannah Arendt. New York: Schocken.

Bentham, Jeremy. 1962 [1787–1802]. "Panopticon; or The Inspection-House," "Panopticon vs. New South Wales," and "A Plea for the Constitution." In *The Works of Jeremy Bentham,* Vol. 4, under direction of John Browring, 1–284. New York: Russell and Russell.

———. 1977 [1787]. *Le Panoptique.* Preceded by interview with Michel Foucault, afterword by Michelle Perrot. Paris: Pierre Belfond.

Bentley, Jerry H. 1996. "Cross-Cultural Interaction and Periodization." *The American Historical Review* 101, no. 3 (June): 749–770.

Bergaust, Erik, and William Beller. 1956. *Satellite!* Garden City, N.Y.: Hanover House.

Berman, Marshall. 1988. *All That Is Solid Melts into Air: The Experience of Modernity.* New York: Penguin.

Bess, Michael D. 1995. "Ecology and Artifice: Shifting Perceptions of Nature and High Technology in Postwar France." *Technology and Culture* 36, no. 4 (October): 830–862.

Betts, Raymond F. 1985. *Uncertain Dimensions: Western Overseas Empires in the Twentieth Century.* Minneapolis: University of Minnesota Press.

Biagioli, Mario, ed. 1999. *The Science Studies Reader.* New York: Routledge.

Bijker, Wiebe E., Thomas P. Hughes, and Trevor Pinch, eds. 1987. *The Social Construction of Technological Systems: New Directions in the Sociology and History of Technology.* Cambridge: MIT Press.

Bilby, Kenneth M. 1990. "The Remaking of the Aluku: Culture, Politics, and Maroon Identity in French South America." Ph.D. diss., John Hopkins University.

Blewett, David. 1995. *The Illustration of Robinson Crusoe, 1719–1920.* Gerrards Cross, U.K.: Colin Smythe.

Blonstein, Larry. 1987. *Communication Satellites: The Technology of Space Communications.* London: Heinemann.

Bloom, Harold, ed. 1988. *Daniel Defoe's Robinson Crusoe.* New York: Chelsea House Publishers.

Blumenberg, Hans. 1987 [1975]. *Genesis of the Copernican World.* Cambridge: MIT Press.

Blunt, Alison, and Gillian Rose. 1994. *Writing Women and Space: Colonial and Postcolonial Geographies.* New York: Guilford Press.

Boas, Franz. 1948. *Race, Language, and Culture.* New York: Macmillan.

———. 1962 [1928]. *Anthropology and Modern Life.* New York: W. W. Norton.

Borel, R. 1992. "CSG: L'Europe avant l'heure." *Latitude 5* 17: 6–8.

Boucher, Philip. 1980–1981. "Shadows in the Past: France and Guiana, 1655–1657." *Proceedings of the Sixth and Seventh Annual Meetings of the French Colonial Historical Society.* Ed. James J. Cook. Washington, D.C.: University Press of America.

Bourdet-Pléville, Michel. 1960. *Justice in Chains: From the Galleys to Devil's Island.* Trans. Anthony Rippon. London: Robert Hale.

Bourdieu, Pierre. 1984 [1979]. *Distinction: A Social Critique of the Judgement of Taste.* Cambridge: Harvard University Press.

———. 1989. *La noblesse d'etat: Grandes ecoles et esprit de corps.* Paris: Editions de Minuit.

Bouyer, Frédéric. 1990 [1867]. *La Guyane française: Notes et souvenirs d'un voyage exécuté en 1862–1863.* Reprint, Cayenne: Guy Delabergerie. Orig. Paris: Libraire de L. Hachette.

Bowker, Geoffrey C. 1994. *Science on the Run: Information Management and Industrial Geophysics at Schlumberger, 1920–1940.* Cambridge: MIT Press.

Bowler, Peter J. 1989 [1983]. *Evolution: The History of an Idea.* Berkeley: University of California Press.

Brami, Joëlle. 1989. "Decembre 79: 'Je me souviens.'" *CNESQUISEPASSE?* 59 (December): 9–13.

———. 1991. "Kourou, en pleine croissance." CNESQUISEPASSE? 65 (April): 12–13.

Bredin, Jean-Denis. 1986 [1983]. *The Affair: The Case of Alfred Dreyfus.* New York: George Braziller.

Brugioni, Dino. 1989. "Impact and Social Implications." *Technology in Society* 11 (Special Issue: Global Impact of Commercial Remote-Sensing Satellites): 1.

Bruleaux, Anne-Marie. 1992. "Les plans de colonisation de la Guyane, 1763–1843." In Archives Nationales, edited catalogue volume, *Voyage aux îles d'Amérique*. Paris: Archives Nationales.

Bruleaux, Anne-Marie, R. Calmont, and S. Mam-Lam-Fouck, eds. 1986. *Deux siècles d'esclavage en Guyane Française, 1652–1848*. Paris: L'Harmattan.

Bulkeley, Rip. 1991. *The Sputniks Crisis and Early United States Space Policy: A Critique of the Historiography of Space*. Bloomington, Ind.: Indiana University Press.

Bullard, Alice. 1997. "Self-Representation in the Arms of Defeat: Fatal Nostalgia and Surviving Comrades in French New Caledonia, 1871–1880." *Cultural Anthropology* 12, no. 2 (May): 179–212.

Burns, Michael. 1991. *Dreyfus: A Family Affair, 1789–1945*. New York: Harper Collins.

Callon, Michel. 1999 [1986]. "Some Elements of Translation: Domestication of the Scallops and the Fishermen of St. Brieuc Bay." In *The Science Studies Reader*, ed. Mario Biagioli, 67–83. New York: Routledge.

Calmont, André. 1987. "La nouvelle donne énergétique en Guyane." *Equinoxe* 24: 1–34.

Calmont, Régine. 1988. "L'impact de l'immigration haïtienne en Guyane." *Equinoxe* 26: 1–48.

Canguilhem, Georges 1989 [1966]. *The Normal and the Pathological*. New York: Zone Books.

Carroll, Lewis. 1971 [1865]. *Alice in Wonderland*. Ed. Donald J. Gray. New York: W. W. Norton.

Cart-Tanneur, Philippe, Bernard Ruff, and Patrick Garrouste. 1989. *La Guyane, terre d'espaces*. Paris: Trameway.

Carter, Dale. 1988. *The Final Frontier: The Rise and Fall of the American Rocket State*. London: Verso.

Carter, L. J., ed. 1962. *Communications Satellites*. London: Academic Press.

Carter, Paul. 1988. *The Road to Botany Bay: An Exploration of Landscape and History*. New York: Alfred A. Knopf.

Castells, Manuel, and Peter Hall. 1994. *Technopoles of the World: The Making of Twenty-First-Century Industrial Complexes*. London: Routledge.

Castor, Elie, and Georges Othily. 1984a. *La Guyane, les grandes problèmes, les solutions possibles*. Paris: Editions Caribéennes.

———. 1984b. *La Région Guyane, 1960–1983*. Paris: Editions L'Harmattan.

CCIG (Chambre de Commerce et d'Industrie de la Guyane). 1993. *Le Developpement: Bulletin de la CCIG* 53 (June).

———. 1994. "Guyane: terre d'Amazonie." Informational brochure.

Cendrars, Blaise. 1958 [1930]. *Rhum*. Paris: Bernard Grasset.

Certeau, Michel de. 1984 [1979]. *The Practice of Everyday Life*. Berkeley: University of California Press.

Césaire, Aime. 1972. *Discourse on Colonialism*. New York: Monthly Review Press.

Chadeau, Emmanuel. 1988. "Government, Industry, and the Nation: The Growth of Aeronautical Technology in France, 1900–1950." *Aerospace Historian* 35 (March): 26–44.

Chaïa, Jean. 1958. *Echec d'une tentative de colonisation de la Guyane au XVI–IIe siècle (Etude médicale de l'Expédition de Kourou, 1763–1764).* Paris: Biologie Médicale.

Chakrabarty, Dipesh. 1992. "Postcoloniality and the Artifice of History: Who Speaks for 'Indian' Pasts?" *Representations* 37 (winter): 1–26.

Chalifoux, Jean-Jacques. 1987. *L'identité ethnique: Questions pour la Guyane.* Cayenne: CRESTIG.

Chamoiseau, Patrick, and Rodolphe Hammadi. 1994. *Guyane: Traces-mémoires du bagne.* Paris: Caisse Nationale des Monuments Historiques et des Sites.

Charrière, Henri. 1970 [1969]. *Papillon.* [Trans. Patrick O'Brian.] St. Albans, U.K.: Panther Books.

Chérubini, Bernard. 1988. *Cayenne: Ville créole et polyethnique, essai d'anthropologie urbaine.* Paris: Karthala.

Chesneaux, Jean. 1972. *The Political and Social Ideas of Jules Verne.* London: Thames and Hudson.

Cittadino, Eugene. 1990. *Nature as the Laboratory: Darwinian Plant Ecology in the German Empire, 1880–1900.* Cambridge: Cambridge University Press.

Clair, Silvie, et al. 1990. *Terres de bagne.* Aix-en-Provence: CAOM/AMAROM. Exhibition catalogue.

Clair, Silvie, Odile Krakovitch, and Jean Préteux. 1990. *Etablissements pénitentiaires coloniaux, 1792–1952: Série Colonies H, répertoire numérique.* Paris: Archives Nationales.

Clarke, Arthur C. 1945. "Extra-Terrestrial Relays: Can Rocket Stations Give World-Wide Coverage?" *Wireless World.* Reprinted in *The Beginnings of Satellite Communications,* by J. R. Pierce, 37–43. San Francisco: San Francisco Press, 1968.

———. 1965. *Voices from the Sky.* New York: Harper and Row.

———. 1968. *2001: A Space Odyssey.* New York: Signet.

Clarke, Thurston. 1988. *Equator: A Journey.* New York: William Morrow.

Clifford, James. 1988. *The Predicament of Culture.* Cambridge: Harvard University Press.

———. 1997. *Routes: Travel and Translation in the Late Twentieth Century.* Cambridge: Harvard University Press.

Clifford, James, and George Marcus, eds. 1986. *Writing Culture: The Poetics and Politics of Culture.* Berkeley: University of California Press.

CNES (Centre National d'Etudes Spatiales). 1970. "La Guyane-Cayenne-Kourou: Quelques renseignments." Diffusion, Information et Documentation, 129 rue Université, Paris 7eme.

———. 1972. *Les bases de lancement/Launching bases.* Conference proceedings.

———. 1978? "Le Centre Spatial Guyanais/The Guiana Space Centre." Bilingual brochure.

———. 1987. "Chiffres." *CNESQUISEPASSE?* 49: 17–18.

———. 1988. "La Guyane et l'espace." CNES/CSG informational brochure.

———. 1990. "Centre Spatial Guyanais: Port spatial de l'Europe." Pamphlet.

———. 1991. "Chiffres." *CNESQUISEPASSE?* 65 (April): 14.

———. 1994. "1964: Conception et naissance du Centre Spatial Guyanais." Press release from future authorized history of CNES and original reports. Also published in *Antilla* 582 (29 April 1994): 21–22.

CNES (Centre National d'Etudes Spatiales) and ESA (European Space Agency). 1994a. "Ariane 5: Ground Facilities in French Guiana." Brochure.

———. 1994b. "Ariane 5: Le Programme." Brochure.

CNES (Centre National d'Etudes Spatiales) with Palais de la Découvert and SEP (Société Européenne de Propulsion). 1991. "L'Espace: Comment ça marche?" Instructional pamphlet.

CNRS/ORSTOM. 1979. *Atlas des Départments Français d'Outre-Mer 4: La Guyane.* Paris: Centre d'Etudes de Géographie Tropicale de CNRS.

Cognat, André. 1977. *Autecume ou une autre vie.* Paris: Editions Robert Laffont.

Cohen, Stephen. 1977 [1969]. *Modern Capitalist Planning: The French Model.* Berkeley: University of California Press.

Cohn, Bernard. 1987. *An Anthropologist among the Historians and Other Essays.* Delhi: Oxford University Press.

Collet, Jocelyn. 1989. "Un tourisme très . . . spatial." *Latitude 5* 6: 25–28.

Collingwood, R. G. 1960 [1945]. *The Idea of Nature.* Oxford: Oxford University Press.

Collins, Guy. 1990. *Europe in Space.* London: Macmillan.

Collins, Harry, and Trevor Pinch. 1998. *The Golem at Large: What You Should Know about Technology.* Cambridge: Cambridge University Press.

Collins, Martin J., and Sylvia D. Fries. 1991. *A Spacefaring Nation: Perspectives on American Space History and Policy.* Washington, D.C.: Smithsonian Institution.

Comaroff, Jean, and John Comaroff. 1992. *Ethnography and the Historical Imagination.* Boulder: Westview Press.

Conkey, Margaret. 1989. "The Place of Material Culture Studies in Contemporary Anthropology." In *Perspectives on Anthropological Collections from the American Southwest,* ed. A. L. Hedlund, 13–31. Tempe, Ariz.: Arizona State University, Anthropology Research Papers no. 40.

Cooper, Frederick. 1994. "Conflict and Connection: Rethinking African Colonial History." *American Historical Review* 99, no. 5: 1516–1545.

———. 1997. "Modernizing Bureaucrats, Backward Africans, and the Development Concept. In *International Development and the Social Sciences: Essays on the History and Politics of Knowledge,* ed. Frederick Cooper and Randall Packard. Berkeley: University of California Press.

Cooper, Frederick, and Randall Packard, eds. 1997. *International Development and the Social Sciences: Essays on the History and Politics of Knowledge.* Berkeley: University of California Press.

Cooper, Frederick, and Ann L. Stoler. 1989. "Introduction: Tensions of Empire: Colonial Control and Visions of Rule." *American Ethnologist* 16, no. 4 (November): 609–621.

———, eds. 1997. *Tensions of Empire: Colonial Cultures in a Bourgeois World.* Berkeley: University of California Press.

Cooper, Gail. 1998. *Air-conditioning America: Engineers and the Controlled Environment, 1900–1960.* Baltimore: John Hopkins University Press.

Coronil, Fernando. 1995. "Beyond Occidentalism: Towards Non-Imperial Geohistorical Categories." *Cultural Anthropology* 11, no. 1: 51–87.

Cosgrove, Denis. 1994. "Contested Global Visions: One-World, Whole Earth, and the Apollo Space Photographs." *Annals of the Association of American Geographers* 84, no. 2: 270–294.

Crawford, Stephen. 1991. "Changing Technology and National Career Structures: The Work and Politics of French Engineers." *Science, Technology, and Human Values* 16, no. 2: 173–194.

Cremins, Tom, and Elizabeth Newton. 1991. "Changing Structure of the Soviet Space Programme." *Space Policy* 7, no. 2: 129–136.

Crosby, Alfred W. 1972. *The Colombian Exchange: Biological and Cultural Consequences of 1492.* Westport, Conn.: Greenwood Press.

———. 1986. *Ecological Imperialism: The Biological Expansion of Europe, 900–1900.* Cambridge: Cambridge University Press.

Croyere, Antoine. 1984. "Comprendre le temps en Guyane." Cayenne: CNDP/CRDP des Antilles-Guyane/CDDP de Guyane.

CSG (Centre Spatial Guyanais). 1994. "Ariane en Guyane." Informational brochure.

CSG (Centre Spatial Guyanais) and CLAMFUK (Club de Lancement de Mini-Fusées de Kourou). 1994. "Lancement de la fusée RG." Informational packet.

CSST (Committee on Science, Space, and Technology). 1989. *Europe 1992 and Its Effects on U.S. Science, Technology, and Competitiveness.* Washington, D.C.: GPO.

Curtin, Philip. 1989. *Death by Migration: Europe's Encounter with the Tropical World in the Nineteenth Century.* Cambridge: Cambridge University Press.

Daget, Serge. 1992. "Main-d'Oeuvre et Avatars du peuplement en Guyane française, 1817–1863." *Revue Français d'Histoire d'Outre-Mer* 79, no. 297: 449–474.

Damas, Léon-Gontran. 1938. *Retour de Guyane.* Paris: Librarie José Corti.

Dattner, A. 1982. *Réflexion sur l'Europe spatiale: Les deux premières décennies et au-delà.* Noordwijk, Netherlands: European Space Agency.

Davis, Hassoldt. 1952. *The Jungle and the Damned.* New York: Duell, Sloan and Pearce.

Defoe, Daniel. 1903a [1719]. *The Life and Strange Adventures of Robinson Crusoe, Part 2: Farther Adventures of Robinson Crusoe.* New York: Thomas Y. Crowell.

———. 1903b [1720]. *Serious Reflections during the Life and Surprising Adventures of Robinson Crusoe, with His Vision of the Angelic World.* New York: Thomas Y. Crowell.

———. 1972 [1719]. *Robinson Crusoe.* Ed. J. Donald Crowly. Oxford: Oxford University Press.

———. 1975 [1719]. *Robinson Crusoe.* Ed. Michael Shinagel. New York: W. W. Norton.

Delaporte, François. 1991 [1989]. *The History of Yellow Fever: An Essay on the Birth of Tropical Medicine.* Cambridge: MIT Press.

Dening, Greg. 1980. *Islands and Beaches: Discourse on a Silent Land: Marquesas, 1774–1880.* Chicago: Dorsey Press.

Derrida, Jacques. 1976 [1967]. *Of Grammatology.* Trans. Gayatri Chakravorty Spivak. Baltimore: Johns Hopkins University Press.

Desobeau, Jean-Michel. 1990. "CSG: Guiana Space Center." *La documentation guyanais.* Cayenne: Saga.

Desowitz, Robert S. 1991. *The Malaria Capers: More Tales of Parasites and People, Research and Reality.* New York: W. W. Norton.

Devèze, Michel. 1968. *Les Guyanes.* Paris: Presses Universitaires de France.

———, ed. 1965. *Cayenne: Déportés et bagnards.* Paris: Julliard.

Dirks, Nicholas, ed. 1992. *Colonialism and Culture.* Ann Arbor: University of Michigan Press.

Dompierre D'Hornoy, M. de (Minstre de la Marine et des Colonies). 1874. *Notice sur la transportation à la Guyane française et à la Nouvelle-Calédonie, pendant les années 1868, 1869, et 1870.* Paris: Imprimerie Nationale.

Donet-Vincent, Danielle. 1992. *La fin du bagne, 1923–1953.* Rennes: Editions Ouest-France.

———. 1993. "La fin des bagnes." *L'Histoire* 168: 104–107.

Doriac, Neuville. 1985. *Esclavage, assimilation et guyanité.* Paris: Editions Anthropos.

Doucet, Louis. 1981. *Vous avez dit Guyane!* Paris: Editions Demoël.

Douglas, Mary. 1984 [1966]. *Purity and Danger: An Analysis of the Concepts of Pollution and Taboo.* London: Ark Paperbacks.

Downey, Gary L., Arthur Donovan, and Timothy Elliott. 1989. "The Invisible Engineer: How Engineering Ceased to Be a Problem in Science and Technology Studies." In *Knowledge and Society: Studies in the Sociology of Science Past and Present,* ed. L. Hargens, R. A. Jones, and A. Pickering, 189–216. Greenwich, Conn.: JAI Press.

Downey, Gary L., and Joseph Dumit, eds. 1997. *Cyborgs and Citadels: Anthropological Interventions in Emerging Sciences and Technologies.* Santa Fe, N.Mex.: School of American Research Press.

Dreyfus, Alfred. 1899. *The Letters of Captain Dreyfus to His Wife.* Trans. L. G. Moreau. New York: Harper and Brothers.

———. 1901. *Five Years of My Life, 1894–1899.* New York: McClure, Phillips.

Dreyfus, Hubert, and Paul Rabinow. 1983. *Michel Foucault: Beyond Structuralism and Hermeneutics.* Chicago: University of Chicago Press.

Duchart, Jean Michel, ed. 1978. "Fournier, Philippe: Un givordin aux bagnes de Guyane, 1853–1858." *Les Cahiers de l'Academie du Souilat* no. 2.

Durand-de Jongh, France. 1998. *De la fusée Véronique au lanceur Ariane: Une histoire d'hommes, 1945–1979.* Paris: Editions Stock.

EDF (Electricité de France). 1992. "Recherche archeologique de Petit-Saut: Trois ans de découvertes, six milles ans d'histoire." Brochure.

———. 1993. "Aménagement hydro-électrique et environnement: Barrage de Petit-Saut en Guyane française." Brochure.

———. N.d. "Barrage de Petit-Saut." Brochure.

EDF (Electricité de France) and CNEH (Centre National d'Equipement Hydraulique). 1993. "Le barrage de Petit Saut et l'environnement." Brochure.

Edwards, Paul N. Forthcoming. "The World in a Machine: Origins and Impacts of Early Computerized Global Systems Models." In *Systems, Experts and Computers*, ed. Thomas Hughes and Agatha C. Hughes. Cambridge: MIT Press.

ELDO (European Launcher Development Organization). 1970? "Eldo Equatorial Launching Base in French Guiana." Informational brochure.

Elias, Norbert. 1978 [1939]. *The Civilizing Process*. Vol. 1, *The History of Manners*. New York: Pantheon.

Embassy of France. 1989. *FAST (French Advances in Science and Technology)* 3, no. 2 (summer). Special Issue: Engineering Education in France.

Entrikin, J. Nicholas. 1991. *The Betweenness of Place: Towards a Geography of Modernity*. London: Macmillan.

Eribon, Didier. 1991 [1989]. *Michel Foucault*. Trans. Betsy Wind. Cambridge: Harvard University Press.

ESA (European Space Agency). 1975. "Convention for the Establishment of a European Space Agency." Legal document.

———. 1987. "European Space: On Course for the Twenty-First Century." Pamphlet.

———. 1988. "Reaching for the Skies: The Ariane Family Story and Beyond." Pamphlet.

———. 1989a. "ESA and Space Science." Informational brochure.

———. 1989b. "Our Inheritance—Our Future: Space. ESA: The European Space Agency." Pamphlet.

———. 1991. "Hermes." Pamphlet.

———. 1992a. "Ariane: A European Success Story." Informational brochure.

———. 1992b. "The Satellites at the Service of the Environment and Development." Brochure for UN conference on Environment and Development.

Escobar, Arturo. 1995. *Encountering Development: The Making and Unmaking of the Third World*. Princeton: Princeton University Press.

Evans-Pritchard, E. E. 1940. *The Nuer: A Description of the Modes of Livelihood and Political Institutions of a Nilotic People*. Oxford: Oxford University Press.

Everett, Charles. 1966. *Jeremy Bentham*. London: Weidenfeld and Nicolson.

Evernden, Neil. 1992. *The Social Creation of Nature*. Baltimore: Johns Hopkins University Press.

Fabian, Johannes. 1983. *Time and the Other: How Anthropology Makes Its Object*. New York: Columbia University Press.

Fanon, Frantz. 1967 [1952]. *Black Skin, White Masks*. Trans. Charles Markmann. New York: Grove Press.

———.1968 [1961]. *The Wretched of the Earth*. Trans. Constance Farrington. New York: Grove Weidenfeld.

Fardon, Richard. 1990. *Localizing Strategies: Regional Traditions of Ethnographic Writing*. Edinburgh: Scottish University Press and Smithsonian Institution Press.

———, ed. 1995. *Counterworks: Managing the Diversity of Knowledge*. London: Routledge.

Faubion, James. 1988. "Possible Modernities." *Cultural Anthropology* 3, no. 4: 365–378.

———. 1993. *Modern Greek Lessons: A Primer in Historical Constructivism*. Princeton: Princeton University Press.

Featherstone, M., ed. 1990. *Global Culture: Nationalism, Globalization, and Modernity*. London: Sage.

Feenberg, Andrew. 1995. *Alternative Modernity: The Technical Turn in Philosophy and Social Theory*. Berkeley: University of California Press.

Feld, Steven, and Keith Basso, eds. 1996. *Senses of Place*. Santa Fe, N.Mex.: School of American Research Press.

Ferguson, James. 1990. *The Antipolitics Machine: "Development," Depoliticization, and Bureaucratic Power in Lesotho*. Cambridge: Cambridge University Press.

Finney, Ben R., and Eric M. Jones. 1985. *Interstellar Migration and the Human Experience*. Berkeley: University of California Press.

Fischer, Michael M. J. 1995. "Eye(I)ing the Sciences and Their Signifiers (Language, Tropes, Autobiographers): InterViewing for a Cultural Studies of Science and Technology." In *Technoscientific Imaginaries: Conversations, Profiles, and Memoirs*, ed. George Marcus, 43–84. Chicago: University of Chicago Press.

Fores, Michael. 1988. "Transformations and the Myth of 'Engineering Science': Magic in a White Coat." *Technology and Culture* 29 (January): 62–81.

Forster, Colin. 1996. *France and Botany Bay: The Lure of a Penal Colony*. Melbourne: Melbourne University Press.

Fortun, Kim. 1999. "Locating Corporate Environmentalism: Synthetics, Implosions, and the Bhopal Disaster." In *Critical Anthropology Now: Unexpected Contexts, Shifting Constituencies, Changing Agendas*, ed. George Marcus, 203–244. Sante Fe, N.Mex.: School of American Research Press.

Foucault, Michel. 1973 [1966]. *The Order of Things: An Archaeology of the Human Sciences*. New York: Vintage Books.

———. 1975. *Surveiller et punir*. Paris: Editions Gallimard.

———. 1979 [1975]. *Discipline and Punish: The Birth of the Prison*. New York: Vintage Books.

———. 1980a. *Power/Knowledge: Selected Interviews and Other Writings, 1972–1977*. Ed. Colin Gordon. New York: Pantheon Books.

———. 1980b. "Truth and Power." In *Power/Knowledge: Selected Interviews and Other Writings, 1972–1977*, ed. Colin Gordon, 109–133. New York: Pantheon Books.

Fox, Richard, ed. 1991. *Recapturing Anthropology: Working in the Present*. Santa Fe, N.Mex.: School of American Research Press.

Franklin, Sarah. 1995. "Science as Culture, Cultures of Science." *Annual Review of Anthropology* 24: 163–184.

French, Howard. 1991. "A Space Center or Not, Some Say It's a Jungle." *The New York Times* (26 April): A6.

Friedland, Roger, and Deirdre Boden, eds. 1994. *NowHere: Space, Time, and Modernity*. Berkeley: University of California Press.

Galison, Peter, and Bruce Hevly, eds. 1992. *Big Science: The Growth of Large-Scale Research*. Stanford: Stanford University Press.

Garland, David. 1990. *Punishment and Modern Society: A Study in Social Theory*. Chicago: University of Chicago Press.

Geertz, Clifford. 1973. *The Interpretation of Cultures*. New York: Basic Books.

————. 1983. *Local Knowledge: Further Essays in Interpretive Anthropology.* New York: Basic Books.

————. 1988. *Works and Lives: The Anthropologist as Author.* Stanford: Stanford University Press.

Gérando, Joseph-Marie de. 1969 [1800]. *The Observation of Savage Peoples.* Berkeley: University of California Press.

Giddens, Anthony. 1993. *The Giddens Reader.* Ed. Phillip Cassell. Stanford: Stanford University Press.

Girardet, Raoul. 1972. *L'idée coloniale en France.* Paris: La Table Ronde.

————. 1983. *Le nationalisme français: Anthologie, 1871–1914.* Paris: Editions du Seuil.

Glacken, Clarence J. 1967. *Traces on the Rhodian Shore: Nature and Culture in Western Thought from Ancient Times to the End of the Eighteenth Century.* Berkeley: University of California Press.

Goonatilake, Susantha. 1984. *Aborted Discovery: Science and Creativity in the Third World.* London: Zed Books.

Gould, Stephen Jay. 1981. *The Mismeasure of Man.* New York: W. W. Norton.

Graburn, Nelson H. H., and Jafar Jafari. 1991. "Tourism Social Science." *Annals of Tourism Research* 18: 1–11.

Graham, Clifford P. 1991. "The Brazilian Space Programme—An Overview." *Space Policy* 7, no. 1: 72–76.

Graves, Robert. 1960 [1955]. *The Greek Myths.* Vol. 1. New York: Penguin Books.

Green, Martin. 1979. *Dreams of Adventure, Deeds of Empire.* New York: Basic Books.

————. 1990. *The Robinson Crusoe Story.* University Park, Pa.: Pennsylvania State University Press.

Greenblatt, Stephen, ed. 1993. *New World Encounters.* Berkeley: University of California Press.

Gregory, Derek. 1994. *Geographical Imaginations.* Oxford, U.K.: Blackwell.

Grenand, Pierre, and Françoise Grenand. 1989. Preface to *Français et indiens en Guyane,* by Jean-Marcel Hurault. Cayenne: Guyanne Presse Diffusion.

Gritzner, Charles. 1963. "French Guiana: Developmental Trends in Post Prison Era." *The Journal of Geography* 62 (April): 161–168.

————. 1964. "French Guiana Penal Colony: Its Role in Colonial Development." *The Journal of Geography* 63, no. 7 (October): 314–319.

Groene, Denis. 1990. "La forêt et le milieu naturel et humain de la Guyane française." *Bois et Forets des Tropiques* 219 (March special on Guyane): 7–12.

Grove, Richard. 1995. *Green Imperialism: Colonial Expansion, Tropical Island Edens, and the Origins of Environmentalism, 1600–1860.* Cambridge: Cambridge University Press.

Guérard, Albert. 1946. *France: A Short History.* New York: W. W. Norton.

Guha, Ranajit, and Gayatri Chakravorty Spivak, eds. 1988. *Selected Subaltern Studies.* Oxford: Oxford University Press.

Gupta, Akhil. 1998. *Postcolonial Developments: Agriculture in the Making of Modern India.* Durham, N.C.: Duke University Press.

Gupta, Akhil, and James Ferguson, eds. 1997a. *Anthropological Locations: Boundaries and Grounds of a Field Science*. Berkeley: University of California Press.

———. 1997b. *Culture, Power, Place: Explorations in Critical Anthropology*. Durham, N.C.: Duke University Press.

Gusterson, Hugh. 1996. *Nuclear Rites: A Weapons Laboratory at the End of the Cold War*. Berkeley: University of California Press.

Hacking, Ian. 1990. *The Taming of Chance*. Cambridge: Cambridge University Press.

Halasz, Nicholas. 1955. *Captain Dreyfus: The Story of a Mass Hysteria*. New York: Simon and Schuster.

Hammel, Ian. 1979. *Les Guyanais: Français en surcis?* Paris: Editions Entente.

Hannerz, Ulf. 1989. "Notes on the Global Ecumene." *Public Culture* 1, no. 2 (spring): 66–75.

Haraway, Donna. 1989. *Primate Visions: Gender, Race, and Nature in the World of Modern Science*. New York: Routledge.

———. 1991. *Simians, Cyborgs, and Women: The Reinvention of Nature*. New York: Routledge.

———. 1997. *Modest-Witness@Second-Millennium.FemaleMan©-Meets-OncoMous™ : Feminism and Technoscience*. New York: Routledge.

Harris, Marvin. 1956. *Town and Country in Brazil*. New York: Columbia University Press.

Harrison, Mark. 1996. "'The Tender Frame of Man': Disease, Climate, and Racial Difference in India and the West Indies, 1760–1860." *Bulletin of the History of Medicine* 70, no. 1 (spring): 68–93.

Harrison, Robert Pogue. 1992. *Forests: The Shadow of Civilization*. Chicago: University of Chicago Press.

Harvey, David. 1989. *The Condition of Postmodernity: An Enquiry into the Origins of Culture Change*. Oxford, U.K.: Basil Blackwell.

Hauzer, M. 1992. "L'Europeanisation du CSG." *Latitude* 5 16: 4–5.

Hayes, Carlton J.H. 1960. *Nationalism: A Religion*. New York: Macmillan.

Hayman, Ronald. 1982. *Kafka: A Biography*. New York: Oxford University Press.

Headrick, Daniel R. 1981. *The Tools of Empire: Technology and European Imperialism in the Nineteenth Century*. New York: Oxford University Press.

———. 1988. *The Tentacles of Progress: Technology Transfer in the Age of Imperialism, 1850–1940*. New York: Oxford University Press.

Hearn, Lafcadio. 1890. *Two Years in the French West Indies*. New York: Harper and Bros.

Hecht, Gabrielle. 1998. *The Radiance of France: Nuclear Power and National Identity after World War II*. Cambridge: MIT Press.

Hegel, G.W.F. 1977 [1806]. *Phenomenology of Spirit*. Oxford: Clarendon Press.

Heidegger, Martin. 1977 [1927–1964]. *Basic Writings*. New York: Harper Torchbooks.

Hemming, John. 1987. *Amazon Frontier: The Defeat of the Brazilian Indians*. London: Macmillan.

Hennigsgaard, William. 1981. "The Akawaio, the Upper Mazaruni Hydroelectric Project, and National Development in Guyana." *Cultural Survival Occasional Paper* 4.

Henry, Arthur. 1989 [1950]. *La Guyane: Son histoire, 1604–1946*. Cayenne: Guyane Presse Diffusion.

Henry, Louis, and Jean Hurault. 1979. "Mortalité de la population Européenne de Guyane française au début du XVIIIe siècle." *Population* 6, nos. 4–5 (July–October): 1087–1100.

Herzfeld, Michael. 1987. *Anthropology through the Looking Glass: Critical Ethnography at the Margins of Europe*. Cambridge: Cambridge University Press.

Hess, David. 1992. "The New Ethnography and the Anthropology of Science and Technology." In *Knowledge and Society: The Anthropology of Science and Technology*, ed. David J. Hess and Linda L. Layne, 1–26. Greenwich, Conn.: JAI Press.

Hirst, J. B. 1983. *Convict Society and Its Enemies*. Sydney: George Allen and Unwin.

Historia. 1986. Special issue on penal colonies, 472 (April).

Hobart, Mark, ed. 1993. *An Anthropological Critique of Development: The Growth of Ignorance*. New York: Routledge.

Holston, James. 1989. *The Modernist City: An Anthropological Critique of Brasília*. Chicago: University of Chicago Press.

Horkheimer, Max, and Theodor Adorno. 1987 [1944]. *Dialectic of Enlightenment*. New York: Continuum.

Hughes, Inc. 1994. "Hughes Space and Communications." Brochure.

Hughes, Robert. 1986. *The Fatal Shore*. New York: Alfred A. Knopf.

Hulme, Peter. 1986. *Colonial Encounters: Europe and the Native Caribbean, 1492–1797*. London: Methuen.

Hulme, Peter, and Neil Whitehead, eds. 1992. *Wild Majesty: Encounters with Caribs from Columbus to the Present Day, an Anthology*. Oxford: Clarendon Press.

Hume, L. J. 1973. "Bentham's Panopticon: An Administrative History 1." *Historical Studies* 15, no. 61: 703–721.

———. 1974. "Bentham's Panopticon: An Administrative History 2." *Historical Studies* 16, no. 62: 36–54.

Humphreys, Margaret. 1996. "Kicking a Dying Dog: DDT and the Demise of Malaria in the American South, 1942–1950." *Isis* 87: 1–17.

Huntington, Ellsworth. 1924 [1915]. *Civilization and Climate*. 3d ed. New Haven: Yale University Press.

Hurault, Jean-Marcel. 1989 [1972]. *Français et indiens en Guyane, 1604–1972*. Cayenne: Guyane Presse Diffusion.

Huyghues-Belrose, Vincent, ed. 1990. *Histoire de la Guyane: La Grande Encyclopédie de la Caraïbe*. Vol. 7. Italy: Sanoli.

Huyghues-Belrose, Vincent, and Anne-Marie Bruleaux, eds. 1988. "L'orpaillage en Guyane: Du siècle des Lumières aux Annés folles." Annotated collection of documents. Cayenne: Archives départmentales.

Ignatieff, Michael. 1978. *A Just Measure of Pain: The Penitentiary in the Industrial Revolution, 1750–1850*. New York: Pantheon Books.

Ingold, Tim. 1993. "Globes and Spheres: The Topology of Environmentalism." In *Environmentalism: The View from Anthropology*, ed. Kay Milton. London: Routledge.

Inkles, A., and D. H. Smith. 1974. *Becoming Modern: Individual Change in Six Developing Countries*. Cambridge: Harvard University Press.

INSEE (Institut National de la Statistique et des Etudes Economiques). 1991. "Movement Demographique, 1982–1990, Antilles-Guyane." *Les Dossiers Antilles Guyane* 17.

———. 1993. *Tableaux économique regionaux Guyane*. Cayenne: INSEE.

———. 1995. *L'impact économique de l'activité spatiale en Guyane*. Cayenne: INSEE.

Isakowitz, Steven J. 1991. *International Reference Guide to Space Launch Systems*. Washington, D.C.: American Institute of Aeronautics and Astronautics.

Jackson, R. V. 1987. "Bentham vs. New South Wales: The Letters to Lord Pelham." University of London Australian Studies Center Working Paper no. 25.

———. 1988. "Luxury in Punishment: Jeremy Bentham on the Cost of the Convict Colony in New South Wales." *Australian Historical Studies* 23, no. 90: 42–59.

Jameson, Frederic. *Postmodernism: Or, the Cultural Logic of Late Capitalism*. Durham, N.C.: Duke University Press.

Jensen, Claus. 1996. *No Downlink: A Dramatic Narrative about the Challenger Accident and Our Time*. New York: Farrar, Straus and Giroux.

Johnson-Freese, Joan. 1990. "Can Germany Afford Reunification and a Space Program Too?" *Technology in Society* 12: 4.

Jolivet, Marie-José. 1982. *La question créole: Essai de sociologie sur la guyane française*. Paris: Editions de l'Office de la Recherche Scientifique et Technique Outre-Mer.

———. 1987. "Nécessité et permutabilité de l'étranger dans la construction identitaire 'créole.'" In *Vers des sociétés pluriculturelles: Etudes comparatives et situation en France,* ed. AFA, 418–427. Paris: Editions de l'ORSTOM.

Jordanova, Ludmila, ed. 1986. *Languages of Nature: Critical Essays on Science and Literature*. New Brunswick, N.J.: Rutgers University Press.

Jules, Jean-Paul. 1994. *Guyane: L'enérgie autrement*. Matoury, French Guiana: RGI.

Kafka, Franz. 1948 [1919]. "In the Penal Colony." In *The Penal Colony, Stories and Short Pieces,* 191–227. New York: Schocken Books.

Kant, Immanuel. 1965 [1781]. *Critique of Pure Reason*. New York: St. Martin's Press.

Kaplan, Martha. 1995. "Panopticon in Poon: An Essay on Foucault and Colonialism." *Cultural Anthropology* 10, no. 1 (February): 85–98.

Kearney, M. 1995. "The Local and the Global: The Anthropology of Globalization and Transnationalism." *Annual Review of Anthropology* 24: 547–565.

Keller, Evelyn Fox. 1985. *Reflections on Gender and Science*. New Haven: Yale University Press.

Kennedy, Dane. 1981. "Climatic Theories and Culture in Colonial Kenya and Rhodesia." *Journal of Imperial and Commonwealth History* 10, no. 1 (October): 50–66.

Kern, Stephen. 1983. *The Culture of Space and Time, 1880–1918*. Cambridge: Harvard University Press.

Kesteloot, Lilyan. 1974 [1963]. *Black Writers in French*. Trans. Ellen Conroy Kennedy. Philadelphia: Temple University Press.

Kincaid, Jamaica. 1988. *A Small Place*. New York: Farrar, Straus and Giroux.

Kingery, W. David. 1996. *Learning from Things: Method and Theory of Material Culture Studies*. Washington, D.C.: Smithsonian Institution Press.

King-Hele, Desmond. 1992. *A Tapestry of Orbits*. Cambridge: Cambridge University Press.

Kingsland, Sharon E. 1993. "An Elusive Science: Ecological Enterprise in the Southwestern United States." In *Science and Nature: Essays in the History of the Environmental Sciences*, ed. Michael Shorthand. British Society for the History of Science Monographs 8: 151–179.

Kipling, Rudyard. 1941 [1912]. *Just So Stories*. New York: Doubleday, Doran.

Kipple, Kenneth F. 1984. *The Caribbean Slave: A Biological History*. Cambridge: Cambridge University Press.

Kiste, Robert. 1972. "Relocation and Technological Change in Micronesia." In *Technology and Social Change*, ed. H. R. Bernard and P. J. Pelto, 72–107. New York: Macmillan.

Klor de Alva, J. Jorge. 1995. "The Post-Colonization of the (Latin) American Experience: A Reconsideration of 'Colonialism,' 'Postcolonialism,' and 'Mestizaje.'" In *After Colonialism: Imperialism, Colonialism, and the Colonial Aftermath*, ed. Gyan Prakash. Princeton: Princeton University Press.

Knorr Cetina, Karin, and M. Mulkay, eds. 1983. *Science Observed: Perspectives on the Social Study of Science*. London: Sage.

Kojève, Alexandre. 1969 [1947]. *Introduction to the Reading of Hegel*. New York: Basic Books.

Kondo, Dorinne. 1986. "Dissolution and Reconstitution of Self: Implications for Anthropological Epistemology." *Cultural Anthropology* 1: 74–96.

Krakovitch, Odile. 1990a. "Les Antillais et les bagnes de Cayenne." *Revue Historique* 575 (July/September): 89–100.

———. 1990b. *Les femmes bagnardes*. Paris: Oliver Orban.

Krarup-Nielsen, Aage. 1938 [1933]. *Hell beyond the Seas: A Convict's Own Story of His Experiences in the French Penal Settlement in Guiana*. Garden City, N.Y.: Garden City Publishing.

Krige, John, and L. Sebesta. 1994. "U.S.-European Cooperation in Space in the Decade after Sputnik." In *Big Culture: Intellectual Cooperation in Large-Scale Cultural and Technical Systems. An Historical Approach*, ed. Giuliana Gemelli. Bologna: Editrice CLUEB.

Kroeber, Alfred L. 1963. *An Anthropologist Looks at History*. Berkeley: University of California Press.

Kroeber, Alfred L., and Clyde Kluckhohn. 1963 [1952]. *Culture: A Critical Review of Concepts and Definitions*. New York: Vintage Books.

Kuhn, Thomas S. 1970 [1962]. *The Structure of Scientific Revolutions*. 2d ed. Chicago: University of Chicago Press.

Kuklick, Henrika, and Robert E. Kohler, eds. 1996. *Science in the Field. Osiris* 11.

Kupperman, Karen. 1984. "Fear of Hot Climates in the Anglo-American Experience." *William and Mary Quarterly* 41 (April): 213–240.

Lafargue, Paul. 1975 [1880]. *The Right to Be Lazy.* Chicago: Charles H. Kerr.

Lagrange, Francis, and William Murray. 1961. *Flag on Devil's Island.* New York: Doubleday.

Laidet, Louis. 1989. "The French Space Program." In *Space: National Programs and International Cooperation,* ed. W. C. Thompson and S. W. Guerrier, 63–78. Boulder, Colo.: Westview Press.

Lambright, W. Henry. 1994. "The Political Construction of Space Satellite Technology." *Science, Technology, and Human Values* 19, no. 1: 47–69.

Laporte, Paul. 1983 [1915]. *La Guyane des écoles.* Cayenne: ATIPA-COGUAC.

Lartin, Philippe, and Stephane Blot. 1988. *Memorial du bagne de la Guyane.* Vols. 1–5. Paris: Editions Orphie.

Latour, Bruno. 1988 [1984]. *The Pasteurization of France.* Cambridge: Harvard University Press.

———. 1993 [1991]. *We Have Never Been Modern.* Cambridge: Harvard University Press.

———. 1996 [1992]. *Aramis or the Love of Technology.* Cambridge: Harvard University Press.

———. 1999. *Pandora's Hope: Essays on the Reality of Science Studies.* Cambridge: Harvard University Press.

Latour, Bruno, and Steve Woolgar. 1986 [1979]. *Laboratory Life: The Construction of Scientific Facts.* 2d ed. Princeton: Princeton University Press.

Laurin, Pierre. 1987. *De Nouméa à Cayenne . . . hier et aujourd'hui.* Joinville: Lionel Hugnet.

Lavery, David. 1992. *Late for the Sky: The Mentality of the Space Age.* Carbondale: Southern Illinois University Press.

Le Clère, Marcel. 1973. *La Vie quotidienne dans les bagnes.* Paris: Librarie Hachette.

Le Goff, Jacques. 1984 [1981]. *The Birth of Purgatory.* Trans. Arthur Goldhammer. Chicago: University of Chicago Press.

Lefebvre, Henri. 1991 [1974]. *The Production of Space.* Trans. Donald Nicholson-Smith. Oxford: Blackwell.

Lemonnier, Pierre, ed. 1993. *Technological Choices: Transformation in Material Cultures since the Neolithic.* London: Routledge.

Leslie, Stuart W. 1993. *The Cold War and American Science: The Military-Industrial-Academic Complex at MIT and Stanford.* New York: Columbia University Press.

Lévi-Strauss, Claude. 1966 [1962]. *The Savage Mind.* Chicago: University of Chicago Press.

———. 1973 [1955]. *Tristes Tropiques.* New York: Penguin.

Levieux, Michel, and Eleanor Levieux. 1980. *Cassell's Colloquial French: A Handbook of Idiomatic Usage.* London: Macmillan.

Lewis, Martin Deming. 1962. "One Hundred Million Frenchmen: The 'Assimilation' Theory in French Colonial Policy." *Comparative Studies in Society and History* 4, no. 2: 129–153.

Lezy, Emmanuel. 1989. *Guyane: De l'autré côté des images*. Paris: L'Harmattan.

Limerick, Patricia N. 1994. "What Is the Cultural Value of Space Exploration?" In *What Is the Value of Space Exploration? A Symposium*. National Geographic Society, Washington, D.C., July 18–19.

Livingstone, David N. 1992. *The Geographical Tradition: Episodes in the History of a Contested Enterprise*. Oxford: Blackwell.

Logsdon, John M. 1995. *Exploring the Unknown: Selected Documents in the History of the U.S. Civil Space Program*. Washington, D.C.: NASA.

Londres, Albert. 1975 [1923–1927]. *L'Homme qui s'evada/Au bagne*. Paris: Union Général d'Editions.

Lowenthal, David. 1960a. "French Guiana: Myths and Realities." *Transactions of the New York Academy of Sciences*, 2d ser., vol. 22: 528–540.

———. 1960b. "Population Contrasts in the Guianas." *The Geographical Review* (January): 41–58.

Loxley, Diana. 1990. *Problematic Shores: The Literature of Islands*. London: Macmillan.

Lüst, Reimar. 1988. "Europe in Space: An Example of Successful European Cooperation." *Center for European Studies Working Paper Series*. Cambridge: Harvard University Center for European Studies.

MacCannell, Dean. 1989 [1976]. *The Tourist: A New Theory of the Leisure Class*. 2d ed. New York: Schocken Books.

Mack, Pamela E. 1990. *Viewing the Earth: The Social Construction of the Landsat Satellite System*. Cambridge: MIT Press.

MacKenzie, Donald, and Judy Wajcman, eds. 1985. *The Social Shaping of Technology: How the Refrigerator Got Its Hum*. Philadelphia: Open University Press.

MacKenzie, John M., ed. 1990. *Imperialism and the Natural World*. Manchester, U.K.: Manchester University Press.

Madders, Kevin. 1997. *A New Force at a New Frontier: Europe's Development in the Space Field in the Light of Its Main Actors, Policies, Law, and Activities from Its Beginnings up to the Present*. Cambridge: Cambridge University Press.

Mailer, Norman. 1970. *Of a Fire on the Moon*. Boston: Little, Brown.

Malinowski, Bronislaw. 1944. *Freedom and Civilization*. New York: Roy Press.

———. 1954 [1948]. *Magic, Science, and Religion, and Other Essays*. New York: Doubleday Anchor.

Mam-Lam-Fouck, Serge. 1987. *Histoire de la société Guyanaise, les années cruciales: 1848–1946*. Paris: Editions Caribéennes.

———. 1992. *Histoire de la Guyane contemporane, 1940–1982: Les mutations économiques, sociales, et politiques*. Paris: Editions Caribéennes.

———, ed. 1997. *L'identité Guyanaise en question: Les dynamiques interculturelles en Guyane française*. Actes du colloque 21 avril 1995. Kourou: Ibis Rouge Editions.

Mannoni, O. 1990 [1950]. *Prospero and Caliban: The Psychology of Colonization*. Ann Arbor: University of Michigan Press.

Marchand-Thébault, Marie-Louise. 1986 [1960]. "L'Esclavage en Guyane sous l'anciene régime." In *Deux siècles d'esclavage en Guyane Française, 1652–1848,* ed. Anne-Marie Bruleaux, R. Calmont, and S. Mam-Lam-Fouck, 11–62. Paris: L'Harmattan.

Marcus, George. 1986. "Contemporary Problems of Ethnography in the Modern World System." In *Writing Culture: The Poetics and Politics of Culture,* ed. James Clifford and George Marcus, 165–193. Berkeley: University of California Press.

———. 1995. "Ethnography in/of the World System: The Emergence of Multi-Sited Ethnography." *Annual Review of Anthropology* 24: 95–117.

———, ed. 1995. *Technoscientific Imaginaries.* Chicago: University of Chicago Press.

Marcus, George E., and Michael M. J. Fischer. 1986. *Anthropology as Cultural Critique: An Experimental Moment in the Human Sciences.* Chicago: University of Chicago Press.

Markham, S. F. 1944. *Climate and the Energy of Nations.* London: Oxford University Press.

Marseilles, Jacques. 1984. *Empire colonial et capitalisme français: Histoire d'un divorce.* Paris: Editions Albin Michel.

Martin, Andrew. 1990. *The Mask of the Prophet: The Extraordinary Fictions of Jules Verne.* Oxford: Clarendon Press.

Martin, Emily. 1994. *Flexible Bodies: The Role of Immunity in American Culture from the Days of Polio to the Age of AIDS.* Boston: Beacon Press.

Marx, Leo. 1964. *The Machine in the Garden: Technology and the Pastoral Ideal in America.* New York: Oxford University Press.

Maugham, W. Somerset. 1963a. "A Man with a Conscience." In *Collected Short Stories,* Vol. 4, 202–220. London: Penguin.

———. 1963b. "An Official Position." In *Collected Short Stories,* Vol. 4, 221–238. London: Penguin.

May, J. A. 1970. *Kant's Concept of Geography and Its Relation to Recent Geographical Thought.* Toronto: University of Toronto Department of Geography.

Mayntz, Renate, and Thomas P. Hughes, eds. 1988. *The Development of Large Technical Systems.* Boulder, Colo.: Westview Press.

McCurdy, Howard E. 1997. *Space and the American Imagination.* Washington, D.C.: Smithsonian Institution Press.

McDougall, Walter A. 1985a. *The Heavens and the Earth: A Political History of the Space Age.* New York: Basic Books.

———. 1985b. "Space-Age Europe: Gaullism, Euro-Gaullism, and the American Dilemma." *Technology and Culture* 26, no. 2: 179–203.

McKeon, Michael. 1987. *The Origins of the English Novel, 1600–1740.* Baltimore: Johns Hopkins University Press.

Mead, Margaret. 1928. *Coming of Age in Samoa: A Psychological Study of Primitive Youth for Western Civilization.* New York: William Morrow.

Memmi, Albert. 1965 [1957]. *The Colonizer and the Colonized.* Boston: Beacon Press.

Ménager, Georges. 1970. *Les quatres vérités de Papillon*. Paris: Editions de la Table Ronde.

Mendelsohn, Everett, and Yehuda Elkana, eds. 1981. *Sciences and Cultures: Anthropological and Historical Studies of the Sciences*. Dordrecht, Holland: D. Reidel Publishing.

Menier, Marie-Antoinette. 1977. "La détention du Capitaine Dreyfus à l'île du Diable, d'après les archives de l'Administration pénitentiaire." *Revue Française d'Histoire d'Outre-Mer* 64, no. 237: 456–475.

Merchant, Carolyn. 1990 [1980]. *The Death of Nature: Women, Ecology, and the Scientific Revolution*. San Francisco: Harper and Row.

Merle, Isabelle. 1995. *Expériences coloniales: La Nouvelle-Calédonie, 1853–1920*. Paris: Belin.

Michaud, Michael A.G. 1986. *Reaching for the High Frontier: The American Pro-Space Movement, 1972–1984*. New York: Praeger.

Michel, Jacques. 1989. *La Guyane sous l'ancien régime*. Paris: L'Harmattan.

Michelet, Jean-Claude. 1981. *La guillotine seche: Histoire du bagne de Cayenne*. Paris: Fayard.

Milani, Felix, and Micha Grin. 1977 [1975]. *The Convict*. Trans. Anita Barrows. New York: St. Martin's Press.

Miles, Alexander. 1988. *Devil's Island: Colony of the Damned*. Berkeley: Ten Speed Press.

———. 1990. "Jungle des rêves Daniel K. Ludwig et le projet Jari." *Version Guyane* 22, no. 4 (June): 22–27.

———. 1994. "French Space Agency in 'Right Stuff' Campaign." Reuters wire story, November 20.

———. 1995. "Dreyfus Grandson Visits Devil's Island." Reuters wire story, April 14.

Miles, Alexander, and Colin Rickards. 1980. "Shackles to Satellites: How Europe Hopes to Beat the Americans at Their Own Game." *Caribbean Business News* 11, no. 1 (January): 5–9.

Miller, D. 1995. "Consumption and Commodities." *Annual Review of Anthropology* 24: 141–161.

Miller, David H., ed. 1977. *The Frontier: Comparative Studies*. Norman: University of Oklahoma Press.

Milton, Kay. 1993. *Environmentalism: The View from Anthropology*. London: Routledge.

Mintz, Sidney. 1974. "The Caribbean Region." *Daedalus* (spring): 45–71.

———. 1985. *Sweetness and Power: The Place of Sugar in Modern History*. New York: Viking Penguin.

———. 1989 [1974]. *Caribbean Transformations*. New York: Columbia University Press.

Mintz, Sidney, and Sally Price, eds. 1985. *Caribbean Contours*. Baltimore: Johns Hopkins University Press.

Mitchell, Timothy. 1991 [1988]. *Colonizing Egypt*. Berkeley: University of California Press.

Mitchell, W.J.T., ed. 1994. *Landscape and Power*. Chicago: University of Chicago Press.

Montesquieu, Charles-Louis de Secondat. 1900 [1748]. *The Spirit of the Laws.* Vol. 1. New York: Colonial Press.

Morton, Peter. 1989. *Fire across the Desert: Woomera and the Anglo-Australian Joint Project, 1946–1980.* Canberra: Australian Government Publishing Service.

Mumford, Lewis. 1963 [1934]. *Technics and Civilization.* New York: Harcourt, Brace and World.

Munroe, J. 1878. "A Visit to One of the Prisons of Cayenne." *Good Works* (October/November?): 746–752.

Naddeo-Souriau, Isabelle. 1986. *Ariane: Le pari européen.* Paris: Editions Hermé.

Nader, Laura. 1972. "Up the Anthropologist—Perspectives Gained from Studying Up." In *Reinventing Anthropology,* ed. Dell Hymes, 284–311. New York: Pantheon Books.

———, ed. 1996. *Naked Science: Anthropological Inquiry into Boundaries, Power, and Knowledge.* New York: Routledge.

Nandy, Ashis. 1983. *The Intimate Enemy: Loss and Recovery of Self under Colonialism.* Delhi: Oxford University Press.

Narayan, Kirin. 1993. "How Native Is a 'Native' Anthropologist?" *American Anthropologist* 95: 671–686.

NASA (National Aeronautics and Space Administration). 1972. *Kennedy Space Center Story.* Washington, D.C.: GPO.

———. 1992. "Spaceport USA." Informational brochure.

———. N.d. "America's Spaceport: John F. Kennedy Space Center." Informational brochure.

Nash, Dennison. 1970. *A Community in Limbo: An Anthropological Study of an American Community Abroad.* Bloomington: Indiana University Press.

Nash, Roderick. 1982 [1967]. *Wilderness and the American Mind.* New Haven: Yale University Press.

National Foreign Assessment Center. 1980. "Ariane: A European Space Launch Vehicle." Springfield, Va.: (CIA) National Technical Information Service.

Needell A., ed. 1983. *The First Twenty-Five Years in Space: A Symposium.* Washington, D.C.: Smithsonian Institution Press.

Neufeld, Michael J. 1995. *The Rocket and the Reich: Peenemunde and the Coming of the Ballistic Missile Era.* New York: Free Press.

Nietzsche, Friedrich. 1974 [1882]. *The Gay Science.* Trans. W. Kaufmann. New York: Vintage Books.

Niles, Blair. 1928. *Condemned to Devil's Island: The Biography of an Unknown Convict.* New York: Grosset and Dunlap.

Nobel, David F. 1997. *The Religion of Technology: The Divinity of Man and the Spirit of Invention.* New York: Alfred A. Knopf.

Norgaard, Richard B. 1994. *Development Betrayed: The End of Progress and a Coevolutionary Revisioning of the Future.* London: Routledge.

Oberg, James E. 1981. *Red Star in Orbit.* New York: Random House.

O'Brien, Patricia. 1982. *The Promise of Punishment: Prisons in Nineteenth-Century France.* Princeton: Princeton University Press.

Oelschlaeger, Max. 1991. *The Idea of Wilderness.* New Haven: Yale University Press.

ONF (Office National des Forêts). 1992. "Dossier Guyane." *Arborescences* 38 (May/June). Office National des Forêts.

Ong, Aihwa. 1987. *Spirits of Resistance and Capitalist Discipline: Factory Women in Malaysia.* Albany, N.Y.: State University of New York Press.

Ophir, Adi, and Steven Shapin. 1991. "The Place of Knowledge: A Methodological Survey." *Science in Context* 4, no. 1: 3–22.

Ordway, Frederick I., III, and Mitchell R. Sharpe. 1982 [1979]. *The Rocket Team.* Cambridge: MIT Press.

Orgeas, J. 1885. *Contribution à l'étude du non-cosmopolitisme de l'homme: La Colonisation de la Guyane par la transportation: Etude historique et démographique.* Paris: Octave Doin.

———. 1886. *La pathologie des races humaines et le problème de la colonisation: Etude anthropologique et économique faite à la Guyane française.* Paris: Octave Doin.

Ortner, Sherry. 1984. "Theory in Anthropology since the Sixties." *Comparative Studies in Society and History* 26, no. 1: 126–166.

———. 1995. "Resistance and the Problem of Ethnographic Refusal." *Comparative Studies in Society and History* 37, no. 1: 173–193.

Orwell, George. 1933. *Down and Out in London and Paris.* San Diego: Harcourt Brace.

Osborne, Michael A. 1994. *Nature, the Exotic, and the Science of French Colonialism.* Bloomington: Indiana University Press.

Palladino, Paolo, and Michael Worboys. 1993. "Science and Imperialism." *Isis* 84: 91–102.

Paradis, Anne. 1989. "Creation d'un bureau local des carrieres au CSG." *Latitude 5* 5: 9–11.

———. 1990. "SOS Missionaires." *CNESQUISEPASSE?* 60 (March): 38–40.

———. 1993. "Les secrétaires dans tous leurs états." *Latitude 5* 21 (July): 25.

Paradis, Anne, with M. Hucteau. 1991. "Ariane ne perd pas le nord." *CNESQUISEPASSE?* 66: 37–38.

Park, Chris C. 1992. *Tropical Rainforests.* London: Routledge.

Parry, J. H., and Philip Sherlock. 1971 [1956]. *A Short History of the West Indies.* 3d ed. London: Macmillan.

Péan, Charles. 1948. *Conquêtes en terre de bagne.* Strasbourg: Editions Altis.

Pease, C. B. 1991. *Satellite Imaging Instruments: Principles, Technologies, and Operational Systems.* New York: Ellis Horwood.

Pedelty, Mark. 1995. *War Stories: The Culture of Foreign Correspondents.* New York: Routledge.

Peet, Richard, and Michael Watts, eds. 1996. *Liberation Ecologies: Environment, Development, Social Movements.* New York: Routledge.

Pels, Peter. 1997. "The Anthropology of Colonialism: Culture, History, and the Emergence of Western Governmentality." *Annual Review of Anthropology* 26: 163–183.

Perrot, Michelle, ed. 1980. *L'impossible prison: Recherches sur le système pénitentiaire au 19e siècle.* Paris: Editions du Seuil.

Pestre, Dominique, and John Krige. 1992. "Some Thoughts on the Early History of CERN." In *Big Science: The Growth of Large-Scale Research*, ed. Peter Galison and Bruce Hevly, 78–99. Stanford: Stanford University Press.

Petit, Jacques, et al. 1991. *Histoire des galères, bagnes et prisons : XIIIe–XXe siecles: Introduction à l'histoire penale de la France.* Preface by Michelle Perrot. Toulouse: Editions Privat.

———, ed. 1984. *La prison, le bagne et l'histoire.* Geneva: Libr. des Meridiens.

Pfaffenberger, Bryan. 1992. "Social Anthropology of Technology." *Annual Review of Anthropology* 21: 491–516.

Phelan, Paul. 1994. "Spaceport PNG." *Paradise: In-Flight with Air Niugini* 107 (November/December): 47–50.

Pick, Daniel. 1989. *Faces of Degeneration: A European Disorder, circa 1848 to circa 1918.* Cambridge: Cambridge University Press.

Pickering, Andrew. 1995. *The Mangle of Practice: Time, Agency, and Science.* Chicago: University of Chicago Press.

Pierce, J. R. 1968. *The Beginnings of Satellite Communications.* San Francisco: San Francisco Press.

Pierre, Michel. 1981. "Les bagnes de Guyane." *L'Histoire* 38 (October): 76–83.

———. 1982. *La terre de la grande punition: Histoire des bagnes de Guyane.* Paris: Editions Ramsay.

———. 1986. "Aller simple pour la Guyane ou la guillotine verte." *Historia* 472 (April): 87–96.

———. 1989. *Le derniere exil: Histoire des bagne et des forçats.* Paris: Editions Gallimard.

Pigg, Stacy L. 1992. "Inventing Social Categories through Place: Social Representations and Development in Nepal." *Comparative Studies in Society and History* 34, no. 3 (July): 491–513.

Pitou, Louis-Ange. 1807. *Voyage à Cayenne, dans les deux Amériques et chez les anthrophages.* 2d ed. Paris: L. A. Pitou.

Pluchon, Pierre. 1982. *Histoire des Antilles et de la Guyane.* Toulouse: Editions Privat.

Poggie, John J., Jr. 1972. "Ciudad Industrial: A New City in Rural Mexico." In *Technology and Social Change,* ed. H. R. Bernard and P. J. Pelto, 9–38. New York: Macmillan.

Ponchelet, Hervé. 1992. "On va (re)marcher sur la Lune." *Le Point* 1055 (5 December): 79–82.

Pool, Ithiel de Sola. 1990. *Technologies without Boundaries: On Telecommunications in a Global Age.* Ed. Eli M. Noam. Cambridge: Harvard University Press.

Poovey, Mary. 1998. *A History of the Modern Fact: Problems of Knowledge in the Sciences of Wealth and Society.* Chicago: University of Chicago Press.

Porter, Theodore M. 1995. *Trust in Numbers: The Pursuit of Objectivity in Science and Public Life.* Princeton: Princeton University Press.

Prakash, Gyan, ed. 1995. *After Colonialism: Imperial Histories and Postcolonial Displacements.* Princeton: Princeton University Press.

Pratt, Mary L. 1991. *Imperial Eyes: Travel Writing and Transculturation.* New York: Routledge.

Pred, Allan, and Michael Watts. 1992. *Reworking Modernity: Capitalisms and Symbolic Discontent.* New Brunswick, N.J.: Rutgers University Press.

Price, Don K. 1988. "Science and Technology Policy in France, 1981–1986." *Minerva* 26: 493–511.

Price, Richard. 1973. *Maroon Societies: Rebel Slave Communities in the Americas*. Baltimore: Johns Hopkins University Press.

———. 1983. *First Time: The Historical Vision of an Afro-American People*. Baltimore: Johns Hopkins University Press.

———. 1990. *Alabi's World*. Baltimore: Johns Hopkins University Press.

———. 1998. *The Convict and the Colonel*. Boston: Beacon Press.

Price, Richard, and Sally Price. 1989. "Working for the Man: A Saramaka Outlook on Kourou." *New West Indian Guide* 63: 199–207.

———. 1992. *Equatoria*. New York: Routledge.

———. 1995. *Enigma Variations*. Cambridge: Harvard University Press.

Price, Sally. 1984. *Co-wives and Calabashes*. Ann Arbor: University of Michigan Press.

Proust, Marcel. 1934 [1913–1927]. *Remembrance of Things Past*. Vol. 1. New York: Random House.

Putz, Francis E., and N. Michele Holbrook. 1988. "Tropical Rain-Forest Images." In *People of the Tropical Rain Forest*, ed. Julie S. Denslow and Christine Padoch. Berkeley: University of California Press.

Pyenson, Louis. 1993. *Civilizing Mission: Exact Sciences and French Overseas Expansion, 1830–1940*. Baltimore: Johns Hopkins University Press.

Pynchon, Thomas. 1973. *Gravity's Rainbow*. New York: Viking.

Rabinow, Paul. 1977. *Reflections on Fieldwork in Morocco*. Berkeley: University of California Press.

———. 1989. *French Modern: Norms and Forms of the Social Environment*. Cambridge: MIT Press.

———. 1994. "On the Archaeology of Late Modernity." In *NowHere: Space, Time, and Modernity*, ed. Roger Friedland and Deirdre Boden, 402–418. Berkeley: University of California Press.

———. 1996a. *Essays in the Anthropology of Reason*. Princeton: Princeton University Press.

———. 1996b. *Making PCR: A Story of Biotechnology*. Chicago: University of Chicago Press.

———. 1999. *French DNA: Trouble in Purgatory*. Chicago: University of Chicago Press.

Racine, Daniel. 1988. "Leon-Gontran Damas and Africa." In *Critical Perspectives on Leon-Gontran Damas*, ed. Keith Q. Warner, 49–62. Washington, D.C.: Three Continents Press.

Ralegh, Walter. 1928 [1596]. *The Discoverie of the Large, Rich, and Bewtiful Empire of Guiana*. Ed. V. T. Harlow. London: Argonaut Press.

Ray, William. 1990. *Story and History: Narrative Authority and Social Identity in the Eighteenth-Century French and English Novel*. Oxford, U.K.: Basil Blackwell.

Read, Donald. 1992. *The Power of the News: The History of Reuters, 1849–1989*. Oxford: Oxford University Press.

Redfield, Peter. 1994. "Remembering the Revolution, Forgetting the Empire: Notes after the French Bicentennial." In *Visualizing Theory: Selected Essays from V.A.R., 1990–1994*, ed. Lucien Taylor, 322–344. New York: Routledge.

———. 1996. "Beneath a Modern Sky: Space Technology and Its Place on the Ground." *Science, Technology, and Human Values* 21, no. 3: 251–274.

Redfield, Robert. 1962. *Human Nature and the Study of Society.* Chicago: University of Chicago Press.

Reingold, Nathan, and Mark Rothenberg. 1987. *Scientific Colonialism: A Cross-Cultural Comparison.* Washington, D.C.: Smithsonian Institution Press.

Relph, E. 1976. *Place and Placelessness.* London: Pion.

Rémondière, André, and Michel Colmenero-Cruz. 1987. "Impact du C.S.G. sur le contexte economique de la Guyane." CNES/CSG working document, July.

Resse, Alix. 1964. *Guyane française: Terre de l'espace.* Paris: Editions Berger-Levrault.

Reuters. 1994. "Norway's Kværner Goes into Space." Reuters wire story, dateline Oslo, June 21.

Revel, Jacques. 1991. "Knowledge of the Territory." *Science in Context* 4, no. 1: 133–161.

Revert, Eugène. 1949. *La France d'Amérique: Martinique, Guadeloupe, Guyane, Saint-Pierre, et Miquelon.* Paris: Société d'Editions Géographiques, Maritimes et Coloniales.

Rickards, Colin. 1968. *The Man from Devil's Island.* New York: Stein and Day.

Robertson, A.F. 1984. *People and the State: An Anthropology of Planned Development.* Cambridge: Cambridge University Press.

Romier, Lucien. 1962 [1953]. *A History of France.* Trans. and completed by A.L. Rowse. London: Macmillan.

Rosaldo, Renato. 1989. *Culture and Truth: The Remaking of Social Analysis.* Boston: Beacon Press.

Rostow, Walt Whitman. 1960. *The Stages of Economic Growth: A Non-Communist Manifesto.* Cambridge: Cambridge University Press.

Rousseau, Jean-Jacques. 1957 [1762]. *Emile ou de l'éducation.* Paris: Editions Garnier.

Rousseau, Louis. 1930. *Un médecin au bagne.* Paris: Editions Armand Fleury.

Roussenq, Paul. 1957 [1934]. *L'enfer du bagne: Souvenirs vécus inédits.* Vichy: Pucheux.

SAGA. 1988. *Esquisses: Généralités touristiques guyanaises.* Cayenne: Studio des Arts Graphiques Appliqués.

Sahlins, Marshall. 1985. *Islands of History.* Chicago: University of Chicago Press.

Sahlins, Peter. 1989. *Boundaries: The Making of France and Spain in the Pyrenees.* Berkeley: University of California Press.

Said, Edward W. 1979. *Orientalism.* New York: Vintage.

———. 1993. *Culture and Imperialism.* New York: Alfred A. Knopf.

Saint-Exupéry, Antoine de. 1943. *The Little Prince.* New York: Harcourt, Brace and World.

Salomon, J.-J. 1990. "What Is Technology? The Issue of Its Origins and Definitions." In *Techniques to Technology: A French Historiography of Technology,* ed. S. Bhattacharya and P. Redondi, 242–284. Hyderabad: Sangam Books.

Sanite, Léon. 1988. "Introduction." *Panda* 35 (December—Special Guyane): 3.

Sauer, Carl Ortwin. 1966. *The Early Spanish Main.* Berkeley: University of California Press.

Savoie, Clovis. 1922. *Histoire de La Nouvelle-Caledonie et de ses dependances.* Noumea, New Caledonia: Imprimerie Nationale.

Scheper-Hughes, Nancy. 1992. *Death without Weeping: The Madness of Hunger in Northeast Brazil.* Berkeley: University of California Press.

Schneider, Jean, and Monique Léger-Orine. 1987. *Frontiers and Space Conquest: The Philosopher's Touchstone.* International Colloquium, Frontiers and Space Conquest, Paris, France, 13–16 January 1987. Dordrecht: Kluwer Academic Publishers.

Schonhorn, Manuel. 1991. *Defoe's Politics: Parliament, Power, Kingship, and Robinson Crusoe.* Cambridge: Cambridge University Press.

Schwartzbeck, Frank. 1986. "Guyane: A Département Like the Others?" In *Dual Legacies in the Contemporary Caribbean: Continuing Aspects of British and French Domination,* ed. Paul Sutton. London: Frank Cass.

Scott, David. 1995. "Colonial Governmentality." *Social Text* 13, no. 2 (fall): 191–220.

Scott, James C. 1990. *Domination and the Arts of Resistance.* New Haven: Yale University Press.

Seaton, George John. 1951. *Isle of the Damned.* New York: Farrar, Straus and Young.

Sécretariat d'Etat aux DOM-TOM. 1976. "Le Plan Vert: Charte de développement de la Guyane." Paris. Official brochure.

Segal, David, and Richard Handler. 1992. "How European Is Nationalism?" *Social Analysis* 32: 1–15.

Semple, Janet. 1993. *Bentham's Panopticon: A Study of the Panopticon Penitentiary.* Oxford: Clarendon Press.

SEPANGUY. 1993. *Forêt Guyanaise: Gestion de l'écosysteme forestier et aménagement de l'espace régional.* Cayenne: Conseil de la Culture, de l'Education et de l'Environnement, Société pour l'Etude, la Protection et l'Aménagement de la Nature en Guyane, Collection Nature Guyanaise.

Serres, Michel, and Bruno Latour. 1995 [1990]. *Conversations on Science, Culture, and Time.* Trans. Roxanne Lapidus. Ann Arbor: University of Michigan Press.

Shapin, Steven. 1994. *A Social History of Truth: Civility and Science in Seventeenth-Century England.* Chicago: University of Chicago Press.

Shapin, Steven, and Simon Schaffer. 1985. *Leviathan and the Air-Pump: Hobbes, Boyle, and the Experimental Life.* Princeton: Princeton University Press.

Shaw, A. G. L. 1966. *Convicts and the Colonies.* London: Faber and Faber.

Shields, Rob. 1991. *Places on the Margin: Alternative Geographies of Modernity.* London: Routledge.

SIK (Syndicat d'initiative, Kourou). 1988. "Le syndicat d'initiative present Kourou." Promotional brochure. Under the direction of Monique Mestrallef.

Silverman, Sydel. 1981. *Totems and Teachers: Perspectives on the History of Anthropology.* New York: Columbia University Press.

Sinclair, Gordon. 1935. *Loose among Devils: A Voyage from Devil's Island to Those Jungles of West Africa Labelled "The White Man's Grave."* London: Hurst and Blackett.

Smith, Merritt Roe, and Leo Marx, eds. 1995. *Does Technology Drive History? The Dilemma of Technological Determinism.* Cambridge: MIT Press.

Soeurs de Saint-Paul de Chartres. 1978 [?]. *250 ans en Guyane.* Rome: STI.

Solzhenitsyn, A. 1963. *One Day in the Life of Ivan Denisovitch.* New York: Lancer Books.

Soop, E. M. 1994. *Handbook of Geostationary Orbit.* Dordrecht: Kluwer Academic Publishers.

Souty, J. L. 1986. "Aux origines de l'histoire guyanaise (XVIe–XVIIe siècles)." *Revue Française d'Histoire d'Outre-Mer* 272: 303–334.

Sponsel, Leslie. 1986. "Amazon Ecology and Adaptation." *Annual Review of Anthropology* 15: 67–97.

Stafford, Barbara. 1984. *Voyage into Substance: Art, Science, Nature, and the Illustrated Travel Account, 1760–1840.* Cambridge: MIT Press.

Starn, Randolph. 1982. *Contrary Commonwealth: The Theme of Exile in Medieval and Renaissance Italy.* Berkeley: University of California Press.

Steedman, Carolyn. 1987. *Landscape for a Good Woman: A Story of Two Lives.* New Brunswick, N.J.: Rutgers University Press.

Steward, Julien H., ed. 1956. *The People of Puerto Rico: A Study in Social Anthropology.* Urbana: University of Illinois Press.

Stewart, Kathleen. 1991. "On the Politics of Cultural Theory: A Case for 'Contaminated' Cultural Critique." *Social Research* 58, no. 2 (summer): 395–412.

Stocking, George W., Jr. 1979. "Anthropology at Chicago: Tradition, Discipline, Department." Exhibition catalogue.

———. 1983. *Observers Observed: Essays on Ethnographic Fieldwork.* Madison: University of Wisconsin Press.

———. 1992. *The Ethnographer's Magic and Other Essays in the History of Anthropology.* Madison: University of Wisconsin Press.

Stoler, Ann L. 1989. "Rethinking Colonial Categories and the Boundaries of Rule." *Comparative Studies in Society and History* 31, no. 1 (January): 134–161.

———. 1991. "Carnal Knowledge and Imperial Power: Gender, Race, and Morality in Colonial Asia." In *Gender at the Crossroads of Knowledge: Feminist Anthropology in the Postmodern Era*, ed. Micaela di Leonardo. Berkeley: University of California Press.

———. 1995. *Race and the Education of Desire: Foucault's History of Sexuality and the Colonial Order of Things.* Durham, N.C.: Duke University Press.

Strobel, Michèle-Baj. 1998. *Les gens de l'or: Mémoire des orpailleurs créoles du Maroni.* Petit-Bourg, Guadeloupe: Ibis Rouge Editions.

Tambiah, Stanley Jeyaraja. 1990. *Magic, Science, Religion, and the Scope of Rationality.* Cambridge: Cambridge University Press.

Taussig, Michael. 1987. *Shamanism, Colonialism, and the Wild Man.* Chicago: University of Chicago Press.

Thamar, Maurice. 1935. "Les peines coloniales et l'expérience guyanais." Ph.D. diss., Université de Paris, Faculté de Droit.

Thiher, Allen. 1990. *Franz Kafka: A Study of the Short Fiction*. Boston: Twayne Publishers.

Thomas, Clive Y. 1988. *The Poor and the Powerless: Economic Policy and Change in the Caribbean*. New York: Monthly Review Press.

Thomas, Keith. 1983. *Man and the Natural World: A History of Modern Sensibility*. New York: Pantheon Books.

Thomas, Nicholas. 1994. *Colonialism's Culture: Anthropology, Travel, and Government*. Princeton: Princeton University Press.

Thompson, Harry. 1991. *Tintin: Hergé and His Creation*. London: Hodder and Stoughton.

Tocqueville, Alexis de. 1955 [1856]. *The Old Régime and the French Revolution*. Trans. Stuart Gilbert. New York: Doubleday Anchor.

Tournier, Michel. 1969 [1967]. *Friday*. Trans. Norman Denny. New York: Pantheon Books.

———. 1972 [1967]. *Vendredi, ou les limbes du Pacifique*. Paris: Editions Gallimard.

Traweek, Sharon. 1988. *Beam Times and Life Times: The World of High-Energy Physicists*. Cambridge: Harvard University Press.

———. 1992. "Big Science and Colonialist Discourse: Building High Energy Physics in Japan." In *Big Science: The Growth of Large-Scale Research*, ed. Peter Galison and Bruce Hevly, 100–128. Stanford: Stanford University Press.

Trigger, Bruce G. 1989. *A History of Archaeological Thought*. Cambridge: Cambridge University Press.

Trouillot, Michel-Rolph. 1991. "Anthropology and the Savage Slot: The Poetics and Politics of Otherness." In *Recapturing Anthropology: Working in the Present*, ed. Richard Fox, 17–44. Santa Fe, N.Mex.: School of American Research Press.

———. 1992. "The Caribbean Region: An Open Frontier in Anthropology." *Annual Review of Anthropology* 21: 19–42.

Tsing, Anna Lowenhaupt. 1993. *In the Realm of the Diamond Queen: Marginality in an Out-of-the-Way Place*. Princeton: Princeton University Press.

Tuan, Yi-Fu. 1977. *Space and Place: The Perspective of Experience*. Minneapolis: University of Minnesota Press.

———. 1979. *Landscapes of Fear*. New York: Pantheon.

U.S. Congress (Committee on Science and Astronautics, U.S. House of Representatives). 1961. Hearings: Equatorial Launch Sites: Mobile Sea Launch Capability. Washington, D.C.: GPO.

Van Heuvel, Jacob A. 1844. *El Dorado; Being a Narrative of the Circumstances Which Gave Rise to Reports, in the Sixteenth Century, of the Existence of a Rich and Splendid City in South America*. New York: J. Winchester New World Press.

Van Loon, Hendrik Willen. 1940 [1932]. *Van Loon's Geography: The Story of the World*. Garden City, N.Y.: Garden City Publishers.

Vaughan, Diane. 1996. *The Challenger Launch Decision: Risky Technology, Culture, and Deviance at NASA*. Chicago: University of Chicago Press.

Verne, Jules. 1958 [1865/1870]. *From the Earth to the Moon and a Trip around It.* New York: Crest Books.

———. 1966a [1870]. *Autour de la lune.* Paris: Librairie Hachette.

———. 1966b [1865]. *De la terre à la lune.* Paris: Librairie Hachette.

———. 1995 [1978/1865]. *The Annotated Jules Verne: From the Earth to the Moon.* 2d ed. Ed. Walter James Miller. New York: Gramercy Books.

Vignon, Robert. 1954. "French Guiana: Looking Ahead." *Caribbean Commission Monthly Bulletin* 7 (June): 251–254.

———. 1985. *Gran Man Baka.* N.p.: Editions Davol.

Villiers, Gerard de. 1970. *Papillon épinglé.* Paris: Presses de la Cité.

Visweswaran, Kamala. 1994. *Fictions of Feminist Ethnography.* Minneapolis: University of Minnesota Press.

Voltaire. 1956 [1759]. *Candide and Other Writings.* Ed. Haskell M. Block. New York: Modern Library.

Von Braun, Werner, and Frederick I. Ordway III. 1976. *The Rocket's Red Glare.* Garden City, N.Y.: Anchor Press.

Wagley, Charles. 1976. *Amazon Town: A Study of Man in the Tropics.* New York: Columbia University Press.

Wali, Alaka. 1989. *Kilowatts and Crisis: Hydroelectric Power and Social Dislocation in Eastern Panama.* Boulder, Colo.: Westview Press.

Wallerstein, Immanuel. 1987. "World Systems Analysis." In *Social Theory Today,* ed. A. Giddens and J. Turner. Stanford: Stanford University Press.

Watson, James M., and Peter F. Meiksins. 1991. "What Do Engineers Want? Work Values, Job Rewards, and Job Satisfaction." *Science, Technology, and Human Values* 16, no. 2: 140–172.

Watt, Ian P. 1963 [1957]. *The Rise of the Novel: Studies in Defoe, Richardson, and Fielding.* Berkeley: University of California Press.

Weber, Eugen. 1976. *Peasants into Frenchmen: The Modernization of Rural France, 1870–1914.* Stanford: Stanford University Press.

Weber, Max. 1946. "Bureaucracy." In *From Max Weber: Essays in Sociology,* ed. H. H. Gerth and C. Wright Mills. Oxford: Oxford University Press.

Weinstein, Brian. 1972. *Eboué.* New York: Oxford University Press.

White, Hayden. 1978. *Tropics of Discourse: Essays in Cultural Criticism.* Baltimore: Johns Hopkins University Press.

White, Leslie. 1987. "Satellites and Gods; or, the Press, the Clergy, and an Anthropologist and Anthropological Approaches to Religion." In *Leslie A. White, Ethnological Essays,* ed. Beth Dillingham and Robert Caneiro, 345–354. Albuquerque: University of New Mexico Press.

White, Luise. 1997 [1993]. "Cars out of Place: Vampires, Technology, and Labor in East and Central Africa." In *Tensions of Empire: Colonial Cultures in a Bourgeois World,* ed. Frederick Cooper and Ann Stoler, 436–460. Berkeley: University of California Press.

Whitehead, Neil L. 1995. "The Historical Anthropology of Text: The Interpretation of Ralegh's Discoverie of Guiana." *Current Anthropology* 36, no. 1 (February): 53–74.

Wild, Wolfgang. 1991. "Cornerstones of German Space Strategy." *Space Policy* 7, no. 1: 5–8.

Williams, Brackette. 1990. "Nationalism, Traditionalism, and the Problem of Cultural Inauthenticity." In *Nationalist Ideologies and the Production of National Cultures*, ed. Richard G. Fox, 112–129. Washington, D.C.: American Anthropological Association.

———. 1991. *Stains on My Name, War in My Veins: Guyana and the Politics of Cultural Struggle*. Durham, N.C.: Duke University Press.

Williams, Donn A. 1975. "Brazil and French Guiana: The Four-Hundred-Year Struggle for Amapá." Ph.D. diss., Texas Christian University.

Williams, Eric. 1970. *From Columbus to Castro: The History of the Caribbean*. New York: Vintage Books.

Williams, Raymond. 1983. *Keywords: A Vocabulary of Culture and Society*. New York: Oxford University Press.

———. 1985 [1973]. *The Country and the City*. London: Hogarth Press.

Williamson, Mark. 1990. *The Communications Satellite*. Bristol: Adam Hilger.

Williamson, Ray A. 1987. "Outer Space as Frontier: Lessons for Today." *Western Folklore* (October): 255–267.

Willis, William. 1959. *Damned and Damned Again*. New York: St. Martin's Press.

Winner, Langdon. 1977. *Autonomous Technology: Technics-out-of-Control as a Theme in Political Thought*. Cambridge: MIT Press.

———. 1986. *The Whale and the Reactor: A Search for Limits in the Age of High Technology*. Chicago: University of Chicago Press.

Winter, Frank H. 1990. *Rockets into Space*. Cambridge: Harvard University Press.

Wise, Steve. 1990. "Space and National Development: Are Brazil and Argentina Examples?" *Technology in Society* 12, no. 1: 79–90.

Wolf, Eric. 1982. *Europe and the People without History*. Berkeley: University of California Press.

Wolfe, Tom. 1979. *The Right Stuff*. New York: Bantam Books.

Wood, Kris. 1995. "Au delà du Spatial—Propulsons la Guyane!" *Le Pou d'Agouti* 14: 30–32.

Worster, Donald, ed. 1988. *The Ends of the Earth: Perspectives on Modern Environmental History*. Cambridge: Cambridge University Press.

Worthington, Richard. 1993. "Introduction: Science and Technology as a Global System." *Science, Technology, and Human Values* 18, no. 2: 176–185.

Wright, Gordon. 1983. *Between the Guillotine and Liberty: Two Centuries of the Crime Problem in France*. New York: Oxford University Press.

———. 1987. *France in Modern Times*. 4th ed. New York: W. W. Norton.

Wright, Gwendolyn. 1991. *The Politics of Design in French Colonial Urbanism*. Chicago: University of Chicago Press.

Wright, Gwendolyn, and Paul Rabinow. 1982. "Spatialization of Power: A Discussion of the Work of Michel Foucault." *Skyline* (March): 14–20.

WWF (World Wildlife Fund). 1988. *Panda* 35 (December—Special Guyane).

Young, M. Jane. 1987a. "Parables of the Space Age—The Ideological Basis of Space Exploration: Introduction." *Western Folklore* 46 (October): 227–234.

———. 1987b. "'Pity the Indians of Outer Space': Native American Views of the Space Program." *Western Folklore* 46 (October): 269–279.

Young, Robert J.C. 1995. *Colonial Desire: Hybridity in Theory, Culture, and Race*. London: Routledge.

Zabusky, Stacia. 1995. *Launching Europe: An Ethnography of European Co-operation in Space Science*. Princeton: Princeton University Press.

Zaconne, Pierre. N.d. (ca. 1876). *Histoire des bagnes, depuis leur création jusqu'à nos jours*. Paris: Gennequin Fils.

Credits

Figure 1. Devil's Island from guard post on Ile Royale. Photo by author, 1990.

Figure 2. Frontispiece to first French translation of *Robinson Crusoe*, B. Picart, 1720, published by L'Honore et Chatelain, Amsterdam. Reprinted from 1721 second edition, by permission of the British Museum (shelfmark 12611.EE.2).

Figure 3. French stamp, 1991. Courtesy of La Poste and Claude Andreotto.

Figure 4. Governor's palace, Cayenne. Photo by author, 1990.

Figure 5. Creole house, Mana. Photo by author, 1993.

Figure 6. French Foreign Legion, on parade in Cayenne. Photo by author, 1994.

Figure 7. Interior of penal colony building, St. Laurent. Photo by author, 1990.

Figure 8. Fiche anthropometrique, Alfred Dreyfus, January 5, 1895. CAOM, Aff. pol. 3350, cote 2 Fi2503. Courtesy of the Centre des Archives d'Outre-Mer, Aix-en-Provence (Archives Nationales France).

Figure 9. Launch of the second Tintin rocket, Kourou. Photo by author, 1994.

Figure 10. Ariane launch. Photo courtesy of the Centre Spatial Guyanais and the European Space Agency.

Figure 11. Villas in Kourou's new town. Photo by author, 1993.

Figure 12. Apartments in Kourou's new town. Photo by author, 1993.

Figure 13. Shack in Kourou's old town. Photo by author, 1993.

Figure 14. Jupiter control room at the Guiana Space Center, 1993. Photo ESA/G. Liesse. Courtesy of the European Space Agency.

Figure 15. Cows in Kourou's new town. Photo by the author, 1992.

Figure 16. Postcard of control panel, Guiana Space Center. Photo CSG/F. Hidalgo. Courtesy of the Centre Spatial Guyanais and the European Space Agency.

Figure 17. Globe outside technical complex of the Guiana Space Center. Photo by author, 1994.

Figure 18. Convicts surprised by a boa constrictor. L. Tobb/E. Lefebvre print from Pierre Zaconne's *Histoire de bagnes*, ca. 1876. Courtesy of Bancroft Library, University of California, Berkeley.

Figure 19. Tour boat leaving Maripasoula. Photo by author, 1994.

Figure 20. Postcard of convicts and guard in the Kourou sawmill, undated (ca. 1900). Courtesy of Editions Delabergerie, Cayenne.

Figure 21. Path of the Stars, Kourou. Photo by author, 1993.

Index

Compositor:	Impressions
Text:	10/13 Sabon
Display:	Sabon
Cartographer:	Bill Nelson
Indexer:	Doug Easton
Printer and binder:	Edwards Bros.